COMPUTER SYSTEMS
DEVELOPMENT

John Wiley
INFORMATION SYSTEMS SERIES

Editors

Richard Boland
University of Illinois at
Urbana-Champaign

Rudy Hirschheim
University of Houston

COMPUTER SYSTEMS DEVELOPMENT: HISTORY, ORGANIZATION AND IMPLEMENTATION

Andrew L. Friedman

University of Bristol, UK
Copenhagen School of Economics and Business, Denmark

with

Dominic S. Cornford

National Computing Centre, UK

John Wiley
INFORMATION SYSTEMS SERIES

JOHN WILEY & SONS
Chichester · New York · Brisbane · Toronto · Singapore

Copyright © 1989 by John Wiley & Sons Ltd,
Baffins Lane, Chichester,
West Sussex PO19 1UD, England

Other Wiley Editorial Offices

John Wiley & Sons, Inc., 605 Third Avenue,
New York, NY 10158-0012, USA

Jacaranda Wiley Ltd, GPO Box 859, Brisbane,
Queensland 4001, Australia

John Wiley & Sons (Canada) Ltd, 22 Worcester Road,
Rexdale, Ontario M9W 1L1, Canada

John Wiley & Sons (SEA) Pte Ltd, 37 Jalan Pemimpin #05-04,
Block B, Union Industrial Building, Singapore 2057

Library of Congress Cataloging-in-Publication Data:

Friedman, Andrew L.
  Computer systems development: history, organization and implementation/
    Andrew L. Friedman with Dominic S. Cornford.
      p.   cm.—(John Wiley information systems series)
  Includes bibliographical references.
  ISBN 0 471 92399 0
    1. Electronic data processing.   2. Computer software—Development.
  I. Cornford, Dominic S.   II. Title.   III. Series.
  QA76.F755   1989
  004—dc20
                                                    89-16589
                                                    CIP

British Library Cataloguing in Publication Data:

Friedman, Andrew L.
  Computer systems development: history, organization and implementation.
  1. Great Britain.   Business firms.   Computer systems
  I. Title   II. Cornford, Dominic   III. Series
  658′05′0941
  ISBN 0 471 92399 0

Typeset by Galliard (Printers) Ltd, Great Yarmouth
Printed and bound in Great Britain by
Biddles Ltd, Guildford and King's Lynn

For Pat

Contents

Series Foreword

In order for all types of organizations to succeed, they need to be able to process data and use information effectively. This has become especially true in today's rapidly changing environment. In conducting their day-to-day operations, organizations use information for functions such as planning, controlling, organizing, and decision making. Information, therefore, is unquestionably a critical resource in the operation of all organizations. Any means, mechanical or otherwise, which can help organizations process and manage information presents an opportunity they can ill afford to ignore.

The arrival of the computer and its use in data processing has been one of the most important organizational innovations in the past thirty years. The advent of computer-based data processing and information systems has led to organizations being able to cope with the vast quantities of information which they need to process and manage to survive. The field which has emerged to study this development is *information systems* (IS). It is a combination of two primary fields: computer science and management, with a host of supporting disciplines, e.g. psychology, sociology, statistics, political science, economics, philosophy, and mathematics. IS is concerned not only with the development of new information technologies but also with questions such as: how they can best be applied, how they should be managed, and what their wider implications are.

Partly because of the dynamic world in which we live (and the concomitant need to process more information), and partly because of the dramatic recent developments in information technology, e.g. personal computers, fourth-generation languages, relational databases, knowledge-based systems, and office automation, the relevance and importance of the field of information systems, and office automation, the relevance and importance of the field of information systems has become apparent. End users, who previously had little potential of becoming seriously involved and knowledgeable in information technology and systems, are now much more aware of and interested in the new technology. Individuals working in today's and tomorrow's organizations will be expected to have some understanding of and the ability to use the rapidly developing information technologies and systems. The dramatic increase in the availability and use of information technology, however, raises fundamental questions on the guiding of technological innovation, measuring organizational and managerial productivity, augmenting human intelligence, ensuring data integrity, and establishing strategic advantage. The expanded use of information systems also raises major challenges to the traditional forms of administration and authority, the right to privacy, the nature and form of work, and the limits of calculative rationality in modern organizations and society.

The Wiley Series on Information Systems has emerged to address these questions and challenges. It hopes to stimulate thought and discussion on the key role information systems play in the functioning of organizations and society, and how their role is likely to change in the future. This historical or evolutionary theme of the Series is important because considerable insight can be gained by attempting to understand the past. The Series will attempt to integrate both description—what has been done—with prescription—how best to develop and implement information systems.

The descriptive and historical aspect is considered vital because information systems of the past have not necessarily met with the success that was envisaged. Numerous writers postulate that a high proportion of systems are failures in one sense or another. Given their high cost of development and their importance to the day-to-day running of organizations, this situation must surely be unacceptable. Research into IS failure has concluded that the primary cause of failure is the lack of consideration given to the social and behavioural dimensions of IS. Far too much emphasis has been placed on their technical side. The result has been something of a shift in emphasis from a strictly technical conception of IS to one where it is recognized that information systems have behavioural consequences. But even this misses the mark. A growing number of researchers suggest that information systems are more appropriately conceived as social systems which rely, to a greater and greater extent, on new technology for their operation. It is this social orientation which is lacking in much of what is written about IS. The present volume, *Computer Systems Development: History, Organization and Implementation*, by Andrew Friedman exemplifies the theme of the series by analysing how the information system function has been shaped by technical, organizational and social forces. It is, to our knowledge, the first comprehensive historical analysis of the information systems function in the modern organization. It will be of special interest to scholars hoping to understand the developmental process of organizational information systems, as well as to managers who are responsible for guiding their future course.

The Series seeks to provide a forum for the serious discussion of IS. Although the primary perspective is a more social and behavioural one, alternative perspectives will also be included. This is based on the belief that no one perspective can be totally complete; added insight is possible through the adoption of multiple views. Relevant areas to be addressed in the Series include (but are not limited to): the theoretical development of information systems, their practical application, the foundations and evolution of information systems, and IS innovation. Subjects such as systems design, systems analysis methodologies, information systems planning and management, office automation, project management, decision support systems, end-user computing, and information systems and society are key concerns of the Series.

Rudy Hirschheim
Richard Boland

Preface and Acknowledgements

This book has had a long gestation period. It began with a research grant from the British Economic and Social Research Council (ESRC) to study management strategies and manpower use in the production of computer software in Great Britain. This work began in the summer of 1980. It led to the 1981 survey of data processing managers, which is discussed in some detail in Chapter 6. The 1981 survey was carried out with the cooperation and support of Computer Economics Ltd. From the beginning of 1982 until the end of 1985 a second ESRC grant was received to allow the research to be extended in two directions. First, we would carry out face-to-face surveys of computer installation managers in several different countries, using similar questionnaires to those developed in Britain. Second, we would carry out further surveys in Britain. The surveys carried out in Britain after 1982 were supported by the British National Computing Centre.

In this book we primarily use British surveys. Surveys have also been carried out in Australia, Denmark, Ireland, Japan, The Netherlands, Norway, Sweden and the USA. The results of these surveys have influenced the interpretations presented in this book, but they are reported on in detail elsewhere (Knudsen, 1984; Friedman, 1984; Friedman and Greenbaum, 1984, 1985; Friedman et al., 1984; Hørlück, 1985; Friedman and Cornford, 1987; Friedman et al., 1988). Some results from the survey carried out in the USA in 1983 are reported in Chapters 11 and 12.

The international project led to the formation of the International Computer Occupations Network (ICON). ICON is a group of computer specialists and academic researchers joining together through a common interest in the organization of the work of those in computer occupations. Representatives from all the countries surveyed as well as Finland and Italy have been meeting regularly to discuss common research projects and to exchange information.

During the first few years of this second project we became increasingly aware of a major change in a large number of the installations we visited. Although user relations have always been an issue in computer systems development, it has often been expressed in terms of pinning the user down with a clear requirements specification. During our earliest interviews in 1980 and 1981 we found that senior computer department staff often berated users for not knowing what they wanted, for not understanding what was possible (and what was not possible), and for a lack of interest in computerization (except when things went wrong).

Through interviews in Sweden, Norway and the USA in 1982 and 1983 and further interviews in the UK during those years we began to perceive a marked increase in senior computer staff's appreciation of user relations issues. Attitudes toward users were more likely to be expressed in terms of the computer department taking specific actions in order to reduce user dissatisfaction with delivered systems. In some installations this was expressed in terms of more computer department staff being allocated to work full time on user relations. More care was being taken over systems implementation. The information centre and hands-on user software were being introduced. Rising concern for user relations was beginning to affect more than the direct user interface. Methods for computer systems development were being affected (such as increased use of prototyping) and the types of people being recruited for systems development work were changing. Job advertisements were beginning to specify that knowledge of particular user-defined systems was required. It seemed that a desire to improve user relations was becoming the major concern among data processing managers.

Certainly all computer installations have not been affected, but during the 1980s the introduction of techniques for improving user relations (or at least evaluation of available techniques) has become the mark of modernity in the computing community. This has been confirmed by more recent interviews undertaken by ICON groups, particularly the Dutch group, which completed a survey in 1987 (see Regtering and Riesewijk, 1987; Friedman *et al.*, 1988). We have come to view this rising concern with user relations as a major shift in systems development management attitudes. We believe this change will continue to be a major influence on the practice of computer systems development during the 1990s. Originally we were going to call this book *Managing the Computer User Revolution*. Eventually we decided that the title should not emphasize our thinking about the current and future situation. Rather it was more important to situate those thoughts in the context of the entire history of computer systems development.

Dominic Cornford worked as a research assistant during the collection of the data and was primarily responsible for the British surveys used in this book which were carried out between 1982 and 1988. He also made important contributions to the writing of Chapters 2, 4 and 5.

I would like to thank the hundreds of computer department managers who gave of their time to be interviewed. Often interviews which were scheduled to take two hours were still steaming along after three or even four hours. In addition, many analysts, programmers and consultants gave us interviews. These were all too numerous to mention here. However, a few particularly helpful people whom we contacted during the project should be mentioned. Richard Sharpe, former editor of *Computing* magazine, was a continual source of ideas and contacts. Ron Campfield and especially Peter Stevens of Computer Economics Ltd were very helpful at early stages of the research. Discussions at ICON gatherings have been very useful. In particular Bjørn Egerth, Kalle Mäkilä, Pelle Ehn and Bo Oberg from Sweden; Trond Knudsen, Ellen Ofstad and Olav Korsnes from Norway; Jens Hørlück, Finn Borum and Eld Zierau from Denmark; Maggie Tierney and James Wickham from Ireland; Markku Sääksjärvi from Finland; Kazushi Ikegami,

Masayoshi Ikeda and Yoshiaki Takahashi from Japan; Hans Doorewaard, Harrie Regtering and Bernard Riesewijk from Holland; and Joan Greenbaum from the USA. Finally, I would like to thank Carol Bates, who was the secretary for the project.

A number of people made helpful comments on drafts of this book. These were Finn Borum, Jesper Strandgaard Pedersen and Mette Mønsted (colleagues on the CHIPS project at the Copenhagen School of Economics), Finn Valentin, Peter Lotz, Jens Frøslev Christensen, Per Vejrup Hansen, Peter Kamedula, Povl-Erik Jensen, Peter Ploughman, Egil Fivelsdal, Arne Grip, Niels Bjørn-Andersen, Hans Doorewaard, Harrie Regtering, Wil Martens and specially Bernard Riesewijk and Kazushi Ikegami. I would also like to acknowledge the encouragement and helpful comments made by Jens Hørlück from Århus University during the latter stages of this book's progress. His comments have allowed me to improve the book considerably. Of course I alone am responsible for any deficiencies in the final product.

Finn Valentin, Gurli Jacobsen and Carla Clausen provided moral support during my stay at the Copenhagen School of Economics, when most of the book was written. Pat Taylor, to whom this book is dedicated, contributed to the American survey; she commented on various parts of the manuscript and she provided continual moral support and encouragement during the long gestation period of this book. Finally, I would like to thank Katie and Sammy for putting up with a tired and grumpy daddy who spent too many hours in front of his 'pecuter'.

Andrew L. Friedman
November 1988

Part 1
BACKGROUND AND THEORY

Chapter 1
INTRODUCTION

This book deals with subjects which would normally be covered in texts on software engineering and the management of information systems development. However, these subjects are not presented with a view to teaching readers how to use techniques or how to choose which ones are 'best'. Instead, pictures of what methods and techniques have in fact been used in the 'field' are presented. We also develop models to illuminate the factors which have stimulated changes in the practice of computer systems development. By doing so we attempt to explain *why* particular software engineering techniques and particular strategies for managing information systems functions are being used. We also use the models to indicate how the practice of computer systems development is likely to change in future. The value of this book to aspiring and practising computer systems developers can be to provide them with a context to their work—one which can provide a deeper insight into the advantages and limitations of currently recommended techniques.

Describing and explaining the way the work of computer systems developers has been changing during the past four decades has led us to deal with subjects which are normally considered in texts on organization theory, the labour process, the sociology of work and the economics of technical change. Specialists in these areas may be interested in this 'case', because it embraces rapidly growing occupations which are at the heart of the information technology 'revolution'. In examining the history of computer systems development we have an opportunity to study the circumstances under which certain important aspects of this new 'technological regime' (Nelson and Winter, 1977) or 'technological paradigm' (Dosi, 1982) are being formed. We can study factors which affect the direction of new computer software technology. While studies of the social implications of new information technology are rather common, there is little written about social effects on the development of new information technology. Such a study may be of interest to those interested in the direction of technological change.

In this chapter we introduce the overall approach towards computer systems development upon which this book is based. It is a historical approach which is also analytical. It is based on models of social change and of management strategies for organizing work. It is also based on particular models of how the diffusion of computers and computer-based systems affect organizations.

We suggest that the myriad ways in which the work of computer systems developers has changed since the 1950s can be understood in terms of a succession of phases. Each phase is marked by a particular critical factor, a particular constraint on the further development and penetration of computer-based systems. Efforts to overcome this critical factor stimulate changes in management strategies towards computer systems developers, changes in the position of systems development activities within organizations and even changes in the orientation of technological changes. Why it is that different critical factors have been the focus of attention during the history of computing is explained by a combination of forces. These include technological changes in hardware and software, changes in the types of systems being developed and types of users, changes in the degree of competition faced by suppliers of computer systems, and continual shortages of skilled and experienced computer systems developers. The models we use to develop these themes are presented in Chapter 3.

In section 1.1 we explain why a historical and analytical approach to computer systems development can provide an important contribution to our understanding of current and future developments. By linking the organization of computer systems development to a range of social, economic and technical factors we can also understand significant differences between different installations. The standard explanation for observed differences in computer installations is simply their age, based on the idea that all such organizations go through an invariant set of stages in their development (see section 2.3). While this evolutionary approach is useful, it must be supplemented with analysis of the interaction between computer installations and their environments. There are good reasons (quite apart from arrested development or perversity) for certain computer installations to display unusual patterns of development.

In section 1.2 we discuss the limitations of our analytical approach to the history of computer systems development. The analytical approach leads us to a higher level of abstraction than would be expected in a historical account. The approach makes generalization easier. It allows the path of computer systems development to be compared more easily with histories of other technologies. However, there are many aspects of the history of computer systems development which we have left out. These are noted. This chapter ends with a guide through the rest of the book.

1.1 RATIONALE FOR A HISTORICAL AND NON-PRESCRIPTIVE APPROACH TO COMPUTER SYSTEMS DEVELOPMENT

Books about computer systems development have been overwhelmingly prescriptive in nature. They have attempted to give their readers what the authors believe to be the most up-to-date, and therefore the best, information about how managers should organize the computer function in order to produce successful information systems. This is not surprising. Within the field there is a preoccupation with state-of-the-art technology, with being, or at least appearing to be, aware of the frontiers of development. Job prospects can often be improved by giving the impression that one's experience is particularly relevant to a new situation. With continual severe labour shortages, even less resources are applied to check up on the relevance of a candidate's experience than in other fields. The speech of practitioners is peppered with jargon. However, we have found in the course of hundreds of interviews that most practitioners are unfamiliar with much of that jargon. New jargon is being generated so quickly and from so many different sources that a high proportion of books about the subject appear with glossaries to guide seasoned practitioners as well as novices. In a field which has come close to being synonymous with 'new technology' among governments, academics and in the media around the world, interest naturally focuses on what is new.

Nevertheless, there are good reasons for examining computer systems development from a historical perspective. First, computers are hardly new. Computers were first built in the 1940s. Computer systems have been developed for business applications since the mid-1950s.

Second, the history of computer systems development has not been linear. Certainly many think of the history of computers in this way. Changes in computers have been distinguished by continually falling prices, rising capacity and miniaturization. While this has stimulated a rapid and continual diffusion of computers into organizations, the path of systems development has not been correspondingly smooth. The lightening of hardware constraints has revealed other constraints on the progress of computer systems development. Since the mid-1960s in particular, reports of unsatisfactory computer systems and project failures have become commonplace. We will argue that constraints on further computerization now primarily arise from demand-side problems, rather than supply-side capabilities. Satisfying user needs currently occupies a large and growing proportion of systems development effort compared with economizing on expensive and unreliable hardware and software. This change is reflected in a significant shift of emphasis in texts on computer systems. It also affects recruitment patterns, skill requirements and work practices of computer systems developers.

If we are interested in understanding how things are likely to change, it is important to understand how things came to be as they are. This would be a 'fairly' simple exercise if changes could always be attributed to a single agent, or if we want to predict changes in activities which have always changed in a linear fashion. Because computer systems development has not been so simple an activity, a more careful history is needed than the usual story of the triumphant march of technical progress in machine capabilities.[1] A more complete forecast is needed than the commonplace prospective of spreading artificial intelligence[2] and automation of systems development activities.[3] The immanent demise of systems developers owing to automation of their specialist tasks (especially the disappearance of specialist computer programmers) has been predicted since the early 1960s (Bosak, 1960; Hopper, 1962). To borrow from Mark Twain (see Chapter 13), reports of the death of the programmers have been exaggerated.

They are still exaggerated. Why computer programming has been a rapidly growing occupation for so long is a major theme to be explored in this book.

A third reason for looking at computer systems development from a historical perspective is that not all installations operate in an 'up-to-date' fashion. Sometimes this is because managers and staff are simply behind the times. Introducing new techniques is expensive and time-consuming. Any diffusion process takes time. However, the environment of certain computer installations discourages the introduction of certain types of 'state-of-the-art' techniques. They are simply inappropriate in certain contexts. For example, developers of computer applications in most user organizations are being encouraged to increase user friendliness of systems, even if it means that systems will require more machine memory and more processing time. Machine capacity is no longer the primary expense for most computer applications. Nevertheless, developers of *systems* software, developers of applications for dedicated equipment such as point-of-sale terminals and bank cash dispensers, and developers of certain applications to run on personal computers, must take into account hardware capacity limitations. They develop systems under environmental conditions which resemble those of the 1950s and early 1960s, not because they are backward, but because the circumstances under which they develop systems are not the same as the majority of computer installations.

There is a general problem in the computing literature of advancing the clock, or of what we have called the 'problem of tenses' (see section 2.3.4). Planned techniques are described as 'implemented'; techniques implemented in one installation or a few truly 'state-of-the-art' sites are described as widespread. This occurs partly because what is new is news. Partly it also occurs because information about what techniques are actually being used in most installations is much more difficult to come by.

The problem of tenses leads to mistaken impressions; that most places have adopted new techniques or are about to do so, and that such techniques are universally appropriate. By examining historical antecedents for various changes which have occurred during the past four decades of computer systems development, we can illuminate links between different environmental circumstances and differences in the way systems development is carried out at present.

A fourth reason for examining computer systems development from a historical perspective is that it allows us to examine the relation between technological change and social change. In particular it allows us to see the extent to which the direction of technological change is shaped by social and economic factors. Certainly the reverse direction of causality, that technical change influences social conditions, is important. However, there has been too great an emphasis on examining the 'implications' of technological change, particularly of changes in information technology.[4]

A bias in our understanding arises in the following way. Studies of *social factors*

either start from a framework of technological influence by defining t
questions in terms of implications or impact of technology,[5] or they are
with a historical perspective and so at least consider technological change as one of
several agents stimulating social change. Studies of the *technology* are largely
historic and their social content is prescriptive. This leads them to take
technological change as given, as exogenous.

The combination of these two approaches leaves the perspective of technological change being influenced by social factors undeveloped. Certainly at the
macro-historical level there is considerable work on social factors affecting technological change. Most notable are studies of the industrial revolution (for
example, Landes, 1969). Also recent work on long waves, or what have been
labelled Kondratieff cycles (50-year general business cycles), has begun to look at
the direction of technological change as affected by social factors (see Freeman, 1983;
Blackburn *et al.*, 1985). Also at the micro level of studies of individual inventions or
inventors there is an appreciation of social factors shaping individual technical
events. However, at the middle level, looking at occupations and constellations of
technologies and industries, there is little (one notable exception is Noble, 1977).[6]

Neglect of the social influences on technological change by writers on
computers and computer systems development is not unusual, although we would
argue that it is extreme. Computer technology seems to be the quintessential
example of the independent and inexorable march of new technology coming to
trample our antiquarian methods of social interaction. In part this is because
computers are seen as a primary example of a distinct invention, the product of
university environments during the war and the immediate post-war years, which
was then 'innovated' by certain more entrepreneurial academics in conjunction
with entrepreneurial private companies. From outside the field it then appears
that the computer simply diffused to organizations which then had to react to the
inevitable consequences of taking on such an expensive and superior technology.[7]
In this way computer technology appears to support a Schumpeterian view of
technical progress.

According to Schumpeter, invention, innovation and imitation are separate
processes (Schumpeter, 1934). Clearly identifiable inventions such as the
computer itself, transistors or integrated circuits are made by inventors in a
research environment (such as the universities or, in the case of transistors, Bell
Laboratories). They are then translated into innovations in a different,
commercial environment. Once 'proven' successful by early adopter en-
trepreneurs, they are imitated more or less rapidly through a diffusion process.

As Rosenberg (1975) points out, this view of technological change focuses on
particular types of improvements: on individual breakthroughs, on major
inventions which lead to a substantial shift in productivity. There is another kind
of technological progress. This is the result of improvements which, although
modest individually, can be of major significance when considered cumulatively.
Among economic historians and sociologists there is considerable support for this

second view. For them technological progress is more accurately described as the cumulation of individually minor improvements (see Gilfillian, 1935; Usher, 1954; Hollander, 1965).[8] More recently this view of innovation has been emphasized by certain economists who argue for an evolutionary approach to the subject (David, 1975; Nelson and Winter, 1982; Elster, 1983; Clark and Juma, 1987).

When we view technical progress as primarily a cumulation of minor improvements, rather than the application of major inventions, then it is easier to see how the direction of technical progress can be affected by identifiable social factors. Rather than trying to explain the antecedents of individual genius we are trying to explain what sustains a swarm of inventive/innovative activity in a particular direction. Much invention is then directly stimulated by perceptions of profit-making possibilities. This means that the strict invention versus innovation separation is inapplicable. It also means that new techniques will follow *perceived* profit opportunities, which will not necessarily coincide with actual profit opportunities. They will be responsive to problems encountered in real productive situations. They will also respond to climates of opinion, identifying the primary problems being faced in any particular field, and created by word of mouth or by trade and academic literature. That is, the direction of technological change can be affected by fashion.

This, as we shall show below, has had an important effect on the direction of technological change in computer systems development. When an 'imitator' organization buys a computer and becomes a computer user organization, it requires specialist staff to develop and maintain computer systems. This staff is normally employed and managed by the user organization.[9] This specialist staff represents *both* inventive and innovative capacity. New methods and techniques can be developed as part of any major project. Sometimes this progress remains confined to individual installations. Sometimes results are published. Both management and technical systems development magazines and journals are filled with articles describing techniques developed during the course of single systems development projects.

When we discuss the direction of technological change in computer systems development, we are also discussing technological change in computers themselves. When any organization buys or leases a computer, they acquire software as well as hardware. They buy a computer system or, rather, what we call below the core of a computer system. We will argue that the important technological changes in the computer system core, in terms of the contribution of computers to increasing productivity in user organizations, have come more and more from developments in the software area, particularly after the introduction of transistors and integrated circuits to hardware technology (for example, operating systems, higher-level languages, database management systems and various generators).[10]

As mentioned above, most studies in the computing field which deal with the relation between technological change and social change define the object of study as discovery of the implications of new technology on social factors. In this book we examine the history of computer systems development in terms of both the spread of computerization and changes in what computerization means. Many of those changes in computerization have occurred because of a continual process of technological change generated largely from within the computing community, even from within what Schumpeter might have regarded as the 'imitator' section of the community, from installations in user organizations. This allows us to focus on the way social and economic pressures on that community can affect the direction of that technological change. Thus we hope to redress the bias towards technological determinism encouraged by studies of the diffusion of computers which treat the computer as a single invariant innovation being introduced into a population of organizations, or by studies of the social implications of the diffusion of computers and new forms of computer technology which by definition preclude the reverse direction of causality, or by studies of the 'invention' of computers, which focus on the big breakthrough which has been of increasingly less importance for understanding what it is that has been diffusing under the label of computers, the cumulation of 'minor' improvements to computer systems core.

1.2 LIMITATIONS OF OUR ANALYTIC APPROACH TO THE HISTORY OF COMPUTER SYSTEMS DEVELOPMENT

The approach to computer systems development taken in this book is analytical as well as historical. Models of the diffusion of computer systems and of the influence of social, economic and technical factors on the pattern of computer systems development are presented. We have not attempted to present a complete history of computer systems development. This has led to a necessary focusing on some aspects of that history, and neglect of others. The set of factors which have been the strongest influences on computer systems development (according to our models) are treated in considerable detail. Also the critical factor for each of the separate phases we have identified has been described in great detail.

One feature of the presentation which may surprise many readers is our attempt to separate issues and descriptions in the *prescriptive literature* about computer systems from description of *actual changes* in the management and practice of computer systems development (note section 5.1 and Chapter 8). We have given the computer literature separate treatment because it is both less important and more important than is usually thought. It is less important because it is not an accurate reflection of computer systems development practice. The problem of tenses means that certain new directions are exaggerated. What sometimes turn out to be blind alleys are often presented as super-highways leading to the future (see Chapter 13). In this sense the computer literature is less important than expected. However, because we believe that new technology and new organizational forms have been generated within the broad computer community, and because we consider the direction of those new developments to be strongly influenced by fashion, then the computing literature can be thought of as one (among several) of the agents of change in this field. In this sense the literature is more important than expected.

Another limitation of this book is that we have focused on computerization of administrative functions and the development of information systems. We have only examined the development of technical systems (software for manufactured goods, CAD/CAM systems, etc.) in terms of the development of software which would normally be sold with any computer destined for the commercial market (operating systems, higher-level languages, generators).

We have also concentrated on the productive activity or labour process of computer systems development, rather than the collection of computer systems which have been developed. This has led us to concentrate on the sites where most people are occupied with computer systems development, i.e. the user organizations, rather than either computer hardware manufacturers or independent software houses and service bureaus. Informatics estimated that in 1976 only between 10% and 15% of all instructions executed on US computers were software purchased from outside suppliers. The rest were produced at in-house departments of user organizations (OECD, 1985, p. 49). In the UK it was estimated that in 1985 74% of skilled software specialists worked in user organizations.[11] We have therefore concentrated on the *occupations* concerned with computer systems development, more than on what may be thought of as the computer systems *industry*. Among those occupations we have concentrated almost entirely on systems analysts and programmers (whom we will often describe collectively as computer systems developers), rather than computer operators, data preparation and control staff or sales staff.

One further limitation of our approach relates to the data sources we have used. We have primarily drawn evidence from US and British sources. We would argue that the history of computer systems development has followed very similar patterns in the USA and Great Britain. Computer systems development is an international activity and systems developers are an international set of occupations. In part this is a consequence of computers emerging at a time of unprecedented inter-penetration of economic and social activity among nations, particularly between those of Europe and the USA. In part it is a consequence of the dominance of a single US-based multinational company in the field of computer software as well as computer hardware. IBM is the largest software producer in the world. It had about 15% of the US software market in 1983 (OECD, 1985, p. 57). Also IBM offers training programmes for systems developers in other organizations. It produces recommendations on how systems development should be organized. Both current and former IBM employees have been very active producers of prescriptive literature.

We are not suggesting that there are no important international differences in computer systems development. International differences are regularly discussed at ICON meetings and conferences, and several studies focusing on such differences have been published (see citations listed in the Preface). There are also considerable differences in approaches to the organization of computer systems development within countries. Rather, we believe differences between Great Britain and the USA to be of secondary importance when considering broad changes over the long term. At times we also refer to European compared with US experiences.[12]

In Chapters 5 and 7, where most detailed emprical evidence is presented, we rely heavily on British data which we have either generated ourselves, or had direct contact with those who generated the data. In those chapters US sources are referred to, but in much less detail.

1.3 A GUIDE TO READERS

In the next chapter approaches to the history of computer systems development which may be found in the literature are discussed and evaluated. Readers who are interested solely in discovering the particular history of computer systems development may skip this chapter, or leave reading it to the end. In Chapter 3 our models of computer systems and of the history of both computer systems and computer systems development are presented. In our model the history of computer systems development is divided into three phases. Chapter 4 deals with the antecedents to the first phase (roughly up to the mid-1960s) and with a description of computer systems development during that phase. Chapter 5 deals with the antecedents to the second phase (roughly mid-1960s to early 1980s), and Chapter 6 presents a picture of computer systems development during this second phase. Chapters 8–9 deal with antecedents to the third phase and Chapters 10–12 describe computer systems development during the third phase. In Chapter 13 we look at the future of computer systems development and in the final chapter we present an evaluation of a number of themes raised earlier.

Chapters 4–12 provide a history of computer systems development, but they are arranged in only roughly chronological order. In Chapters 4, 6 and 10–12, pictures of computer systems development in each of the three phases are presented. Broad factors which we believe have driven changes in the practice of computer systems development characteristic of each phase have also been treated chronologically in Chapters 4, 5 and 7–9.

Chapters 5–12 are most firmly related to the material covered in texts commonly classed as software engineering management and the development of management information systems. Those interested in gaining a historical perspective on these subjects may wish to read Chapters 1 and 2 and then move on to Chapter 5. In Chapter 13 we look at the future for computer systems developers, and in particular we address the prediction that these occupations will soon disappear due to automation or due to users taking over systems development tasks. Finally, in Chapter 14 we return to the issue of generalizability and relations among changing technology, management strategies and the social and economic environment associated with computer systems development.

The computing field is marked by the circulation of an enormous body of jargon. Several terms have changed over the years as new equipment has been introduced and as new applications have been developed. In order to avoid confusion we have chosen to use certain terms throughout this book, even though the terms popularly used have changed. The strongest example is our use of the terms 'computer systems' and 'computer systems development'. As noted above we have concentrated on the computerization of administrative functions and the development of information systems. During phase one these activities would have been carried out in what would have been called computer departments or electronic data processing departments. In phase two those departments would have been called data processing departments or management information services. With phase three, in addition to the titles of phase two, many are called management services departments or information systems departments or information services departments.[13] As a concession to this change in jargon, we will use the term 'computer departments' when referring to phase one, 'data processing (DP) departments' when referring to phase two, and 'information systems (IS) departments' when referring to phase three (and beyond). However, we will stick with the terms 'computer installation', 'computer systems', 'computer systems development' and 'computer systems developers' throughout the book. Finally, note that in the UK computer service bureaus, software companies selling custom-made software and software companies selling software packages are called 'the computer services industry'. We will follow this terminology.

ENDNOTES

1. In addition to books devoted to this subject, such as those of Bernstein (1981) of Shurkin (1984), most texts on computer-related subjects have a short rendition of this theme.
2. Such as Feigenbaum and McCorduck (1983).
3. Such as Couger et al. (1982).
4. Some of this emphasis has occurred in response to recent substantial financial incentives from governments and research councils looking for policy guidelines. This work is not, in itself, misguided, but it tends to reinforce the view that technology determines social behaviour. Admittedly, many of the serious studies actually produced in recent years on this topic have 'discovered' that technological changes do not 'determine' social changes. Effects of new technology are mediated by social factors, such as the market situation of potential adopting organizations (Stoneman, 1983), or the industrial relations climate into which the technology is introduced (Wilkinson, 1983). The same technology introduced into different situations leads to different behaviour.
5. In the information technology field this bias is clearly illustrated in the excellent and well-received books edited and written by Tom Forester during the 1980s (1980, 1985, 1987). These books all begin with the presumption that a revolution in microelectronics or information technology has transformed society. Note the title of his latest book, High-Tech Society: The Story of the Information Technology Revolution. We do not deny that information technology has had a profound influence on late-twentieth-century society. We do argue against treating the appearance and development of information technology as exogenous.

6. Neglect of factors which affect the direction of technological change may be in part attributable to the dominance of neoclassical economics. In neoclassical economics technological change is firmly treated as exogenous. At one point (Hicks, 1932) it was thought that a change in the relative prices of factors of production (say a rise in the price of labour relative to capital) would stimulate inventions which economize on the factor which has become relatively expensive (i.e. labour-saving technological change). However, as several economists have correctly pointed out (Salter, 1960; Fellner, 1962; Samuelson, 1965), in a purely competitive situation firms have no market incentive towards either labour-saving or capital-saving innovations. They are interested in any innovation that will reduce costs, but under perfectly competitive conditions no factor is more expensive then another from the individual firm's perspective. This is because each firm pays each factor of production the value of its marginal product. If there is a change in the cost of any factor, it is assumed that an instantaneous and perfect adjustment in the number of units of that factor employed by each firm is made such that the equation of prices paid for the factor and the value of its marginal product is restored. While many neoclassical economists admit that the real world is not characterized by perfect competition, most seem to believe that the real world works in a way that can be understood by using models based on perfect competition. The consensus on induced directions to technological change which emerged in the economics literature of the early 1960s has almost completely erased this topic from the economics literature. An important exception to which we will refer below has been Rosenberg (1969, 1975, 1982).

7. This also seems to be the view of Richard Nolan, or at least one interpretation of his view. Nolan is a well-known figure inside the field (see section 2.3.3).

8. There have, of course, been major shifts in the direction of technological progress occasioned by a major technological breakthrough. However, these breakthroughs were rarely recognized as such and rarely did their initial introduction provide substantial increases in productivity. This is because fundamental technological changes in production processes require a periphery of related improvements to affect the overall productivity of major activities or enterprises. Rosenberg points to the 'breakthrough' of changing the position of steamboat wheels from the side to the end of the steamboat. Initial improvements in efficiency were meagre because further features of the design of steamboats needed to be altered to make better use of the new position of the wheel. These later changes could only be discovered by development work carried out by early adopters of the new wheel position. Braun and Macdonald (1982) tell a similar story about the beginning of the transistor. For a long time the old technology of vacuum tubes continued to be more efficient because of the well-developed periphery of technical improvements which had already been made to the design of the vacuum tube. As we shall see in following chapters (especially Chapters 5, 6 and 8), computers and new computer systems have often been failures because of inadequate peripheral improvements such as unwieldy operating systems or inadequately structured programming techniques.

9. An exception to this practice is in Japan, where much of this work is subcontracted out. This system allows user organizations to acquire computer systems at greatly reduced costs, but it may also lead to reduced innovative activity in that sector. It may help to explain why Japanese software achievements have not matched their success at computer hardware and hardware components (see Friedman, 1987a).

10. Although hardware cost/performance improvements have certainly continued since the introduction of integrated circuits.

11. Estimates were made by the Institute for Manpower Studies at Sussex University. They estimated that 15 000 skilled programmers, systems analysts and electrical engineers

would be working in computer hardware firms, 35 000 in computer software and service bureaus and 142 000 in computer departments of computer user organizations (Anderson and Hersleb, 1980).

12. Perhaps we should refer to northern European experiences. Through the ICON research programme we have comparable data from six European countries, but these are all in northern Europe (Scandinavian countries, Great Britain, Ireland and the Netherlands).

13. We recognize that in many large organizations the IS function covers a larger unit than a department, often a division, but we will normally use the term 'department'.

Chapter 2

APPROACHING THE HISTORY OF COMPUTER SYSTEMS DEVELOPMENT

2.1 PREVIOUS APPROACHES TO THE HISTORY OF COMPUTER SYSTEMS DEVELOPMENT

Three different approaches to the history of computer systems development are well known in the literature. The first, and most common, may be called the *hardware generations approach*. The history of computers is divided into a series of generations of computer hardware technology, each marked by major changes in the basic components of computers. The first generation was based on valve technology, the second on transistors, the third on integrated circuits and the fourth and fifth on larger and larger scale integrated circuits. Changes in computer software, in organization of computer specialists work and, for some, in the general social implications of computers have derived from changes in component technology according to this view.

The second approach concentrates on the history of data processing within individual firms. This approach assumes that there is a standard way that organizations react to the introduction of computer technology, and a natural progression of applications for which computers are used. Once computers are introduced into any organization the computer resource will develop through a series of stages which are essentially the same for all organizations. We will call this the *organization stages approach*. This approach is generally associated with Richard Nolan. Nolan does not allow for differences in size, industry or management culture to affect the progression from one stage to another. He did once state that firms which introduce computers at different dates will move through the stages differently (Nolan, 1979, p. 116), but all firms still are assumed to go through the same stages. The implications of going through stages differently has been left unexplored. Therefore, if we were to write the history of computing with only the stages as our guide, we would view that history as the changing configuration of stages through which existing computer users are progressing. All we would need to know is when organizations began to computerize and how fast they progress from stage to stage in order to analyse the general state of computing organization at any time.

The third approach begins with the organization of computer specialists' work. According to this approach the work of computer specialists may be viewed as a labour process like any other. There are general laws which mark the development of all labour processes in capitalist societies. In particular, there is a tendency towards breaking up jobs into smaller and less skilled components. Conceptual work (requiring judgement and skill) is separated out from most jobs and concentrated among fewer people in order to reduce average wage costs. The majority of jobs are thereby deskilled. According to a number of authors (Braverman, 1974; Kraft, 1977; Greenbaum, 1979; Kraft and Dubnoff, 1986) the history of computing organization may be viewed as following this deskilling path. We will call this the *labour process approach*.

We believe that there is an element of truth to each of these approaches. Each by itself is inadequate. Furthermore, taken as a general basis for understanding the history of computer systems development, each will lead to serious misunderstandings. In the following three sections the approaches will be dissected in order to extract what we believe is worth retaining.

2.2 HARDWARE GENERATIONS APPROACH

By far the most common approach to the history of computer systems development has been to concentrate on changes in computer hardware technology. Computer history is divided into generations, each representing a significant advance on previous generations in terms of the speed, reliability and capabilities of the equipment.

2.2.1 Hardware Components Basis

The key element distinguishing one generation from another is usually taken to be the type of basic electronic components used in the hardware (see, for example, Rose, 1969; Walter and Walter, 1970; Nashelsky, 1972; Hayes, 1978; Bartree, 1981). Digital computers are basically a huge set of electronic switches which either allow the passage of an electrical pulse or block that passage. In first-generation computers these switches were made using vacuum tubes (or valves). The distinguishing characteristic of second-generation computers is normally taken to be the use of the discrete transistor in the range of computers which were introduced from 1958. The introduction of integrated circuits, i.e. planar transistors or transistors made as an integrated part of the flat surface of a material, marked the third generation of computers. The third generation of computers were introduced in 1964 (RCA Spectra 70) and 1965 (IBM 360).

These three generations represented a clear way of distinguishing quite different machines. While the heart of the computer (a complex set of switches) remained the same, changes in the design and materials used in the basic components clearly had a direct effect on the capacity, speed and reliability of those machines. As the quality of individual components improved, the factors limiting performance shifted to the interconnections between switches. This encouraged further integration of components to eliminate interconnections or to reduce their presence as separate entities. This, in turn, stimulated changes in the character of communication between computer users and the machine. Communication with the computer became quicker (through multiprogramming and on-line facilities), more user-friendly (with more English-like languages) and automated (with monitors and operating systems removing certain basic housekeeping from the activities to be carried out by each application program).

In this sense the hardware generations approach provides a credible way of summarizing more general changes than improvements in component technology. Not only were changes in the hardware design stimulated by component improvements, but also the character of the computer user's interaction with the machine was altered by improved basic components. This, in turn, led to changes in the organization of work of computer specialists and to changes in the management of the computer resource. We are primarily interested in the history of computer systems development and we have drawn a connection between hardware generations and that history. Such connections are not made in computer science or management information systems textbooks, primarily because they do not examine the history of computer systems development explicitly. Rather they describe the current state of systems development, and elsewhere they describe the history of computer hardware as a series of generations. The generations are primarily used as a descriptive rather than an analytical device.

Table 2.1 shows the way the generations were viewed in 1969 (Walter and Walter, 1970). The connections between hardware component technology and the organization of computer specialists' work is easily identified. For example,

TABLE 2.1 Computer hardware generations

Generation	Hardware components	Software	Method of processing	Most significant controlling parameter
1	Vacuum tubes	Machine language, subroutines, assemblers	Batch	Interconnection of different components
2	Transistors	Add high-level languages, monitors, macro-assemblers	Batch	Interconnection of different components
3	Integrated circuits	Add operating systems, on-line real-time multiprogramming systems, data management systems	Batch + on-line	Interconnections of integrated circuits

Source: Walter and Walter (1970).

during the first generation, with the use of unstable and large vacuum tube circuits, it was pointless to build huge memories into computers because of the necessary size and cost. Computers were also relatively slow in operation. The relative lack of memory and slow speed meant that a very high premium was placed on the efficiency of the program. In order to write highly efficient programs, detailed knowledge of the computer and how it functioned was required. This affected the kind of person who could be employed as a programmer (high technical education background) and the way their work could be organized (research or academic type of atmosphere).

Couger (1982) draws an explicit parallel between improvement in computer hardware and improvement in systems development techniques, based on the idea of successive generations. Systems development techniques lagged behind hardware evolution by one generation during the 1950s. During the second generation of hardware techniques, computer-oriented systems development techniques were only in their first generation. When Couger writes about systems development techniques he is referring, particularly in these early years, to techniques for systems analysis and design, not programming. According to Couger, this lag only slightly diminished during the 1960s. It was during the late 1970s and early 1980s that the gap began to close.

> The fifth generation of system techniques has been developed almost in parallel with the fifth generation of hardware. System professionals are finally utilizing the power of the computer to aid in analysis and design of computer applications. (Couger, 1982, p. 8)

Interestingly this was published in 1982, but Couger dates both fifth generations from 1985 (see Table 2.2).

Couger implies that the improvements in hardware stimulated improvements in systems development techniques. The content of Couger's generations of systems development techniques will be discussed and evaluated in Chapter 14.

The term 'generation' of computers was popularized by hardware manufacturers who wished to emphasize the technical advances of their latest machines

TABLE 2.2 Generations of hardware and systems development techniques

Generations	Hardware	Systems development techniques
First	1940–1950	1950–1960
Second	1950–1963	1960–1970
Third	1963–1979	1970–1980
Fourth	1979–1985	1980–1985
Fifth	1985–	1985–

Source: adapted from Couger (1982, p. 8).

over previous ones. Even after the second generation there were doubts about whether what the manufacturers were calling the latest-generation computers really represented the same sort of qualitative change from the current generation as between the current and previous generations.[1] Rosen (1969) reported that new computers introduced after 1965 and most that remained on the market after that year were called third-generation computers by their manufacturers. After IBM announced that its 360 series was the third generation of computers, other manufacturers could not afford to keep anything so out of date as a second-generation computer on the market, at least not one which was labelled as second-generation vintage.

The tremendous success of IBM's third-generation computers led manu-facturers to try on the fourth-generation label at the earliest opportunity. Informatics and the University of California at Los Angeles held a large symposium on fourth-generation computers in 1969 (Gruenberger, 1970). Many commentators after 1969 described only three generations. For example, Sanders (1973) does not mention a fourth generation. Anderson (1974) does not go beyond the third generation in his original edition or in the second edition (1978). Greenbaum (1979) also considers computers at the time of writing to be of the third generation.

Continuing with the component basis to computer generations entails defining the fourth generation in terms of the packing density of integrated circuits used in computers. The number of circuits packed on to a given planar transistor, or chip, has grown considerably since they were first introduced. The chips used in early IBM 360s contained dozens of switches. By the early 1970s chips being used in computers had hundreds of circuits and were called LSI, or large-scale integrated circuits.

Until recently, those who continued to believe in the component basis to the generations associated the fourth generation with LSI circuits. On this basis the fourth generation is deemed to have begun during the period 'entering the 1970s' (Nashelsky, 1972) or around 1975 (Hayes, 1978). Certainly the effects of greater packing density of components on size and cost of computer hardware have been almost as dramatic as the introduction of transistors or integrated circuits. Nevertheless, packing density did not rise suddenly. The introduction of LSI circuits in the early 1970s did not represent a qualitative change from the components used in the late 1960s. Packing density rose steadily from small-scale integrated circuits (SSI) through medium-scale integrated circuits (MSI) to large-scale integrated circuits. Furthermore, the density growth continued after the early 1970s. By the late 1970s thousands of circuits were being placed on a single chip, called VLSIs or very large-scale integrated circuits. Since then VLSIs have become even more 'VL'. Sometimes they are called ULSI (ultra-large-scale integration). Perhaps in the future they will be called SLSI (super-large-scale integration) or FLSI (fabulously large-scale integration).

The technical distinction between generations based on different packing densities of components is less clear than that based on completely different forms of components. Fourth-generation computer systems (defined as MSI- and LSI-based) were less easily distinguishable from earlier systems. Generally, even manufacturers have resisted the temptation to call computer systems fifth generation simply because they use VLSI components. Currently (1989) microcomputers incorporating VLSI chips are advertised as fourth-generation systems. (For example, ACT uses the phrase 'Go 4th' to advertise its Apricot, microcomputer range.)

The generations approach is still being used today, but the general consensus seems to be that the fifth generation should be defined more in terms of a change in the types of applications computers are used for, rather than characteristics of the hardware. Fifth-generation systems are commonly associated with expert systems or artificial intelligence. Even fourth-generation systems are often associated more with software or communications technology than with the hardware components. Fourth-generation systems are distinguished by the use of real-time systems, sophisticated database management systems and very high-level languages. These technologies were available during the time of earlier component generations (see Table 2.1), but they did not become widely used in administrative data processing until the late 1970s and early 1980s (Friedman and Cornford, 1981, 1985). [2]

2.2.2 Evaluation of the Hardware Generations Approach

The analytical specifications of the generations approach are rarely made explicit. Normally the generations are used as descriptive historical labels, merely a convenient way of summarizing long-run technical changes. Nevertheless, there is an implication that even if improvements in component technology did not directly cause changes in hardware design, in software, in systems development techniques and in the organization of the computer function, at least they created the conditions which allowed wider developments to occur.

During the early years of computer systems development, it clearly was the basic hardware which limited computer usage. Almost from the outset of business computing, many recognized a wide range of potential uses to which the computer could be put. The gap between perceived theoretical possibilities and concrete technical attainments was very high. However, as the limitations due to unreliable, large and expensive components were lifted, the power of new developments in component technology have waned. One clear indication of this has been the confusion and uncertainty concerning the dating and characteristics of the fourth generation.

There is a tradition of attributing social changes to technological changes in the academic literature as well as in general parlance. The hardware generations approach accords with this tradition. It enjoys the positive aspects of this tradition and suffers from its limitations. On the positive side, the line of causality runs from a clearly identifiable phenomenon—the use or spread of a technique or set of techniques—to social phenomena. Also, there is considerable evidence of correlations between technical and social factors. Nevertheless, the correlations are not perfect. There have been times when the character of the hardware technology was a critical influence (particularly during the 1950s and early 1960s), but there have always been other factors. For example, even during the early years of computing there were severe labour shortages. This was partly because of factors which had nothing to do with hardware technology. Many scientists, especially mathematicians, looked down at computer programming as an 'impure' scientific activity. Also the mere fact of computing being a new activity meant that there would be a lag before institutions for training appropriate staff could be established or before existing institutions could redesign courses to meet new requirements. We will argue that factors other than hardware technology have become relatively more important during the past 25 years.

The danger of an approach which emphasizes a single determining factor over a long time period is that it can become insensitive to changes in the relative importance of that factor. The hardware generations approach implies that developments in component technology, or at least in hardware technology, will always be the key factor allowing us to make sense of computer developments. The result has been considerable confusion after the mid-1960s, when component technology in particular diminished in importance.

Our approach to the history of computing will incorporate the influence of developing hardware technology, particularly of component technology, but only as one among other potent factors. Clearly, in the early days of computing it was hardware cost and reliability which primarily limited the spread of computer applications. Improvements in hardware technology therefore influenced many other aspects of computing during that time. Nevertheless there were other influences, even during the 1950s. After the mid-1960s these other influences dominated. The discussion of other approaches to the history of computing which follows will help us to specify these other influences and to develop a more balanced approach.

2.3 ORGANIZATION STAGES APPROACH

2.3.1 Churchill, Kempster and Uretsky's 1969 Hypothesis

The origin of the stage hypothesis appears to have been a study of administrative computer-based information systems by Churchill, Kempster and Uretsky in 1969. They proposed four stages in the development of computer departments based on four types of computer applications. The types of applications are related to two dichotomies concerning management. The first is the view that the chief functions of management are planning and control (Urwick, 1949). Planning is the 'higher' end of the dichotomy. It involves recognizing problems, searching for solutions, evaluating and selecting from among alternative solutions and forming an implementation plan. Control, the 'lower' end, involves ensuring implementation occurs, coordinating the operation of the plan, recognizing problem areas and feedback to planning.

The second dichotomy concerns the environments managers must deal with. They are classified as either structured, meaning routine or programmed, or unstructured, i.e. ill-defined or intuitive. 'Higher'-level management normally deals with unstructured environments. This dichotomy is taken from Simon (1960).

The two dichotomies lead to four categories of management. The lowest level of management involves controlling highly structured activities. The highest level involves planning unstructured activities. In between are either planning highly structured activities or controlling relatively unstructured activities. These four categories relate to the four types of computer applications as shown in Figure 2.1.

Type 1 applications are simply replications of clerical systems which were already being carried out by manual methods. They are 'more of the same but faster and cheaper' (Churchill *et al.*, 1969, p. 7). Type 2 systems involve either integrating type 1 systems that had previously been treated separately, or developing new, more comprehensive or more timely reports on routine operations of the firm. A key distinction between type 2 and type 1 systems was that type 2 systems allowed data to be gathered and integrated across functionally separated boundaries of the organization.

A major break occurs with type 3 systems. Type 3 and type 4 systems are oriented towards what they call managerial rather than clerical activities. The essence of management-oriented systems is that they involve either unstructured environments or planning functions. Clerical activities involve both structured environments and control functions. Type 3 applications either involve developing a simple system to replace a number of previously separate activities or

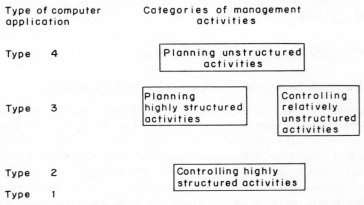

FIGURE 2.1 Computer applications and management activities

they insert decision-making programs directly into the information-processing routines. Type 4 applications involve simulations, or processing ad hoc inquiries to previously unspecified management problems.

According to Churchill *et al.*, their four types represent four stages in the development of computer applications. They qualify this by stating that the 'categorization, while closely related to sophistication, does not require a strict ordering in time' (p. 7). However, they expect the majority of applications to follow the order of types. For example, they state that by the end of the first four or five years of computer use, the major share of applications programmed in all 12 of the companies they surveyed could be considered as type 1 applications (p. 7).

Also the authors emphasize the old adage that you must learn to walk before you can run. One of their major conclusions is that the successful approaches to types 3 or 4 applications are distinguished by the following three characteristics: first, the existence of top-level management support; second, mutual understanding between systems staff and user managers; and third, a good database on which to build (p. 141). It is through the successful development of type 1 and type 2 systems that these requirements are fulfilled.

Churchill *et al.*'s organization stages are based on the following three premises: first, that there is a natural progression of applications sophistication; second, more sophisticated applications require a basis in less sophisticated applications: third, this basis can only be acquired by actually developing these less sophisticated applications in-house. Types 1 and 2 applications not only provide a material basis (the database) for more sophisticated managerially oriented systems, but also the process of their development in-house and the experience of their successful implementation builds up both top management support and an understanding between computer staff and user management.

The authors make some attempt to relate types of computer applications to the internal organization of computer departments, although this aspect of their study is not emphasized. For example, the authors formulate a loose connection between stages of computerization and the location of the computer organization. They observe that in stage 1 the computer group was usually part of the accounting department, since type 1 applications were routine, highly structured activities fulfilling accounting functions. After stage 1 accounting retained control over the computer in some firms, but in others it was moved to a higher level. Computer managers reported directly to the chief financial executive or to the vice-president of administration. In one case the computer group was moved from under the controller and then back again (p. 134). Regarding the direct management of the computer group, the authors state that to the extent that the computer resource is devoted to types 1 and 2 applications, managing the computer is similar to managing factory production or an assembly operation. To the extent it is devoted to types 3 and 4 applications 'its management problems are more like those of an R and D operation' (p. 125). No evidence is presented for this proposition, and we would argue that it is hard to justify.

Whether justified or not, Churchill *et al.* did clearly develop the notion of organization stages based on accumulation of increasingly sophisticated computer applications. Furthermore, they proposed some connections between stages and both the organizational position of the computer group and internal characteristics of computer departments.

2.3.2 Nolan's Early Version of the Stages Hypothesis

Richard Nolan developed the stages approach to computer growth and management during the 1970s. In earlier versions of the model (Nolan, 1973; Gibson and Nolan, 1974) four stages were proposed. The stages are derived from the long-term pattern of computer budgets observed by Nolan in only three companies. This is characterized by an S-shaped curve. All S-shaped curves have three 'turning' or inflection points (see Figure 2.2). From these three turning points four stages were derived. In his 1973 article Nolan called them initiation, contagion, control and integration. In the 1974 article the stages were called initiation, expansion, formalization and maturity. We will concentrate on the 1974 version.

The turning points not only mark the boundaries of different stages, but they also correspond to likely crises in the life of computer facilities. Movement from stage to stage is seen as a series of lurching steps involving disruption to computer users and instability within computer departments.

In the initiation stage the computer is introduced on the basis of cost savings for clerical operations. The computer is usually located in the department where it is

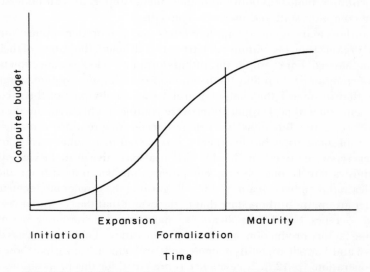

FIGURE 2.2 The S-shaped curve and stages of growth

first applied. Growth is slow. Partly this is because of the limited range of applications attempted. Partly it is also because of management uncertainty or even hostility concerning the computer as a potential change agent. The key problem which generates the S-shaped curve and its attendant crises is that the computer is introduced without a long-term assessment of its impact on personnel, on the firm's organization or on its strategy (pp. 78–79).

The lack of a long-term plan in stage 1 means that during stage 2 an explosion of contagious unplanned growth occurs in computerization. The combination of excess hardware capacity and technically oriented systems analysts, who are over-optimistic about what can be achieved because of stage 1 successes, stimulates strong supply-side pressures for expansion. The emergence of computer use as a status symbol or a sign of progressive management among user managers provides strong demand-side pressure for expansion. Lack of formal controls over project selection, systems development and computer budgets results in cost overruns and hiring of large numbers of professionally oriented computer specialists who are difficult to manage. A loose working environment develops. Basic maintenance and database work are neglected in favour of more glamorous and technically sophisticated new applications. A general explosion of data processing budgets occurs.

The time of reckoning eventually comes and stage 2 turns into stage 3. By the end of stage 2 top managers become aware of the runaway computer budget, 'more likely than not, ... suddenly' (p. 83). This stimulates 'drastic measures'. Elaborate and cumbersome quality control procedures for all aspects of systems development and operations work are imposed. Formal priority setting and management reporting systems are introduced. Chargeout systems are established to impose market-like discipline both on users and on computer departments. Firing the DP manager and replacing him with a more administratively oriented person will often be a key component of the drastic measures.

These measures create a climate where many systems analysts and programmers will either leave or they will 'hunker down', i.e. they will reduce their effort, attend to short term goals and, in effect, work to the rules of the new systems even if this reduces efficiency. The drastic measures become counter-productive. Too much control results in under-utilization and failure to realize the potential of the computer resource.

The solution to this problem is not to introduce new controls in a partial way. 'In managing changes as pervasive as these there is probably nothing worse than doing the job halfway' (p. 84). The stronger the set of informal controls and structures which had been established in stage 2, the more difficult the introduction of formal controls in stage 3 will be. Nevertheless, the more resistant staff are to formal controls, the stronger is Gibson and Nolan's advice to fire them. The solution is not to be soft on existing staff.

The authors recommend several steps that should be taken. First, high-level steering committees should be established to set priorities and curb expansion.

Second, the computer function should be divided up. A centralized core should contain hardware resources and functions such as operations, programming, research and testing. The systems analysts should be decentralized to work closely with users on new applications. These steps are appropriate for firms in stage 3 but, for 'the company wise enough to employ these suggestions at the outset of stage 2, the trauma of stage 3 may be almost entirely avoidable' (p. 86). Therefore, the real 'solution' to the problems of stage 3 is to avoid the mess altogether. For DP managers lucky enough to read Gibson and Nolan's article while they are still in stage 1, the solution is to implement their stage 3 suggestions immediately.

The maturity stage is not brought on by a crisis. Rather it represents the eventual settling of the computer function into the well-planned, effective and flexible resource which it always should have been. Middle managers within the computer department have been trained and habituated to formal control procedures. Close relations with users are only undertaken by specialist analysts located in user departments. The computer manager, now called the MIS (management information systems) manager rather than the EDP (electronic data processing) manager, has a sound relation with top management because they talk the same language, i.e. the language of 'meaningful, detailed plans' (p. 87). The computer function has grown up and can now provide a career path into general management at top levels.

The dynamic of Nolan's stages approach is different from that of Churchill *et al.* For the earlier group it is the progression of increasingly sophisticated types of computer applications that define the stages. For Nolan it is management's short-term reactions to a large-scale and poorly understood technical event, the introduction of the computer, which drives computer users through the stages. Management of the computer function can be compared to a pendulum, reacting to a technological 'push'. First there is excessive and uncontrolled expansion (stage 2), then swinging excessively towards cost control and formalization (stage 3), before settling down to some steady-state or equilibrium level of expenditure, flexibility and formality. In general, the order of applications development follows a pattern similar to Churchill *et al.*'s, but not strictly. Gibson and Nolan mention three types of applications. First are applications which reduce general and administrative expenses by replacing clerical personnel. Second are those which reduce the cost of goods such as inventory control systems. Finally there are applications that can increase revenues and facilitate managerial decision making such as on-line customer service systems and financial planning models.[3] Nevertheless, these do not drive the S-shaped curve, rather they are taken up as allowed for by the prepotent stages.

The first two types of applications are carried out in stages 1 and 2. Stage 3 would coincide with initiation of the third type of application. Nevertheless, they are not taken up during stage 3. These applications are harder to envision and define than previous applications. They are seen as more risky and in the cost-control atmosphere of stage 3 they are not taken up. Only cost-reducing applications such as purchasing control and scheduling systems are attempted at this stage. It is only by stage 4, when the firm is mature enough to handle them, that the more sophisticated management decision and customer-related systems are developed.

We can also relate Nolan's stages approach to the hardware generation approach. Gibson and Nolan accept that technical change occurs throughout the stages. They state that the S-shaped curve 'seems to have been primarily driven by developments in hardware technology in the second- and third-generation systems' (p. 88). They do not mean that changes in management strategies, organization or personnel associated with the computer function have changed during that growth period as a clear reflection of changing hardware technologies. By 'driven' they mean that falling hardware costs have allowed the computer to be applied to more complex applications and this has caused computer budgets to grow. In contrast to the limited role they attribute to technical change as firms moved from stage 1 to stage 4, Gibson and Nolan end their article with the expectation that software developments around database technology are likely to provide a new push of the management pendulum and to start off another S-shaped curve in future. For Gibson and Nolan, technological changes provide the initial push and may sustain the S-shaped curve, but the shape of the curve and the character of the stages which emerge from it are formed by a series of crises within each organization. In this they seem to be following the notion of cycles of evolutionary and revolutionary growth which one of their Harvard colleagues proposed as a general model for growth of all organizations, independent of any particular technical changes (Greiner, 1972).

2.3.3 Nolan's Later Six-stage Model

Nolan extended the stage model from four to six stages, rather tentatively, in a book about chargeout policies. In that book he also explicitly refers to the S-shaped curve as a learning curve (1977b, p. 20), and he uses the concepts of organization control or slack (borrowed from Cyert and March, 1956) to characterize the environment created by management for dealing with computer functions. These new themes are more comprehensively dealt with in Nolan's 1979 *Harvard Business Review* article. In this article Nolan inserted two new stages between stage 3 and 4 and reverted to his 1973 labels for stages 2 and 3. The new model was based on two S-shaped curves, tracking DP budgets (Figure 2.3).

Around the middle of stage 3 a basic transition occurs from management of the computer to management of the company's data resources. This represents the realization of the prediction Nolan made at the end of the 1974 article, that there would be a new S-shaped curve stimulated by database technologies. This makes stage 4 now look like stage 2. In stage 4 users get interactive terminals and support required for using the new database technology. The cost controls established

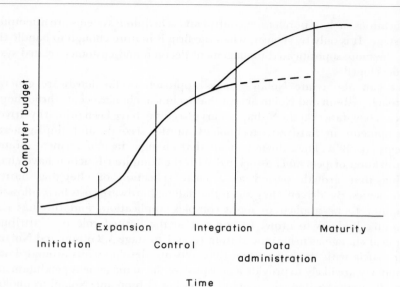

FIGURE 2.3 Nolan's six-stage model

during stage 3 are ineffective for containing a new budget explosion because those systems of planning and control were

> 'designed for internal management of the computer rather than for control of the growth in use of it and containment of the cost explosion. (Nolan, 1979, p. 120).

Stage 4 differs from stage 2 in that it is much more exclusively based on demand-pull pressures. The end user becomes the driving force because of perceived real profit advantage due to advances in database systems which were promised in stage 3. In stage 2, on the other hand, it was primarily supply pressures from overly optimistic and technically oriented computer specialists that drove the firm to over-expand DP budgets. The explosive growth of DP budgets is counteracted in stage 5 by top management tightening up external (user-managed) planning and control systems. The problem of uncoordinated user data collection leading to data redundancy is solved by data administration. This is overseen by a senior management steering committee.

Stage 6, maturity, is reached when external equilibrium between user demands for user-managed projects, and the ability to use new data effectively, matches internal equilibrium between the benefits of innovation within DP and the costs of that innovation.

The other major change in the model from the 1974 version is the incorporation of a control versus slack dichotomy into each of the stages. The difference between those two management-created environments is that financial and performance control systems are present only in the control environment. In the slack environment, incentives to use DP in an experimental manner are present. These incentives are identified as committing 'more resources to data processing than are strictly necessary to get the job done. The extra payment achieves another objective—"nurturing of innovation"' (p. 117). In stages 1–3 it is management of the computer which is the focus of the balance between control and slack. In stages 3–6 it is management of data resources. In both cases the balance changes from low control and low slack, first to high slack and low control when budgets are expanding quickly (stages 2 and 4), and then to low slack and high control when budget growth is being retarded (stages 3 and 5). The process ends in stage 6 when a balance is achieved through high slack and high control. This aspect of the model is not clear.

The very labels—control and slack—suggest a single dimension with control representing 'more' and slack 'less'. Nolan presents insufficient detail to allow us to understand what he means either by the low-slack and low-control situation of stage 1 or the high-slack and high-control situation of stage 6. It is likely that he means the core–periphery situation recommended in the 1974 version for stage 4. The core represented high control through the formal methods established during stage 3. The periphery of systems analysts located in user areas represented flexibility through sensitivity to new applications. The latter may be what Nolan means by high slack. In spite of specifying both high slack and high control as characteristics of maturity, it is clear that Nolan associates more formal planning and control systems both with later stages in the model and with good management practice (in the sense that the earlier these systems are introduced the better). One attempt to test Nolan's model specifically presumed an association between increasing formalization and more 'mature' DP departments to be a major testable prediction arising from the Nolan model (Goldstein and McCririk, 1981). The prediction was not supported by their tests.

2.3.4 Evaluation of the Organization Stages Approach

Organization stages and 'external' developments

We are primarily concerned to evaluate the stages approach as a guide for understanding the overall history of computer management and use. We accept that the models were not specifically intended for this purpose, but the stages approach has been used to locate the general state of computer use in a historical context. For example, Nolan characterizes the situation at the time of writing the 1979 article as one in which 'roughly half of the larger companies are experiencing stage 3 or 4' (1979, p. 121), and on this interpretation he predicts 'an explosive stage 4 type period of DP budget expansion in the next two to five years in most companies' (p. 122). Also by considering organization stages in relation to overall long-run developments, a powerful critique of the stages approach to developments within firms emerges.

The basic problem with the organization stages approach is that it does not incorporate interactions between the experiences of computing within organizations and external factors. Relevant external factors include the experiences of other individual firms as well as general changes in knowledge of computer capabilities and management as expressed in the computer literature. Nolan's knowledge of experiences of certain organizations leads him to summarize their history as a series of stages. He then generalizes his description of these stages from organizations he has observed to all organizations. The obvious question is, why do organizations which computerize later still make the same mistakes as earlier ones? Why do latecomers not benefit from the experience of pioneer organizations, or at least from Nolan's advice? Even more important, rapid technological change in computers has meant that the initial technology which newcomers face is different from that which pioneers had to adjust to.[4]

Nolan becomes aware of these problems by the time of writing his 1979 article. He states, 'a company that began to automate business functions in 1960 moved through the stages differently from a company that started to automate in 1970 or 1978' (p. 116). Nevertheless, this statement seems to be added as an afterthought. How firms of different computer vintages might move through the stages 'differently' is not discussed, nor does Nolan entertain the possibility that the stages themselves may be specific to certain vintages of computer users and certain types of organizations.

Nolan's empirical base is heavily biased. It is likely that nearly all began to automate their business functions before 1970. The entry cost of computerization has fallen dramatically and continuously since the mid-1950s (see Chapter 4). This means that late-entrant companies have been significantly smaller than earlier computer users. As we shall demonstrate, size of company, and particularly size of computer group, strongly affects management of computer staff (see section 12.1.1).

Churchill *et al.*'s sample was biased in the same way as Nolan's, if not more so. They stated that all companies in their sample had at least five years of experience with computers. Their data were gathered either in 1967 or 1968. Therefore it is likely that most of their sample began computerization before 1960. This qualification should be borne in mind when considering empirical evidence for the stages approach.

Empirical support for the organization stages approach

There have been many attempts to test aspects of Nolan's models empirically. These have been summarized by King and Kraemer (1984) and by Benbasat *et al.* (1984).

Lucas and Sutton (1977) found that the S-shaped budget curve was absent from their sample of 29 government computer departments. They found that computer budgets grew in a linear fashion (stable percentage increases). Lucas and Sutton admit that their results may not be generalizable to private-sector budgets, nevertheless they do not support Nolan's stages model.

A number of features to be expected of firms closer to maturity have been tested against either age of computer facilities or an amalgam of criteria discerned from Nolan to indicate maturity. These include items such as expenditure on hardware, degree of formalism in planning, budgeting and monitoring, user awareness and capabilities, and senior management involvement with information systems. The results generally have not supported the Nolan model. For example, Goldstein and McCririk (1981) found that the emergence of a formal data administration function, which should only emerge in stage 4 (1974 version of Nolan's model) or stage 5 (1979 version), was not strongly correlated with maturity criteria. Drury and Bates (1979) found no significant correlation between chargeout system usage and maturity.

In his 1973 article Nolan had indicated that more managerial and less technical skills would be associated with later stages. Benbasat *et al.* (1980) found no significant correlation between maturity and desirability of more generalist rather than specialist skills by DP managers or systems analysts. Work by Drury, reported in Benbasat *et al.* (1984), found no significant positive correlation between length of computer experience and presence of steering committees.

There has been some evidence in favour of Nolan's model. Ein-Dor and Segev (1982) found that when information systems groups originated in low-level staff departments or in operational departments they were eventually moved up the organizational hierarchy. Nevertheless, almost half of their sample (22 out of 45 firms) did not move their information systems group. In most of these (15), the information systems group was originally located at a high level (either as an autonomous unit or in administrative services).[5] Sääksjärvi (1985) concluded that Nolan's model was a good descriptor of the average pattern of changes in a sample of 130 major Finnish data processing installations, but that it was unable to predict developments.

We can explain other empirical failures to validate the stages hypothesis by bringing external historical factors into the analysis to supplement or even to supplant internal stages. Benbasat *et al.* (1980) did not find a correlation between organizational maturity and desirability of generalist skills because a large majority of both systems analysts and MIS managers perceived generalist skills to be more valuable than specialist skills. This is because there has been a widespread shift in emphasis within the computer world towards greater sensitivity to user demands. This has been generated by technological and social factors which are not simply organization specific (see Chapter 11). We suspect that if Benbasat *et al.* had carried out their survey in the 1950s or even the 1960s, they would have obtained different results, at least for the attitudes of systems analysts. As Sääksjärvi puts it: 'The Nolan model is confined within the limits of its own historical background' (1985, p. 188).

Perhaps the empirical assessment most supportive of Nolan is Drury (1983). In his 1979 article Nolan specifies six types of benchmarks by which one can identify which stage a firm is at (p. 121). Drury collected data about these benchmarks from 144 firms. The results of his study were negative in the sense that the benchmarks did not clearly classify the firms into consistent stages. Nevertheless, all pairs of benchmark variables were positively correlated, indicating that generally more mature firms would be at more 'mature' levels on each of the benchmarks. Therefore there seems to be a general rise in all of the benchmarks as experience with computers accumulates, even if the benchmarks do not increase at the same rate as each other or within each of the stages.

The empirical studies indicate some degree of independent organization-tied development, but support for a consistent set of stages has not been forthcoming. A major hindrance to this enterprise is the absence of any systematic or verifiable evidence in Nolan's own published work.

The maturity concept and organizational learning

One often-expressed theoretical criticism of Nolan concerns his maturity concepts (Drury, 1983; Benbasat *et al.*, 1984, pp. 484–485; King and Kraemer, 1984, pp. 471 and 473). The basic criticism is that the concept of maturity implies an eventual static position for the computer function. In 1974 maturity was reached by stage 4, but in later work maturity is not achieved until stage 6. How can 'maturity' mature? Surely only by observers such as Nolan declaring maturity prematurely. This is a much weaker criticism of Nolan than it appears to be. If maturity is treated as an 'end state' and the model is likened to a 'life-cycle' model, such as is used to describe changes in living organisms (birth, growth, maturation), then the model is severely compromised by the theorist returning to print with a declaration of postponed maturity. This is the interpretation which King and Kraemer put forward (1984, p. 471). It is an interpretation based on the label Nolan uses—'maturity'—as opposed to the way he uses the concept, which is better labelled equilibrium. Nolan's model of the firm is one based on a biological analogy, but it is the homeostasis analogy rather than the life-cycle analogy. The introduction of computers is seen as an event or a stimulus from the outside world which upsets the equilibrium or stable balance within firms. The turbulence so created is eventually calmed by appropriate planning and control mechanisms. 'Appropriate' mechanisms are learned by experience—not through simple accumulation of truth, but through a gradual dampening of excessive short-term reactions. In the end a stable balance is regained. The new equilibrium is 'mature' in that the firm has now weathered the technological storm, a storm which it had to face up to because of competitive pressures.

In this sense 'maturity' can be a state to which the computer function returns several times. Clearly this is what Nolan meant. As early as 1974 he suggested that the fourth stage was unlikely to be the last one. While it is therefore wrong to criticize Nolan (as do King and Kraemer, 1984, p. 471) for post hoc theorizing when he adds a further S-curve in later models, we can criticize him for assuming that the only cause of disruption to a firm's equilibrium comes from outside. Crises can develop out of tensions between workers and managers, between managers of different operational departments, between staff and line managers, or between top managers and middle managers, without major external upheavals to spark them off. In fact Greiner's model (1972), which seems to have influenced Nolan, specifies a series of crises generated simply by organization growth. If crises can be both internally and externally generated, the notion of equilibrium, and especially of maturity, can be quite misleading.

Technological determinism and the stages approach

King and Kraemer also criticize Nolan for overstating the dominance of technological change as the primary driving force behind the growth of computing through the stages (p. 471). In particular they accuse Nolan of ignoring demand-side factors such as the need for maintenance and enhancement of existing systems, demand among users for computing as a political resource and the appeal of computing simply for status or as an 'entertaining' technology. This is only partially justified. Nolan explicitly points out that users develop a fascination with the computer and view it as a status symbol in stage 2 (Gibson and Nolan, 1974, p. 81). The controls introduced in stage 5 are needed to contain demand according to Nolan (1979, p. 118). The only change in technology which explicitly affects the Nolan model, apart from the presence of the computer itself, is the emergence of database technology. The weakness of Nolan is not his over-emphasis of technological change, but rather his lack of detailed treatment of this change.

The problem of 'tenses'

Churchill *et al.* make an extremely pertinent point at the outset of their book. Of the computing literature they say 'Descriptions of "what we have done" shade into "what we are now doing" which, of course, immediately lead to "what we plan to do" next week, next month or next year' (1969, pp. 3–4).

We have noticed this problem of tenses in the writings of computer development observers as well as participants. In fact, we believe that Churchill *et al.* also suffer from this problem. This is not because they overestimate the current state of development in the firms they surveyed, but rather because they do not adequately qualify their conclusions as applicable only to the types of firms they have examined. While anonymity was guaranteed, the authors could have told us more about the characteristics of the firms they surveyed, especially their size. The authors list typical computer configurations in their appendix, distinguishing on the basis of size of system. It is likely that the majority of the population of installations existing at the time of their survey would have been what they called small or medium-sized installations. Nevertheless, it is clear that most, if not all, of the author's sample were drawn from large-scale installations (all of their sample had at least five years' experience with computers).

The same problem exists with Nolan's work. Herein lies the danger of taking the stage which the reported sample had reached at the time of writing up as a good estimate of the state of computer development at that time.

The problem of tenses must be qualified in the following way. The tendency for the literature to *anticipate* events in the field refers primarily to positive technical events; to the existence and diffusion of new techniques, and to the potency of new techniques to overcome problems and increase efficiency or effectiveness. Negative effects of technical events are more likely to be *delayed*, to be reported after a cumulation of bad experiences. Those generating new techniques have a vested interest in reporting in anticipation of events. It can be useful for marketing those techniques. Those experiencing positive effects of new techniques have a vested interest in reporting them quickly. It can be useful for marketing themselves and their organization. However, those experiencing negative effects of new techniques or other problems are likely to be reluctant to rush to report their experiences, at least until they are able to assure themselves that the problems they face have not been generated by their own incompetence.

Later in this book we will rely on the computing literature to provide evidence for the major concerns of computer systems developers and their managers. We believe that the problem of tenses, to which Churchill *et al.* referred, may apply to these issues in reverse.

Nolan's model and management strategies

Nolan takes on Cyert and March's dichotomy of control or slack environments which management can create. He suggests one positive characteristic of a slack environment—nurturing innovation—but he clearly believes the most appropriate environment to be that of control. The set of crises which generate the stages emerge due to a lack of foresight. With planning and control mechanisms at the outset, the problems could have been avoided. Also, maturity (the 1974 version) does not involve slackening off on excessive formal controls of the previous stage (stage 3), but rather either the habituation of existing staff to such controls or the replacement of resisters by staff who will accept the controls.

The very terms 'control' and 'slack' imply that control indicates the presence of positive management techniques, while slack is their absence, a negative state from management's point of view. Even if the formulation of alternative environments is rather one-sided, the recognition of available alternatives—that there is no one best way to manage the computer resource throughout its entire history—is a strong addition to the stages model. The notion that different stages require, or are associated with, different managerially created environments gives further substance to the stages model. We have already criticized Nolan's particular formulation of the control/slack distinction (section 2.3.3). Here we note that by proposing a particular control/slack combination as appropriate for each of the stages, Nolan does imply that there is one best environment within each stage.

Description and prescription in Nolan's model

One of the major problems in evaluating the stages approach is the difficulty in distinguishing description from prescription in Nolan's model. Subsequent tests of the stages approach test Nolan's model as a *description* of how characteristics of computer management, organization and personnel will change as the function matures. This is partly justified in that Nolan, at least up to 1974, considered the stages to result from a lack of long-term planning, certainly not the result of a development path prescribed by Nolan. Nevertheless, the 1979 model contains much stronger short-term *prescriptive* elements. By 1979 changes tracked by the turning points of the budget S-curve are seen as inevitable. The job of managers is seen as one of creating the control/slack environment appropriate to each stage, rather then avoiding the disruption of moving from stage to stage. To the extent that Nolan's model represents prescription, the success of any test could be interpreted as a measure of Nolan's influence on the computing world.

The vague line between description and prescription in Nolan's work has worried critics. King and Kraemer seem to complain that the particular control/slack balance, which Nolan suggests should be pursued at particular times, is not prescriptive enough. He is assuming managers will know in what direction their organization is headed in its use of computing.

> In fact most policies are probably reactive, developed in response to problems experienced with computing ... simply categorizing policies in this way does not indicate what policies managers should follow (1984, p. 472).

This is a rather contorted criticism. King and Kraemer are either criticizing Nolan for being descriptive and inaccurate or they are criticizing him for not being concrete or detailed enough in his prescriptions. Either Nolan's suggestions are too good, too efficient, requiring too much foresight, or Nolan is criticized for not giving a more concrete indication of how managers might decide what policies they should follow. The former interpretation is probably closer to King and Kraemer's intent. At another point they criticize Nolan for not taking conflict and inconsistencies over organizational goals into account. This would imply that the best way to manage according to certain groups in the firm may not be shared by others.

2.3.5 Building Blocks from the Organization Stages Approach

The organization stages approach, in spite of its lack of empirical support, has been judged positively in the literature for its provision of 'interesting and testable hypotheses' (King and Kraemer, 1984, p. 474). The elements of this approach which we will build on are the following.

First is the notion of a hierarchy of computer applications based not only on increasing levels of sophistication but also on the outputs of lower types being necessary inputs for higher types. This represents a useful contribution from Churchill *et al.* When this is combined with their connection between types of applications being developed and characteristics of the DP organization and personnel, we have an important counterbalance to the supply-side technological view of the generations approach.

Second is Nolan's proposition that managerial reaction to technological disruptions or opportunities require many years to sort out. This allows a clear appreciation of management failure because of attention to short-term problems and provides a healthy corrective to the economists' view of unproblematic diffusion of new technology.[6]

Third, Nolan's introduction of managerial choice in terms of the control/slack environments they can create provides a useful tool for summarizing managerial strategies towards computer functions. The concept of 'slack' will be refined so that the strategy based on slack represents a more credible alternative to the control environment strategy.

Finally is Nolan's recognition that factors external to the organization should also be taken into account. This insight will be transformed from a qualification to a keystone of the analysis.

2.4 LABOUR PROCESS APPROACH

2.4.1 The General Approach

The labour process approach is based on the proposition that the work of computer specialists can be analysed in the same way as any other work situation. Furthermore, proponents believe that there are certain long-term tendencies common to all work situations. These tendencies are the product of social institutions, not technology. In fact technological developments, whatever their specific form, will have broadly the same social consequences. In a sense the technology is treated as an intervening variable by which social institutions fulfil a general destiny. Rapid technological change has the effect of speeding up movement along the predestined path. In this sense, the labour process approach is diametrically opposed to the hardware generations approach.

The social institution at the heart of all work situations is the employment contract—the people who will do the work contract to sell their capacity to work for particular periods of time. In return they agree to accept the directives of the agents of the employing firm (the managers) during the period of employment. Unlike other contracts, the essential bargain of the employment contract does not involve exchange of physical goods or even specific services for money. While wages may come to be tied to production targets according to strict rules, these rules may change during the contract period. It is the right to make and to alter rules and to expect some degree of compliance which the employer gains by offering an employment contract. When productivity is rising quickly, particularly if it is due to the introduction of new technology, it will be against the firm's interests to tie wages to productivity changes. Wage levels will primarily be affected by general national or regional social factors—notions of 'proper' standard of living, comparisons with similar groups, seniority, skill levels, labour market conditions and strength of worker organization.

Because wages are not strictly tied to productivity levels, it is very much in management's interest to improve productivity. One way to do this is to intensify the work, to push employees to work faster, or to reduce the porosity of working time by cutting down break times or instruction periods, or time required to switch work tasks. A second method, one which is less likely to encounter strong resistance by employees, is to introduce new equipment or reorganize the flow of work, or to automate certain tasks, so that the same number of workers can produce more, quite apart from whether they work faster or more continuously.

Another method of achieving productivity growth is particularly emphasized with the labour process approach. Changes in production methods can do more than improve the productivity of a given set of employees. They can also reduce either the number of employees required or the skills required of any set of employees. This latter effect is particularly important when employees required in a firm are highly skilled. Skilled employees are often highly paid. They are usually in short supply on the labour market. Training is expensive and time-consuming. Also they are often organized in unions based around their skills. Sometimes their organizations will be able to control the flow of new skilled workers on to the labour market by controlling training. Inevitably such employees will control the pace and procedures of their work more than less-skilled workers simply because their work will be more complex. Therefore supervisors and managers, who are further away from the work, will be less likely to understand it. This job control will be enhanced by informal and formal organization among skilled workers.

According to the labour process approach, the principal method by which managers have dealt with this situation is to divide up the labour process so that jobs requiring primarily conceptual activities are separated from those requiring mainly the execution of orders. Furthermore, conceptual activities are concentrated among fewer and fewer people. The best-known advocate of this approach to management was Frederick Taylor. The three basic principles of what he called 'scientific management' were, first, to gather workers' traditional knowledge and systematize it in order to discover the 'one best way' to carry out that work. The second principle was to formulate rules based on that knowledge in a planning or layout department, separated from the factory floor. The third was to instruct individual workers, in writing, in advance, exactly what they should do, when and how to do it (Taylor, 1911).

Two chief advantages accrued to managers who followed this method. First, they would wrest overall control over the labour process away from workers. This would make it possible to measure productivity, which would also make it easier to increase productivity, especially by intensifying the work. Managers would be able to order employees to work faster with less chance of being told, or at least convinced, that it was not possible. The second chief advantage for managers was that the majority of workers employed would require fewer skills. Less-skilled workers would be cheaper to employ as well as more controllable. This is sometimes known as the Babbage effect. By dividing skilled work into different component processes, each requiring different degrees of skill, the employer need only pay for workers with the particular components of the skills required, rather than for all-round craftsmen. The overall wage bill would thereby be reduced (Babbage, 1832).

The modern labour process approach to analysing the history of work effectively began with Braverman (1974). According to Braverman, the Babbage effect and Taylor's scientific management methods were not simply theories of how managers might organize the labour process. Rather they represent the actual practice of management. They are made necessary because of the nature of employment contracts as described above and because of competition. The drives to raise productivity and to reduce costs are not fuelled primarily by the greed of employers. If an individual employer cannot raise productivity or reduce costs in line with competitors, and refuses to do so, he will lose his market to others.

While these pressures have been inherent in the social structure of the economy since the beginnings of capitalism, according to Braverman they became more intense around the end of the nineteenth century, when science was brought more closely under the wing of industry. No labour process is immune from these pressures and Braverman explicitly cites the development of computer specialists' work as a modern example.

2.4.2 Computer Specialists and the Labour Process Approach

In the times before commercial applications of computing, i.e. from 1946 until the early 1950s, computer specialists carried out a wide range of rasks. They analysed problems to be solved by the computer. They transformed these problems into a language that the machine could understand (i.e. they programmed the machine). They operated the machines and often maintained them. They directly entered their data and programs into the machine. Gradually analysis, programming, operating and key punching were divided off. Breaking up the overall set of tasks into these job categories allowed specialists without all-round skills to be hired. Braverman also notes that within each of these broad job categories a myriad of new titles indicating different specialisms had arisen, particularly since the mid-1960s (1974, pp. 329–331).

These divisions represent a clear separation of conception from execution work according to Braverman. The analyst is the employee who primarily carries out the conceptual activity. The analyst instructs the programmer through the program specification or 'spec', which is normally written. There is considerable variation in the amount of detail contained in the spec. It is possible for the spec to be so detailed that the programmers' work becomes quite mechanical. In these cases programmers will often be called coders. The term 'coder' is often used in a pejorative sense among computer specialists.

Operators, even more than programmers, will carry out work with little conceptual content. Not only are their tasks spelled out in considerable detail, but the timing of their work is largely paced by the hardware. Education requirements, average salaries and promotion prospects are substantially better for analysts compared with programmers and operators. Finally, key-punch operators simply enter the data into the computer. This work requires very little skill. It is poorly paid and almost completely done by women. Braverman suggests that these divisions have improved employer's control over the labour process in computer departments as well as keeping overall wage costs below what they would have been (pp. 337–348).

Braverman's suggestions about applying the labour process approach to computer specialists have been taken up by Joan Greenbaum (1976, 1979) and Phil Kraft (1977). Kraft follows the labour process approach most assiduously and we will concentrate on his analysis.

Kraft concentrates on the joining of mass production techniques to the division of labour as the primary characteristic of 'all modern industrial workplaces' (p. 52). The key is the production of a standardized product. If the product is standardized, then the labour process can also be standardized. This implies deskilling for Kraft. Work, made up of separate but independent tasks, is transformed into a larger number of simpler, routine and unrelated tasks. Routinized subtasks are then parcelled out to workers who do a few of them over and over again. These workers require much less skill.

According to Kraft the initial fragmentation of computer specialists' work occurred in the early 1950s, when Systems Development Corporation (SDC), a spin-off of the Rand Corporation, set out to train 2000 programmers needed for the SAGE project. The SAGE project was part of the US government's early-warning system against an air attack from Russia. There the distinction between analysts and programmers was established. Kraft gives the SAGE training programme prominence because it was so large a project. He estimates that it meant a doubling of the number of programmers in the US at that time (p. 37).

From that point attempts to routinize programming work were vigorously pursued. Major efforts were expended to develop a programming language that was so simple as to allow staff, who were not computer specialists, to deal directly with the computer. Kraft cites Robert Bosak, who at a symposium in 1959 stated that the 'ultimate [aim] is to remove the programmer entirely from the process of writing operational programs' (Bosak, 1960, p. 213). Efforts during the 1950s were not successful, but according to Kraft the real breakthrough occurred in the early 1960s with the development of structured programming. Kraft likens structured programming in its potential effects on programmers to the restrictions and control which mass production methods have had on industrial work (pp. 52, 59 and 99).[7]

The effect of structured programming is to limit the number of paths one can travel to reach a solution to a computer-programming problem. Dividing the problem into modules can also have a Babbage-type effect if different people are assigned to write different modules. Many data processing managers in fact do not distinguish modularization from structured programming. According to Kraft, with structured programming (and modularization) managers could have 'programmers who worked like machines' (p. 57). It means 'a standardized product made in a standardized way by people who do the same limited tasks over and over without knowing how they fit into a larger undertaking' (p. 59). Routinization and deskilling of programming has been furthered by several other management techniques that were also developed during the 1960s, according to Kraft. The two main techniques are the widespread use of packaged or 'canned' programs and the reorganization of programming work, particularly using the 'chief programmer team'.

Canned programs are ready-made programs that will deal with all or part of an application problem in a standard way. The advantages to managers are that they need not employ their own people to create a solution. The canned program, like any mass-produced product, is likely to be much cheaper than one that is custom made.[8] Kraft believes that canned programs have been written carefully enough in the first place to allow 'a whole new and less expensive sub-occupation of packaged program modifiers' to be created (p. 55). Chief programmer teams are discussed in section 5.5.6. For Kraft it is clear that the chief programmer specializes in conceptual activities, but the rest specialize in execution, in taking orders and carrying out what is, at most, semi-skilled work.

Kraft is certain that the use of these techniques is either widespread (structured programming, modularization, canned programs) or spreading quickly among large organizations (chief programmer teams). He is certain that where introduced they are making programming work more routine and deskilled. As stated above, Kraft also believes that, ultimately, programming work will resemble assembly-line work. Nevertheless, his assessment in 1977 is that this destiny has not yet been reached. He is rather ambivalent about how close to assembly-line work programming has become. At one point he states:

> Programming, even coding, is still primarily a mind-skill and there are few hard and fast rules of behavior which managers can compare against an efficiency expert's model in order to check performance. (p. 62)

Later he states:

> What is most remarkable about the work programmers do is how quickly it has been
> transformed ... divided and routinized, it has become mass-production work
> parcelled out to interchangeable detail workers ... The great and growing mass of
> people called programmers ... do work which is less and less distinguished from that
> of clerks or, for that matter, assembly line workers. (p. 97)

About the future direction of the programming labour process Kraft is quite clear.
Work fragmentation and programmer deskilling will continue and intensify
(p. 103). The long-run pattern of the labour process in computing is precisely the
same as in blue-collar or traditional clerical occupations. The pattern does not
reflect technological factors, but rather it occurs because of social institutions.[9] In
fact Kraft implies that the technology has been developed in response to the social
imperatives. Structured programming, canned programs and the chief
programmer team are techniques or technologies that have been developed and
have widely diffused. They were not invented by independent geniuses and then
taken up because they were found to be more efficient than any of a larger number
of available, independently generated, inventions. Rather they were stimulated by
a particular set of socially generated needs and desires; the need to deskill and
routinize work. This is derived from the need to control the labour process, which
is derived from the desire to make profits using wage labour (employment
contracts).

Kraft, following Marglin (1974), distinguishes between techniques that
improve efficiency and those that improve management control. For Kraft the
techniques described above are primarily about control. He notes that the
'management literature on programmers displays a general concern with
developing techniques to get the people managers manage to do what they are
told, not simply how to write better programs' (p. 4).

Even if one thinks of technology only as hardware, Kraft's argument implies a
reverse direction of causality from the usual technological changes yields
social implications approach. Kraft points out that during the 1960s more and
more of what had originally been software components of computer systems were
being 'wired into' the machine. For example, if a particular computer is always
going to be programmed using one or very few high-level languages, it will save
considerable machine capacity to wire in the compiler function (the program that
transforms individual high-level language statements into machine code). Kraft
implies that an important effect of this is that, even if programmers wished to write
code in lower-level languages (which allow more scope for unstructured
programming), and have the required skills, they would be barred from doing so.
A further effect would be to eliminate many programming tasks altogether. Kraft
states, 'one strategy involves getting rid of programmers whenever possible by
wiring in more and more software in *smart machines*' (p. 62).

2.4.3 Evaluation of The Labour Process Approach

The labour process approach attributes both social changes and technological changes to social factors. In this we believe it to be a useful corrective to the technological determinism implicit in the hardware generations approach. A further advantage of the labour process approach is that it seems to accord with certain facts. Clearly separation of conception from execution occurred with the separation of computer systems developers (analysts and programmers) from operators and data preparation staff. Also within the computer systems development group, the facts, at least as presented in the 1970s by Braverman *et al.*, seem in accord with the labour process approach. Recently Kraft and Dubnoff (1986) have presented evidence from a survey in the Boston area of the USA which they claim shows a strong division of labour among analysis and programming specialists along lines of conception versus execution. 'The people who make the decisions and set the specifications rarely write code or manuals or test software' (1986, p. 192).[10]

The average programmer in the mid-1970s appeared to be less skilled than the majority of programmers in the 1950s or even the early 1960s. Certainly many computer departments introduced procedures in the 1960s and 1970s that were designed by people who claimed they would raise programmer productivity, and allow less-skilled people to carry out programming. Since the mid-1960s at least, the software productivity gap has been a frequent subject in the computer and management literature (see Friedman and Cornford, 1981). This has partly been stimulated by labour shortages and subsequent relatively high salaries for programmers. Nevertheless, we will present evidence from the 1980s which shows that the trends towards further routinization and deskilling, which were confidently predicted in the 1970s, have not occurred. Many data-processing managers who introduced these procedures later abandoned them. Many never introduced them. Many only introduced them in a partial way and for purposes other than deskilling of programmers.

The major problem with the labour process approach, particularly as represented in Kraft's work, is that it takes on Braverman's theoretical approach uncritically. Braverman has been subjected to substantial criticisms, and the theoretical base of labour process analysis has developed accordingly (see Thompson, 1984, for a survey of this literature). A primary weakness of Braverman's approach is that he does not allow any scope for different managerial strategies for organizing work. Social institutions determine a unique path for management to pursue. The employment relation combined with competition in product and labour markets push managers to deskill work by separating conception from execution in all instances. This confuses the goal of stable and high profits with one strategy for dealing with labour in order to achieve that objective.

We have noted that Nolan distinguishes *two* sorts of managerial strategy (creating control or slack environments). Nolan argues that a clear relation exists between different managerial strategies and different stages of computer development within each firm. We will argue that computer managers have not consistently chosen the deskilling path or the control path for computer staff. Moreover, we will give evidence for general moves towards integrating job categories and both recruitment and encouragement of generalists, rather than narrow specialists, in computer departments in recent years (Chapters 11 and 12).

2.5 INTEGRATING HARDWARE GENERATIONS, ORGANIZATION STAGES AND LABOUR PROCESS APPROACHES

We have indicated advantages and disadvantages of each of the three approaches that have been used in the past to portray aspects of the history of computing. We will draw on the strengths of each approach and, hopefully, avoid their weaknesses.

Consider the hardware generations and the labour process approaches. *Both* technological changes in hardware and the desire to cut labour costs have been driving forces during the history of computing. Nevertheless, we believe that the strength of these stimuli has not been evenly distributed throughout that history. During the earliest years computer hardware was the critical factor, although software costs were still important. By the late 1960s the balance had shifted to software costs. Both hardware generations and labour process approaches ignore a further factor, one which has always been notable. This is the difficulty of developing computer systems that are really useful. High hardware and software costs can limit the growth of computerization. Poor quality of delivered systems can have the same effect. Recently, system quality has become a more important issue than cost in many computer departments. Problems with giving users or clients what they really need have grown in importance because of changes in the degree of prior knowledge about the value of a system. Systems being produced today are no longer simply replacements for pre-existing manual systems. The analysis and particularly the design content of new systems has grown. This results in a greater weight being placed on the quality of delivered systems.

This change in the character of delivered systems has been emphasized in the organization stages approach, particularly in the original Churchill *et al.* version. Moves towards what they consider to be higher-order computer applications have occurred, not only within individual firms but also in the computer world in general. The consequences of these changes have been particularly important influences on management strategies towards computer staff in recent years.

Another element that we draw from the organization. stages approach, particularly from Nolan's work, is the notion of breaking our historical account into stages, or rather phases. Nevertheless, the mechanisms generating those phases are different from Nolan's stages, which occur because of over-reaction within firms to technological disruptions. In contrast, our phases are generated by the gradual alleviation of what is regarded as the primary limitation to computerization in any one phase, and the revelation thereby of a different limiting factor—one which had always been present, but one which was masked by the strength of the previous primary limiting factor.

In the following chapter aspects of each of the three approaches that we consider to be positive are integrated with theories from outside the computing literature into a series of models. These models will then be used to guide our examination of the history of computer systems development.

ENDNOTES

1. For example, Rosen says, 'The distinction between second generation and third is not nearly as clean-cut [as between first and second]' (1969, p. 29, brackets added).
2. A variant of the hardware generations approach was used by Eaton and Smithers (1982). They stick to three generations for the period up to 1980. While they denote changes in component technology as the basis for moving from one generation to another, they take a wider view of the distinguishing hardware for each generation. They also prefer the label stages, although they do identify their first three stages with the traditional generations (p. 14). The first period, which they date as 1950–1960, they describe as being identified with one-off technology. The second period (dated as 1960–1970) they call the mainframe era; the third period (1970–1980) the mini era. Following this line, the distinguishing characteristic of the fourth period is the microcomputer or personal computer, and the basic component technology is the VLSI circuit (not LSI). This fourth stage begins in 1980. While the component technology is still important, Eaton and Smithers shift attention to steps in the size of the basic hardware in order to identify different generations or stages of computer history.
3. In this Nolan follows Anthony's general hierarchy of business activities (Anthony, 1965, pp. 15–19).
   (a) Strategic planning—deciding on objectives of the organization, on changes in these objectives, on the resources used to attain these objectives, and on the policies that are to govern the acquisition, use and disposition of these resources.
   (b) Management control—assuring that resources are obtained and used effectively and efficiently in the accomplishment of the organization's objectives.
   (c) Operational control—assuring that specific tasks are carried out effectively and efficiently.
4. Nolan's stages approach to computerization is reminiscent of Walter Rostow's famous stages of economic growth. According to Rostow (1960), all developed economies have passed through five stages. Rostow predicts that economies developing in future will also pass through the same five stages. Rostow labels his stages as follows: (1) the traditional society; (2) preconditions for take-off; (3) the take-off; (4) the drive to maturity; and (5) the age of high mass consumption. Some criticisms of Rostow's approach can also be applied to Nolan's approach. For example, Rostow has been criticized for not allowing that later countries to develop must do so in a world of already existing developed countries with which they must interact. This can lead to different growth patterns compared with the pioneer countries. We have noted that Nolan too neglects differences between organizations that acquired computers early and latecomers. On the other hand, Rostow has been criticized for his weak specification of mechanisms to link stages in the order he suggests. Nolan's pendulum responses to an initial technical shock is somewhat more convincing.

5. We may be able to explain Ein-Dor and Segev's results by bringing external factors into the analysis. It may be that, originally, new computer departments were placed in operational departments or in low-level staff departments. Certainly this is supported by evidence from earlier studies (Churchill *et al*. 1969). The computer group in these firms was moved in response to accumulated experience within these firms, as predicted by Nolan. Firms that computerized later may have benefited from the experience of pioneer firms and thus realized how important computers would be to a wide range of potential user departments. Therefore latecomers skipped earlier stages of the process altogether and located their computer departments centrally and at a high level from the outset. These firms did not change the location of their computer group because they did not experience a crisis of location as specified by the stages model.

6. For an excellent summary of economists' views on the diffusion of new technology see Stoneman (1983).

7. For a discussion of structured programming see section 5.4.3.

8. Also, the canned program is likely to be written by more highly skilled programmers than the average user firm can afford. The disadvantage is that the problem at hand may not be 'standard'. Either this will have to be accepted and the problem made to 'fit' the solution, or the user firm will have to try to modify or add on to the canned program. In some cases this will be difficult because of lack of access to the people who wrote the original program. If canned programs are well designed and well written, they may be easily modified to fit the needs of different clients, at least within the limits of variations anticipated at the time of creation of the package. This means that the skills required of the programmer who adapts the package will be significantly reduced.

9. 'The transformation of programming is not the result of technological imperatives inherent in the logic of programming or computing. Programming has changed because managers, concerned about profits, have set about systematically and carefully to change it' (Kraft, 1977, p. 97).

10. For a critique of Kraft and Dubnoff's interpretation of their own evidence see Friedman (1987b).

3

...ᴳ A MODEL OF THE PHASES OF COMPUTERIZATION GROWTH

We use four different types of models to guide our analysis of the history of computer systems development. The first is a map representing the 'position' of computer systems development activities within user organizations. This form of representation will allow us to demonstrate the broad pattern of change in these activities. The second model provides a way of summarizing broad management strategies for controlling the computer systems development process. This model is derived from general studies of management strategies for maintaining authority over employees.

These two models represent the phenomena we wish to explain in a comparative static sense. That is, we will present a series of 'snapshot' pictures of both the place of computer systems development activities within organizations and the way these activities are managed at different points in their history (see Chapters 4, 6 and 10–12).

The third model is of the agents of change, of the forces stimulating changes in those snapshot pictures over time. It is our contention that changes in technology have had an important but variable effect on computer systems development activities. Technology is not the only agent of change and at times other agents have been more influential. Along with changes in technology we consider changes in types of computer applications, types of users of applications, and changes in competitive conditions on markets for computer services and for computer-skilled labour.

These three models provide the foundation and rationale for our fourth model— a model of the diffusion of computers to organizations and of the spread of computer applications within organizations. We divide the history of computer systems development into a number of phases, each dominated by a particular factor constraining further computerization. This model is used to summarize the timing of changes in the pictures of computer systems development presented. It provides an overall structure to our historical presentation.

The four models are described in the following four sections of this chapter. In the fourth section a preliminary discussion of the relation between technological change and the phases is presented. This theme will be taken up again in Chapter 14. The chapter ends with a brief discussion of the interrelations among the models.

3.1 THE POSITION OF COMPUTER SYSTEMS DEVELOPMENT IN ORGANIZATIONS

A distinguishing characteristic of the computer is its flexibility. It can be programmed to carry out different functions. In order to fulfil this capability the computer must be programmed. Even if programs are also purchased, the programs need to be run. Often programs must also be adapted to the specific requirements of the organization, and maintained. Even if a computer is purchased with a full set of programs that are deemed adequate for the organization's needs, those needs are likely to be continually re-evaluated, because of the wide range of possible applications to which the computer may be put. The effect of the programming and operating requirements of the computer has been that organizations wishing to acquire a computer have also had to hire considerable staff along with the machine. Typically, an entire new department has been set up in order to carry out the functions necessary to transform a machine, representing wide capabilities, into specific systems for meeting specific objectives. Essentially, this department mediates between the computer and the expressed needs of the organization.

Originally mediating between the computer and the uses to which it would be put was not considered to be a specialist set of activities. During the 1940s almost all computers were located in research organizations. Computer users had the mathematical and engineering skills required to make the computer 'work'. Even then some degree of specialization between scientists who worked more closely with the machines and those more closely working on problem formulation occurred, at least informally. With the coming of business computing[1] the gap between the sorts of skills required to program the computer and the skills possessed by people who wished to make use of the computer widened tremendously.

A representation of computer systems development in organizations must therefore take into account three elements.

(1) The computer itself, which is purchased from outside the organization. We refer to this as the *computer systems core*. This core includes software as well as hardware. Traditionally this software has been called systems software (as distinguished from software related to the application of the computer to a particular problem or application software). How much of the bought-in core is software will vary between firms at any one time, depending on hardware manufacturers' policies and on the sophistication of purchasers. The software proportion has increased enormously during the history of computerization, primarily due to the inclusion of more and more sophisticated operating systems software.

(2) The needs or problems to which the computer is being applied; the uses of the computer or what are often called *computer applications* as well as the *users*.[2]

(3) The activities mediating between the computer and the applications to be computerized. This we have labelled the *mediating process*.

We believe that these elements can be usefully represented as concentric shapes (Figure 3.1). The content of each of these three elements has changed considerably since the beginnings of business computing, as have relations among them. We will be examining each of these elements and their interconnections for each phase in the history of the computerization process. However, we shall focus on the mediating process, and particularly on the activities of systems development.

The complex of concentric shapes is surrounded by an environment external to the organization. This external environment is dealt with in our third model. Note that the external environment can directly impinge on all three basic elements of the model. It need not be 'filtered' through outer rings of the model.

3.1.1 The Mediating Process

The mediating process includes a wide range of activities. Until recently the mediating process has been identified almost entirely with a single department, usually called the data processing, electronic data processing, computer or computer services department, or a specific division called management information systems or information services. We will normally use the term 'computer department', although in citing studies that use other labels we will follow their terminology.

The heart of computer departments has traditionally involved three main types of activities: systems analysis, programming and operations. We may think of them as three stages between users and the computer systems core (Figure 3.2).

Systems analysis may be defined simply as the analysis of an activity or system to determine it and how the system may be improved using computer systems (Longley and Shain, 1985, p. 327). This involves taking user requirements, which

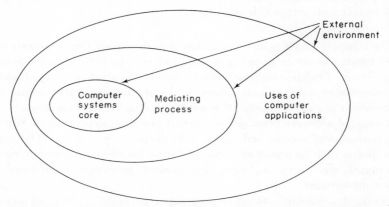

FIGURE 3.1 Computer systems development in organizations

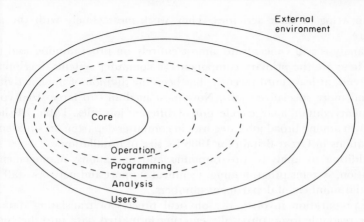

FIGURE 3.2 The mediating process

may be presented in a wide variety of guises, and translating them into a formalized set of requirements specifications capable of being satisfied by a computer system. Then it involves evaluating those specifications in terms of cost-effectiveness and feasibility for actually meeting user needs. Systems analysts also normally carry out tasks that should properly be called system design. This involves a more detailed specification of how the system will operate (design of input, processing and output flows; design of controls and of documents to be produced). These activities of systems analysts occur at early stages in the development of computer systems. Systems analysts will also normally take an active role in the delivery of systems to users. This will involve handing over documentation and may also involve training users or supervising this training.

Programming may be defined simply as the process by which a computer is made to perform a specialized task. This involves creating a formal sequence of instructions that can be recognized and implemented by a computer. Sometimes this is called coding. Programmers test and correct or debug their own programs, although once they believe programs to be acceptable they may be further tested and debugged. Programmers will not only work on new systems. They will also test the work of others and they will revise and improve programs in response to problems or new requirements. This is called maintenance and enhancement. Traditionally programmers have been distinguished from analysts in that analysts normally receive their instructions from users whereas programmers normally receive their instructions from analysts (or others within the computer department, such as project leaders or chief programmers).[3] Finally, most programmers also carry out some analysis and design. Received specifications for particular programs, or for parts of programs (called modules), will not usually be sufficiently detailed to allow immediate coding.

Operators monitor and 'work' the computer. They set up peripheral units and maintain a log of their activities. They work most closely with the physical hardware.

Our analysis will concentrate almost entirely on programming and analysis tasks. These are the primary components of computer systems development. A major trend, at least until recently, has been the division of these activities into more and more specialized jobs. Now most medium- to large-sized computer departments contain a large collection of different job titles. Table 3.1 shows the breakdown among broad job categories in computer departments situated in user organizations in Great Britain for 1986 by size of installation.

In addition to analysis, programming and operations, management, data preparation, systems programming, technical support and network staff involve substantial numbers of department numbers.

Data preparation involves the physical process of translating data into a machine-readable form, physically entering formatted data into the computer, taking information out of the computer as well as checking the accuracy of entered data and ensuring that output goes where it is expected to be received. In the early years of computing, these tasks were separated off from the primary systems development work and given to employees with little education or experience. Although still formally part of many computer departments, data preparation staff are separated from the rest of computer systems developers by the rarity of career progression from data preparation into other jobs in the mediating process. In addition, data preparation jobs are extremely boring and unsatisfying. Data preparation staff are almost entirely women who receive substantially lower salaries than other computer department staff. These jobs have been increasingly

TABLE 3.1 *Distribution of computer department staff in user organizations by installation size*

Job category	Small installations, <11 systems developers (%)	Medium-sized installations, 11–30 systems developers (%)	Large installations, >30 systems developers (%)
DP management	21	14	8
Systems analysts	6	11	13
Analyst/programmers	17	16	11
Programmers	11	13	15
Systems programmers/technical support	2	5	9
Network staff	0	2	4
Operations	28	21	25
Data preparation	25	18	15

Note: Systems developers includes systems analysts, analyst/programmers, programmers and systems programmers.
Source: NCC 1986 survey.

bypassed in recent years by on-line facilities that allow direct entry and direct display of output, and by the availability of cumulated databases built up from earlier applications. In spite of these trends, which date from the early 1970s, substantial numbers of data preparation staff remain in computer departments.

Technical support is a disparate collection of jobs, most of which have been growing rapidly over the past twenty years. The largest group—the one that has been established as a separate job category for longest—is systems programmer. Systems programmers are responsible for what is known as systems software, its evaluation, development and maintenance. Systems software is usually bought in from outside; often it is purchased with the hardware. It is therefore included in our definition of computer systems core in most cases. As the computer systems core has come to include more and more complex systems software supporting more hardware devices and more potentially incompatible software, the need for systems programmers has grown. Systems programmers will often work closely with outside suppliers of computer systems core. Most of their work is to modify and maintain software produced elsewhere, rather than building substantial new systems.

Technical support also includes database administrators and data analysts. They are responsible for the planning, design and maintenance of the organization's database. They supervise systems using the database. They resolve user conflicts and ensure the integrity and privacy of the data, while providing efficient data access. They evaluate possible enhancements to database software.

Network staff are responsible for the planning, implementation and control of data communications. They monitor the teleprocessing network and deal with user inquiries. They support remote terminals and may be involved in user education.

By and large there are a high proportion of managers. The span of control is small. Also most senior systems developers, classed as analysts, programmers or technical support staff, have some management responsibilities.

Note that the proportion of systems programmers, other technical support staff and network staff is highly correlated with installation size. They account for 13% of large installations and only 2% of small ones. The proportion of managers is negatively correlated with installation size.

A substantial proportion of systems developers are now called analyst/ programmers. This practice has grown substantially since the late 1970s. Note that the proportion of systems developers accounted for by analyst/programmers is inversely correlated with installation size (see section 12.1.1).

3.2 MANAGEMENT STRATEGIES: RESPONSIBLE AUTONOMY AND DIRECT CONTROL

The model we use to describe management strategies for organizing the work of computer systems developers and for maintaining authority over these specialists is based on two general types of strategies: responsible autonomy and direct control. Particular management groups are viewed as occupying a continuum from extreme responsible autonomy to extreme direct control. Each type of strategy has its own underlying philosophy.

The guiding principle of the responsible autonomy strategy is that with it managers treat employees in a way that aims to encourage employees to believe that their aims are the same as those of management. The motivation principle underlying the responsible autonomy strategy is loyalty.

The key advantage of the responsible autonomy strategy is that it makes it easier to take advantage of the peculiarly human characteristics of employees. Workers are, potentially, very flexible. You can get people to carry out work that is difficult to specify in advance either because it is poorly understood or because conditions are changing too quickly. The primary method of doing this is to encourage employee loyalty towards the organization, to encourage a belief that employee and manager interests are the same. In part this is done by offering side rewards such as company sports facilities, social activities and perks. Also more careful screening of recruits is carried out to ensure that new staff 'fit' into the organization culture. It is also done by designing working procedures and organization structures in order to allow employees to act relatively autonomously and to give them responsibilities. Finally, and most important, it requires a clear commitment to employment security.

Responsible autonomy strategies are of limited usefulness when competitive conditions require large-scale lay-offs to ensure the organization's survival. Flexibility in working procedures is bought, in part, by a loss of flexibility in moving employees into and out of the organization. It is difficult to convince people that they are all part of one big company family when many are being thrown out. Responsible autonomy strategies are most useful to management when technical and supply conditions, or changes in product demand, necessitate rapid changes in working procedures, but when employment security can be convincingly offered to the vast majority of employees.

Direct control strategies are ones where managers try to treat employees as though they were no different from other inputs to the organization. They are based on an engineering view of labour management. It is direct control types of strategies which Braverman and Kraft describe. Managers try to limit the scope for independent employee initiatives by close supervision, by dividing work into small tasks, by reducing the conceptual content of the majority of jobs, and by concentrating on purely financial means to motivate employees.

Although direct control types of strategies are commonly pursued, they have serious limitations. By removing most decision making from work sites, more transmission mechanisms between planners and executors are required. By actively discouraging initiative on the part of most employees, a potentially profitable resource is foregone. By treating people like machines, boredom, reduced effort and resistance are encouraged. On the other hand, direct control strategies can be advantageous when labour supply is high and when employee organization is weak. Also, when managers are competing on the basis of easily measurable labour costs, rather than on the basis of product quality or quick responses to sudden changes in required product mix, direct control strategies are likely to be relatively advantageous (Friedman, 1984).

There is a substantial body of opinion which distinguishes different managerial strategies towards workers. Two influential pioneer studies in this field were by McGregor (1960) and by Burns and Stalker (1961). McGregor calls his strategies X and Y (or rather theory X and theory Y). Burns and Stalker call theirs organic and mechanistic management. Essentially, theory X and mechanistic management correspond to the direct control strategy; theory Y and organic management with the responsible autonomy strategy.[4]

Those distinguishing different strategies do not propose that they are randomly distributed across different management groups, purely reflecting personal tastes. Many who advocate such dichotomies prescribe one strategy (usually the responsible autonomy type) as 'better' than the other.[5] However, several studies provide evidence that strategic directions chosen are systematically affected by factors such as technology (Burns and Stalker, 1961; Trist, 1971), competitive conditions in product and labour markets (Friedman, 1977; Lutz, 1982), and employee strategies (Friedman, 1977).

In the next section we discuss factors that have stimulated changes in management strategies as well as changes in the position of computer systems development in organizations. In Chapter 6, when we present pictures of the labour process of computer systems developers, the ways these broad management strategies are pursued in practice are described in more detail (see section 6.1).

3.3 THE AGENTS OF CHANGE

Each of the three approaches to the history of computer systems development described in the previous chapter has a different fundamental change agent, a different factor which may be thought of as driving the history, of stimulating long-run changes. It is technical improvements in hardware, and particularly hardware components, for the hardware generations approach. Changing types of computer applications drive Churchill *et al.*'s version of the organization stages approach. Management's (over)-reactions to the initial introduction of the computer drives Nolan's version of organization stages. For the labour process approach it is the fundamental character of employment contracts in a capitalist society that pushes managers to deskill labour and thereby 'drives' the history of work organization in computer systems development.

There is value in all of these approaches and we will draw some insights from each. The most important difference between our approach and all of the others is that we consider several different agents of change to have had separately identifiable and important influences on the history of computer systems development. In addition, we believe the primary agents of change proposed by most of these approaches need to be modified.

The hardware generations contribution needs to be redefined in terms of technical improvements to purchased computer systems core, rather than hardware alone. This is effectively what proponents of the hardware generations approach are doing when they define the fourth generation in terms of high-level languages. However, we believe the identification of the fifth generation with artificial intelligence, particularly interpreted as expert systems, violates the consistency of the generations approach. 'Expert systems' refers to the uses to which computers are put. Defining the fifth generation in this way gives the impression that uses to which computers are put had not changed significantly until the fifth generation, or at least that such changes as occurred before the fifth generation were not significant compared with the leap between fourth and fifth generations.

The second agent of change we wish to consider is changes in types of computer applications typically being developed in computer departments of user organizations. This may be thought of as changes in character of demand for computer systems development output. We consider that progression of types of computer applications that Churchill *et al.* described to be a primary change agent. This is the progression from computerizing lower-level management control functions to computerizing higher-level management planning and strategic functions, and the progression from dealing with structured activities to dealing with unstructured ones.

This trend is not independent of improvements in computer systems core technology. Dramatic cost/performance improvements to delivered computers provided the capacity required for complex and large development projects that lay at the higher end of this progression of applications. However, improvements in core technology after the 1950s were not *necessary* preconditions for this process. Military and scientific applications to computerize planning functions and less-structured activities were attempted long before major improvements in cost/performance ratios were achieved. We have already referred to the SAGE project, carried out in the early 1950s as an early, important example (section 2.4.2). Simulation exercises and other sophisticated modelling applications were also attempted by the scientific community during the 1950s. Quite apart from computer systems core improvements, the accumulation of past successful applications provided the databases and the confidence required to tackle more difficult applications. Without core improvements these 'higher' applications would have been attempted by fewer organizations.[6] Nevertheless, we believe this smaller business computer-using community would have eventually moved on to these types of applications. Computerization has not been limited by lack of vision as to what might be achieved, as a multitude of works of science fiction from the 1930s and especially from the 1950s attest. Since the Second World War the US government, and particularly the US military, has not been seriously held back for lack of ambition to make those visions real, or lack of funds to attempt to fulfil those ambitions.

The third agent of change we wish to consider is the condition of the labour market. This factor has been neglected in other historical accounts. Labour shortages have affected computer systems development work throughout the history of business computing. There have been periods when shortages have been less acute than others. At the beginning of business computing the labour shortage was less acute because of available supplies of relatively poorly paid staff with experience in academic and military installations. Also hardware suppliers provided training and staff. However, these sources could not satisfy the enormous rise in demand for computer staff from the 1960s. Alternative sources of supply have generally provided educated potential computer systems developers, but staff with field experience have been in continual short supply. On-the-job experience has always been far more highly prized than formal training in this field. This is a major reason for the persistence of labour shortages, in spite of efforts by governments (particularly from the early 1980s in Europe) to increase supply through expanding computing education.[7] One important effect of labour shortages has been to encourage responsible autonomy types of strategies towards computer systems developers.

A fourth agent of change we will consider is the nature of competition which computer installations face in the 'market' for their output. This may seem a strange factor to include, given that we are concentrating almost entirely on computer systems development carried out in departments within user organizations. However, departments within organizations are not completely protected from market forces. The services they provide can be obtained from external suppliers, and there may be more than one source of such services within an organization. We will argue that these alternative sources of supply have only become important in the 1970s and 1980s. This factor will be discussed mainly in section 9.3.1.

These four factors may be thought of as external to the mediating process in computer user organizations. They are significant factors in the environment of the mediating process. The labour process approach to computer systems development is more directly concerned with the work of computer systems developers. It proposes that managers try to increase their control over all labour processes and to decrease labour costs, primarily by deskilling workers. This proposition should be modified. Managers in the private sector have an incentive to maintain and improve profits. Markets impose pressures both to improve revenues, perhaps by improving the quality of the product, and to reduce costs. Pressures on public sector organizations may be less continuous than market pressures, but under certain political regimes they may be even more severe, such as the public sector squeezes during the late 1970s and 1980s in the UK, and non-defence public sector squeezes in the USA during the 1980s. Those who strictly follow Braverman's labour process approach are right to suggest that these ures stimulate changes in the way work is organized. They are right to emphasize cost reduction as being particularly important for the interplay between management and labour, at least for labour not directly involved with customer or client contact. However, strategies to reduce labour costs may have adverse effects on product quality. Also, strategies to reduce labour costs by deskilling labour may stimulate such adverse reactions by employees that labour costs are increased, rather than reduced, by raising labour turnover rates or by reducing effort levels. We would argue that many different types of strategies may be pursued. Furthermore, we believe that these strategies can be usefully categorized as ranging from extreme direct control to extreme responsible autonomy. Different types of managerial strategies pursued in computer installations will have different dynamic effects on the work of computer systems developers.

There is a wide range of different ways computer systems development activies may be organized. The interplay of computer managers' strategies for organizing the mediating process, and reactions to those strategies (by top managers, by users, and especially by computer systems developers themselves), leads to compromises and changes in strategies. This, in turn, leads to further reactions, further compromises and further changes in strategies. This internal interplay is certainly affected by external factors, but it is not uniquely determined by them.

Nolan's organization stages approach is driven by one set of actions and reactions which are internal to organizations into which computers have been introduced. For Nolan, the stages of data processing growth depend on changes in the way the organization copes with a new, potentially very advantageous technology. Alterations between slack and control, or responsible autonomy and direct control strategies, towards systems developers depend on the growth and size of organization resources devoted to computer departments.[8] They depend on the attitude of top managers towards advantages and costs of computerization. For Nolan, they are not affected by falling hardware costs, changes in the types of systems being developed or labour market pressures.

We wish to modify Nolan's approach by allowing management strategies towards systems developers to depend on external factors as well as internal ones. We also want to allow for internal factors in a way that does not regard them all as unique to each installation. Many internal tensions have always been present in computer installations and are common to most installations. At particular times certain tensions have received special attention by computer managers. They become the key issue or set of issues that drives initiatives by computer managers to change working procedures. The particular set of issues that receives such attention *may* arise out of internal crises within computer departments, as suggested by Nolan. They may also arise from external pressures. Often crises in many different installations coincide. There then appears to be a crisis in the entire computing field. This crisis will resonate throughout the field via communication among systems developers and managers of systems developers. Opportunities for such cross-communication are ample in this field. Conferences on new and old issues abound. Proceedings from an enormous number of these conferences appear in book form. In addition, the computing press is large and widely read (particularly because of interest in advertised job vacancies). In spite of each installation being different because of different internal personnel and different individual histories, differences can be subjugated when a particular issue becomes prominent in the computing literature.

This media exposure may not affect installations where the issue is of no intrinsic interest. However, where the issue is just one of many concerns, the resonance provided through the computing literature may lead to the issue receiving more attention than it would otherwise be given. In this way the computing literature will both reflect real issues and stimulate greater concern for particular issues.

Fashion seems to play a substantial role in general management strategies and practice.[9] Causal observation leads us to assume that it is at least as important among computing managers. Many data processing and information systems managers have no formal management training. Interviews with these managers often revealed their enthusiasm for testing their own methods against what others were doing, and their anxiety to appear familiar with the latest initiatives receiving attention in the computing literature.

Our view of changes in computer systems development therefore contains two different categories of change agents. The first are external factors: technological changes in computer systems core, changes in types of applications and market pressures. The second are internal pressures. These arise from the interplay between management strategies and internal reactions to these strategies. They arise from the success or failure of specific initiatives for dealing with fundamental management responsibilities[10] as they are influenced by a changing environment (as summarized by the three external agents of change we have identified). It is our contention that this constellation of external and internal factors has led to systematic changes in the sets of issues of most concern to computer managers. Furthermore, a combination of analysis of the external agents of change and a careful reading of the computing literature can reveal these changes. This model of change in the management and organization of computer systems development is summarized in Figure 3.3.

The static picture presented in Figure 3.3 uses the structure by which we described the position of computer systems development in organizations (Figures 3.1 and 3.2). The dynamic picture treats the same elements of the model in a way that demonstrates long-run changes in the primary set of issues of concern to computer managers. Each era or phase of the history of computer systems development is characterized by a different set of issues of concern to computer managers and systems developers. This is reflected in the computing literature and stimulated by it.[11] The effect of this set of issues on the computing field is to stimulate new management initiatives in order to deal with the issues. This involves both the more rapid diffusion of techniques already available and stimulation of invention and innovation of *new* techniques. In this way the computing field itself may be thought of as affecting the *direction* of technological change in computer systems development. The introduction of these new techniques helps to relieve the major issues of concern. Changes in the external agents and experiences with new techniques generated in one phase eventually lead to a turn of the helix. Eventually they lead to a major shift in the set of issues of major concern in computer departments, and a major shift in the issues highlighted in the computing literature. These ideas are given more substance in the next section when we discuss the particular character of different phases in the history of computer systems development that we have identified.

3.4 THE PHASES OF COMPUTERIZATION[1][2]

We believe that the history of computer systems development can be understood in terms of three phases of computerization. These phases are each defined by a 'critical factor,' or problem that has limited the development of computerization during that period. The effects of efforts to overcome that factor have particularly shaped the character of the activities that mediate between the computer and computer applications (Figure 3.2). The types of people recruited into computer departments, management strategies for organizing their work, and relations between computer department staff, users and top managers, have changed in ways which, we believe, can be easily understood with reference to these different phases of computerization. We will also argue that the primary concern of each phase has affected the emphasis of new technology. It has affected the direction of

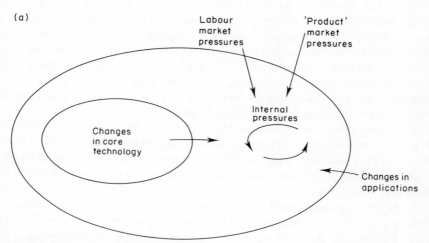

FIGURE 3.3 Phases of computer systems development. (a) Static picture

technological change. The three phases we have identified have been dominat
by constraints on further computerization due to:

(1) Hardware constraints: hardware costs and limitations of capacity and
    reliability.
(2) Software constraints: productivity of systems developers, difficulties of
    delivering reliable systems on time and within budget.
(3) User relations constraints: system quality problems arising from inadequate
    perception of user demands and inadequate servicing of their needs.

The different 'shades' shown in the dynamic picture of change in computer
systems development represent these three phases (Figure 3.3). The dating of these

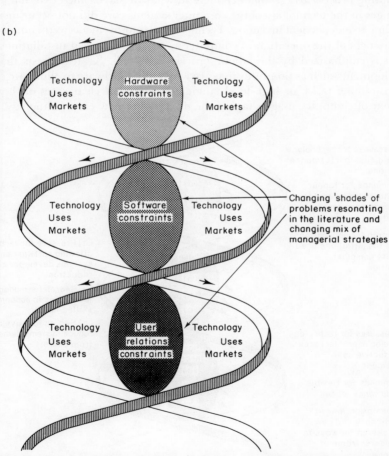

FIGURE 3.3 Phases of computer systems development. (b) Dynamic picture

phases cannot be made too precise because we are dealing with a large and heterogeneous collection of organizations. However, we would roughly consider the first phase, when hardware constraints dominated, to have been from the beginning of computerization until the mid-1960s.[13] The second phase was from the mid-1960s until the beginning of the 1980s. At the time of writing we consider the field to be in its third phase—the phase of user relations constraints. In Chapter 13 we will discuss the future for computer systems development and consider whether a fourth phase is discernible.

Figure 3.4 shows a different aspect of the phases of computerization from that demonstrated in Figure 3.3. In Figure 3.3 we concentrated on the influence of external factors on the mediating process. This is insufficient by itself. The mediating process also *generated* changes in what we have called external factors. Changes in the technology of the computer systems core did not occur merely in response to independent invention. Technological improvements were stimulated by experiences of the operation of computer systems core in real installations. This point is emphasized by the labour process approach. Kraft suggests that new developments such as programs that are wired into hardware to eliminate certain programming tasks, or high-level languages, represent clear cases of the social context of computer usage shaping the direction of new core technology.

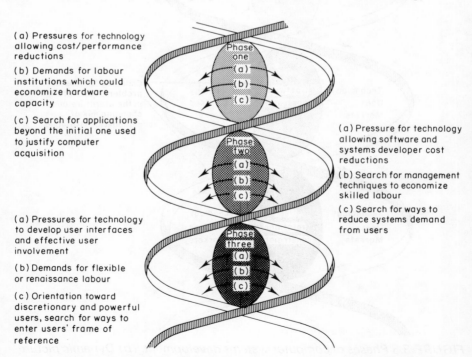

(a) Pressures for technology allowing cost/performance reductions

(b) Demands for labour institutions which could economize hardware capacity

(c) Search for applications beyond the initial one used to justify computer acquisition

(a) Pressure for technology allowing software and systems developer cost reductions

(b) Search for management techniques to economize skilled labour

(c) Search for ways to reduce systems demand from users

(a) Pressures for technology to develop user interfaces and effective user involvement

(b) Demands for flexible or renaissance labour

(c) Orientation toward discretionary and powerful users, search for ways to enter users' frame of reference

FIGURE 3.4 Technologies: effects of computer systems development

As noted in section 1.1, innovation does not simply happen as a once-and-for-all occurrence which is then diffused in its complete form throughout the economy. Rather we view technical progress as primarily the cumulation of minor improvements. The direction of these improvements depends on perceived profit opportunities, which are responsive both to real production problems and to climates of opinion about which problems are most 'important' and about what types of solutions are likely to alleviate the problem. This process of demand-led innovation is likely to be more important in areas of an economy where the innovative process is encouraged at the point of contact between new techniques and the organizations in which they are used. This has been especially the case with computerization. In the computing field problems with the operation and utilization of computers, and opportunities to improve usage by developing new techniques, are easily transmitted to people with the competence to carry out invention and innovation. Many computer departments at user organizations sell products they have developed in-house to outside clients of their parent organizations. Also many independent software houses and service bureaus have been established by individuals and groups from computer departments in user organizations. This is because the competencies required for 'innovation', for systems development, reside within those organizations, in the mediating process. The transmission process is also encouraged by staff interchange between established computer systems core supplier firms and the larger user organizations.

So far we have been referring to technological change in computer systems core. However the mediating process uses techniques, it has a technology apart from purchased computer systems core. Some of these techniques are common to any labour process, such as forms of monitoring or staff evaluation. Others are more tied to computerization, such as the chief programmer teams or structured programming methods.

In each phase of computerization, the computer-using community has generated new technology themselves and stimulated new technology among supplier organizations. However, the types of technology being stimulated in different phases have not been the same. The 'direction' along which technology has progressed has altered somewhat in response to the primary concern of each phase and the mix of managerial strategies being pursued within computer installations.[14]

The turn of the helix from phase one to phase two encouraged new techniques that saved on software development costs and which supported direct control types of management strategies. Techniques to support responsible autonomy strategies were also stimulated, but less forcefully than in phase one. The turn of the helix from phase two to phase three stimulated techniques that would allow greater user involvement in computer systems development and encourage end user computing. During phase three techniques to support responsible autonomy strategies in relation to computer systems developers have been further developed, and emphasis on direct control techniques has waned.

The model of the phases of computerization presented so far must be qualified in a number of ways. First, all three limitations have been present from the outset of computer diffusion. During the earliest period of computer system diffusion there were problems of programming costs and ensuring that delivered systems were really useful, but these were overshadowed by hardware cost and reliability problems. By the third generation of computer hardware, hardware cost problems had been sufficiently eased to reveal other problems as limitations to further computerization. We argue that a similar process has been occurring since the end of the 1970s. Now software costs have eased somewhat. Hardware costs have continued to fall. More important, changes in the types of systems being developed, changes in the types of people using computers, and changes in the way computer systems are being used have increased the visibility of a different problem. This is the problem of delivered systems quality, or of giving users or clients systems that are really needed.

Second, after one limiting factor ceases to be primary, the issue is not dropped. Certain people will still regard it as primary to them. For example, hardware capacity limitations are still a primary constraint on the developers of operating systems and on the producers of packages for personal computers. Managers and systems developers in computer installations that specialize in these areas are not likely to change their practices to reflect the constraints of new phases.

This is particularly important for understanding the effect of the phases of computerization on the generation of new technology in this field. The central constraint of each phase stimulates an academic or scientific estate as well as a set of development and consultative companies dedicated to developing and diffusing new methods for overcoming those constraints. When the problem falls from its primary place among the concerns of most computer systems developers, the 'market' for these new methods is reduced, but it does not disappear. Furthermore, those involved in research efforts in this direction do not easily shift their emphasis in response to market changes. Academic research does not require a ready market. Those who began their research career working on certain problems along certain lines do not easily write off their invested intellectual capital in that area. Therefore a stream of new techniques designed to alleviate all three constraints continues to flow, particularly from the academic and research and development communities today.

Third, the installations that do change their practices will not change at once. The transition between phases will be gradual, just as the diffusion of any new technique takes time. There will be considerable inertia in any computer installation, as there is in all organizations. New developments may rightly be regarded as the product of temporary changes in fashion and of doubtful value. With many new techniques coming on to the market, all accompanied by inflated claims from vendors, evaluation becomes a difficult and costly exercise without evidence from outside objective sources. As noted above, all three limitations continue to be present in different sections of the computing community. This continues to stimulate new techniques to alleviate each of the three constraints. The diffusion path will therefore often depend on idiosyncratic personal networks among computer managers and specialists. Also, some will be disappointed with new techniques, perhaps because claims for them were inflated, perhaps because of unexpected resistance from computer staff or users, perhaps because they were not 'properly' implemented. These experiences will also be fed into networks and will affect the diffusion process. We shall show that the introduction of the best-known techniques designed to alleviate the constraints of phases two and three (structured programming and greater user involvement in computer systems development) were by no means smooth (or irreversible).

Although our primary mechanism generating phases is different from Nolan's stages, within each phase we believe that over-reactions occur. In particular, the computer literature tends to overemphasize the degree to which changes are occurring. This coincides with the problem of tenses denoted by Churchill *et al*. By cultivating access to the largest and most technically sophisticated organizations, the computer press gives the impression that changes these pioneers are making will be quickly emulated by others. Worse still, they do not recognize pioneers as such and they assume that when any organization introduces something new, all organizations are doing so at the same time. Also they regard these changes as irreversible, or they extrapolate along the direction of these changes unjustifiably. We would argue that academic commentators have also misreported tenses. Kraft, in particular, over-represented changes towards deskilling programmers that have been, at least partially, reversed in recent years.

3.5 LINKS BETWEEN THE MODELS AND THE HISTORICAL NARRATIVE

In Parts Two and Three which follow, a history of computer systems development is presented that is guided by the models described in this chapter. We present separate discussions of four aspects of the history of computer systems development:

(1) external agents that stimulated changes in phases;
(2) the literature around the primary problem each phase represents for the organization of the work of computer systems development;
(3) the techniques developed to 'solve' the primary problem of each phase;
(4) snapshot pictures of the practice of computer systems development in user organizations.

What can be observed at any point in time is a complex pattern, with installations exhibiting a wide range of technologies, management strategies and reactions. By providing separate threads of narrative on each of these four strands we present both a history of computer systems development and an analysis of that history. This analysis will be used in Chapter 13 when we discuss the future.

It is also important to recognize that the history presented below is a simplified one (as is every presentation of historical material). The selection and interpretation of the historical material has been guided by the models presented above. These have been derived from the author's prior knowledge and opinions, from theoretical material, from an initial survey of the material, and from the process of writing the history. All presentations of historical material are selective. What is selected depends on the assumptions and frameworks or models exercised by the historian. We label our historical approach as analytical because we have made (at least some of) the underlying assumptions and models explicit, and we have attempted to show connections between the models and the material. The snapshot pictures are particularly important because the survey basis of these pictures is less selective. They allow the models to be 'tested'.

ENDNOTES

1. We use the term 'business computing', as distinguished from 'scientific computing'. In the early computing literature the term 'commercial computing' was often used. We will not use this term because of its association with a particular sector of business activity—what has often been called the tertiary sector.
2. We will show that the term 'users' covers a wide range of roles which can be played by a large number of people (section 7.3).
3. Recently more programmers have been receiving requests directly from users, particularly in the role of providers of user support (often in support of user programming as well as providing 'hot-line' facilities for users when systems appear to malfunction).
4. For arguments in favour of distinguishing strategies rather than philosophies or styles see Friedman (1989).
5. Notably, those known under the label of the human relations school of management thought (see section 8.2.3).
6. Without these cost/performance improvements in computer core, a social effect of computer diffusion might have been to stimulate more dramatic centralization of firms and of industries than occurred in the 1960s and 1970s.
7. Nevertheless there have been periods since the 1950s when the labour shortage has eased. In the UK there were short periods when computer systems developers were being laid off, in 1971/72 and 1981/82.
8. Nolan's dynamic factor is internal to user organizations, but not to the mediating process. His dynamic is driven by the organizational environment.
9. The eagerness with which US corporate executives have latched on to new management fads from the 1950s was nicely summarized in a cover story for *Business Week* magazine (Byrne, 1986).
10. To achieve a satisfactory level of 'return' for the organization, through the management of computer systems developers and other computer-related resources.
11. With appropriate adjustments of the timing as noted in Chapter 2 (on the problem of tenses, section 2.3.4).
12. The term 'computerization' is a cumbersome one. It is being used to denote direct effects of the growth of computer applications within organizations, as well as the diffusion of computers to new organizations. The term 'computer expenditure' might have been simpler, but we wish to embrace more than the cost of computer core. We also want to emphasize the process that arises after computers are purchased. When an

organization purchases (or leases) a computer, it is buying in a *process* for dealing with the organization's problems based on the capabilities of the computer, rather than a fixed *commodity*. By itself the computer is useless. It is a machine that is capable of dealing with a wide range of problems, but something further is needed to allow these capabilities to be realized.

13. The end of phase one can be clearly identified with the third generation of computers, which were properly launched with the IBM 360 series in 1965.

14. The direction of technological change is not entirely determined by demand pressures. We suggest that there have been certain characteristics of the overall computing technology paradigm or technology system that have also contributed to the direction of technological change in this field. These characteristics, as well as a more general model of the direction of technological change, are discussed in Chapter 14.

Part 2
PHASE ONE AND PHASE TWO: HARDWARE AND SOFTWARE CONSTRAINTS DOMINATE

Part 2

Chapter 4
PHASE ONE: HARDWARE CONSTRAINTS

Our analysis of the external forces that have shaped computer systems development concentrate on three areas: computer technology, the uses to which that technology is applied, and the labour market for computer specialists. During the first phase we consider the cost and capacity of computer hardware to have been the major constraint on the spread of computerization (Figure 4.1). We will therefore begin our discussion of the first phase of computing by looking at the technological developments that occurred between the beginning of the computer age and the mid-1960s. The applications for which computers were used and the ways in which these uses were constrained by the hardware and other factors will be considered next. Then we will examine the labour market for computer systems developers. Finally, we will discuss the organization of the mediating process of applying computers to business uses and how this process was affected by these agents of change.

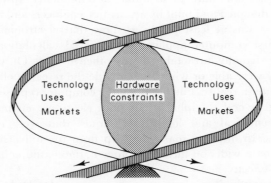

FIGURE 4.1 Phase one: hardware constraints

4.1 PRE-BUSINESS ORIGINS: THE UNIVERSITY MACHINES[1]

The first digital electronic computer is normally considered to have been the ENIAC (electronic numerical integrator and calculator) computer. It was developed by Presper Eckert and John Mauchly from the Moore School of Engineering at the University of Pennsylvania in 1946. ENIAC was built for the

US Army. It contained some 18 000 vacuum tubes and occupied 1800 square feet of floor space. The programming of ENIAC was done by means of wired connections, plugboards and switches. All input and output of data was in the form of punched cards.

The first stored program computer to become operational was EDSAC (electronic discrete sequential automatic computer) in early 1949 at Cambridge University in the UK. The major advance that this represented over ENIAC was the use of the mercury delay line memory with a storage capacity of 512 words. The mercury delay line memory allowed a program to be stored electronically within the computer. Not only was this faster than the physical 'programming' that was required in ENIAC, but it also allowed a library of programs to be accumulated on punched cards or paper tape that could be fed into the computer whenever they were required. The physical programming of the computer in terms of altering the circuits was thus automated.

Other university machines were also important for the early development of the computer. The University of Manchester's MARK I [2] pioneered cathode ray tube memory and magnetic drum memory devices in 1950. Project WHIRLWIND at MIT in 1951, sponsored by the US Air Force and the Office of Naval Research, was the first application of magnetic core memory.

The role of the universities and the sponsorship of university projects by the military, particularly in the USA, were crucial to the beginnings of data processing. [3] It is interesting to note that business applications of electronic computers did not stimulate these initial developments. Instead the earliest computers were designed and built by academics, engineers and mathematicians. Their motivation was at least partly to show that electronic computing was possible. The first computer applications involved calculations that were so lengthy as to be virtually intractable to any other method. Only the universities and the military were able or willing to provide the research effort necessary to make the computer a reality. Furthermore, the computer represented a device at the forefront of several disciplines, not only electronic engineering but also advanced mathematical and logical techniques that were current only in academic circles. In order to make the leap from the university and military environment into the wider business environment, the computer had to be justified in terms of cost-effectiveness.

The first computer built as a business venture was the UNIVAC I, designed and built by Eckert and Mauchly, who formed their own company to do so. During the early 1950s the computer-manufacturing industry began to expand with entrants from the fields of office machinery, electronic components and equipment, and new companies devoted entirely to computer manufacture.

The early computer industry serviced two rather distinct sets of users with different problems. Users of computers for technical calculations required a computer that would carry out complex calculation with great accuracy. The amount of data involved was relatively small, but the actual numbers involved were very large (for accuracy) and the amount of computation was great. Users of computers for business purposes required a computer that would carry out simple calculations on very many, relatively small, numbers. For these users accuracy was important only to the nearest cent, or unit of production, or percentage point. In the early years these two requirements could not be met economically in one computer. Large manufacturers such as IBM produced separate models tailored specifically to scientific or business uses. By the early 1960s hardware technology had progressed sufficiently for a single general-purpose computer to provide sufficient accuracy required by technical users and the data handling required by business computers.

4.2 TECHNOLOGICAL CHANGE IN COMPUTER SYSTEMS CORE

4.2.1 Hardware Performance

The pace of technological change, particularly of the hardware, was extremely rapid during the first 15 years of business computers. This period encompasses the first three 'generations' of computers, as defined by the technology of their logic circuits. The evolution of logic circuit components from valves through discrete transistorized components to integrated circuits gave rise to remarkable increases in the speed and capacity of the logic circuits. Comparisons of performance between computers are highly problematic, but we can illustrate the scale of the improvements in logic circuit performance. The time required for an addition sum on a first-generation business computer such as the UNIVAC I was in the region of 500 microseconds. By the time of the third-generation machines in the mid-1960s, addition times were less than 1 microsecond.

The transition from valves to transistors also brought about considerable improvements in the reliability of computers and in their power consumption. Valves are delicate components containing a heating element that consumes power and gives them a limited lifetime, in much the same way as an electric light bulb. In a computer containing many thousands of valves, both power consumption and frequency of breakdowns were high. Progress in logic circuits also reduced the size of the computer, from the 1800 square feet of ENIAC in the late 1940s to a few square feet for a minicomputer in the early 1960s.

Logic components are only one element of the computer system. With the stored program computer the size, reliability and speed of access to memory was a major parameter determining performance. Moreover, the size of the memory was important for programming the computer, as we shall see later. The earliest computers had very limited primary memory, utilizing the Williams cathode ray tube (CRT) or mercury delay lines. The UNIVAC computer utilized the mercury delay line and had a capacity of 1K words of 12 bits in length.[4] Another first-generation memory device that was used in the IBM 650 was the magnetic drum memory. Information was recorded on and read from the surface of a rapidly rotating drum. This gave the 650 a memory capacity of around 4K words. This method of memory access was much slower than CRT memory, but much cheaper. The major memory advance of the first phase was the introduction of the magnetic core store in 1956. Although magnetic core was invented by the WHIRLWIND project in 1951, it was relatively expensive to manufacture. After its introduction in 1956 in the IBM 704 and 705 and the UNIVAC 1103, this memory medium became the standard in high-priced computers.

It is interesting to note that already there were commercial trade-offs being made between performance and price in the design of computers. The IBM 650 was the most popular business computer of its day, although it was by no means the largest, fastest or the most technologically advanced.

Improvements in core design and production processes led to rapid gains in the size and access times for these memories, as well as a fall in the price per bit. By the early 1960s magnetic core was standard for the working memory in most business data processing computers. The major importance of the advances in core memory came from the ability to provide much larger memories with rapid access time. The magnetic core on the WHIRLWIND computer had an access time of 12 microseconds and a capacity of 2K 16-bit words. By 1965 a medium-range third-generation computer such as the IBM 360/40 could be purchased, with memory sizes ranging from 16K to 256K 8-bit bytes. A top-of-the-range IBM 360/67 would have memory of up to 2000K bytes with an access time of 0.5 microsecond.

Gains in computer performance that were achieved by these advances in electronic components were obviously very important in expanding the uses of computers. During the 1960s many studies appeared with methods for evaluating computer performance, primarily intended to aid computer selection by prospective purchasers. Because of radical changes in computer design—word length, instruction sets, input–output handling, etc.[5]—this was not a simple task. Examples of these studies can be found in Hilleglass (1965), Arbuckle (1966), Calingaert (1967) and the Auerbach Standard EDP Reports. The measures of performance varied in complexity. Simple formulae estimated the power of the computer as a function of memory size and access time. More complicated formulae included the number of arithmetic operations per second. The most complex involved setting up a number of 'benchmark' programs and comparing computer time necessary to process them on different computers. The common factor in these studies was that they concentrated on a narrow definition of hardware performance in technical terms.

The emphasis placed on computer performance was highlighted in a study of how prospective computer-using companies selected their computer (Schneidewind, 1967). When asked to rank eight selection criteria in terms of their importance, computer users ranked objective measures of hardware performance and software performance above other criteria such as cost, manufacturer support, compatibility with existing hardware, potential for growth or delivery time. At the bottom of the list was the availability of applications programs. Stoneman (1976) also comments on the tendency for computer manufacturers to compete in terms of performance in narrow technical terms. This emphasis is entirely consistent with our notion of phase one as a time when the spread of computers was constrained by hardware capacity. The important issues in the minds of those who were responsible for selecting a computer were how big is it and how fast will it go? The reason for this emphasis on hardware performance was that the cost of the hardware represented a very high proportion of the cost of the total application.

4.2.2 Cost/Performance Ratios

A number of studies during the 1960s combined measures of computer performance with measures of cost (rental or purchase prices) to reveal the effect of technological change on cost/performance ratios. Studies by Armer (1965), Skalkum (1967) and Knight (1963, 1968) are reported in Sharpe (1969). These studies all agree on the substantial effect of technological progress on cost/performance ratios. The cost-effectiveness of the central processing unit (CPU) and memory in new computers increased by a factor of 10 every 4 years over the period 1953–1965. Knight's study expressed this statistic in two alternative ways, which are easier to digest. There was an average improvement in CPU and memory of 80% per year. For given performance levels, there was a 55% reduction in cost per year.

Considering the role of technological progress as one strand in the history of computer systems development, changes in the cost/performance ratio and the absolute cost of computers may have been more important than improvements in absolute performance levels. Increases in absolute performance increased the speed with which computers could process existing applications and made more complex applications, requiring rapid computation, technically feasible. However, reductions in the absolute cost of computers meant that smaller firms or smaller units within firms could contemplate the acquisition of a computer. Reductions in cost/performance ratios affected the economic viability of both more complex applications, which required increasing quantities of computer power, as well as relatively simple applications with lower expected benefits. However, the most important implication of the changing cost/performance ratio was its effect on the cost structure of the computer department.

The price of an average computer fell by about 75% between 1953 and 1964. Lecht (1977) estimated the price of an 'average' one-off computer in 1953 at $3 000 000, compared with the price of an IBM 360/40 in 1964 at $700 000. Increases in cost-effectiveness of the hardware cited above were not matched by corresponding increases in cost-effectiveness in the development of software. In a study of the computer requirements of the US Air Force it was estimated that hardware costs in 1955 represented more than 80% of the total costs of an average computer application. By 1965 this had fallen to 50% of the costs (Boehm, 1973).

4.2.3 Uneven Technological Progress and Compensating Changes

So far the discussion of technological change has concentrated on the central processing unit (CPU) and primary memory of the computer. These were the areas in which advances in electronics led to rapid technological progress. However, the hardware of a computer system also consists of peripheral devices for input and output of data and auxiliary memory devices for storing large quantities of data.

The major input and output devices of the early computers were punched card, magnetic tape and paper tape readers, and the line printer. These devices, unlike the CPU and memory, were electromechanical (rather than electronic) devices. Their speed was hampered by constraints such as mechanical inertia of moving parts and the strength of materials. Thus from the earliest computers the input and output processes acted as a constraint on the efficient utilization of the CPU and memory. In technical and scientific applications, where there is considerable calculation and relatively little data input and output, the problem is not very pronounced. Business applications typically consist of large volumes of data on which relatively simple calculations are carried out. The proportion of input/output operations to computational operations is very high. Therefore there were long periods of time when the CPU was tied up with relatively slow input/output operations.

The electromechanical basis of input/output devices also meant that technical progress was slower in this area than in the CPU and memory. The initial problem of slow input and output became further aggravated by uneven technological change. The extent of the distortion induced by technological change can be seen from a comparison of cost/performance ratios of CPU and memory on the one hand, and tape drives, paper tape readers and printers on the other. Schneidewind (1966) estimated that the cost-effectiveness of tape drives and card readers improved by a factor of ten, and line printers by a factor of three, in the decade from 1956 to 1965. Cost-effectiveness of CPU and memory increased by a factor of about 400 during the same period.

Hardware manufacturers went to considerable lengths to devise ways of getting around the constraint placed on overall performance by input/output devices. One early method employed high-speed buffers. The buffer was a memory which could receive and hold data from slow input devices and into which data could be stored for output. Slow data transfer could continue between the buffer and input/output devices while the CPU operated separately. Spooling was another method. Output went to a magnetic tape, a relatively fast memory device, and was then transferred to a printer off-line from the computer. In second-generation machines the control of input and output operations was given to the data control unit. This was essentially a second computer within a computer, which was limited to handling input and output operations.

The earliest operating systems were built by users.[6] During the 1950s specialized operating systems were developed for military and industrial real-time systems and for airline booking systems. The first general operating system, or 'monitor' as such systems were first called, was produced by General Motors Research Laboratories for its IBM 701. The idea of building operating systems spread mainly through the IBM users group (SHARE). By 1957 many users had developed operating systems for the IBM 704 (Rosin, 1969; Grosch, 1977). These operating systems allowed a set of jobs to be grouped together in an input batch on tape. Each program would be written to branch back to the operating system when it completed its processing, and at that point the operating system would begin loading the next program automatically. Operating systems were developed by users outside the IBM circle as well as other manufacturers during the late 1950s. Most users were developing their own operating systems or doing major adaptations of those provided by manufacturers or other users (Weizer, 1981, p. 120). However, at that time there was considerable debate over whether operating systems were worth the machine capacity they tied up and the development and maintenance they required.

From 1960 onwards computer manufacturers began to provide increasingly complex operating systems that would help to optimize the overall utilization of the computer. The most important advance in these operating systems was the development of multiprogramming. Multiprogramming systems enabled the CPU to be switched automatically from the processing of one program to another, whenever the first program became tied up in input or output. The operating system is itself a program that resides permanently in the computer's memory. It imposes a cost by reducing the remaining memory that is available. However, the development of the operating system meant that the overall utilization of CPU and memory grew and total 'run time' for a number of programs was reduced.

The discovery and exploitation of operating systems were 'the significant events of this stage in the history of programming', according to David Sayre, Corporate Director of Programming at IBM. Sayre's statement, made at a series of lectures celebrating MIT's centennial year in the spring of 1961, is worth citing at some length:

> The method is to give to the machines themselves the ability to determine how their own hardware resources should be employed. Then the programmer can ignore this matter, and at the same time, machines which differ in their hardware can be made to look alike. This ability is carried in a large body of programming (automatic coding systems, automatic operating systems and so forth), supplied by the computer manufacturer with the machine. Already this body of programming sometimes exceeds 100 000 words, particularly if it does a really good job of controlling the machine's hardware. From another point of view, it can be said that the manufacturer is beginning to supply a new kind of machine, composed partly of hardware and partly of *software* (the term that is beginning to be used for the body of programming which we are discussing). Such composite machines are rich enough in the control information they contain to resemble one another closely even though they consist of very different hardware arrangements and even though they cover a

wide range of prices and performances. What we have here can be thought of as a clear instance of machine intelligence being substituted for human intelligence in one part of the programming problem. (Sayre, 1962, p. 275; emphasis and parentheses as in the original)

The importance which IBM attributed to operating systems was soon to be confirmed by the enormous resources which IBM poured into the development of the operating system for their 360 series of computers from 1964 (see section 5.1.1).

The development of operating systems has been important for a number of reasons. First, as Sayre clearly states, what manufacturers came to supply could no longer be viewed simply as a machine meaning hardware alone. Rather, the core item supplied came to be a *computer system* in which both software and hardware were essential components. Note that the term 'software' did not become well known until this occurred during the 1960s and that at first that term applied to what is now called systems software alone. It did not include applications software, the major output of the mediating process.[7] Figure 4.2 illustrates this change in computer systems core in terms of our model of the position of computer systems development in organizations.

Second, another way of looking at the new computer systems core was that it was beginning to take over certain of the activities previously carried out by

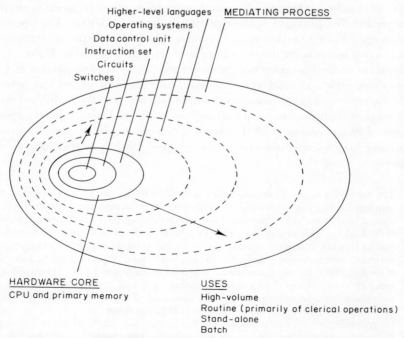

Higher-level languages   MEDIATING PROCESS
Operating systems
Data control unit
Instruction set
Circuits
Switches

HARDWARE CORE
CPU and primary memory

USES
High-volume
Routine (primarily of clerical operations)
Stand-alone
Batch

FIGURE 4.2 Phase one changes in computer core

programmers in user organizations as part of the mediating process. As hardware manufacturers discovered that more and more effort required to produce computer-based systems had to be undertaken on-site at user organizations, they were forced to take over more of these functions in order to sell their machines.

Third, this incorporation of certain mediating process functions into the computer systems core had direct effects on skills required of systems developers in user organizations (see section 4.5.3). Finally, the development of operating systems was also a particularly good example of the way in which uneven technological progress in the elements of a computer system could give rise to further changes in the technology. Progress in electronic components, both in terms of cost and capacity, gave rise to enormous increases in the power of the computer. The development of 'systems software', of which the operating system is an example, allowed the power of the computer to be harnessed to make the overall computer system more efficient.

The other major development in systems software during phase one was the development of computer languages. These were developed to use the power of the computer to reduce the overall cost of computer systems, both hardware and software costs.

In the model of systems development summarized in Figure 4.2, at the heart of the computer are the electronic binary 'switches', the most general and simple devices. Surrounding the electronic binary switch is the 'circuitry', which takes a collection of switches and places them in a configuration that constitutes the CPU and memory. The CPU is clearly a much more complex device in terms of its function(s) than the electronic components from which it is constructed.

The functionality of the computer is defined by its 'instruction set'. This is the set of binary codes by which the CPU can be instructed to carry out tasks such as reading a byte of data from memory, carrying out basic arithmetic or logical functions and sending the result to memory or an input/output device such as a visual display unit or printer. This level of functionality is perhaps the minimum level at which we could call the device a 'computer', yet at this level the computer is still a very general device with relatively simple functions. Surrounding the CPU is the software, which presents a collection of computer instructions to the CPU in a configuration that constitutes the computerized part of the system and provides an interface with the outside world.

4.2.4 Computer Language

The most basic operations that the computer can carry out are known as the instruction set of the computer. Typical instruction set commands would be to bring a word of data from memory to a location in the CPU (known as a register) or to add the contents of a location in memory to the contents of a register in the CPU. The instructions are presented to the CPU in the form of a binary code. This code specifies the instruction and may also specify a particular register in the CPU, a location or locations in main memory, and the location of the next instruction to be carried out.[8] The format of the instruction varies from computer to computer, as does the size of the instruction set. The sequence of coded instructions is known as machine code.

The earliest stored program computers were programmed exclusively in this machine code. Each program consisted of a sequence of numeric codes defining the operations to be carried out and the location of the operands. Programmers had to 'remember' (or look up) the numeric code for each instruction. They also had to make note of the location of the instructions in memory for the creation of loops and branches within the program.

Alterations to the program would cause changes in these locations, which would then have to be corrected and checked through the program. The location of data within the memory also had to be noted and checked when changes occurred. The fact that machine codes had no psychological link to the operations that they initiated, and the complexity and need for continual checking of addresses in memory, meant that machine code programming was time-consuming and highly error-prone.

It was soon realized that the computer itself could translate mnemonic (memory-aiding) representations of the instruction set into their binary equivalents and also keep track of locations within memory. The programs that were developed to carry out these functions were known as assemblers and the syntax of mnemonic codes that they provided were called assembly or assembler languages.

Instead of having to remember a numerical code for an instruction, the programmer would have mnemonic codes such as ADD, SUB, MPY which were consistent within the program rather than the physical memory. The assembler program translates assembler language instructions, written by the programmer (called the source program), into numeric machine code instructions (called the object program). This could then be executed by the computer. For our analysis an important characteristic of a language is what is known as the *level* of the language, meaning the degree to which it is abstracted from the computer procedures that it initiates. This concept of language level is important whether we are discussing impacts on productivity or on skills. Assembler languages are 'low-level' languages in that there is a one-to-one correspondence between the mnemonic assembler commands and the basic instruction set of the computer.

The major impact of assembler languages on productivity was that they reduced the incidence of error and made programs much easier to check and to alter. Their impact on the skills (other than memory skills) of programmers was negligible since they still manipulated the same set of instructions in writing the program.

As the cost of software development grew, the shortcomings of assembler language became increasingly evident. These shortcomings were of two quite distinct kinds. First, just as each new computer model had its own instruction set, so each model had its own assembler language. This meant that programs written on any one computer could not be run on any other model. A change of computer required recoding all programs. It also meant that very large computer users, with many different computers, found themselves developing programs for essentially the same application over and over again. As the computer age progressed, the quantity of developed applications programs grew and user firms began to look for ways of protecting this growing investment in software. This consciousness of the software investment became more evident as the cost of software relative to hardware also grew. Eventually, during the late 1950s, this led to increasing demands from users for a 'universal' computer language that would allow programs (and programmers) to be transferred between computers with relative ease.

A second shortcoming of assembler languages is that they are 'machine oriented'. The syntax and vocabulary of assembler languages are restricted to the basic operations of the machine's instruction set. The only concession that is made to human programmers and human users in the provision of mnemonic labels for the instructions. Many of the functions that were required in writing applications programs were very commonly used and required the same set of assembler instructions on each occasion. It soon became clear to the users of computers that a higher level of language, with a syntax and vocabulary relating more closely to their applications, would make the computer easier to use and vastly improve the productivity of programmers. The potential of high-level languages to do away with the need for programmers to have knowledge of the detailed workings of the computer was also noted. As early as 1959, Robert Bosak, a consultant in data-processing management, could say:

> In the area of programming language, developments will make it possible for programs to be written and modified more efficiently, both from the standpoint of man-hours and elapsed time required. It will also make it possible for less highly trained personnel to program the computer. (Bosak, 1960, cited in Kraft, 1977, p. 27)

The first high-level language, FORTRAN, was developed for scientific and mathematics applications in 1954. COBOL, designed for business applications, was developed in 1959. It is interesting to note that the pressure for the development of both of these languages came from computer users. FORTRAN was defined and developed by John Backus under the auspices of both IBM and the IBM users' association SHARE. COBOL was developed during 1959 and 1960 under the sponsorship of the US Department of Defense, probably the largest computer-using organization in the world. In 1960 the Department of Defense laid down an edict that all data processing computers that it purchased must be supplied with a COBOL compiler.[9]

The major drawback of high-level languages was their relative inefficiency in terms of the way programs written in these languages used the computer systems core. Because higher-level languages adopted a more generalized solution to the coding of problems, it was not possible to write high-level language programs that would fully exploit the capacity of a specific computer to meet a specific problem. The generality of high-level languages enabled applications programs to be written relatively quickly and with relatively little knowledge of the computer, but the resulting programs ran more slowly than their counterparts written directly in assembler. There was thus a trade-off established between productivity in programming and efficiency of machine use.

Within the scientific and technical computing areas the lack of efficiency in machine use was relatively unimportant. Many scientific programs are 'one-off' programs written for a specific purpose. Any individual program occupies the computer for a relatively small proportion of the time. Therefore the proportion of program development cost to hardware cost at a scientific or technical installation is relatively high, favouring the use of any method of cutting program development costs at the expense of machine efficiency. Within the business environment the computer typically runs relatively few programs or applications over and over again. Therefore programs in these installations which are written in a high-level language pay the cost of inefficient machine use many times over.

Recognition of the need for high-level languages and their invention and development can clearly be placed within our first phase of computerization. However, their widespread adoption for business applications did not really occur until the latter half of the 1960s—until phase two. There were a number of reasons for the relatively slow adoption of high-level languages, most of which relate in some way to the costs incurred in terms of machine utilization.

First, the inefficiency of programs written in high-level languages and the need for a complex compiler program to translate them into machine code meant that high-level language facilities were initially provided only for the larger computers. During the 1960s much of the growth in computing came from the spread of smaller, cheaper computers into relatively small organizations.

Second, existence of the capacity constraint, particularly on very early machines, had imbued computer systems developers with the concept that a 'good' program was an 'efficient' program, rather than a 'cheap' program. It took a considerable time before the economic reality of increasing software costs was able to overcome this prejudice.

Third, much of the impetus to develop high-level languages was derived from the compatibility argument. The 'high level' of high-level languages was to act as a bridge between the different machine codes and assembler languages on different machines. This argument was compelling for very large users such as the US Department of Defense, who possessed many computers running similar applications. For users with only one computer, compatibility offered the prospect of long-term gains when transferring from one computer to another in the future, or for the sharing of computer programs with a wide community of other users through user organizations. However, these benefits were less tangible and certainly more difficult to quantify than the clear cost in terms of machine efficiency.

Fourth, there was an element of risk involved in adopting a particular new language because a number of new languages were appearing during this period.[10] It was not immediately obvious that one language would become very widespread, yielding all the advantages of compatibility. Furthermore, manufacturers were also offering programs enabling later models of their computers to emulate earlier models and run programs which had been developed for the earlier machines. In such a rapidly changing technological environment many firms adopted a wait-and-see approach before deciding which technology would become firmly established.

Fifth, the decision to adopt a high-level language meant planning for a higher level of machine capacity and was thus a capital investment decision taken at relatively infrequent intervals.

The widespread adoption of COBOL as the major language for business data processing did not occur until the late 1960s and early 1970s—not until phase two. Therefore, in terms of our model of the development of the computer systems core presented in Figure 4.2, the outer ring—compilers for translating high-level languages—were not widely distributed until phase two. Also operating systems available in phase one were generally primitive compared with those associated with the third generation of hardware (see section 5.4.1).

4.3 COMPUTER USES AND COMPUTER USERS

4.3.1 Problem Solving Versus Data Processing

The distinction between problem-solving and data processing uses is particularly important to appreciate when examining the early years of computing.[11] ENIAC, the first electronic computer, was designed for the calculation of shell trajectories and was later used by the Los Alamos atom bomb project engineers for making complex calculations. Because of their speed of calculation, early computers were applied to many problems in science and engineering. Here theoretical knowledge had produced mathematical models whose solutions were too long-winded for human computation. Calculating rocket trajectories, analysis of stress in complex structures, seismic data analysis and aerodynamics were all early technical uses of the computer.

Business data processing grew rapidly from the mid-1950s, and by 1960 business uses had overtaken scientific uses, both in terms of market size and the number and value of installed computers. The distinction between business and scientific computers which existed up to the mid-1960s allowed the ratio of scientific to business applications to be estimated. Between 1960 and 1964, 86% of IBM computers produced were nominally business computers. The percentage of business computers by value was somewhat lower, at 71%, due to the larger average size and cost of the scientific machines (Sharpe, 1969).

The proportion of installed computers within different industry sectors also gives some impression of the types of computer applications and their relative importance. Stoneman presents estimates of the installed value of machines in the UK, broken down by industry grouping for the years 1962–1970. The relative proportion of the installed UK computer populations within each industry sector for 1962 and 1970 is presented in Table 4.1.

Industries have been aggregated into three groups: group A, representing

TABLE 4.1 Proportion of UK installed computer base by value for 25 industry sectors

Industry	% of UK installed computer value	
	1962	1970
Group A: high technical use		
Computer manufacturers	14.2	9.9
Aircraft manufacturers and guided weapons	5.3	1.9
Armed services	3.6	2.6
Atomic energy	5.2	0.8
Research establishments	4.9	3.4
Universities	8.5	5.6
	41.7	24.2
Group B: moderate technical use		
Chemicals, rubber, glass, plastic, paints, cosmetics	5.4	6.8
Electrical engineering	5.5	4.9
General and construction engineering	3.9	11.1
Oil	4.3	1.5
	19.1	24.3
Group C: low technical use		
Ferrous and non-ferrous metals, mining, quarrying	3.4	3.6
Financial, banks and building societies	4.6	7.3
Food, drink, tobacco, retail, wholesale mail order	4.1	7.3
Government departments	4.7	2.1
Insurance and assurance	3.5	3.5
Local government	3.2	6.8
Motor industry	3.3	2.1
Public bodies	1.3	2.8
Public utilities	4.9	3.1
Transport	2.0	2.4
Textiles, clothing, furniture, toys	na	3.5
Publishing, printing, paper, book clubs	na	3.0
Sports, leisure, TV, films, hotels	na	1.0
Other	4.2	3.0
	39.2	51.5

Source: Computer Survey and Stoneman (1976).

industries where technical applications are likely to dominate; group B, representing moderate technical use; and group C, representing industries where technical applications would be low or non-existent. The trend between usage in 1962 and 1970 clearly shows the growing importance of business compared with technical applications.

4.3.2 Business Applications

The J. Lyons Company, a chain of tea shops, developed their own computer, LEO (Lyons Electronic Office), in collaboration with the EDSAC computer team from Cambridge University. In January 1954 the first business DP application in the UK, the payroll for J. Lyons, was processed on the LEO computer. Payroll is the business application 'par excellence' of the first phase of computerization. As well as being the most frequently computerized application during this period, it embodies many of the characteristics of all early business applications.

A firm acquiring an early computer basically acquired a device for carrying out large numbers of simple arithmetic operations extremely rapidly. The advances in data storage and data access that would make the computer a suitable media for storing information, and the advances in communications that would make the computer system suitable for the transmission of data, still lay in the future. The early applications of the computer were largely confined to areas of the firm's information processing that conformed most closely with the computer's capabilities—applications that involved simple arithmetic operations on a large number of transactions. These were primarily *high-volume*, *routine*, clerical activities.

There are a number of reasons why these activities were the first to be computerized. The importance of *high volume* was directly related to the cost of carrying out the process without a computerized system and thus the potential gains that the system could offer. High-volume activities would tend to be high-cost activities and would thus be likely to attract management attention when looking for direct cost savings. It has been suggested that in some firms rapidly increasing volume of transactions was the overriding reason for computerization in the 1950s. For example, the following is quoted from an internal IBM memo written in 1971:

> At the dawn of the electronic data processing era, pioneer users of EDPM (insurance companies, large banks, Federal Government, airframe and defense industries), in the main, were not motivated by displaceable cost considerations. Sheer transaction volume (or complexity of computational requirements) were such that punched card technology was inadequate regardless of the quantity utilized. (Quoted in Greenbaum, 1979, pp. 14–15)

High volume was also important in terms of the efficient use of the computer. Since computers could only process one task at a time, processing many small applications would require much greater loading and unloading of programs. During this time the computer would be unproductive. Processing only one application at a time, and the need to utilize the computer as efficiently as possible, also meant that most applications were batch applications.[12]

The element of *routine* was important for a number of reasons. First, in order to process an application the computer requires completely detailed instructions as to how it should perform in any eventuality, i.e. the operation must be reduced to a routine. If a particular operation is already mainly routine then applying the computer to it is relatively simple. Systems analysis then consists of observing the existing routine, rules and procedures, and transferring them to the computer. If the operation is not routine, systems analysis must either impose a routine on to the operation, or alternatively introduce flexibility and room for human intervention into the system. The possibility of flexibility and human intervention exists with today's on-line real-time systems. In batch systems, where the user had no direct contact with the computer, this was not possible.

Routine operations also tend to be simple operations. Relatively few steps are involved and few decision criteria must be followed in taking those steps. Clearly there is a direct relation between the simplicity of the operation and several other factors such as the size of the program, the capacity of the machine required to run the program, the time it will take to run and, therefore, the processing cost.

Clerical automation systems

The types of operations that fulfilled criteria of high-volume, routine, arithmetic manipulation were mainly clerical office activities or office activities that had been partially automated through use of mechanical office equipment. The number of clerical office workers had been growing rapidly from early in the twentieth century. In the UK in 1920 they represented 6% of all workers. By the early 1960s they represented 14% (Friedman, 1977, pp. 203 and 222). They thus represented a growing element in firms' overall costs. Furthermore, their work had already been subdivided, rationalized and deskilled to a large degree (Braverman, 1974).

Thus clerical functions were ripe for computerization, both because the tasks were technically suitable and because there was a strong economic incentive. The computerization of clerical procedures offered clear-cut cost savings by the reduction in clerical manpower. Cost savings could be easily calculated, and apart from some procedural adjustments little in the company had to change.

So far we have only mentioned clerical labour saving as the cost justification for computer systems. Faster processing of data could also lead to direct cost savings in other directions. Stock control systems are a good example of an application where direct cost saving could be obtained through faster processing. If a stock control system reduces the lag between stocks running low, re-ordering and replenishment of stocks, then overall levels of stocks can be maintained at a lower level. Cost-saving systems of this type were also popular in phase one. However, the stock control system, with its indirect cost benefits, is somewhat different from a simple clerical automation scheme. The major difference is that it is the information output from the system (rapid identification of falling stocks) rather than the system itself (such as cheap processing of a payroll) which yields the cost advantage. This brings us to the use of the computer system as a producer of information.

Management information systems

In Chapter 2 we discussed Nolan's use of Anthony's general categories of business activities to distinguish different computer applications; operational, control and strategic applications. Large-scale clerical activities in a firm are mainly operational systems. They process data to produce operational outputs such as payslips, invoices, payments or ledgers. Most of these activities also produced information output, usually in the form of reports to management, to enable management to monitor activity. Therefore these clerical activities were also, in part, control systems. Churchill *et al.* recognized this implicitly in their classification of computer systems. Type one systems—those with the lowest level of management information—were those systems where control information to management from the computer system was the same as the control information from the pre-existing clerical system.

The necessity for even the simplest operational systems to produce some element of control information led to an early realization that the computer had great potential for enhancing management information. There is a clear logical priority between computerization of operational clerical procedures first, and then computerization of management information. The product of operational systems is the processing of transactions or data. The product of management information systems is information. The latter is basically the same data, structured and manipulated in such a way that it is useful for management control or strategic functions. Once operational systems have been computerized, the infrastructure of basic data is then available in a computer-accessible form. Computerized management information systems use the computer to structure and manipulate the data in order to produce information. The advantage of the computer is that data, once collected, can easily be structured in many different ways with different degrees of detail. From the early 1960s onwards the computing literature and manufacturers' publicity extolled the virtues of the computer for providing management with more and better information to increase control and decision making.

Along with Churchill *et al.*, the McKinsey Corporation (1968) also carried out a survey of the state of computerization in the USA in the late 1960s. The companies surveyed were all relatively large, mature users of computers, whose data processing systems could be expected to be relatively sophisticated. Both surveys reported that most of the companies in their samples had computerized many of the clerical elements of routine administrative and accounting operations, but that very few had made significant progress beyond this type of system. The Churchill study was explicit in pointing out the lack of impact of increased availability of information on line managers' own work, even though these line managers recognized the impact of the computer in changing the organization of their departments and the work of their clerical subordinates.

The progression from clerical automation systems to management information systems was hampered by a number of factors. First, benefits from management information systems were difficult to quantify and thus heavy additional expenditure on both hardware and software was difficult to justify. As hardware prices fell, it became easier to justify the increased hardware capacity that was required to run management information systems.

Second, although it was relatively easy to see how any specific information could be derived from existing data (the technical capacity existed), it was not easy to see what that specific information should be. The tasks of management are, by definition, not routine tasks. Their information requirements are both difficult to specify and can change very rapidly. Clearly the task of systems analysis becomes much more complicated when the system has first to be both routinized and computerized. Not only is it more complicated, but also it is more 'politically' sensitive. Management information systems imply a rationalization of the routine aspects of management decision making. This was resisted by managers who felt that their role in the organization was threatened. This is particularly true of systems providing control information about low-level management. Because the labour of these managers has not previously been routinized and deskilled, and because of their position in the organizational hierarchy, they could hold up the process of computerization more easily than their clerical subordinates.

Independent versus integrated systems

Another major advance in the character of systems that was mooted in the early 1960s, but not widely achieved during phase one, was the integration of systems. Integration of systems has implications both at the operational and the managerial level. At the operational level, for example, order entry and billing systems could be integrated with production scheduling and inventory management systems. At a managerial level, decision making, and particularly high-level decision making, is often based on information from many diverse areas within the firm and on information from the external environment. If the computer is to fulfil its management information role effectively, it must consolidate information from these different areas within the firm.

Both the Churchill and the McKinsey studies found that the level of integration of systems was low:

> Computer systems have been a significant factor in a number of administrative applications, but they have been undertaken largely as separate systems. The next great step will be their integration. (Churchill *et al.*, 1969, p. 112)

The major problems with integrated systems, as with management information systems, are their complexity and the difficulty of quantifying their benefits. Integration of computer systems requires enormous standardization of the way in which data is coded and stored in different departments. It enforces changes in working practices so that different functional areas of the organization accommodate each other in a way that independent systems do not. It also makes much greater demands in terms of the hardware required to service the application within an acceptable time frame.

4.3.3 Phase One Systems

Let us summarize the major characteristics of phase one systems. From a technical point of view they were batch systems, centralized within data processing departments, with no direct user interface to the computer. In terms of their place in the organization they were cost-saving applications, usually replications of clerical operations and usually independent of each other. In terms of specific application areas, accounting, payroll, stock control and sales processing were most commonly computerized. The proportions of UK installations processing various applications in 1964 are summarized in Table 4.2.

There were exceptions. The SAGE (semi-automatic ground environment) project produced an on-line real-time system for collating, analysing and disseminating data in the event of an airborne attack on the USA. This was developed in the mid-1950s. A number of airlines also developed on-line real-time flight reservation systems during the 1950s. Finally, there was the increasingly sophisticated systems software being developed by the hardware manufacturers. The existence of these projects tends to suggest that limitations were not purely

TABLE 4.2 Frequency of computer applications

	%
Financial accounting	40
Management information services[a]	54
Payroll	59
Invoicing and billing	36
Stock control	40
General statistics	28
Production control	19
Other office work	12

[a] We suspect that management information services (MIS) in this case includes any reports to management. Certainly the questionnaire form from which this data was generated did not specify the detail of management information, or whether this information was 'new' information, or information which had been produced by clerical procedures. At the time when the survey was carried out MIS was a 'buzz-word' which needed closer definition before it could be usefully interpreted. Interpretation of the other headings is much easier and more reliable.
Source: Department of Employment (1964, Appendix 11).

technological, but actually a matter of economics. For those organizations which wanted or needed very advanced systems badly enough, they could be designed and built.

Churchill *et al.* commented on a 'long plateau in systems development which seems to occur between Type 2 applications and those more central to management' (1969, p. 9). In most of the companies that they visited, initial operational computer systems were developed in the first four or five years, followed by a period of relative stagnation. During this period the DP department was mainly concerned with conversion of existing systems from one generation of computers to another.

This applications plateau was not a necessary logical outcome of computerization within the organization. The order of first applying the computer to clerical systems, followed by integration of systems and management information applications, is a logical ordering and therefore allows a reasonable prediction of the organization stages approach to computerization. The plateau or period of slow progress was caused by social and economic problems, as well as the state of technology at the time. Neither the technology or cost of computer hardware, nor the techniques of systems developers, were sufficiently advanced to cope adequately with the problems of computerizing new and unstructured areas or with the complexity of integrating systems. In Chapter 5 we will discuss these social and technical problems in more detail.

Figure 4.3 shows two pictures of the position of computer systems development in business organizations. The first picture shows the development of the computer systems core and applications as we believe actually occurred in most installations. The second picture presents the impression one is likely to have got about the field from the computing press in the early 1960s, according to Churchill *et al.* Certainly compilers to deal with COBOL or FORTRAN became available, and some extremely large and complex computer projects were being attempted during phase one. However, this sophisticated software was being developed by hardware manufacturers and a small number of very sophisticated user organizations. As we will show in the next chapter (section 5.1), it was around these projects that types of concerns we have associated with phase two were first expressed publicly.

4.4 LABOUR MARKET PRESSURES

The origin of the computer in the universities, and the predominance of research and technical applications among very early uses of the computer, had important influences on the organization of work in early computer installations. Within academic or research environments prospective computer users were scientists, mathematicians or engineers. They usually developed their own programs and operated the computer themselves. Where a degree of specialization had taken place, those who became computer specialists came from a science, mathematics or engineering background. There was little prospect of any strong direct control

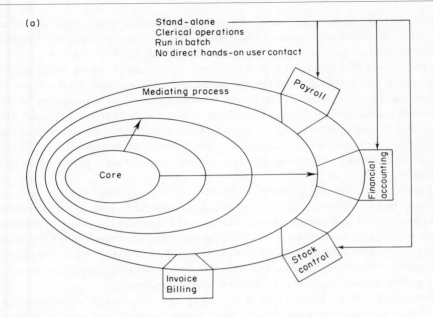

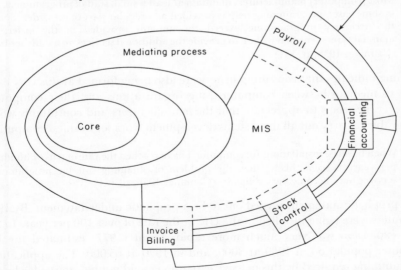

FIGURE 4.3 Phase one changes in applications. (a) Development of core and applications during phase one. (b) View of computerization from the computing press

strategies being applied to their work because computer activities were viewed as research. Research and academic activities are two areas where direct control forms of management are notably absent (Burns and Stalker, 1961).

The spread of the computer to the business environment, which began in the mid-1950s and gathered pace rapidly in the early 1960s, threw up a new set of problems. In the business environment computer 'users' were managers in the computer-using organization. They were the users in that they defined the desirable overall objectives that computerization should achieve and they had the authority to instigate a computer application. Clearly, managers as users did not have the necessary skills to apply the computer to their own problems as did scientists.

Furthermore, the development of business data processing systems involved writing large complex programs, entailing considerable man-years of effort. Unlike scientific and research users, managers did not have the desire to develop their own applications, even if they could acquire the necessary skills. Computer users were thus separated from the computer itself by a need to delegate the task of systems development to others. The data processing operation grew up in business computing to mediate between the users and the computer.

Computer manufacturers realized that computer sales were dependent on this mediating process very early on and they played a substantial role in the first decade of computerization:

> Most [computer] manufacturers maintain at least a small staff of programmers, and in some cases, programming help is provided as a regular part of the order. Should the necessary programming exceed the amount provided in the order, the manufacturers are often willing to provide the additional services on a daily fee basis. (Canning, 1956, p. 131)

Canning indicates that consulting firms were also being formed at this very early stage to mediate between computer-using organizations and their computers. However, he seems to appreciate that the manufacturers and consultants would not be able to carry out all the systems development work for business computing:

> When business installations [of computers] have reached the rate of tens or hundreds per year, as seems likely, then the problem of obtaining suitable programming services may become very difficult. (Canning, 1956, p. 131)

That prophetic statement turned out to be a prophetic understatement. By 1960 computers were being installed in the UK at the rate of over 100 per year. In the USA expansion was very much more rapid. Lecht (1977) estimated the US computer population in 1959 at 3000, and in 1970 at 65 000. The applications programming required by this massive expansion could not be catered for by the manufacturers or by the rapidly growing consultancy sector. User firms had to become increasingly self-reliant in developing their own systems and finding their own staff.

Although labour shortages have existed throughout the era of business computing it would seem that during the 1950s this was not considered to be a pressing problem in computer user organizations. Computer manufacturers and the scientific computing community were well established and provided well-trained recruits. Even if computer staff had to be paid more than other employees of comparable age and experience, staff costs represented a small proportion of computer application costs (no more than 20%, according to Boehm's estimate for 1955). Hardware cost and performance were much more pressing problems. However, during the 1960s this situation changed.

4.5 THE ORGANIZATION OF COMPUTER SYSTEMS DEVELOPMENT WORK

4.5.1 The Literature

Anyone wishing to glean a detailed picture of the organization of computer systems development work in very early computing departments from the literature will be disappointed. There is very little on the subject up to the mid-1960s. Then the volume of literature on organization of work explodes. Issues of personnel selection, division of labour, monitoring, control and productivity all subsequently receive considerable attention. The relative lack of literature on the labour process of computer systems developers during the 1950s, and its subsequent growth in the late 1960s, is strong evidence for our formulation of phases one and two. The early literature concentrates on the hardware aspects of computing. A literature concentrating on systems development costs and other labour process issues emerged later, when they became a constraining factor.

4.5.2 Staff Recruitment and Training

The emergence of the computer or electronic data processing department in organizations immediately generated new issues for management, particularly concerning recruitment. The mediating role of this department meant that knowledge both of the organization and of the computer was required. Canning poses the question as to whether it is easier for managers to become good programmers than it is for experienced programmers to learn the intricacies of the business. There are really a number of separate issues involved in this question. First, how closely involved should managers be in the selection of a computer and the design of computer systems? Their involvement is clearly desirable because of their knowledge of the organization and their clear sight of its objectives. Canning himself suggests that delegation of these tasks will be necessary because of the time needed to acquire computer skills and the volume of work in systems design and programming. Second, given that delegation is necessary, should internal staff be trained or should experienced computer staff be hired? If internal non-management staff are used, is there any benefit from their knowledge of the organization's existing procedures, or are they merely a convenient labour pool? Canning does not answer these questions himself. He merely states: 'Management must decide whether to have existing company personnel do all of the programming or whether to hire experienced programmers during the early planning and training phases' (1956, pp. 129–130).

It seems that most organizations setting up a data processing department adopted a combination of strategies. They would employ some experienced programmers or take advantage of manufacturers' programmers both to provide a core of technical expertise and to train existing company personnel in computer techniques. A major source for experienced computer programmers was from the scientific and academic fields, where a large proportion of the early computers were situated. Both the manufacturers and the users themselves recruited experienced computer programmers from these areas in the 1950s and early 1960s. These programmers, coming from the research environment into the business environment, brought with them their own working customs, which were largely accommodated by organizations who were anxious to obtain their technical expertise.

The types of existing personnel who were trained in programming would depend on the type of organization. Accounting and clerical staff were one obvious source because of the frequency with which computers were applied in those areas. Technical and engineering staff had an education background with a mathematical bias which suited them to computer tasks. Organization and methods staff, where such departments existed, had both a technical background and a suitable perspective on automation and systems within the organization. People were drawn from very many areas of the organization into the DP department, and many regarded it as an unlikely accident that they became 'involved' with computers.

In the early 1960s the pace of computerization quickened. The numbers of computers doubled every two years throughout the decade. The need for computer staff grew commensurately and the recruitment net was spread wider. Some organizations came to administer programmer aptitude tests to all their employees in their search for computer staff.

The formal training of computer staff was mostly in the hands of the computer manufacturers during the 1950s. The same business forces that induced them to provide applications programs with their machines also induced them to provide training for user organizations. They could not sell computers without providing training. The training provided by IBM in particular was renowned for its high quality. Organizations trying to recruit would use the promise of IBM training as a lure for potential employees (Kraft, 1977, p. 36). On the other hand, computer hardware manufacturers, and especially IBM, provided staff as well as hardware and software to customers as part of their marketing strategy. Sometimes these people remained formally employed by IBM, but worked on-site at key customers for years. Many eventually joined user organizations formally, often taking key positions. With this strategy hardware manufacturers encouraged customer loyalty.

The other major form of training was on-the-job training. Programming was very much a craft, with the consequence that some of the skills required of programmers could only be learned by experience. On-the-job training requires a core of experienced programmers who can correct and educate the less experienced in the course of their work. This master–apprentice structure was only complemented by formal training, not supplanted by it.

4.5.3 Automation and Programming Skills

By the early 1960s a few had begun to see that software was beginning to overtake hardware as the limiting factor in computerization growth:

> It is becoming clear that the limiting factor in the growth of the use of machines is beginning to be mankind's ability to instruct machines in complex activities and not the machines' raw information-processing power. (Sayre, 1962, p. 274)

However, the solution to the problem at that time was conceived in hardware terms, in terms of automation:

> These circumstances naturally produce an intense pressure to economize on human intelligence in programming by developing machine intelligence as a substitute, so as to trade what is plentiful for what is scarce. (Sayre, 1962, p. 274)

The same principle by which electronic and chemical technology of computer switches substituted for wires and connections in the circuitry of computer components (when computer generations changed from a transistor basis to integrated circuits) and by which electronic devices were used to substitute for electromechanical input/output devices, would be applied to substitution of computer systems core for programming effort. Rapid technological progress in one area, or one medium, would lead to that area engulfing areas of slow technological progress. This could be done either by directly replacing the slowly developing medium with a rapidly developing one, or by using the functions performed in rapidly developing media more intensively to avoid relying on functions performed in slowly developing media (such as by spooling or multiprogramming, as noted above, section 4.2.3).

Operating systems and other forms of systems software substituted processing power (or what Sayre called 'machine intelligence') for human intelligence. They automated certain parts of systems development. However, the effect of these forms of automation was not to deskill programmers. The programming tasks taken over by systems software during phase one were similar in type to the sorts of business applications computerized during phase one: high-volume, routine, clerical-type activities (see section 4.3.2). It was in these less-skilled tasks that the comparative advantage of automation lay. Grace Hopper, one of the first who recognized the coming software constraint, clearly stated the automation schedule as seen from a phase one perspective at the MIT centennial lectures in 1961:

> After the systems analyst has produced his flow chart, a programmer appears in the scheme of things to make the run charts and write the run specifications. His charts go to a coder who writes machine instructions, and these machine instructions go to the operator who runs the computer. Work in automatic coding has concentrated on getting rid of the coder. We have not yet tackled the job of automatic programming ... One step further is automatic system design, and this too may be attempted within the next ten years. (Hopper, 1962, p. 272)

It was the less-skilled coding work that would be automated. In the rapidly expanding computer systems development environment which has existed since the 1950s the consequences of automation on development staff were to require updating and upgrading of skills, rather than either deskilling or redundancy. As we shall see in the following chapters, although substantial advances in automation were indeed achieved during the past 30 years, the process of automating human intelligence has not proceeded so quickly as Grace Hopper expected, and its effects have not been so complete. Factors other than the rapid pace of technological progress in the computer systems core also influenced the computerization process in later phases.[13]

4.5.4 The Work of Computer Systems Developers and Management Strategies

Many descriptions of computers begin with the observation that the computer is basically a set of switches that can be altered between two states: on and off. This observation, out of context, may be misleading, giving no hint of the capabilities or limitations of the computer. Nevertheless, as a description of the computer itself it has two redeeming features.

First, it emphasizes the binary nature of the computer, with its use of binary arithmetic and Boolean logic. Second, it emphasizes the fact that the computer is in essence a collection of very simple devices (simple, that is, in terms of their function). The complexity of the computer derives from the very large number of simple devices and its ability to complete very many simple binary operations in a very short time. Third, it allows an appreciation of the proposition that computers cannot think for themselves without human intervention, i.e. they must be programmed.

The task of developing a computer system is thus to take this general, functionally simple device and apply it to a specific and functionally complex application. This definition of computer systems development, as moving from the general to the specific and the simple to the complex, is essential for understanding the changes that have occurred in the nature of systems development.

The process of programming consists of combining the relatively simple instruction set of the computer to make a complex program. Because of the simplicity of the instructions and the complexity of the resulting system there are many ways of combining the simple instructions to achieve the same end result. Each program is unique. Generally the greater is the gulf between the simplicity of the instruction set and the complexity of the end system, the more ways there are of combining the instructions to achieve the same desired result. The existence of many different solutions to any particular program objective is an important facet of the programming activity since it introduces a high degree of discretion into the programming process.

The types of computers available during phase one, particularly in the 1950s, were very expensive to buy and expensive to run. They required a lot of space. They also required a controlled environment because they generated a lot of heat. They were rather unreliable and this meant a lot of downtime. Substantial effort was required to maintain the hardware. Perhaps the most significant feature of these machines, in terms of their effect on programming, was their relatively slow speed and limited primary memory capacity. The mark of a good programmer was one who could write programs that ran quickly and that required little memory space. Programmers developed subtle and complex tricks to 'squeeze' more out of the machine's capacity. Few could follow what a virtuoso programmer was doing. This meant that programmers were often treated as wizards or magicians. Programming was widely regarded as an 'art'.

By the 1960s the notion of the talented programmer as an artisan with innate qualities and sometimes almost mystic skills had taken a strong hold. D. E. Knuth observed:

> The process of preparing programs for a digital computer is especially attractive because it not only can be economically and scientifically rewarding, it can also be an aesthetic experience much like composing poetry or music. (Knuth, 1968)

The inherently creative character of systems development work, attributable to the high level of discretion that programmers in particular had to exercise, placed a clear limit on the extent to which direct control strategies could be pursued. The responsible autonomy style of work in academic and research organizations was carried over to business environments because the character of the work in the new environment was similar, at least in the early years of computing. Managers of computer departments in business organizations had to rely on the skill, discretion and goodwill of systems developers. In those years it was common for managers of computer departments to have come from accounts or finance departments of organizations and therefore to have little detailed understanding of the work of computer specialists. Wide productivity differentials among computer systems developers (which were revealed in the computing literature only in phase two) had to be tolerated because of the difficulty of accurately measuring the productivity of these creative processes.

For the individuals who were drawn into computer programming during phase one, the work itself represented a major advantage. A computer program is a well-defined product. When you have written it you can test it, and derive satisfaction from seeing it work. Programming is a creative activity and an individual activity. As just noted, there are very many ways to solve any particular problem. Decisions have to be made continuously as to how to approach each problem. Programming is also a craft activity in that a program can always be improved, made to run faster, occupy less space in memory, use fewer statements. The extent to which a program excels in these areas is largely dependent on the skill or craft of the programmer. Enid Mumford stresses the importance of these factors in creating high job satisfaction among computer programmers (Mumford, 1972). Certainly for many people moving from traditional, and hence rationalized, jobs in other areas of the organization, the relative freedom from strict rules and procedures and the scope for individual skills must have presented a strong contrast.

In addition to the inherent character of the work, the glamour of working with new technology and the prestige attached to an occupation which was in high demand rapidly set skilled computer workers apart from other workers in the organization. Salaries reflected the high levels of demand for their skills and rose rapidly. The new skills of computer workers were not specific to an individual organization or industry, but a passport to jobs in other organizations and other industries. Increasingly computer systems developers began to identify more with their skills and the technology they were implementing than with the organizations employing them. This situation, always more prevalent with external recruits to computing than internal transfers, became exacerbated as external recruitment of trainees was increasingly used to staff the growing DP departments. It had two major effects.

First, labour turnover grew as people 'job-hopped' between organizations to gain promotion, higher wages or a technical challenge. Second, the data processing department became increasingly remote from the users. Users could not understand the technical jargon of computer specialists, and the computer staff themselves were more concerned with getting programs to run and the computer to function than they were with the effects of the system on the users.[14]

Management problems caused by the increasing power of computer staff, both in terms of their market strength and their possession of technical expertise which the user organization needed, began to come to the fore during the early 1960s. They mark the transition from phase one to phase two and will be discussed in the next chapter. Problems caused by misunderstandings between computer specialists and users and by disappointed users have only recently become major issues. They represent one of the major problems in phase three, which will be discussed in Part Three.

4.6 COMMENT

According to Bergland, writing from a software engineering perspective (see section 5.5), programming was in its 'golden age' during the 1950s:

> The approach was to take a small group of highly qualified people and solve a problem by writing largely undocumented code maintained by the people who wrote it. The result was inflexible and inextensible code, but it was adequate to the demands of the time. (Bergland, 1981, p. 14)

Buxton (1978) called it 'cottage industry' programming.

We will show how this form of organization was increasingly judged inadequate to the demands of the time from the late 1960s. However, we will also show that, while a consensus developed as to the general nature of the problem with the way computer systems development was organized, there has been much disagreement over how to solve this problem.

ENDNOTES

1. Short versions of the early history of computing are available in many general texts on computers. A good account can be found in Rosen (1969).
2. This should not be confused with the electromechanical calculator developed by Harvard and IBM during the 1940s, also called MARK I.
3. For an example of the importance of the military for the development of the transistor, see Braun and Macdonald (1982).
4. In the computing field large numbers are common. It has become standard practice to cite measurements in terms of K (1000s). To cite numbers in terms of K seems to be taken as a sign of technical sophistication. A mark of the prosperity of the field is the use of K when citing salaries. Occasionally we will indulge in this practice.
5. See section 4.2.4 for an explanation of these terms.
6. Weizer defines an operating system as follows:
   > An operating system is an integrated set of systems programs whose major function is to manage the resources of a computer system at both the macro and micro levels. Such functions as resource scheduling, I/O control and error recovery, memory management, processor management, task and job scheduling, system error recovery, and security can all be considered integral parts of an operating system. (1981, p. 120)
7. Applications software was usually produced within computer user organizations.
8. There are also instructions for reading data from input channels and writing data to output channels.
9. COBOL (COmmon Business Oriented Language) was first demonstrated in December 1960 by the CODASYL committee (COmmon DAta SYstems Language) set up by the US Department of Defense. During 1961 and 1962 most American computer manufacturers announced their intention to produce COBOL compilers. Grace Hopper, a leading CODASYL member, was careful to note that 'COBOL would not make top-rate programmers out of second-rate personnel' (Hopper, 1962, p. 38).
10. The cover of a 1960 issue of the *Communications of the Association for Computing Machinery* showed a drawing of the Tower of Babel, each brick being a different language (referred to by P. W. Abraham in Greenberger, 1962, p. 282).
11. We have already examined this distinction with respect to the different demands that these broad types of applications make on the computer and the consequent parallel development of scientific and business computers during the 1950s (section 4.1).

12. Transactions are collected and recorded manually over a certain time period (for a payroll this might be weekly or monthly). They are then processed together in a batch.
13. The automation strategy can be easily represented with our model of the position of computer systems development in user organizations. Ultimately the mediating process would be engulfed by expanding computer core (Figures 4.2 and 4.3).
14. At the 1961 MIT lectures Grace Hopper related the following anecdote concerning COBOL:

    > When it recently became possible to use the English language to write programs, an Air Force colonel was heard to say, 'Now we can take back command of the Air Force from those damned programmers.' (Hopper, in Greenberger, 1962, p. 285)

Chapter 5

PHASE TWO: SOFTWARE PROBLEMS DOMINATE

As noted in Chapter 2, change in technology is often viewed as an exogenous factor in computing histories. Scientific advances in the basic technology, through solid-state electronics and integration, have been strong external stimuli, particularly during the first few generations of computer hardware, but the characteristics of computer technology as actually sold to computer users and the way that technology was actually used within computer user organizations have been affected by other factors. They have been influenced by the uses to which computers were put, by market forces and by characteristics of the internal organization of the computing function.

Rapid growth in the number of potential or viable computer applications (due largely to the fall during phase one in both hardware cost/performance ratios and absolute cost of the computer systems core), stimulated an enormous growth in demand for staff to carry out the mediating process. This meant that the average experience level of computer systems developers continued to be low. Also rapidly growing demand for staff could not easily be matched by a similar growth in the supply of systems developers. Severe shortages appeared. Shortages gave those individuals who had acquired systems development skills and experience considerable market power and independence. This provided an incentive for the computer-using organization to find ways of limiting the organization's dependence on the individual systems developer.

With fewer limitations on cost and performance of the hardware, more complex and grandiose schemes for computer systems could be attempted. Many marginal applications that became potentially viable were not the simple replications of existing clerical manual systems that had dominated during phase one. Many were attempts at integrating systems from different parts of the organization, providing new functions, particularly information and management support functions. These systems were not only technically more complex owing to their size and the interconnections between different systems, they were also more complex in their organizational implications and effects.

The combination of increasing complexity of systems and the relative inexperience of systems development staff led to late deliveries of systems, escalating costs and failed software projects. Failure of systems developers to deliver on their promises brought about a general loss of confidence on the part of senior management. It brought about a desire to improve control over the computerization process in general and over the systems development process in particular. This came to be known as the software crisis, or the software bottleneck, or the problem of lagging software productivity (and especially of unsatisfactory programmer productivity).

The essence of the second phase was that systems development or software costs and performance came to displace hardware costs and performance as the major constraints on the spread of computerization. This, in turn, led to rapid change in the nature of the systems development process, in markets, in computer uses, and in the character of new computer technology itself. Referring to our diagram of the phases model, by the mid-1960s the concerns of computer systems developers had 'turned' (Figure 5.1). As we will show in the following section, clear evidence for this turn may be found in the computing literature from the late 1960s. This in turn affected the direction of innovation.

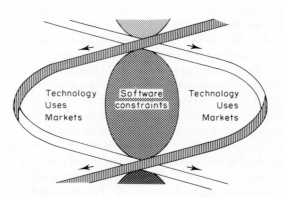

FIGURE 5.1 Phase two: software constraints

Computer hardware manufacturers had an incentive to find ways of either removing the need for some of the skills or increasing the productivity of the skilled. This resulted in the emergence and the eventual widespread adoption of high-level languages, utilities, generators and systems software, such as database management systems and teleprocessing monitors. Another consequence of these changes was the emergence of the independent software-producing sector and the increasing commodification of software in the form of software packages. It also affected management strategies towards computer systems developers.

After discussing the computing literature on software productivity problems, we will examine reasons why software problems came to dominate the computing literature from the late 1960s. Then we will examine reactions to these perceived software problems, in terms of both changes to the organization of work within computer installations and changes in the direction of technological change.

5.1 EMERGENCE OF CONCERN ABOUT SOFTWARE PRODUCTIVITY IN THE COMPUTING LITERATURE

The importance and the general nature of the 'software crisis' was first recognized by those who were involved in the area of systems programming and real-time systems. These were the largest and most complex systems development projects that were being tackled. Most contributors to this literature were academics or they worked for hardware manufacturers or the military. From these sources awareness and articulation of concern spread to business users.[1] Edsger Dijkstra, regarded by many as the father of structured programming, cited a particular date for the public emergence of the software crisis:

> Only a few years ago this was different: to talk about a software crisis was blasphemy. The turning point was the Conference on Software Engineering in Garmisch, October 1968, a conference that created a sensation as there occurred the first open admission of the software crisis. (Dijkstra, 1972, p. 120)

Dijkstra's declaration was slightly overstated. We have noted that as early as the 1961 MIT conference key figures in the computing world were aware of software problems on the horizon. The term 'programming bottleneck' was used by G. W. Brown[2] at the conference (Brown, in Greenberger, 1962, p. 278). However, as noted in Chapter 4, this was regarded as a new technical challenge that would soon be met. Dijkstra was right to emphasize the reluctance of computer specialists to admit that there was a software crisis. During phase one computers were viewed with great suspicion by many potential users. The computing community was anxious to emphasize progress and high expectations to potential investors as well as to customers. Over-optimism associated with rapid expansion and an enthusiastic computing press undoubtedly led many project leaders and computer department managers to regard many problems which they faced as due to factors particular to their own installations. As such they would have been reluctant to own up to them.

The Garmisch conference was important not only because of the open admission of software crisis expressed, but also because many of the key figures in the international software world attended: from manufacturers, users and the universities.

5.1.1 The Garmisch Conference of 1968[3]

In the keynote speech, A. J. Perlis (Computer Science Department, Carnegie-Mellon University) emphasized the importance of the conference theme in terms of growing sections of society which would be affected by the consequences of defective software. Their ability to forgive the software community was inversely proportional to their ignorance of the difficulties faced by software specialists, according to Perlis. One purpose of the conference was to reduce such ignorance, especially ignorance on the part of military users, who were at that time still the largest users of computer software. The conference was sponsored by the NATO science committee.

Recognition of a crisis was stimulated by certain software failures which had led to very public disasters. Dark references were made to air crashes and large banking errors reflecting 'an uncritical belief in the validity of computer-produced results' (R. M. Graham, Project MAC, MIT, and A. Opler, IBM, New York, p. 121):

> There is a widening gap between ambitions and achievements in software engineering ... The gap is arising at a time when the consequences of software failure in all its aspects are becoming increasingly serious. Particularly alarming is the seemingly unavoidable fallibility of large software, since a malfunction in an advanced hardware–software system can be a matter of life and death, not only for individuals, but also for vehicles carrying hundreds of people and ultimately for nations as well. (E. E. David, Bell Telephone Laboratories, and A.G. Fraser, Mathematical Laboratory, Cambridge University, p. 120)

Many conference participants reported experiences of large projects which had been disappointing in three main ways. The projects ran on long after their estimated deadlines. They cost much more than their budgets allowed. They resulted in systems that did not match performance expectations anticipated at the beginning of the projects:

> Today we tend to go on for years, with tremendous investments to find that the system, which was not well understood to start with, does not work as anticipated. We build systems like the Wright Brothers built airplanes—build the whole thing, push it off the cliff, let it crash, and start over again. (Graham, p. 17)

> Programming management will continue to deserve its current poor reputation for cost and schedule effectiveness until such time as a more complete understanding of the program design process is achieved. (K. Kolence, Boole and Babbage Inc., Palo Alto, p. 123)

Most participants expressed the belief that there was indeed a software productivity problem. Although even on this point some believed the conference was too pessimistic about the software productivity crisis (R. C. Hastings, IBM, Rochester, New York, p. 120; H. R. Gillette, Control Data Corporation, p. 120). There was disagreement about the causes of the problems. Suggested solutions were varied, often contradictory, and debated with vigour.

Causes of the crisis

Many reasons were suggested for software problems. For many the problems were primarily due to the increasing size of software systems that were being attempted at that time. The most notable example of an early software project running into problems was the development of the operating system for the IBM 360 family of computers (OS/360). This project, which was crucial to IBM's computer strategy, ran into serious problems in the mid-1960s. The system finally emerged late, cost several times the initial estimates and was widely criticized in terms of its performance, until several subsequent releases of the software had cleared up most of the more serious bugs. IBM's problems with OS/360 were well known to Garmisch Conference participants:

> Production of large software has become a scarce item for management. By reputation it is often an unprofitable morass, costly and unending. This reputation is perhaps deserved. No less a person than T. J. Watson said that OS/360 cost IBM over 50 million dollars a year during its preparation, and at least 5000 man years investment. TSS/360 is said to be in the 1000 man year category. It has been said, too, that development costs for software equal the development costs for hardware in establishing a new machine line. The commitment to many software projects has been withdrawn. This is indeed a frightening picture. (David, p. 67)

> Many of us would agree that Multics and TSS/360 have taken a lot longer to develop than we would have wished, and that OS/360 is disappointing. (Perlis, p. 121)

Why were these projects so difficult and disappointing? One reason may be associated with the problem of tenses and salesmanship. These large projects were too ambitious. Basic software systems were increasingly being used by hardware manufacturers as a competitive tool for selling new computers. This led to unrealistic promises being made by computer hardware manufacturers' sales offices. Promises were unrealistic because the research nature of software systems development was not properly appreciated. It is difficult to estimate time constraints if the research content of projects is high. The systems being attempted were so large that it was difficult to tell beforehand what the research content was (F. Genuys, IBM–France, p. 72; R. M. McClure, Southern Methodist University, Dallas, pp. 72 and 123; H. A. Kinslow, Computer Systems Consultant, Ridgefield, Connecticut, p. 122; S. Gill, Imperial College, London, p. 123). All projects involved some aspects that were new. In addition, many elements of projects that had been done before would have to be done a new way, because the hardware technology had changed substantially since the previous project. Manufacturers were being caught by their own anticipatory claims for new computer systems core under development.

Second, it was difficult to estimate the ultimate size and cost of systems once they were under way, because it was difficult to measure progress:

> Only one thing seems to be clear just now. It is that program construction is not always a simple progression in which each act of assembly represents a distinct forward step and that the final product can be described simply as the sum of many sub-assemblies. (A.G. Fraser, Mathematical Laboratory, University of Cambridge, p. 86)

Fraser complained that he experienced the classic problem of measurement whereby the measuring effort interferes with what is being measured. In a large project they kept totals of the number of subroutines classed as tested, and compared this with the total number of subroutines in the final product. This led to a rise in programmer productivity, measured by the time taken to produce a tested subroutine, but a fall in the quality of those subroutines. At the heart of the measurement problem of large systems production is the interdependency of different programmers' work. An error in one part of the system will have consequences on work for the system produced by others, and error correction can seldom be left as a localized activity. This means that interface details between different parts of the system will have to be altered regularly. Fraser went so far as to say

> One might even suggest, a little dangerously perhaps, that rapid change to interface descriptions is a sign of good progress. (p. 87)

If such changes must occur then it is easy to see why it was hard to identify observable events to mark real progress towards the final completion of a project. Thus it was difficult to report the extent of progress (Kolence, p. 87).

Third, there was the problem of managing large numbers of people. Some conference participants simply stated that projects requiring more than a certain level of manpower usually resulted in disaster (J. N. Buxton, University of Warwick, UK, p. 68; David, p. 39).

> The reason that small groups have succeeded in the past, and that large groups have failed, is that there is a need for a certain structure of communication and a structure of decision making in the development of software. (T.B. Pinkerton, University of Edinburgh, p. 43)

Clearly the seriousness of problems of estimating the research content of new projects, of measuring progress during projects and of managing staff were directly related to the large size of many of these projects. However, rapidly changing technology was also an underlying force exacerbating problems. Three further problems were widely discussed at the conference; we will deal with each of these in greater detail later in this chapter.

First was the problem of inadequate documentation. In part this was identified as a management problem. Programmers find documentation boring. They neglect it or they document their work too long after they have finished, when memory has faded. In part, inadequate documentation was considered to be a technical problem. Notation and procedure were developing so quickly that individuals were making up their own forms of description. These led to communication problems. More detailed standards were required (David, p. 60; E. W. Dijkstra, Technological University, Eindhoven, Netherlands, p. 61; P. Naur, A/S Regencentralen, Copenhagen, p. 90; J. Nash, IBM UK laboratories, p. 93). Standards are discussed more fully below (section 5.5.1).

A second problem, according to some, was that too much time was being allotted to coding and too little to design and testing. Coding was begun too soon (R.S. Barton, Consultant in System Design, Avalon, California, pp. 60–61; McClure, p. 73). However, this was a highly contentious point. Others believed that it was impossible to leave coding until design was perfectly completed because the design specifications were never correct. It is only by coding that you come to realize how the design is deficient (Kinslow, p. 32; D. T. Ross, MIT, p. 32). Methods of ordering stages in systems development projects and of monitoring progress through those stages received considerable attention in the latter half of phase two (see section 5.5.4 and 7.2).

Inadequate manpower was the third problem identified. In particular, a general lack of programming competence was bemoaned (Barton, p. 57; Perlis, p. 86). This was clearly blamed on the labour shortage (see section 5.2.2):

> in software projects, talent is often so scarce that marginal people are welcomed. (David, p. 83)

'Solutions' suggested

Beyond more documentation, more standardized documentation, and more time to be budgeted for testing, all other suggested solutions to software problems were subjected to vigorous criticisms. Several said that the solution to problems associated with large projects was not to attempt systems which required more than some specific level of manpower, but Perlis noted that there was a high demand for certain large and complex software systems. These could only be done by many people 'each of whom does a mole's job' (p. 68).

Most who spoke about high-level languages recommended that they be used (David, p. 56; Graham, p. 57; Ross, p. 57; McClure, p. 58; B. Randell, IBM, Yorktown Heights, New York, p. 58; P. M. Kjeldaas, Kjeller Computer Installation, Kjeller, Norway, p. 55; B. Galler, University of Michigan, p. 59). Claims for high-level languages were that they reduce machine dependence, are easier to read and change, and increase programmer productivity. However, it was noted that they were still rarely used (Randell, p. 58). Some preferred lower-level languages for hardware efficiency (Kinslow, p. 58) and for debugging (Perlis, p. 57). Kolence made the point that installations that settle on a single high-level language restrict themselves to a limited structural class of programs, because each higher-level language has some particular design features built into them. They are not so general as lower-level languages (p. 59).

The key recommendation of the conference organizers, that projects and programmers be managed using more traditional engineering tools, was hotly debated. They knew this would be controversial. The software engineering argument for solving the software crisis was as follows. First, standardization of program structures, particularly via modularization, was recommended. Second, there should be a specific ordering of stages in the systems development process. Third, design and programming procedures should be standardized. These recommendations would increase the observability and measurability of systems development and thereby increase management control.

Modularity and rigid specification of interfaces were considered essential design concepts for maintainable systems, according to Gillette (p. 39).

> Each program designer's work should be scheduled and bench marks established along the way so that the progress can be monitored ... The yardstick should measure both what has been designed and how, from the standpoint of meeting the design requirements. Programmers should be required to flowchart and describe their programs as they are developed, in a standardized way. The bench marks for gauging the progress of the work should be a measure of both the documents and program produced in a given amount of time. (J. A. Harr, Bell Laboratories, Naperville, Illinois, p. 88)

Harr's recommendations came from his experiences with one particular large project, producing real-time software for electronic switching systems. He presented further details of the organization structure, type of personnel, the structure of group meetings and measures of programmer output in words per man-year for this project. While no one doubted Harr's description, reaction to his proposed generalization from this case was highly critical. Others had either tried such methods or heard of such methods being applied. Their experiences were very different:

> I know of one organisation that attempts to apply time and motion standards to the output of programmers. They judge a programmer by the amount of code he produces. This is guaranteed to produce insipid code—code which does the right thing but which is twice as long as necessary' (McClure, p. 88)

Smith noted that at Scientific Data Systems rigid standards were imposed on software production:

> They begin with planning specifications, go through functional specifications, implementation specifications, etc. etc. This activity is represented by a PERT-chart with many nodes. If you look down the PERT-chart you discover that all the nodes on it up until the last one produce nothing but paper. It is unfortunately true that in my organisation people confuse the menu with the meal. (pp. 88–89)

As pointed out above, several participants stressed that the high research or creative content of software development means that you cannot assume that you can design a system and specify it adequately and completely before you code and test. Kinslow suggested that an interative process between design and coding is not only common, but necessary (p. 32). Ross went so far as to say that the most deadly thing in software is the concept that you can specify what you are going to do in advance, and then that you can do it (p. 32).

5.1.2 Software Crisis and the General Business Community

By the early 1970s the problems of systems development in the business data-processing area were also having an important impact. A government review of the state of computerization in the UK in 1972 reported:

> ... some of the more ambitious systems for improving decision-making by management, involving the coordination of data on all aspects of a business (integrated databases), have not yet generally made the progress once expected. Furthermore, recent economic stringencies and disappointment with some ill-conceived systems have recently slowed the pace of installing office computers and EDP systems. (Department of Employment, 1972)

These problems stimulated a non-academic audience for management theorists and consultants on management of the systems development process, particularly among managers in large computer user organizations. Two collections of articles, both published in 1970 in the USA, provide a fair sample of the types of issues that were attracting attention and the type of treatment they received. *Computers and Management* (Sanders, 1970) provided an overview of a number of the organizational issues concerned with introducing computers, including the changing applications of computers, controlling the computer function and computer personnel issues. *On the Management of Computer Programming* (Weinwurm, 1970) was more precisely concerned with the problems of the systems development process.

In his introductory note Weinwurm expresses the growing concern about the systems development process:

> It comes as a distinct shock to the uninitiated that for an activity that accounts for the expenditure of several billion dollars a year in the USA alone, the management of computer programming is still something of a black art.

Later in the same introduction he notes growing awareness in US government circles of a need to monitor and improve the quality of systems development in the administration. In a law passed in 1965, the US Bureau of the Budget was charged with monitoring and coordinating information processing management within government and developing policies, standards and techniques in this area. The Department of Commerce was charged with the development of both technical and management standards for information processing (US Public Law 89–306, cited in Weinwurm, 1970).

The US government was (and still is) the largest computer user in the world, with much greater experience as a computer user organization than any other. It is therefore not surprising that the concerns that were soon to emerge in smaller and less experienced organizations should emerge first in the US government. However, by the early 1970s, the stories of problems associated with developing computer systems, and the malfunctions which occurred once they had been developed, were becoming very widespread. They were even appearing in the popular press; in publications as diverse as *The Wall Street Journal, Dun's Review, Fortune, The Economist,* and *Playboy* magazine. For example:

> We have seen over the past twelve years some incredible blunders. Twinkling lights, spinning tapes and pastel cabinets seem to have a mesmerizing effect on some managers. In a pell-mell rush to be among the first to play with a new toy, enormous sums have been wasted. (Hershman, 1968, p. 26)

For many the problems of managing large software products was most graphically presented by Frederick Brooks in his book *The Mythical Man-Month* (1975). Brooks' basic hypothesis was as follows. Poor estimation techniques and poor monitoring techniques led to late delivery of large software projects. However, these problems were exacerbated by a tendency to equate effort with progress and a presumption that men and months were interchangeable. These fallacies led project managers to add manpower when projects were slipping behind schedule. Complex interrelations among the parts of a large systems development project and communication requirements among the staff meant that extra training was required for the additional manpower. This, and the need to rush, meant more errors and, of course, further delays. Therefore adding manpower to a late job makes it later. The idea of a man-month, of a trade-off between men and months, is a myth (1975, pp. 14–25).

The slump in the UK computer market of 1970–1971 provided the strongest possible evidence of this growing disenchantment with computer systems. Reacting to the slump, an article in *The Economist* characterized the computer as the 'accident prone miracle' (1971). It related a number of stories of computer projects that failed to deliver systems, or systems that were unable to carry out their stated function. This article was quoted as evidence of the increasing disenchantment of senior management with computerization in a later publication in the UK by Ward (1973).

Ward's analysis clearly relates growing disenchantment with the computer at that time to failings in the systems development process, and in particular to the supply of systems staff with 'appropriate skills':

> The ability to realize the tremendous potential of computers will be directly proportional to the supply of competent and dedicated staff prepared to make a career in e.d.p. (Ward, 1973, p. xiii)

The problem for Ward was one of availability of suitable computer systems developers who were skilled in both technical and business implications of computer systems. His prescriptive passages stressed staff selection and training techniques.

Many of the issues dealt with by technical specialists and academics at the Garmisch conference were soon reflected in the business literature. However, there were differences in emphasis. In the business literature the software problems were more likely to be considered problems of management, rather than problems of technology. For example, while the academics bemoaned the absence of techniques for predocumentation as a solution to the generally agreed problem of inadequate documentation, business managers were worried about *excess* documentation and time wasted on producing and digesting documentation (Orlicky,[4] 1969, p. 122; Dearden, 1972, pp. 90–99: Adams, 1973, p. 4).

While business managers also complained about shortages of computer specialists and incompetent programmers, they were more likely to blame computer managers for software failures:

> The quality of project management is more important than the quality of technical talent used. (Orlicky, 1969, p. 126)

5.2 AGENTS OF CHANGE: GENERATING SOFTWARE PROBLEMS

Changes in technology, increasing complexity in the types of applications attempted and growing labour shortages all contributed to the software crisis. The rapid improvement in the cost/performance ratio of hardware throughout the 1950s and the early 1960s was chronicled in the previous chapter. This continued throughout the 1960s and 1970s. Over the same period there were some advances in the development of software which also tended to bring down software costs, and increase the productivity of software developers. More generalized systems software was developed, adding higher-level functions which did not need to be developed for each individual application. Higher-level languages became available, which also offered higher-level functions than machine code and assembler languages.

However, there were also countervailing forces, tending to increase software costs. More complex applications were attempted and many of these large projects ran into severe problems. Problems with testing and debugging a system tended to increase geometrically, rather than arithmetically, with the size of the system. Testing and debugging large systems came to occupy almost half of the total development effort.

The net effect of these different cost tendencies was a very significant shift in total system costs towards software. In the article by Boehm cited above (section 4.2.2), it was estimated that the proportion of computer systems costs in the US Air Force that could be attributed to software had risen from less than 20% in 1955, to 50% in 1965 and to 70% in 1970 (Boehm, 1973). It was forecast to increase to over 90% by 1995 (see Figure 5.2).

Boehm suggested that these results were also characteristic of other organizations. He also noted certain implications of this growth in proportion of software costs. The *absolute* increase in systems development costs, and in particular the problems of estimating software development costs and time-scales, was

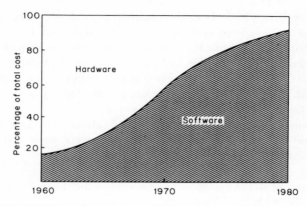

FIGURE 5.2 Software and hardware costs compared

leading to increasing management interest in the systems development process, both in the air force and elsewhere.

Couger and Zawacki present somewhat different figures for the business computing sector, but the direction of change is similar to Boehm's:

> Personnel costs occupy a significantly higher proportion of the DP budget each year. In 1970 they were only 30 percent of the total budget. Five years later the proportion was 40 percent. In 1980 personnel costs amounted to over 50 percent of the total DP budget. (1980, p. 3)

There is general acceptance of the picture shown in Figure 5.2 in the computing field. Boehm's graph is widely cited. Frank (1983, p. 253) presents 13 examples of the graph published in the ten years since Boehm's article, as well as a very similar graph he produced for a *Datamation* article published five years before Boehm's graph (Frank, 1968). However, according to Frank, the graph depicts a *myth*. The proposition that software represents a growing proportion of total data processing expenditures is a myth. Cragon (1982) also considers the proposition to be a myth.

Why might it be a myth? Certainly the cost of hardware of a given performance level has fallen much more quickly than the cost of producing software of a given performance level. However, hardware manufacturers have responded to this potential dramatic fall in the unit cost of their products by producing machines with much greater performance capacities. Users have steadily upgraded their hardware. Hardware manufacturers have also produced far cheaper machines, but these have either been bought by new users, who could not afford previous machines, or they have been bought by existing users in addition to new, higher-performance machines, rather than as replacements. In addition, hardware has been substituted for relatively more expensive software in the process of computer systems development (see section 5.4 below). We regard this latter factor as an effect of the growing proportion of DP budgets attributable to staff costs which are primarily software production costs, rather than a denial of the higher software to hardware ratio.

It is difficult to be precise about the long-term pattern of the software/hardware cost ratio because comparable figures over time are not available and because of definition problems. Frank admits that many different ratios can be constructed, depending on what economic issue or situation is being studied.[5] For our purposes the key distinction is between purchased computer systems core and mediating process expenditure on computer systems development (this would include payments for external services, other than packaged software, as well as direct staff costs). It is difficult to disagree with the pattern shown on the graph for the period before 1970, i.e. for the period which covers phase one and the early years of phase two. We presented circumstantial evidence that personnel costs were relatively unimportant during phase one in the previous chapter. Also this was the part of the graph based on Boehm's experience. However, we do agree with Frank that since 1970 there has not been a dramatic change in the ratio. Nevertheless, there is evidence for a steady rise in the ratio of software to hardware costs and the ratio of mediating process cost to that of purchased computer systems core.

In the May 1981 issue of *Datamation* a ten-year comparison of their annual DP budget surveys was presented. In the budget year 1972 the ratio of software (personnel, purchased software and external services) to hardware (computer hardware and data communication equipment) was 53/47.[6] Comparable figures for 1976 and 1980 were 57/43 and 62/38. Figures for budget years 1984 and 1988 were 59/41 and 75/25.[7] The ratio of mediating process to computer systems core costs rose similarly.[8]

5.2.1 Market Relations and Output from Computer Departments

In phase one the typical supplier of systems was the hardware supplier. Computer departments in user firms arose from the inadequacy of that source of supply. Hardware manufacturers may have sold their wares on the pretext that they were supplying user needs for systems; however, manufacturers were either not able to perform the mediating functions between the computer systems core and user needs, or they were not interested in carrying them out.

By late phase one the typical configuration in user organizations was for there to be a centralized DP department with a *monopoly* in computer systems supply to user departments. In most organizations the monopoly was so strong that no financial records were kept which would allow user departments or senior management to know the cost of supplying particular applications. Even if cheaper or better suppliers were available, DP department clients would not have been able to judge better or cheaper. Not only was actual competition absent, but also barriers to evaluating potential competition developed. Costs from internal sources could not be established easily. This made comparisons with potential external sources difficult.

Only 39% of the sample in the CEL 1972 survey charged users for systems analysis and programming and only 10% were run as a profit centre. This was in spite of the statement by 45% of the sample that they provided DP services to organizations outside their company, although incomes from this source were, on average, only 4% of the DP budget.[9]

It was only from 1969, with unbundling, that a substantial software industry emerged, first in the USA and a few years later in Europe.[10] Therefore from the beginning of the 1970s it was possible for user organizations to purchase systems and applications software from a growing software industry, rather than producing it in-house. Many predicted the rapid demise of in-house computer systems development. However, rapid growth of the software industry has occurred alongside rapid growth in DP departments within user organizations. It was estimated that US firms spent only 2% of their DP budgets on external software in 1978.[11]

5.2.2 Growth of Systems Demand and Labour Shortages

Rapid growth of installed computers during the 1960s led to a strong demand for systems development staff and to severe shortages. Brandon estimated a shortage of 30 000 DP managers, 35 000 systems analysts and 60 000 programmers in the USA in 1967 (1967, p. 37). In the UK a government report estimated a shortage of some 4000 systems developers by 1972.

Rapid growth in demand for systems development staff generated a major recuitment drive in the 1960s. In order to recruit and train large numbers of systems developers, it was first necessary to identify the individuals who had the potential to become computer programmers. Although many of the earliest systems developers were mathematicians and engineers, it was clear that the massive demand for systems developers could not be met from these sources. Furthermore, it was also clear that for most programming tasks advanced mathematical skills were not necessary. The capabilities which were deemed necessary were strong logical and reasoning capabilities and good attention to detail. With these basic inherent capacities the potential recruit could be trained to become a computer programmer.

The first programmer aptitude tests were developed before 1959 at IBM. The 1959 revised test issued by Hughes and McNamara at IBM became the standard. This test was designed to screen individuals to see if they had the required logical and reasoning abilities to become programmers. By the mid-1960s the IBM programmer aptitude test, or 'PAT' as it came to be known, was the most commonly used selection test.[12] The growing need was such that at many organizations anyone who could pass the aptitude test screen was assured of entry into the field of data processing. Many other selection criteria that would normally be imposed on staff entering an organization were ignored.

Shortages were exacerbated by the time required for a new recruit into the systems development area to become a productive member of a systems development team. Formal training on courses supplied mainly by the manufacturers themselves did help to fill the gap. However, a period of on-the-job training and experience has always been regarded as an essential part of the programmer's or systems analyst's education. The period of relatively unproductive learning on the job has long been reckoned to be around 18 months.

The initial period of on-the-job training and experience gathering was particularly important in the early days of systems development, when there were relatively few formalized rules and procedures that could be taught. Programming was viewed largely as an individualistic craft activity, with the characteristically long learning curve associated with a craft. Many of the developments in the technology and management strategies for systems development have been attempts to formalize the craft skills and thus to shorten the informal learning curve.

Having 'trained' staff was just the beginning of software productivity problems associated with labour shortages. Salaries for staff that had acquired the critical 18 months to two years of experience were rising quickly. Shortages also meant that managers could not be choosey about systems developers, especially programmers. This, and the creative nature of the activity, meant that there were enormous differences in productivity among experienced programmers. At the Garmisch conference David cited a now well-known study by Sackman *et al.* in which 12 programmers with 2–11 years of experience were tested on a specific logic problem (1968, p. 6). The performance variation ranged from a minimum of 5/1 for the size of coded program to 25/1 for actual coding time used and 26/1 for debug time used (David, in Naur and Randell, 1969, p. 83).

> In managing software projects the real problem is 'spot the lemon and spot the lemon early.' (Opler, in Naur and Randell, 1969, p. 84)

The difficulty with spotting the lemon early was that there would be many programmers performing significantly less well than the others. There was a range of productivity levels and therefore many lemons, or near-lemons. Also labour shortages made it difficult for managers to get rid of less than satisfactory staff.

Another effect of the shortage was that systems developers with any technical expertise tended to be promoted very rapidly. Generally poor management in the software field was mentioned at the Garmisch conference. In part this was attributed to little experience of large projects, but it was also attributed to the immaturity of the field. Lack of software management theory meant lack of software management training. This led to a lack of software management specialists (Kolence, in Naur and Randell, 1969, p. 123). Programmers were promoted into management because they were good programmers, rather than good managers. This led to 'emotional management' (McClure, in Naur and Randell, 1969, p. 123). One participant cited the 'Peter principle', that 'people are eventually promoted to their final level of incompetence' (David, in Naur and Randell, 1969, p. 62).

If systems developers were not promoted internally, it was easy for them to find higher rates of pay and more senior technical management positions through the labour market. Many projects suffered badly or foundered completely during the late 1960s and the 1970s, because essential staff left projects prior to completion, or because of inexperience among project managers and staff.

By the late 1960s the problems associated with staffing computer development projects were not merely those associated with finding and keeping systems development staff in an expanding market. There was also an increasing communication gap and worsening relations between computer systems development staff and the rest of the organization. There were many reasons for this.

Many young staff were recruited into the growing activity and soon found themselves in positions of considerable responsibility and seniority. Because of rapid growth, the demand for their skills and the glamour of working with the new technology, many of the new recruits into systems development seemed to regard themselves as a race apart from the staff in the other parts of the organization.

Their working practices were different from those of other departments in many ways. They often worked at odd hours, late into the night, developing new systems when the computer was not running the firm's existing systems. The language of systems developers was full of the jargon of the emerging technology and not widely understood outside the DP department. Chandor (1976) summarized many people's attitude towards DP staff, describing them as 'high priests of the new technology' and the fledgling DP department as 'the cuckoo in the nest'.

The emerging stereotype of the systems developer was the long-haired, 'hippy' programmer, who identified more closely with the technology that he was developing than the users for whom he was developing it; and who identified more closely with the emerging computing profession than the organization that employed him.

Richard Brandon expressed a popular (although somewhat hysterical) image of the programmer of the late 1960s and early 1970s:

> The average programmer is often excessively independent to the point of mild paranoia; he can be egocentric, slightly neurotic, and bordering on a limited schizophrenia. The incidence of beards, sandals and other symbols of rugged individualism or nonconformity are notably greater among this demographic group... (Brandon, 1970, p. 9)

Brandon laid much of the blame for the recruitment of this 'management problem' on the process of programmer selection by aptitude tests:

> Many people with the aptitude to pass numeric or spatial relations tests lack the ability to become effective and productive members of a programming group. As a result, selection of personnel by these tests often tends to segregate individuals whose

personality characteristics are very strong and sometimes negative. Furthermore, because the programmer has absolute control over his product and his productivity, his incapacity for mature cooperation with management can preclude effective control. (Brandon, 1970, p. 11)

Brandon's view is that the programmer selection criteria, and by implication the skills necessary for computer programming, tended to attract recruits with certain undesirable attributes (from a management perspective). Brandon's condemnation of the programmer aptitude test may have been misguided. Aptitude testing is still widely used today, along with other personnel selection criteria. However, nonconformism is much less evident among computer specialists, particularly if dress is taken as an indicator. It seems more likely that rapid growth in demand for systems developers happened to attract young people into the emerging occupation at a time of particular social change among young people.

Whichever view one takes, it remains clear that by the late 1960s management of the systems development function was perceived as a serious and growing problem by many observers. This problem had become the major limitation to continued expansion of computerization.[13]

5.3 REACTIONS TO SOFTWARE PROBLEMS

Problems posed by the systems development process were approached from a variety of angles. One approach was to automate systems development functions. There were two variants of this approach. One was to substitute hardware for software. The other was to incorporate systems development functions into the computer systems core, to substitute bought software for the activities of systems developers in the mediating process (such as adoption of high-level languages). The second, and more direct, approach was to attempt to improve management strategies for the systems development process within user organizations. This approach received most attention in the literature, particularly the labour process literature.[14]

5.4 AUTOMATION AND THE ROLE OF SYSTEMS DEVELOPMENT TECHNOLOGY

As noted in Chapter 3, there were some in the early 1960s who foresaw both the coming software productivity problem and a clear solution to that problem. The solution was to continue to automate, to use expected rapid advances in hardware technology to incorporate systems development activities into the computer systems core (Bosak, 1960; Hopper, 1962). However, as we have shown in this chapter, in spite of continual and significant improvements in hardware technology, by the beginning of the 1970s the computing world had become famous for failures: dangerous system errors, late deliveries, spectacular budget overruns and abandoned projects. High expectations were not fulfilled.

Nevertheless there were notable achievements during the 1960s and 1970s. These are summarized and evaluated in the next three subsections.

5.4.1 The Operating System and Computer Languages

In Chapter 4 we described the beginnings of high-level languages, particularly COBOL and FORTRAN, in the late 1950s. It was not until the early 1970s that COBOL became established as the dominant high-level language for writing business DP applications.

The fact that a COBOL compiler[15] is a piece of software rather than hardware is not essential. What is important is the interface between the computer and the systems developer. Many low-level programming tasks, such as comparing the values of two variables and acting on the outcome, which would take many statements in machine code or assembler language, can be accomplished with one statement in COBOL.

This may be viewed as a movement of the computer systems core closer to the final system (as described in Figure 4.3). Another way of looking at this process is to regard part of systems development tasks as having been automated, as the computer systems core taking over part of the mediating process.

The introduction and spread of COBOL and other high-level languages was technically dependent on the expanding capacity of computers and on the improvements in the cost/performance ratio of the hardware. With high-level language compilers there was a definite price to be paid (in terms of program efficiency), for the benefits of reduced systems development time and labour costs. The benefits of high-level languages were well aired at the Garmisch conference. According to E. E. David of Bell Laboratories, high-level languages reduce errors, increase programmer productivity and therefore require fewer programmers. They improve the readability of source code and can reduce machine dependence (increase portability). They can be more flexible, i.e. easier to change (David, in Naur and Randell, 1969, pp. 55–57). Graham stated that the advantages of higher-level languages show up particularly in large projects, with more complex tasks. They increase programmer productivity. They make programs easier to understand and thereby allow managers to 'move people around easier, or replace them easier' (Graham, in Naur and Randell, 1969, p. 57).

Although COBOL was first developed in the early 1960s it did not become well established during the 1960s. In spite of their clear advantages, high-level languages were not the great breakthrough that would allow programming to be done by users who were not computer specialists. D'Agapeyeff, director of Britain's largest independent computer services company, Computer Analysts and Programmers, made the following general criticism:

> In aiming at too many objectives the higher-level languages have, perhaps, proved to be useless to the layman, too complex for the novice and too restricted for the expert. I

maintain that high-level programming languages have, to this extent, failed. (D'Agapeyeff, in Naur and Randell, 1969, p. 55)

Randell, of IBM, blamed slow growth of high-level languages on project managers seeking to optimize easily measurable criteria on which they expected to be judged; measures such as minimizing core store used or maximizing speed. Long-term advantages such as portability and ease of recoding were ignored (Randell, in Naur and Randell, 1969, p. 58). This position clearly showed tensions created by the transition from phase one to phase two.

It was only during the early 1970s that COBOL became the primary programming language for business applications. COBOL was used in 70% of UK installations, according to a survey carried out by the Department of Employment in the UK in 1971. However, it was often used only to a limited extent, as a second or third language (Department of Employment, 1972). By 1975 a National Computing Centre survey of the UK user population reported 92% of installations using a high-level language, usually as their major applications development language (Hansen and Penney, 1976, pp. 10–13).

Since the widespread acceptance of COBOL for business applications development during the early 1970s, there has been considerable speculation about the next generation of computer languages for applications development. These are the so-called fourth-generation languages or 4GLs.

There are still applications today which are programmed directly in assembler language or machine code.[16] For these applications the improved system performance which can be achieved with assembler programs, or the constraints on system efficiency due to hardware limitations, outweigh the benefits of developing the system in a higher-level language. These are typically real-time applications in areas such as control systems or communications and would include the operating systems of most computers and other systems software. Alternatively, they may be software applications such as packages which are going to be reproduced many times and where a small improvement in performance can justify a significant outlay in development time and cost.

In the DP or IS function in the user organization it is only common for assembler language or machine code programming to be carried out by the systems programmers, who may be trying to optimize the performance of the system as a whole or improving the performance of key sections of applications which run very frequently. In all of these areas, the hardware constraint on the development process that characterized the first phase of computerization continued throughout phase two (and phase three, although in a smaller proportion of locations).

Nevertheless the widespread adoption of high-level languages for most programming is one of the distinguishing features showing the shift in emphasis away from machine efficiency and pure hardware considerations and towards software cost and programmer productivity. As such it is one of the major indicators of the transition to the second phase of computerization.

5.4.2 Utilities, Generators and Database Management Systems

In addition to the growth of high-level languages, a number of classes of software tools and utilities were developed to aid the systems development process during the 1970s. These tools or utilities may be language-like in that they provide a programmer with a form of syntax for instructing the computer at a higher level of functionality. However, they differ from computer languages in that each is usually applied to a very specific range of computer applications.

Certain types of functions are common to many computer applications. One such common function is the sorting of data into a certain order so that it can be processed sequentially. The requirement for sorting data files rapidly and efficiently led software developers to develop sorting utility programs. These can be 'called' by the programmer to sort large data files. The programmer does not have to write a new program each time a sort is required.

Another category of development aid which was becoming common in the late 1970s and early 1980s was the program generator, of which the most common type has been the report program generator. Many DP applications, particularly those concerned with providing management information, manipulate data to produce reports. Report program generators provide a syntax for specifying the contents and the layout of a report. They provide functions such as totals, averages, comparisons, selection of data records on specified conditions and many other functions that are required to manipulate data to produce a report. They also provide a simple format for specifying the layout of the report, the position of the information on the printed page, titles, etc. This allows a report program to be developed in a much shorter time than using COBOL for the entire program.

With the advent of on-line data collection, where data are entered directly into the computer, generators for developing data entry 'screens' were also developed. The function of the data entry screen is very similar to the report in that it provides the interface between the user and the system, in this case for inputting data as opposed to outputting information or reports. The function of the screen generator is thus very similar to the report generator. It allows the programmer to define the appearance of a screen, to collect data from a user, to check it for consistency and to store·it in the appropriate computer files, instead of accessing data from files, manipulating it and providing information to the user.

Technically, generators can work in different ways. Some are effectively very high-level languages, where the statements that the programmer produces are compiled to produce machine code, which can then be processed by the computer. Others take the input of the programmer and translate it into a high-level language such as COBOL, which is then compiled to produce machine code. As far as the programming process is concerned, these technical differences in the way that the generator produces a working program are unimportant. What is important is that the process of developing the report program or data entry program has been partially automated.

In addition to the language-like facilities and tools there have also been software tools developed that act as extensions to the operating system of the computer. The most important generic type of systems extending the functions of the operating system have been database management systems.

A data base management system is a software program for managing the storage and efficient access to data held on the computer. All data are recorded by the database management system (DBMS). The programmer no longer needs to specify (or even to know) the physical location of the data or the form in which the data are stored. The DBMS allows the systems developer to access an individual item of data from many different points of view without the need to store the data item many times over.

For example, a data record with details of a transaction, such as an order for goods or services, may be accessed by a program to calculate a salesman's bonus, a program to send an invoice to the customer, a program to check on stocks and inventories, etc. The DBMS allows the same physical record of the data to be viewed as an item in the salesman's file, an item in the file of outstanding invoices and an item in the file of orders to be processed.

The DBMS is a development which occurred relatively late in phase two. In the NCC 1975 survey 32% of organizations reported using one compared to 59% in a survey of comparable organizations in 1981 (CEL 1981 survey, see Data Appendix). The major impetus for developing DBMSs and for individual organizations acquiring one was largely technical and related to the types of applications that were developed. In particular it came with the development of 'on-line' systems for data capture and data inquiries, which emerged as the major development in many organizations' DP during the 1970s.

There have been a very wide range of software tools and utilities developed which have automated or obviated parts of the systems development process. The techniques by which they produce executable programs have varied, as have the means or the syntax by which the programmer instructs them to produce the executable code. However, they can all be viewed as part of the same process, that of applying the computer itself to the systems development process.

In general, whenever an identifiable and relatively standardized function such as report generation, screen generation, data management or transaction processing became sufficiently widespread and well understood, software tools would emerge to assist the programmer in the programming of the function. These languages' tools or utilities removed the lowest-level coding functions from the programmer or coder and automated them completely.

The ultimate evolution of this process of identifying standardized functions and computerizing them is the applications 'package'. Applications packages, such as payroll programs or accounting ledgers, emerge where the function of the entire system to be computerized is sufficiently standardized across a large number of organizations to enable one program to be used, with only minor modifications, by a large number of different organizations.

The trend towards using packaged, 'off-the-shelf' or what Kraft called 'canned', systems, emerged first in the USA in the early 1970s, and only later in the UK and the rest of Europe. It is a reaction to the high cost of developing one-off bespoke systems using traditional development methods. As such it was encouraged by the spread of cheaper hardware into smaller organizations, which occurred earlier in the USA. This aspect of computerization will be examined more fully in Chapter 9.

5.4.3 Interactive Programming

The other major technological change which affected the systems development environment and the productivity of the systems developers was the application of the computer to the mechanics of systems development. In the mid- to late 1970s, with the growth of computer power available and particularly the enormous virtual memory available, the actual process of writing, editing and changing a program became more highly computerized. Early in phase two the programming process consisted of writing a program with a pencil on paper, punching the program on to cards, handing the program to the operators to be queued for compilation and testing, fetching the printed output with the results of the test run, amending the program and then going through the iterative process again until the program was tested and functioning to some level of acceptance.

By the late 1970s most program development beyond the design stage was carried out at a computer terminal. The programmer types the program directly into the computer at a terminal, using a program editor with powerful facilities for manipulating and amending the text of the program.[17] The program is then compiled at the programmer's command, with the results of the compilation and error messages transmitted directly to the programmer. Once the program is successfully compiled it can be tested, running with test data files created by the programmer from the database management system, and the test results transmitted directly to the programmer's terminal.

The productivity gains offered by interactive programming have been steadily enhanced by adding more and more tools to assist the programmer with the systems development task. These tools include facilities to assist in the systems documentation process, to check the program syntax and logical structure, and many other detailed aspects of the development process. In the 1980s these software-based systems development tools are being combined together into packages and referred to as a 'Programmer's Workbench' or 'IPSE' (Integrated Programming Support Environment).

5.5 STRATEGIES FOR DIRECT CONTROL OF THE LABOUR PROCESS

Although significant advances in the automation of systems development tasks were achieved during phase two, a different set of strategies were also being pursued in computer installations at that time. This was to try to wrest control over of systems development work in a more direct way, by reducing the discretionary content of the work through standardization and routinization, as discussed by Kraft (see section 2.4.2). However, we will argue that this strategy was not pursued as strenuously, nor did it succeed so completely as Kraft suggested.

During the very early years of systems development a number of factors combined to permit or even encourage the discretionary aspect of computer programming (discussed in section 4.5.4). The relatively high cost of hardware and the absolute capacity constraints in terms of available memory meant that a high premium was placed on program efficiency (minimizing computer time required to run a program, or minimization of memory requirement).

Program efficiency was achieved by tailoring the program very specifically to the capabilities of the particular computer and the demands of the particular system. Any set of programming rules, laying down general procedures, would tend to preclude this tailoring procedure and incur penalties in terms of program efficiency.

As we saw in the previous chapter, many programmers evolved their own obscure techniques and tricks for improving the performance of their programs. Programming was widely regarded as an 'art'.

Dijkstra described a phenomenon which aptly summarizes this attitude towards programming, the phenomenon of 'one-liners':

> It takes one of two distinct forms: one programmer places a one-line program on the desk of another and either he tells what it does and adds the question, 'Can you code this in less symbols?'—as if this were of any conceptual relevance!—or he just says, 'Guess what it does!' (Dijkstra, 1972, p. 123)

Dijkstra was actually citing this as a criticism of a language (probably APL) for allowing such obscure constructions, but it is symptomatic of the 'clever tricks' attitude. Many of the management theorists writing about computing at this time were well aware of the problem presented by programming as a creative activity.

Gerry Weinberg (1971) coined the term 'egoless programming'. This would be the remedy for many of the problems in systems development. With egoless programming the individual programmers would curtail their *individual* creative instincts to some extent, and operate more as part of a team. In particular, creative programmers' possessive relationship towards their program should be weakened or broken.

Weinberg clearly considered the discretionary nature of programming, and the many individual approaches that it permitted, as a problem. Weinberg's answer was to remove some individual discretion by promoting a team or consensus approach to systems development.

Other methods took a more direct approach, by actually limiting the scope of the choices available to the systems developers. These included the development of programming and systems development standards, and latterly structured programming and design methodologies. Connected with these methods were recommended ways of dividing up work tasks and types of organization structures which would contribute to ensuring that discretionary working practices would not be channelled in unproductive ways.

5.5.1 Standards

The term 'standards' has two rather different meanings in computer jargon. When used to describe the *industry at large* 'standards' usually refers to technical cooperation and coordination (or more frequently the lack of it) between different manufacturers, or different countries. Standards, in this sense, have been a thorny issue throughout the history of computers. Although a high degree of standardization is beneficial to the users of computers, it is not necessarily in the interests of computer hardware manufacturers. Lack of standardization between manufacturers tends to 'tie in' user organizations to particular manufacturers. The users' investment in software and hardware that is not compatible with the offerings of rival manufacturers can provide a strong incentive to remain with the existing manufacturer.

There have been a number of notable subjects for standards, and many where standards have not yet been achieved. One common standard is the 'ASCII' (American Standard Code for Information Interchange) standard, which defines the binary codes by which alphabetic and numeric characters and symbols are commonly represented in computers. The evolution of languages is another area which has been subjected to some form of standards. The CODASYL (Conference on DAta SYstems and Languages) committee is responsible for defining additions and changes to the COBOL language. Every ten years or so a new definition of the language is published which is referred to by the year of its publication, hence COBOL72, FORTRAN77. During the 1980s there has been increasing pressure for standardization to simplify communication between computers.

Inside an organization, standards can refer to 'standardization' between different teams or individuals. However, it is also used in the wider sense of the rules governing all aspects of the DP activity. There are a number of distinct roles that standards fulfil in the systems development process. For our purposes it is useful to distinguish standards on the basis of the motivation behind their imposition. These can be divided into three major types.[18]

(1) the desire for coordination when there is more than one individual involved in a project;
(2) the desire for more management control;
(3) the desire to improve quality or performance, either of the producers or the product.

It can be difficult to distinguish which of these motives lies behind any particular standard. Standards can be motivated by several of the considerations above. Also, imposing a standard to increase coordination may incidentally increase control or performance. However, it is useful to keep the perspective of these three basic motivations when discussing the emergence of standards.

Coordination standards

Coordination standards are, on the face of it, the simplest and least controversial types of standards. In a large team or department certain standard practices are adopted. These concern the naming of variables, how reports or programs are to be laid out, and defining a consistent style of practice and procedure. As projects grew larger and more complex, with more and more people involved and spread over longer periods of time, the value of coordination standards became more and more apparent. These standards certainly affected the discretionary activity of the systems developer, but not in a very significant way. Certainly they reduced the individual artisan aspect of programming work in terms of the form of the program, but they had little effect on the content of the work. Coordination standards were likely, on balance, to increase skills, particularly for less-experienced staff. Learning a consistent style for naming variables or for layouts, and learning how such standards facilitated communication within a project group or a department, were part of the critical on-the-job training that came to be highly valued on the labour market. Even more experienced staff could benefit from such standards because the standards were continually evolving as new procedures and practices were generated by new applications and by changing technology. Senior programming staff would generally be involved in developing these standards. Rather than creating personal procedures, senior staff would have to develop management skills by creating procedures that were both applicable to more than the specific problem they were working on as well as communicable to less experienced staff.

Of course, the effect of coordination standards on development staff was not necessarily positive. Such standards could be established by remote management, particularly in larger installations. They could be treated as invariant laws that had to be followed. In installations with long-standing teams working primarily on maintenance and minor enhancements to old systems, such procedures could lead to the atrophy of programmer creativity and a diminution of one dimension of programmer skills; although with severe labour shortages such installations would have had to pay above the going rate or suffer high turnover of staff with the critical two years of experience. In installations where new projects and new technology were continually being introduced, remotely initiated, static coordination standards would likely be ignored by programmers, usually with the tacit support of project leaders and other middle managers.

In most cases coordination standards appear to have been continually developing, flexibly applied, a positive contribution to programmer skills and of little consequence for management control over development staff. However, these standards were a necessary precondition for allowing the work of developing a system to be shared among a number of systems developers.

Management control standards

Standards or rules to improve management control over the systems development process began to emerge in the management literature of the mid-1960s. Dick Brandon's book, *Management Standards for Data Processing* (1963), was the first comprehensive guide. Brandon dealt with all types of standards, but for Brandon standards were all part of a necessary direct control strategy towards DP. Brandon was one of the first to formulate phase-two problems in terms of the need for direct control management strategies.

> Because of the imbalance of supply and demand, salaries in the field have risen dramatically. The average annual salary of skilled data processing technicians has increased by almost 50% since 1958. The turnover rate in the industry has increased correspondingly, further causing severe problems in many established installations. Management has therefore been forced to the realization that *tighter control* and *management intervention* are both required in computer implementation. Management must become more aware of the problems and of the solutions and exercise direct control over every aspect of the operation. It is this control that demands the establishment and enforcement of standards. (Brandon, 1963, pp. 5–6; emphasis in original)

> methods standardization requires that each programmer create programs in a uniform manner, understandable to all others, with the basic minimum of documentation produced *during* the programming effort, not afterwards. This will ultimately result in much better personnel relationships; programmers are no longer indispensable—therefore they can now be fired and promoted more easily. (Brandon, 1963, p. 19; emphasis in original)

Most of these management control standards are concerned with making the workings of the systems development process and the work of individual systems developers more visible to managers. Many of the techniques and standards are common to widely different labour processes, with the basic objective of giving managers improved information about the process and the people that they are trying to manage.

The problem of elastic development times was tackled by work measurement techniques such as worksheets to record the effort expended on particular tasks by particular individuals. In some organizations the information from this procedure was used to generate productivity standards measured in lines of 'code' per day expected from programmers. In this way performance of individuals could be monitored and assessed. The estimation of future development times could be improved. Another common practice was to set targets in terms of job completion times. However, since the programmers and analysts were often the only people qualified to estimate the time to complete a job, they were very often involved in setting their own targets.

Project control techniques were another form of management control standard that grew in importance at this time. Breaking projects down into separate, identifiable phases that could be targeted, monitored and identified as complete was one way of identifying slippage on projects at a relatively early stage. Typically projects would be broken down into phases such as feasibility analysis, systems analysis, systems design, programming, program testing, systems testing, implementation and maintenance. Theoretically, each phase of the project could have a target date for completion and be identified as complete. At each phase documents or other products could be defined that should be produced and could be inspected to ensure their completeness.

Later in phase two, as problems between users and systems developers proliferated, it became common for users to be asked to 'sign off' these intermediate products as having been produced to their satisfaction. In practice, however, most systems development projects would not follow such a simple sequential model. Most projects would actually follow an iterative process involving several of the phases outlined above. Problems in later phases of development projects would involve revision of the earlier phases (these issues are dealt with in detail in sections 7.3 and 11.3.2).

Although these standards received considerable attention from the theorists and were widely implemented in many organizations to some degree or another, there is little evidence to suggest that they had more than a slight impact on the problems of systems development at the time. The main problem with these general techniques for improving management is that they did not tackle the specific detailed activities involved in the systems development process. Without understanding and controlling the detailed activities in a production process it is not possible to gain more than a superficial level of management control. The problem for those trying to increase management's direct control of the systems development process at that time was that there was no well-formulated theory of the development process. It was widely discussed and thought of as an art.

Brandon's standardization vision, like Hopper's automation vision, was flawed, and for similar reasons. Neither appreciated the rise in complexity and discretion consequent on developing applications beyond the simple replacement of existing manual systems. For Brandon the imposition of methods and performance standards would lead to direct control of the DP labour process. Standardization would allow 'time and motion' to be applied to DP work (1963, p. 19). This did not happen during the 1960s. Even Kraft (1977) allowed that it was only with the development of *structured programming* methods during the late 1960s and early 1970s, and with their proliferation during the 1970s, that substantial progress towards achieving direct control occurred, although this too is open to doubt.

Quality and performance standards

The development of standards aimed at improving the quality of systems and the performance of systems developers was also hampered by the lack of any systematic understanding of the process of analysis and programming. To make matters worse, the parameters by which quality and performance were measured were themselves changing as a result of the changing balance in systems costs between hardware and software.

The problems of late systems which failed to meet users' requirements and were difficult to maintain forced a recognition that the concept of system quality must change. System quality had been measured in terms of the technical efficiency of the system, the compactness of the code and the elegance of the algorithms used. Increasingly it came to be measured by the promptness of the delivery, the extent to which it matched users' needs and the ease with which it could be altered and maintained.

The issue of maintenance in particular was one where standards were applied relatively early. If the discretionary nature of systems development meant that there were very many ways of solving any particular design or coding problem, it also meant that it was very difficult for one programmer to pick up a program written by another to complete or amend it. A number of factors further aggravated this problem.

First, the increasing complexity of systems, and particularly the growing tendency to integrate systems, meant that it was often necessary for one systems developer to be able to understand in detail the systems developed by another for their programs to work together harmoniously. Second, by the late 1960s the simple fact that an increasing number of installations had been in existence for a number of years meant that there was a growing load of systems maintenance to be carried out. The tight labour market meant that the staff who developed a particular system had often left the organization by the time it needed maintaining, and not infrequently before it had even been completed.

Organizations involved in substantial software development projects saw themselves becoming more and more dependent on *individual* systems developers, over whom they had very little control. One way of trying to reduce that dependence on the individual was to try to make the work of one more comprehensible to those who might follow by introducing standards for documentation.

Documentation standards are almost universally applied by DP management, and almost as universally detested by systems developers. The objective of the documentation is to provide instructions about the system's use for the users and to provide information on the structure and design of the system for the system's maintainers.

The systems documentation for future maintainers normally takes the form of the design documents (systems specification, program specifications, program flow charts, etc.) and detailed comments inserted in the body of the programs to clarify what is being done at each stage and why. The production of documentation is a detailed and time-consuming task. It is also relatively boring compared to the business of actually designing systems and writing programs. Documentation, at least finished and detailed documentation, is also not essential in the short run, when the primary objective is to get a system functioning before the project deadline arrives. Nevertheless the importance of documentation, as a means of reducing the organization's dependence on the individual or individuals who developed the system, stimulated the widespread adoption of documentation standards in DP departments.

Other quality and performance standards were less generalized and widespread prior to the development of structured programming and systems design methodologies. Although there was a real concern with quality and performance, there was no established set of procedures for ensuring high quality or high productivity. There were a number of techniques that were widely used as part of the systems development process, for example program flow charts that provided a graphical representation of the flow of the logic in a program. However, these techniques did not provide any real discipline in the systems development process, or limit the discretion of the systems developers. This situation did not change until the development of structured programming techniques, which began in the late 1960s.

5.5.2 Systems 'Engineering' and Structured Methods

Systems engineering methods represent the most serious attempts to transform the systems development process from an individualized 'art' to a formalized 'discipline'. The organizers of the Garmisch conference drew attention to what they regarded as the need for software manufacture to be based on the 'theoretical foundations and practical disciplines that are traditional in the established branches of engineering' (Naur and Randell, 1969, p. 13). The organizers intended the engineering emphasis of the conference to be 'provocative'. This did indeed promote considerable debate at the conference. However, as Dijkstra acknowledged (section 5.4.2), the organizers were also particularly successful at provoking greater interest among the international computing community in structured programming techniques, which were surfacing around the time of the conference.

During phase two the systems engineering approach became associated with structured methods. Three types of structured methods may be identified, each relating to a different phase of a systems development project (or a different phase in what is called the computer system life cycle, section 7.2). Taking them in the order in which they were developed and popularized, the three broad categories of structured methods are as follows.

(1) Structured programming. This concerns the configuration of the code (such as formatting conventions and limitations on which statements are permissible)

and the procedure for constructing the code (following test plans, cross-referencing, use of debugging tools).

(2) Structured design. This concerns the formal procedures for transferring requirements specifications into program or module specifications to be coded (such as refining the logic of the structure, functional decomposition, interface checking, establishing test plans and acceptance criteria and test cases).

(3) Structured analysis. This concerns the procedures for defining user requirements 'evaluating user requests, carrying out a feasibility study, producing a 'correct' requirements specification).

5.5.3 Structured Programming

Structured programming has become a generic term, often only indicating the presence of any sort of rules or procedures. Glass labelled structured programming computing's 'Universal Elixir, circa 1974' (1977, p. 3). However, most have come to associate it with limitations of the types of statements that the computer programmer can use. The best example of this is the well-known stricture against GOTO statements (Dijkstra, 1968).

The evolution of structured programming

Structured methods grew out of a number of debates in the late 1960s, concerning the design of computer systems. It is important to stress in this context the changing criteria by which systems were judged. A review of structured programming methods that appeared in 1973 summarizes the changing emphasis:

> The primary requirement to be met in software development has always been to perform the function specified for the software. But where at one time secondary emphasis was placed only on software efficiency, that is core and time required, today three other factors are recognized as requiring special emphasis. These factors are reliability, maintainability, and extendibility. The emphasis on these factors has increased because their economic importance has been recognized. (Donaldson, 1973, pp. 50–52)

There are a number of basic techniques involved in structured programming, with the primary objective of making the programs easier to understand and thus easier to test, maintain and extend.

The first key concept is 'flow of control' in the program. A computer program is a set of instructions which are carried out in sequence. There are a number of instructions which can alter the normal sequential processing of instructions. These are required for parts of the program which have to be repeated (iterative procedures) and for selecting different actions based on different conditions (conditional branches). In a large system with many iterative procedures and conditional branches the flow of control can become very complex, making the program very difficult to follow.

Much of the early attention of the structured programming theorists centred around the unconditional change of control flow, or GOTO statement, which diverts the computer to another part of the program. Analysing the logic flow in a large unstructured program, containing many GOTO statements, has been compared to analysing the topology of a plate of spaghetti.

Dijkstra is usually credited with being the first person to emphasize the need for structure, in order to achieve the aims of producing reliable, maintainable and extendible software. A paper delivered to the 1965 IFIP (International Federation for Information Processing) conference contained most of the seeds of the structured programming revolution.[19]

> ... each programmer who wants to produce a flawless program must at least convince himself by inspection that his program will terminate. In a program in which unrestricted use of the goto statement has been made, this analysis may be very hard on account of the great variety of ways in which a program may fail to stop. After the abolishment of the goto there are only two ways in which a program may fail to stop: either by infinite recursion, i.e. through the procedure mechanism, or by the repetition clause. This simplifies the inspection greatly. (1965, p. 216)

Other academic programmers and mathematicians also contributed to the evolution of the theory of structured programming. A paper by Bohm and Jacopini (1966) proved the assertion that *any* program logic could be constructed from three basic control flow structures: sequence, selection and iteration (see Figure 5.3).

Conventions for the layout of programs have made structured programs easier to read. The code lying within a logical structure (i.e. a do-loop or an if-then-else construction) is physically indented compared to the previous and subsequent code. When the source code is printed out the logical structures are clearly visible as indented sections in the listing of the program, and it is possible to see the level of the program logic at any point in the program.

A number of other conventions regarding program structure have been adopted to increase readability or maintainability of systems. One example is that a

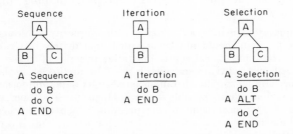

FIGURE 5.3 The three basic control flow constructs. Note: this notation is recommended by Michael Jackson (1975)

program or module should have a single point of entry and a single point of exit. If it does not then it is probably carrying out several functions and should be written as several programs. Another example is that programs or modules should be restricted to a particular size, often expressed as a number of lines of code (e.g. 50) or one printer page.

The concept of limiting the control flow structures, and especially elimination of GOTO statements, attracted much of the attention in the structured programming debate. However conventions on layouts, the 'single entry, single exit' rule for programs and modules, and the limitations on module size were also important restrictions placed on the structure of the systems. Most of these techniques were eventually packaged up and touted with the grandiose label of 'methodologies'.

5.5.4 Structured Design: Modular Programming and Top-down Development

The concept of modular programming, i.e. breaking a system down into program modules that could be coded separately, represents an age-old method for handling complexity; break up into manageable bits.[20] Modular programming was not only essential for handling complexity, it was also essential in some form for involving many people in a large programming project. The traditional method for breaking down a system into subprograms or modules is to define modules by their function. Most systems design naturally proceeded by a process of analysis of the problem and subdivision into functions, a process known as 'functional decomposition'. After a certain degree of functional decomposition, usually at the stage of defining the functions of the modules, this top-down, analytical process was replaced by a bottom-up, programming process of writing code. A number of amendments were suggested to this traditional process.

The concept of 'stepwise refinement' suggested that the process of decomposition should continue until a level of functionality is reached that is the same level of abstraction as that of the programming language. The concept was explained by Nikolas Wirth, the designer of the PASCAL programming language:

> Our most important mental tool for coping with complexity is abstraction. Therefore a complex problem should not be regarded immediately in terms of computer instructions, bits, and logical words, but rather in terms of entities natural to the problem itself, abstracted in some suitable sense. In this process an abstract program emerges, performing specific operations on abstract data, and formulated in some suitable notation—quite possibly natural language. The operations are then considered as the constituents of the program which are further subjected to decomposition to the next 'lower' level of abstraction. This process of *refinement* continues until a level is reached that can be understood by a computer, be it a high level programming language, FORTRAN, or some machine code. (Wirth, 1974, p. 249; emphasis in original)

Rigorous application of stepwise refinement will 'automatically' generate structured programs. The concept of stepwise refinement illustrates the very flexible boundary between the *analytical* process of systems design and the *synthetic* process of writing program code. This is particularly important when we consider the evolution of higher and higher levels of programming languages. The higher-level languages enable the 'final' level of refinement to be at a higher level of abstraction, closer to the original statement of the problem. In this way it is possible to see 'traditional' programming skills being squeezed by an extension of the analytical process on the one hand and an evolution of the programming language on the other.

Another development in the area of systems structure that affected the development process was the notion of 'top-down development'. The structuring of the system, particularly the single-entry, single-exit constraint on modules, enhanced the hierarchical nature of the system. At the 'top level' there is the command and control program which calls lower-level modules into operation. These may, in turn, call lower and lower levels of modules or subprograms, each with their own discrete independent function.

The top-down development method prescribed an ordering for the development of these modules, starting with the highest-level control module and proceeding to lower and lower levels. At each stage the emerging system can be tested with dummy programs to represent the actions of the lower levels of programs that are not yet developed. Because of the strict hierarchy of the program modules, each level can only have an impact on the lower levels of the system. This enabled the process of testing to proceed continuously, with no risk that subsequent developments could engender problems in the higher-level modules. This is in contrast to the bottom-up development procedure. Here low-level program modules for specific functions are developed and tested and then combined with higher-level modules until the entire system is assembled and tested.

The top-down and bottom-up development methods both rely on some form of functional decomposition to define the modules. The difference is in the order of developing and testing the entire system. With the top-down development method strictly applied, there should be no need to change the high-level modules once they have been developed and tested as a result of the influence of the lower-level modules. With the bottom-up development method the lower-level modules, which have been developed and tested satisfactorily *as independently functioning programs*, may need to be amended when they are combined together and tested *as an entire system*. By and large it is top-down development that is emphasized in the literature.

The process of functional decomposition is not itself a rigorous procedure. There are many different ways of splitting a particular process into functions, thus leading to many different system structures for the same problem. For example, you can decompose with respect to the order activities occur in time, or with respect to data flow, or logical groupings, or access to a common resource, etc. The criterion by which you decompose will lead to cohesion of the system according to that criterion. For example, decomposition by time produces modules such as initialize, process and terminate, leaving a structure with temporal cohesion. Clustering functions that access a shared database contributes to the definition of abstract data types and leaves a structure with communicational cohesion. As Bergland notes, functional decomposition was the most popular of structured methods, because of its general applicability. However, because there are so many ways to proceed with functional decomposition, by itself its effects are variable and unpredictable (1981, pp. 19–20).

The standard references for structured design have been Meyers (1975) and Yourden and Constantine (1975) in the USA and Jackson (1975) in Europe. These methods generally evolved after the early work on structured programming. Broadly, structured programming was the hot topic in the literature of the early 1970s, while structured design was the topic of the late 1970s. Structured design is largely related to the basis for modularization of the system, with the objective of ensuring the maximum independence between the modules. Sometimes structured design is known as modular design. Maximizing independence of the modules ensures that changes in one module cause the minimum of changes to other modules in the system. The desire for 'extensibility' and maintainability were key stimulators for the spread of structured design (see section 4.6).

A key concept which complements the notion of designing independent modules in a top-down manner is that of 'information hiding' associated with Parnas (1972). A modular structure should develop in a top-down fashion whereby at each step the modules are defined as bundles of functions and data which belong together. The detail of one module does not have to be 'seen' by people working on other modules. This becomes a key principle for organizing large numbers of designers and programmers to work on the same system, but independent of each other (see section 5.5.6).

5.5.5 Structured Analysis

The key references for structured analysis in the late 1970s were Ross (1977), Ross and Schoman (1977) and especially DeMarco (1978). Although structured analysis was the last of the elements of structured methods to be popularized, it is logically prior to the other structured methods. This 'contradiction' has not gone unnoticed in the software engineering literature:

> Structured Methods in systems and software projects are top down methods developed from the bottom up. Our current emphasis on Structured Analysis techniques has evolved from an initial emphasis on structured programming. This emphasis needs to be tempered with a very basic fact, namely that analysis, of any kind, is the logical FIRST step, not the last step, in implementing systems. (Hruschka, 1987, p. 421)

There was a clear reason for this. Structured methods were conceived as technical procedures which would lead to the application of engineering techniques to systems development by their originators. They would lead to the use of techniques which had been developed for the design and construction of physical entities. Although coding is one of the later phases of a project, it is close to the computer systems core. Of the three elements of structured methods, analysis is furthest from the core, least associated with the physical machine and least machine-like. The direct control approach is to make the labour process more machine-like, more stable, predictable and thereby, more controllable. This approach may well be least appropriate for activities that involve dealing with people, negotiation and uncertain outcomes.

Systems analysis involves dealing with people who are likely to have both vague and contradictory ideas about what they require. Also what they require is likely to change. By the time those concerned with software productivity began to confront systems analysis procedures, more and more were beginning to realize that solving the wrong problem may be more serious than solving problems unproductively (Ross and Schoman, 1977, p. 5).

The literature on structured analysis came to be dominated by a search for the 'best' way to represent user requirements, the right requirements definition language. We will deal with this quest in Part Four (section 8.2.6, 10.2 and 11.3.2).

5.5.6 Chief Programmer Teams and the Division of Labour

The chief programmer team represents the organizational form that complements the standardized and fragmented programming tasks created by structured programming and modularization. The chief programmer team was largely developed by analysts at IBM. The nucleus of the team contains three people, a chief programmer, a backup programmer and the programming librarian. The chief programmer designs the system of programs and, in particular, decides on how to modularize it. He or she is ultimately responsible for the coding. The backup programmer works with the chief programmer as a cross between an understudy and an apprentice. The backup should be as skilled as the chief, but the key ideas all come from the chief. The backup helps the chief and in so doing becomes totally familiar with the design and procedures developed by the chief. The main role of the backup is to take over if the chief should leave. The programming librarian carries out all of the documentation work as well as providing a communication channel to protect the chief from distracting, inessential interruptions to his or her creative efforts.

The remainder of the organization structure based on the chief programmer team is the additional programmers who carry out the small-scale work assignments designed by the chief. The chief programmer strictly adheres to structured programming principles and so the majority of programmers receive only fragments of the system which they are to code in a standardized manner. Proponents of the chief programmer team compare it to a surgical team (Baker, 1972, p. 339).

5.5.7 The Impact of Structured Methods

By reducing the scope for error and by making error detection and correction easier, structured methods could increase the predictability of the systems development process. Structured methods could also substantially reduce the costs of systems development, particularly in the areas of testing, maintaining and enhancing systems.

Initially the structure in structured programming referred mainly to the program itself. The question was asked, is there a most desirable structure or set of characteristics for a given program? Once the desirable attributes of a structured program had been relatively well defined, it became possible to define methods or a set of rules for programmers and systems designers to follow to achieve this desirable structure. That is, the process of programming and systems design became structured.

The promotion of structured programming and structured design as part of a management strategy encouraged the coupling of the technical elements with more overtly management-oriented elements, and the sale of the whole as a structured systems development methodology. The methodology could be sold in the form of training courses, seminars or books. The 'management' elements of such a strategy are procedures such as design or coding reviews, where the designer or programmer is required to submit the program design or code for review by peers or superiors. The methodologies also contain elements of documentation, often in the form of graphical representations of the program or systems, which are required as intermediate products in the development process, thus increasing the visibility of the process to managers.

The impact of structured programming on the task of systems development and the work of systems developers has been widely debated in the labour process literature. The debate has centred in particular on the deskilling effects of structured programming. Kraft interprets structured programming as the routinization and deskilling of the programming process:

> For managers the advantages of this sort of programming are enormous. If there are only a few predetermined ways of ordering a program's logic, considerably less skill, training and experience are required to grasp the major logical tools of the trade ... Structured programming, in short, has become the software manager's answer to the assembly line, minus the conveyor belt but with all the other essential features of a mass-production workplace: a standardized product made in a standardized way by people who do the same limited tasks over and over without knowing how they fit into a large undertaking. (Kraft, 1977, pp. 62–63)

Dijkstra, on the other hand, takes a completely different view of the impact of structured programming on the programmer.

> The first effect of teaching a methodology—rather than disseminating knowledge—is that of enhancing the capacities of the already capable, thus magnifying the difference in intelligence. In a society in which the educational system is used as an instrument for the establishment of a homogenized culture, in which the cream is prevented from rising to the top, the education of competent programmers could be politically unpalatable. (Dijkstra, 1972, p. 125)

In our view the impact of structured programming on programming skills is more complex.[21] A comment frequently made by programmers we interviewed regarding the structured programming debate was that they had always implicitly used many of the concepts enshrined in structured programming techniques. It is also important to note that the development of structured programming, particularly in its early stages, was firmly in the hands of academic and scientific programming practitioners, not managers or management theorists.

The impact of structured programming on the programming labour process lay in its ability to reduce the dependence on any *individual* programmer. Standardized working methods, as opposed to individual 'clever tricks', and increased clarity and readability of programs meant that programming work could be more easily transferred between one programmer and another. Similarly, top-down design and other procedures for program modularization also increased the scope for the division of labour in programming projects, although they do not necessarily specify the character of the division of labour.

Reduced reliance on the individual programmer did permit increased management control over the labour process. However, as Kraft himself admits, the organizational importance of structured programming stems from its 'social application' in the workplace and not from the techniques or methodology themselves.

Bergland (1981) also seems to propose a connection between the social application of structured methods and the techniques themselves, but his argument is something of an upside-down version of Kraft's caution. Three elements of the structured approach to computer systems development, or what he calls software engineering techniques, ought to be distinguished explicitly. These are the actual (well)-structured system, composed of (well)-structured programs, the structuring of the development process, and the support tools used in the development process. These are what were normally considered to be the key elements of a structured methodology in the late 1970s. According to Bergland, these items may be regarded as a pyramid, with structure of the programs as the base and the support tools on the top. The base is the single most important determinant of systems development costs. However, Bergland notes that the concepts which people tended to apply first were items such as teams, design reviews and program libraries, i.e. items relating to the top two elements of the pyramid. Most were what Vyssotsky (1979) characterized as techniques for dealing with programmer 'crowd control' according to Bergland. That is, they tended to concentrate on the social application, rather than the underlying technical structures. Bergland cautions that while these higher-level items 'can be implemented relatively quickly, their major benefits can only be realized in the context of a well-structured program' (1981, p. 14).

While Kraft presumed that structured methods would diffuse rapidly, Bergland, writing four years later, is able to observe that the introduction of these methods was not straightforward and their impact was not as great as expected. By the end of phase two, although most DP managers claimed to be using structured methods, the integrated pyramid described by Bergland was not what DP managers had in mind. Instead, as we will show in the following chapter (section 6.4.2), techniques from all these layers of the pyramid were implemented piecemeal in most installations. This has had a significant effect on the diffusion of computer-aided software engineering (CASE) techniques during phase three (see section 13.5.1).

5.6 RESPONSIBLE AUTONOMY STRATEGIES

Responsible autonomy strategies received relatively little attention in the computing literature during phase two. This is not surprising given the considerable freedom computer systems developers enjoyed during phase one. Nevertheless, two particular names were associated with responsible autonomy strategies towards DP staff during phase two. They were Enid Mumford in England and Dan Couger in the USA. Broadly following the humanistic strain of general management thought (see section 8.2.3), both consider job satisfaction to be the key factor stimulating labour productivity. Mumford became more sympathetic to end users after discovering extremely high levels of job satisfaction among computer specialists in studies carried out early in phase two (see section 6.2).[22] Couger, basing his opinions on surveys carried out late in phase two (around 1978) argued that job satisfaction was an area where substantial improvements could be made by managers of computer specialists.

Couger and Zawacki (1980) expressed the phase-two problem in the following way. The expanding backlog of work was a major cause for concern in the typical DP department. This backlog was not being reduced because of rising system complexity, rising demand for systems from users, labour turnover, rising maintenance costs from accumulated past systems, and a shortage of qualified people (pp. 2–4). The problem was indeed one of staff productivity, but the solution was to increase staff motivation, rather than to automate or deepen direct control over them. Increasing staff motivation could be achieved by raising job satisfaction. This would reduce labour turnover. It would also alleviate the general staff shortage by making existing staff more productive.

According to Couger and Zawacki, attempts to solve the labour turnover problem by raising salaries and fringe benefits had been 'calamitous'. Only by satisfying the special needs of computer personnel could managers hope to retain them and to improve productivity, and thereby to alleviate the expanding backlog problem. They noted that DP professionals (analysts, programmer/analysts and programmers) had higher 'growth needs strength' and lower 'social needs strength' than other professionals.[23] They all demanded training and to be allowed to attend conferences. On the other hand, because their training proceeds from a foundation in programming, where success depends on interaction with the computer, rather than other people, both analysts and programmers have low social needs strength.[24] In order to motivate employees with this combination of characteristics Couger and Zawacki considered it essential to design high-scope tasks (tasks with a high degree of skill variety, task identity, task significance, autonomy and feedback). They recommend the use of achievement-oriented but also participative leadership styles.[25] These styles and task definitions are generally what we have called responsible autonomy strategies (see section 6.1).

5.7 CONCLUSION

Figure 5.4 shows the effect on computer systems of the considerable progress achieved through automation strategies during phase two. We could present two different pictures. One picture would be of a few installations that embraced the most advanced automation techniques available, where computer systems core

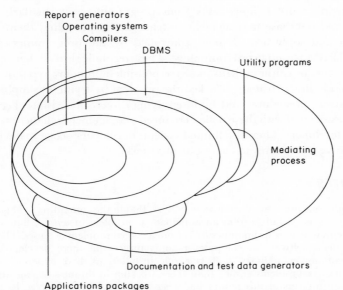

FIGURE 5.4 Phase-two changes in computer core and the mediating process

embraced the major applications programming effort via general packages. However, most installations had only a few very specific packages. By the end of the 1970s, most had a selection of software tools and utilities. The vast majority were using COBOL as their primary language. Many were acquiring packages (notably statistical packages and report generators) for carrying out specific work using fourth-generation languages. Most had a DBMS, very recently acquired, but with very little of their database on it (see section 9.1.3).

Expansion of the core was substantial compared with the early 1960s. However, the shortage of labour to carry out mediating process activities was at least as great during the late 1970s as it has been in the late 1960s. Although much traditional programming work had been automated, increased demand for new systems and the further spread of computers to smaller organizations meant that demand for programmers was still buoyant. However, automation *did* affect the composition of demand. The pressure of demand for applications programmers eased, but demand for systems programmers began to grow very quickly. The computer systems core had expanded unevenly. New software core did not completely surround old core. Considerable effort was required within computer user organizations to maintain and adapt the growing proportion of computer systems core that was software, much of which was not being supplied (or supported) by hardware manufacturers.

The effects on programmer skills and discretion of the two main approaches for dealing with software productivity problems during phase two were in opposite directions. The automation strategy attacked the problem of productivity either by removing more tedious tasks from programmers (particularly operating systems and database management systems) or by providing them with more powerful and sophisticated tools, controlled by the programmers themselves (particularly interactive programming). These technological changes encouraged DP managers to continue with loose, responsible autonomy types of strategies.

The more direct strategy attacked the problem by trying to simplify tasks, by standardizing procedures and by intensifying direct supervision. Technological changes associated with these policies reduced management reliance on individual systems developers. They also limited systems developers' scope to devise unusual and creative procedures to carry out their tasks.

ENDNOTES

1. Consider our proposition from section 2.3.4, that in the computing field good news or marketing news suffers from an anticipatory 'problem of tenses', but bad news or problems with new techniques suffers from a lagged problem of tenses. Those working on systems software at computer manufacturers and those developing real-time applications in military and research installations had experienced software productivity problems earlier than those working in business organizations. Large software projects of this nature had been attempted in the 1950s. Recognition of software productivity problems was therefore 'late' in spheres where software costs had

long been a substantial proportion of overall development costs. In the business community, experiences of substantial software costs compared with hardware costs was more recent.

2. Professor of Business Administration, Professor of Engineering and Director of the Western Data Processing Center at the University of California at Los Angeles.

3. Unless otherwise stated, all page number references in this section refer to the report on the conference by Naur and Randell (1969). Affiliations will be given when conference participants are first referred to.

4. Joseph Orlicky was IBM's Manufacturing Industry Education Manager. However, he joined IBM after 11 years in industrial management. His book *The Successful Computer System* (1969) was written from a business manager's perspective. Many of the issues Orlicky raised had their major impact on the computer community ten years after his book was published.

5. For example, should software provided by hardware manufacturers, which is 'bundled' up with the hardware, be included as software or hardware? Are all DP department personnel costs to be included in software (including operators and secretaries)?

6. This figure, and all the ratios presented in this paragraph, exclude a figure presented under the heading of 'other' expenses (presumably mainly space rental and office consumables).

7. These figures were from the March 1985 and April 1988 issues of *Datamation*. The 1988 figure undoubtedly overstates the trend. The underlying questionnaire changed between 1987 and 1988. The ratio for the 1987 budget year as reported in the April 1987 issue was 52/48.

8. If we define expenditures on the mediating process as personnel, external services and other costs for DP installations, and expenditures on computer system core as hardware, software and data communications, the figure for 1972 was 55/45, for 1976 it was 59/41, and for 1980 64/36. Figures for 1984 and 1988 were 56/44 and 73/27.

9. A high proportion of these were financial institutions supplying payroll systems to the financial institutions' customers.

10. From the second generation of hardware, computer manufacturers supplied software along with hardware. The systems software that was provided was included in the price of the hardware. It was not invoiced separately; it was 'bundled'. In 1969 the US Department of Justice required IBM to unbundle its software and hardware, to invoice them separately.

11. Figures cited in OECD, 1985, p. 52.

12. According to a survey of 483 firms in the USA and 98 in Canada carried out in 1966, 60% used the IBM programmer aptitude test (PAT). Almost all firms (87%) reported using some selection test, but only PAT had widespread use. The next most popular test was only used by 11% of the sample (Dickmann, 1966, pp. 15–27). This usage is remarkable considering that during the mid-1960s several research papers were published which showed that no selection test consistently predicted job performance. These studies were summarized by Mayer and Stalnaker (1968).

13. The deceleration of growth in DP departments and attempts to impose 'drastic measures' to control project selection, the systems development process and computer budgets were ably described by Nolan in 1973 and 1974 (see section 2.3.2). He took these observations to be a sign of changes in a set of stages which proceeded due to a logic internal to specific computer departments and dependent upon their age. However, the problems his 'control' or 'formalization' stage were intended to correct were being experienced throughout the computing world, not merely in the very first computer user organizations. Staff shortages, training problems, lack of managers with training and experience of managing, along with the technical problems associated

with large-size projects and rapidly changing technology, were being experienced by established computer departments and newcomers alike. Staff shortages were likely to be even more severe for newcomers, because they lacked an internal experience base from which to train inexperienced recruits.

14. A third approach was to farm out the problem to specialist companies and to employ contract staff for specific projects. The growth of the independent software-producing sector represented this market reaction to the problem.

15. The program which translates statements in the COBOL instruction set into statements in the CPU's instruction set.

16. According to our NCC 1985 survey of user organizations in the UK (see Data Appendix), 9% of installations were using assembler languages, although usually as a second language behind COBOL.

17. Often an existing program will be copied and then edited on the screen.

18. Brandon distinguished two types of standards within organizations. *Methods standards* concern the establishment of uniform practices and common techniques. *Performance standards* concern measures that make it possible to review performance of personnel and equipment (1963, p. 2). A fourth type of internal standard may be motivated by marketing considerations. Particular clients may already use certain procedures which may have to be followed in order for new development work to be of value to them.

19. Yourden said of Dijkstra's 1965 paper, 'If structured programming can be thought of as a revolution, then surely Dijkstra's landmark paper, "Programming Considered as a Human Activity," published in 1965, marks its beginning' (Yourden, 1979, p. 1). However, Knuth (1974) argued that the first published remarks about harmful GOTO statements came from Naur (1963). He also claimed that the first person to practise the programming style which is now known as structured programming was D. V. Schorre of UCLA in 1960 (Knuth, 1974, p. 264).

20. Strictly following modular programming leads to programs with the following characteristics (Bergland, 1981, p. 17):
    (1) they are composed entirely of modules;
    (2) they implement a single independent function;
    (3) their modules perform a single logical task;
    (4) their modules have a single entry and exit point; and
    (5) each module is separately testable.

21. Note that skill required for jobs ought to be thought of as affected by both the range of tasks people carry out and judgement or discretion they exercise over that range (see Fox, 1974).

22. In addition she noted the lack of sympathy these computer specialists had for preserving or stimulating job satisfaction among end users (Hedberg and Mumford, 1975).

23. People who are high in growth needs strength are people with a strong need for personal accomplishment, for learning and developing beyond where they are now, for being stimulated and challenged. People with a low social needs strength have a 'low proclivity to social interaction' (Couger and Zawacki, 1980, pp. 20–23).

24. Compared to other personnel, 'to be successful, programmers need far less skill in verbal communication' (Couger and Zawacki, 1980, p. 26).

25. Couger and Zawacki allow that incongruence between task scope and growth needs strength (GNS) may be compensated for by certain leadership styles. For example, if high-GNS staff are given low-scope jobs, supportive leadership can 'minimize dysfunctional consequences' (1980, p. 120).

Chapter 6

PHASE TWO: STRATEGIES FOR DEALING WITH THE SOFTWARE BOTTLENECK

Two pictures of work in data processing (DP) departments are presented in this chapter. Both are based on evidence from Great Britain, although US studies are also referred to. The first picture shows the situation *early* in phase two. It relies on surveys carried out between 1969 and 1972 by Computer Economics (Peat, Marwick, Mitchell and Computer Economics, 1972), by Hebden (1975) and particularly by Mumford (1972). The second picture shows the situation *late* in phase two. This description relies largely on two surveys which the authors carried out in 1981. These snapshots of early and late phase two will be supplemented by information from a survey carried out in Britain in 1975 (Hansen and Penney, 1976). The surveys used in this chapter are described and compared in the Data Appendix.

The picture early in phase two is comparatively straightforward. Computer programmers and systems analysts are universally described as enjoying what Mumford calls 'almost ideal job characteristics' (1972, p. 183). Jobs are distinguished by variety and creativity. Little real control is exercised over their work. Salaries are high. Job satisfaction is high. The only cloud on this picture from the computer specialist's point of view is the lack of promotion prospects for more experienced specialists. In particular, promotion from higher-level, management-oriented functions within DP departments into general management is unlikely.

The second picture is more complex. The 1970s were a period of rapidly growing concern with staff issues on the part of DP and senior management. That the first large-scale surveys of DP staff should have been undertaken at management schools early in phase two is symptomatic of this concern (Mumford at the Manchester Business School, Hebden at Salford University). Computer Economics is a private firm set up in 1968 to survey salaries of DP staff and to sell the results to managers. Its establishment in the late 1960s is evidence that growing concern with staff issues, particularly staff costs, in DP departments had penetrated practising managers as well as management theorists.[1] Computer Economics has been carrying out salary surveys twice a year with unbroken regularity from 1969 to the present.

The message of crisis from the Garmisch conference and from other pronouncements in the literature, as well as unsatisfactory experiences within many computer installations, led to more conscious management practice during the 1970s. Most of the literature emphasized the need to wrest control away from computer specialists. Accountability and visibility in systems development work and the need to reduce management's reliance on individual programmers was emphasized. Direct control types of strategies were most commonly recommended. A bewildering array of packaged techniques, methods, methodologies, aids and tools that claimed to break the software bottleneck appeared on the market. According to some accounts these techniques were rapidly diffusing during the 1970s (Kraft, 1977; Greenbaum, 1979). However, what we find by 1981 is not a straightforward new picture where the responsible autonomy of phase one had been replaced by direct control. Certainly techniques which attempted to make it easier to replace staff, to lower the cost of individual programming tasks and to standardize productivity levels had diffused extensively. However, in addition, in some DP departments, more structured responsible autonomy strategies were being implemented. More conscious and more sophisticated techniques had been introduced during the 1970s which emphasized staff retention and raising individual productivity by providing sophisticated tools. Also a small, but influential, literature developed which emphasized a responsible autonomy strategy of increasing job satisfaction in order to improve computer systems developers' motivation and to reduce labour turnover (Couger and Zawacki, 1980).

The picture late in phase two is therefore a mixed one. In most departments elements of the new direct control techniques had been introduced (but often only on a voluntary basis or as mere formality). On the other hand, many departments were extending the career structure and providing sophisticated tools and substantial training for more experienced staff.

6.1 DESCRIBING THE LABOUR PROCESS OF SYSTEMS ANALYSTS AND COMPUTER PROGRAMMERS

The two management strategies introduced in section 3.2, direct control and responsible autonomy, are general labels for describing the types of approaches managers can take towards controlling staff. We want to use these general terms to help to illuminate broad changes in management policies towards systems developers.

These types of management strategies are best thought of as labels for end points of a continuum, or as two directions towards which management can move. Any particular manager or set of managers pursue a diverse set of policies towards their staff. It is not a simple matter to identify and measure strategies from evidence of individual policies and practices by themselves.

Some policies can directly express responsible autonomy or direct control. For example, Brandon's recommendation for how managers should apply standards was expressly to directly control all aspects of systems developers' work (section 5.5.1). On the other hand, McClure at the Garmisch conference stated that attempts to apply time and motion standards to the output of programmers is guaranteed to produce insipid code (see section 5.1.1).

On this evidence identifying whether computer installation managers are pursuing a direct control strategy or not would seem to be a fairly easy matter of discovering whether or not management standards were being imposed. However, standards may be introduced for reasons other than to achieve direct control over staff. They may be introduced simply to satisfy customer specifications or to allow compatibility between project groups or compatibility with work at other installations. Also the same standards may have different implications for management control depending on how they are applied. Standards which are rigidly enforced by careful monitoring and accompanied by strict penalties for non-compliance will lead to much greater management direct control over the labour process than standards that are treated purely as a formality. Therefore we must allow that introducing standards and achieving direct control are not equivalent, although the presence of standards may be taken as evidence for direct control, especially if accompanied by evidence that standards are strictly imposed.

The difficulty of identifying which type of managerial strategy is being pursued is compounded by the fact that standards are not the only policies designed to increase management's direct control over the work of systems developers. Structured programming, design and analysis techniques were other methods that were recommended to increase direct control during the 1960s and 1970s. As with standards, each of these policies could be introduced for reasons other than to achieve direct control and each could be applied with varying intensity. However, whether or not these policies are introduced, and how strictly they are imposed, may also be taken as evidence for direct control. Therefore in order to discover which type of strategy for controlling staff managers are pursuing, and in which direction they are moving if they are changing their strategies, a collection of control policies must be considered.

Measuring and identifying managerial strategies is even more difficult than this. Certain management policies that are not normally thought of as motivated by control considerations can also contribute to increasing direct control or responsible autonomy. One example are policies concerning staff recruitment, training, promotion and lay-offs, which we have labelled as employment relations. These are usually considered to be management reactions to product and labour market conditions and to the technological requirements of the labour process. However, as we shall see, policies on these issues can clearly contribute to direct control or responsible autonomy strategies and can be motivated by these considerations. Good promotion prospects and training can encourage staff to consider their aims and management's aims as the same. Reluctance to lay off staff and careful recruitment procedures can clearly affect management's ability to maintain a credible responsible autonomy strategy. On the other hand, lay-offs, or the threat of lay-offs, can be used as part of the punishment aspect of a direct control strategy for keeping staff in line.

The way tasks are organized are a second set of policies which may not be considered as motivated by control considerations but which have important consequences for management control strategies. Before the labour process literature emerged, issues such as the division of labour were considered as purely reflecting exogenously determined technological requirements. However, there are many who argue not only that control considerations can influence these decisions (Marglin, 1974), but also that such decisions determine the technology chosen (Noble, 1977; Rosenbrock, 1979). To say that technology is determined by management control considerations is as misleading as saying that management policies are determined by technology. In fact they are mutual influences. Moments in the history of computer systems development when the direction of influence has been stronger in one direction or the other have already been indicated. During phase one, technological influences dominated. However, in Chapter 5 we argued that during phase two the desire for greater control over both systems developers and over the systems development labour process dominated; that this desire influenced which technologies were introduced into computer

TABLE 6.1 Management strategies, policies and strategic dimensions

Strategies	Responsible Autonomy—Direct Control		
Categories of policies	Task Organization	Employment Relations	Control Structure
Subcategories of policies	Types + form of inputs Method of transformation Scheduling + organization structure Tools + machinery available	Charting the individual's progress through the firm: Recruitment Training Promotion Separations	*Layers of control* Instruction + direction Monitor Evaluate + reward (punish) *Phases of control* Initiation Process Results
Strategic dimensions	Task length Task variety Task originality	Dependency on particular staff Employment protection of individuals	Degree of detail Degree of formality Monitor people or work Evaluate by reward v. punishment

installations and influenced which technologies were developed. It influenced the direction of technological change.

In the pictures of systems development work early and late in phase two which are presented below, three sets of management policies will be considered. They are, first, the way tasks are organized, the division of labour and computer installation organization structures; second, employment relations; and third, control structures. For each, dimensions of policies that reflect management control strategies will be emphasized.

Dimensions of task organization which are particularly relevant for the managerial control strategies are task variety, task length and task originality. Tasks designed to be short, invariant and repetitive may be considered as a prerequisite for successful direct control strategies. On the other hand, computer installation managers often try to attract and keep staff, particularly programmers and systems programmers, by offering challenging and original ('state-of-the-art') work.

Relevant dimensions of employment relations policies are the dependency of managers on particular staff and how carefully managers try to protect the employment security of staff. How easily may staff be replaced? How much disruption can be caused by individual employees either leaving or performing in an uncooperative manner? The relevant dimensions of control structures are how detailed and formal they are and whether they involve evaluation and motivation by punishment or by reward. These sets of policies and the strategic dimensions associated with each are illustrated in Table 6.1.[2]

6.2 THE SITUATION EARLY IN PHASE TWO: SPECIALIST AUTONOMY BY DEFAULT

Our hypothesis is that during phase one it was responsible autonomy types of management strategies that were used to maintain authority over computer specialists and to organize the structuring of their work. Furthermore, we would argue that the lack of general experience with managing computer specialists, as well as the small number of them, both in total and in relation to the resources devoted to hardware, all contributed to an absence of thought-out techniques, relating either to responsible autonomy or to direct control at that time. These characteristics should be clearly visible in studies of computer specialists carried out at the beginning of phase two.

6.2.1 Task Organization

Originality and variety of tasks for programmers and particularly for systems analysts were very high early in phase two. Mumford notes the considerable confusion expressed in the computer press at the time over just what the detailed functions of systems analysts ought to be (Mumford, 1972, p. 56).

This is partly because the job of systems analyst had only been separated out from programming late in phase one in many departments. It is also partly due to the immense variety and creative content of systems analysts' work. The analysts Mumford interviewed described their jobs as to devise solutions for line management's problems and to examine the existing methods and improve these using computer techniques. 'I need an overall appreciation of hardware and software available and of techniques needed to deal with routine problems and not so routine problems,' said one analyst in a user firm (Mumford, 1972, p. 35). It was in the user firms that the jobs of systems analysts were in fact relatively narrow compared with analysts interviewed in computer hardware manufacturing firms or computer services firms. In the latter firms analysts dealt directly with the organization's customers. This meant dealing with very different environments.

Mumford found that the task content of programmers' jobs also contained a high degree of originality, although somewhat less variety than for the analysts. At the heart of the programmers' job is the writing of instructions for computers. Nevertheless, the majority also tested, implemented and maintained their programs (1972, p. 35). Particular jobs carried out by programmers were therefore long as well as varied. This made it difficult to control programmers' working practices. In fact the 90% syndrome often characterized programmer reports of progress on jobs. That is, the task would seem to be 90% finished for 90% of the time. This is because testing and implementation often took longer than expected. Mistakes discovered at this late stage generated recoding and possible redesign work that had not been anticipated when tasks were first assigned:

> A standard joke in the industry is that a program typically remains 90% debugged for about 25% of the total implementation time. (Kolence, in Naur and Randell, 1969, p. 60)

As with analysts, task variety in hardware manufacturers and consultancy firms was greater than in user organizations. Manufacturer and consultancy firms had more interaction with customers and required a more comprehensive knowledge of hardware and software. In the consultancy firms programmers also investigated programming techniques in general and designed packages.

The structuring of work was also found to be rather lax. 'All firms avoided tight job specifications,' Mumford notes (p. 104). Jobs were specified, but only within broad limits, and in the consultancy firms it was explicitly recognized that jobs were 'very flexible and likely to change from day to day' (p. 104). However, all but one organization in Mumford's sample had written manuals specifying quality standards and work procedures.

This accords with results of the Computer Economics survey in which 96% of the sample had an internal standards manual (Peat, Marwick, Mitchell and Computer Economics, 1972, p. EIII). Although specific procedures formally existed, it is clear from Mumford's sample that these procedures were not vigorously enforced by DP management. The main complaints of programmers and analysts were about *too little* rather than too much control. Only a minority of staff had criticisms about controls, except in one services firm where 57% of staff had complaints. However, these complaints were directed against the ineffectiveness of controls rather than their existence (Mumford, 1972, p. 109).

Mumford's general conclusion was that DP staff were extremely satisfied with their jobs. The work itself was the primary factor. In answer to the question 'have you ever regretted your decision to become a programmer (analyst)?' an overwhelming majority answered no (90.2%). Of those who had no regrets, 61.7% said this was because they liked the work, and this was often expressed as satisfaction with the variety of the work (Mumford, 1972, p. 160). When pressed further and asked 'what aspects of your work do you find most rewarding?' (p. 171), 44% of the programmers said getting output from a program or system (13% of analysts) and 50% of the analysts said seeing a project in successful operation (19% of programmers). Mumford was aware of the gathering tendency towards direct control in DP, but contrary to Kraft she concluded that in the UK, in 1969, the effect was negligible. She states:

> Data processing is an area where the philosophy of the job reducers and job simplifiers—the followers of Taylor—has not been accepted; although there are already indications that some managements are attempting to achieve better work control through splitting up EDP activities into small, specialist sections. (p. 175)

On the contrary, she presents a glowing report of the task content of computer specialists, 'computer work as referred to by our programmers and systems analysts appears to possess almost ideal job characteristics' (p. 183).

These findings from Great Britain, that considerable task variety and lax control over task definition were the norm early in phase two, are supported by a US study. Cross (1971) reports American programmers as intrinsically motivated and desiring to set their own work schedules (reported in Loseke and Sonquist, 1979, p. 175). According to a survey carried out in 1964 in New York, only 27% of computer programmers' time was spent performing activities which directly resulted in the generation of programs (reported in Mayer and Stalnaker, 1968). Programmers were away or out for 15% of their time and spent 32% talking or listening. In a similar study performed by the same researcher (Bairdain, 1964) on engineers in a research laboratory, it was found that a much higher percentage of time was spent on activities which directly resulted in the production of a piece of work (45%).

The one technique clearly established by early phase two that went some way towards direct control was the division of labour between analysts and programmers. This was the major management control technique developed during phase one. At the beginning of phase two almost all installations had separate job titles. Furthermore, most separated analysts and programmers into different sections. This created problems from the outset. The wide variety of job tasks required of development groups meant that it was difficult in practice to establish a satisfactory boundary between the two jobs. The absence of clearly defined task boundaries between them was seen as a problem by 24% of programmers and 11% of analysts in Mumford's sample (p. 177). However, while the task boundaries between systems analysts and programmers was seen as a problem by some, the main spheres of activities for the two groups had been separated sufficiently to have led Hebden to conclude that the groups should be regarded as two distinct occupations, rather than two segments of a single occupation (1975, pp. 127–130). The majority of programmers (74%) spent less than 10% of their working time with users, compared with only 19% of analysts. Programmers were more concerned with the technical side of the work, particularly with the hardware configuration. Analysts were particularly concerned with users and senior management. As a result there was a significant difference between the two groups in terms of whether they identified with their occupation or with the organization. For example, 62% of programmers and 47% of analysts hoped they would be holding a job within DP in ten years' time (Hebden, 1975, p. 112). Also 93% of programmers unambiguously chose members of their occupation as the reference group to whom they would look for evaluation of their work, compared with 55% of analysts (p. 114).

US sources on the division of labour between analysts and programmers support the British results. Brandon complained that 'the tasks of analysis, programming and even operations and control are not defined, and uniform standards are effectively non existent' (Brandon, 1968, in Sanders, 1970, p. 339). However, Berger and Wilson, using a questionnaire containing 186 task statements, found that they could differentiate between experienced analysts and experienced programmers (Berger and Wilson, 1967, reported in Mayer and Stalnaker, 1968, pp. 140–141).

A further division of labour within the programming group emerged early in phase two. This was between systems programming and applications programming. As operating systems emerged in the second- and third-generation hardware, the need to maintain (and enhance) such systems grew. In general, computer department work that was near to the hardware tended, at first, to be provided by hardware manufacturers. However, slow and unreliable service led larger installations gradually to hire or train their own systems programmers.

As with the division of labour between programmers and systems analysts, that between applications and systems programmers could be used as an instrument for deepening direct control. It could be part of a strategy of fragmenting the mediating process into pieces with unequal skill requirements in order to allow the less-skilled parts to be filled with cheaper labour (the Babbage effect). This would imply a greater separation of conception from execution and a need for more careful supervision of staff—the Braverman/Kraft hypothesis. However, the separation of functions may simply be a means of retaining staff by offering a clear promotion ladder. Hebden notes that a number of organizations in his sample were developing twin career ladders for DP staff. The analysis ladder would lead into general management; the programming ladder into development work in systems programming (p. 129).

Hebden's analysis implies that the division of labour between analysis and programming had become quite strict by the end of the 1960s. This was a necessary first step for developing techniques to deskill programming work. Hebden reported that only 18% of programmers hoped to proceed into systems analysis, and less than 40% of the systems analysts entered via programming or a combination of systems and programming (p. 129).

The Computer Economics Survey, carried out in 1972, just a few years after Mumford and Hebden, showed the beginnings of a trend towards reintegrating programming and analysis functions. This did not involve reintegration within single individuals at this time, but rather organizational integration into project teams. Of the Computer Economics sample, 34% of installations had switched from organizational structures that kept programmers and analysts in separate groups to project teams containing both between 1970 and 1972 (p. HXIII); 52% were so organized at the time of the survey. Computer Economics reported that the proportion of companies using project teams was stabilizing. One at least reported to have changed back to separating groups of analysts from programmers. The project team form of organization was most common in government and utilities (76%) and the lowest in manufacturing (43%) (p. 35).

Clearly quite early in phase two problems with too strict a separation of programming and analysis were being faced. Instead of the separation leading to rapid deskilling and direct control of programming (as occurred with data preparation staff), the initial reaction of many DP managers was to reintegrate the functions in project teams. According to Computer Economics, a further reason for the use of project teams was to 'overcome the problem of lack of management involvement' (p. 35). We would interpret this as a concern for management involvement in the combined work of programmers and analysts, i.e. systems development and maintenance, rather than concern with the adjudication of programmers' (and analysts') performance of their narrower roles within systems development and maintenance. In part this can be explained by the continuing staff shortage both for programmers and analysts. In part it was also due to relative lack of progress in finding techniques which genuinely deskilled programming work.

6.2.2 Employment Relations

During the late 1960s two management views towards DP staff developed. The first was to view DP staff as complex prima donnas, people who carry great responsibility but who are without the wisdom of age (Yearsley, 1969, pp. 30–31). The other view was that they were an essential resource and that staff retention was a key factor for successful computer use (Gillis, 1968, pp. 24–26). Early in phase two the latter view was widely held, but relatively little was done about it. Mumford comments:

> Formalized career paths with built-in training opportunities are essential if expensive computer staff are to be retained. Increasingly firms will have to abandon attempts to recruit experienced staff and shift to a policy of taking on graduates with the expectation that by the time they have completed their training programme there will be jobs waiting for them. (1972, p. 59)

Certainly this had not happened during the following few years. Computer Economics reported that 55% of the programming staff in their 1972 sample of user organizations were recruited externally. Only 28% came into programming from other DP positions and 17% from non-DP positions within the organization. Of analysts 42% were recruited externally, with 24% from non-DP positions within the organization. So the promotion route from within DP up to analysts' positions applied only to one-third of DP staff in user organizations. Also 31% of DP management were recruited externally and, surprisingly, 28% were recruited from non-DP positions within the organization (Peat, Marwick, Mitchell and Computer Economics, 1972, p. HXII).

The problem for many DP specialists was promotion. Few of Mumford's sample aspired to positions beyond DP management (p. 192); however, a substantial minority considered their promotion prospects within DP to be poor or nil. This was particularly so in user organizations for programmers (26%) and analysts (46%). Analysts in particular mentioned career blockage as a reason for wishing to leave their present employers (p. 207). For programmers a desire for wider DP experience was mentioned more often. This was particularly important for programmers in user organizations and in computer service firms. It was also important for analysis in user organizations (p. 96).

Brandon gives the impression of similar promotion problems in the USA:

> To the uninitiated it appears as if there is a typical promotion chain operating within the data processing structure. After all, there are five job families with ascending skill requirements, and nothing appears more reasonable than to promote
>
> clerical staff to operations
> operators to programmers
> programmers to systems analysts
> analysts to managers, and
> managers to?
>
> This logic does not survive the recognition that the *prerequisites* for each job are different, thereby invalidating the ability of an individual to progress through the chain. (1968, in Sanders, 1970, p. 340)

The career blockage problem was the most important reason for high labour turnover among DP staff. For analysts the problem was the difficulty of finding DP management positions within their organizations. The problem arose in part due to the rapid promotion of DP staff through the positions available within job families in the DP departments. This, in turn, occurred first because of the rapid turnover of staff, which left relatively recent DP specialists at the top of the experience ladders within DP departments, and second, because of the strong bargaining power of DP staff. Both of these factors can be attributed to the general shortage of experienced DP staff in the labour market. The difficulty of replacing experienced staff who left meant that threatening to leave was a powerful bargaining tool for computer specialists. The ease of getting another job meant that leaving jobs commonly occurred. However, one clear additional reason for the career blockage problem was the relatively short promotion ladder within DP departments.

Mumford reports an average length of service for programmers in individual DP departments and within computer manufacturer and computer services organizations of two years for programmers and two years and eight months for analysts. Of programmers, 46% reported that they were thinking about leaving the organization, first in order to gain wider experience in DP, and second to gain promotion. Of analysts, 45% were thinking of leaving, first for promotion, and second to gain wider experience in DP (1972, p. 96). These high turnover figures reinforced DP managers' reluctance to train staff from scratch. The result of the pattern was that DP salaries, while beginning rather low, quickly rose with experience, particularly once two years of experience was approached. A consequence was that rather young people began earning rather high salaries. Mumford notes that managers regarded these salaries as too high and in user firms they reported that this distorted traditional company salary differentials and caused problems with personnel managers (p. 207).

6.2.3 Staff Control

As indicated above, responsible autonomy strategies dominated in DP departments early in phase two. Tasks contained a high degree of variety and originality. Although formal procedures existed, they were not rigidly enforced. Programmers and analysts were extremely satisfied with their work. Although a fairly strict division of labour had developed between analysts and programmers, there was still considerable movement between job roles. There were also some tendencies for the two roles to be organizationally recombined in project teams. The responsible autonomy strategies were stimulated by rapidly rising demand for computer-based systems, as senior managers and line managers came to see the advantages of computer-based systems, particularly those relatively straight-forward replacements of manual systems.

Beyond finding good staff, the major problems facing DP managers early in phase two were keeping within budgets and the related problem of producing systems on time. These became more visible failings of DP departments as queues for systems lengthened and as DP budgets expanded. These, in turn, were widely being recognized as symptoms of inadequate control over the systems development process during phase two, and they came to be thought of as symptomatic of lack of control over DP staff as well. Mumford paints the following picture of control structures used early in phase two:

> The main problem was that it was hard to check work where it originated and mistakes were unlikely to show up until a system was implemented in a user area. When data processing managers were asked how long it would take before substandard work became apparent the answers ranged from one week to twelve months. (pp. 104–105)

Three different methods were noted for controlling work. The first was to specify different staff to check over work. The second was to have a tight set of working procedures. The third was to have a very precise specification against which work could be tested. All departments had checking procedures, usually by the person doing the job, by the person to whom the work was passed for further processing and by the unit supervisor. However, without this checking process being carried out by specialized auditors, or alternatively unless the checking process was supplemented by tight working procedures or a very detailed specification, DP management would be thrown back on relying primarily on the creativity, precision, care and good motivation of the staff who actually carried out the work. Even these latter methods are rather weak attempts to impose direct control if specifications change in the development process, and this was common according to the Computer Economics survey (1972, p. 23).

Only in one of the hardware manufacturers were there what Mumford called a tight set of working procedures to check against, and only one other manufacturer had a special work-checking section within DP. The user organizations and computer services firms relied on the employees themselves and their supervisors (Mumford, 1972, p. 105). Only 15% of respondents to the Computer Economics survey replied that regular efficiency checks of DP functions were carried out by specialist auditors (Peat, Marwick, Mitchell and Computer Economics, 1972, p. EV). They comment that this figure is 'surprisingly low, particularly when it is considered that senior management outside DP often have only limited knowledge of the work performed within the DP department' (p. 27).

An absence of strong structural controls, in the form of strict working procedures or precise and inviolable task specifications and a lack of specialized personnel to monitor staff, meant that control was highly concentrated in the hands of direct supervisors. One indication of the importance of personal supervision was the short span of control exercised by first-line supervisors in Mumford's sample. In the user organization a third of all programmers and analysts had supervisory responsibilities of some kind. All but one of these supervisors had less than six staff under their control (p. 115). Mumford's interviews with these supervisors clearly reveals their bias towards responsible autonomy strategies for performing their role. 'Supervisors were very conscious of the need for cultivating personal responsibility in their staff", 'the consensus of opinion amongst the supervisors was that supervision, to be effective, must be loose and employee-centered' (p. 115). An example of supervisor comments reported by Mumford states the strategy very clearly:

> One must not be strict. One must give freedom but staff must feel they can approach one for help when necessary. As a supervisor one is only interested in the end result. They can work as they please. (p. 115)

One of the most common methods of supervision was the setting of targets for staff. This was always done jointly with the staff involved. Monitoring staff then involved simply noting how well staff did against the mutually set targets.

All firms used some form of employee appraisal to control staff performance in Mumford's sample. This was carried out annually in the user organizations, and either annually or more frequently in computer hardware and services firms. Formal employee appraisal systems were in use in 81% of the user organizations Computer Economics surveyed. Such appraisals were carried out annually in 69% of cases and every six months in 32% (1972, p. EVI). However, the assessments were overwhelmingly used when considering positive incentives, such as salary reviews (95%) and promotions (90%), rather than for negative strictures such as dismissal (49%) and redundancy (25%).

The really striking results from Mumford's survey occurred when she asked employees their opinions on how they reacted to controls imposed on them and how they thought work might best be controlled. In general the DP staff regarded supervisors as resource people rather than controllers. The few complaints about supervision were 'about too little supervision rather than too much' (p. 121). In one of the user organizations, for example, 25% of systems analysts wanted supervisors to set targets and believed that supervisors were not very good at setting them. Programmers at one of the computer services firms complained that 'supervisors did not provide them with sufficiently clearly defined work structure. Work organization was too free and easy' (p. 122). Staff who complained were not in favour of tight structural controls, but they wanted more guidance.

Similar criticisms were made of higher-level DP management. Concerning this level of controls, a surprisingly large number of Mumford's sample of analysts and programmers approved of formal controls (58%; p. 107). Criticisms about formal controls were more often that they were ineffective rather than that they were tried. Only in one organization, the government department, were there criticisms that there were too many formal controls (pp. 108–109).

6.3 LIKELY DEVELOPMENTS DISCERNIBLE EARLY IN PHASE TWO

Mumford notes that there was considerable management disquiet about the degree of freedom enjoyed by DP staff. This was echoed by many US sources, as reported in the previous chapter. Mumford reported that one of her user organizations was experimenting with a work measurement scheme for programmers by which worksheets were filled out accounting for activities carried out every half hour. She reported that some programmers found this exercise irritating and they questioned the accuracy of the activity analysis sheets that were emerging from the exercise (p. 116). The computer press at the time was very concerned both with work measurement (Mumford reference, 1972, p. 115, footnote 18) and with structured methods (Weinwurm, 1970). This suggests that we would find a significant move towards direct control by the end of phase two.

Mumford also reports another tendency (Mumford reference, 1972, p. 117, footnote 14). This was to move the DP department away from one based on functional division of labour between analysts and programmers, and towards what was called a federal form of organization based on project teams composed of computer generalists. A project team would handle the entire project from start to finish. It would be responsible for every aspect of the project. More important, the team would set its own standards. As Mumford notes, this high degree of responsible autonomy would work only if the DP staff were 'experienced and mature' (p. 117). Therefore tendencies towards more consciously worked out strategies towards DP staff were discernible early in phase two. Organizations were moving away from the phase one concentration on hardware selection and evaluation, which had bred a kind of management by neglect policy towards personnel and which, by default, tended towards responsible autonomy.

One further development discernible early in phase two was that the career blockage problem would stimulate some policy initiatives. Career blockage was a major reason cited for systems developers thinking of quitting, as Mumford demonstrated. Labour turnover, especially among more experienced systems developers, was a major headache, especially in large projects. This was one factor stimulating new technology, especially structured techniques aimed at improving system maintainability. Another way of tackling labour turnover was to reduce the labour shortage. Kraft (1977) described the explosion of training facilities, particularly for programmers in the USA. However, there is another way of dealing with labour turnover if it is substantially stimulated by career blockage. That is to develop career structures for systems developers. In the USA, Kaye (1971) predicted that corporations would soon begin to promote computer specialists into upper management levels, although he saw it as a consequence of rising DP department budgets and as a solution to the problem of poor relations between DP departments and the rest of the organization. Other American writers clearly suggested that internal recruiting and training of DP staff should be introduced in order to reduce labour turnover (Yoritz and Stanback, 1967; Davis, 1969; Tomeski, 1974).

6.4 THE SITUATION LATE IN PHASE TWO: DIRECT CONTROL?

Our primary hypothesis about management strategies during phase two is that it was direct control types of strategies which were emphasized. However, the impact of new techniques to support direct control strategies was, in our opinion, far *less* than many observers writing during the 1970s predicted. The rising software to hardware ratio of costs, the general growth of DP department budgets, and frequent experiences of serious overruns on important projects, brought software costs to the attention of top managers as well as DP department managers. It became important for DP department managers to be seen to be doing something about these issues. The shift in emphasis among DP department managers towards strategies for managing people, and away from the near-exclusive interest in hardware selection and support of phase one, led to further articulation of *both* direct control and responsible autonomy strategies.

6.4.1 A Note on Data Sources

The primary source of our data was a mailed survey which was carried out during June–October 1981 in Great Britain. This was a survey of firms participating in the Computer Economics Ltd (CEL) salary survey. Therefore the population from which our sample was drawn was similar to that upon which the Computer Economics 1972 report was drawn ten years earlier. Also some of the questions asked in 1981 were based on the 1972 survey. A summary of the results of this survey were reported in Friedman and Cornford (1982b). This will be referred to as the CEL 1981 survey. In developing this questionnaire 42 DP managers and computer services firm executives were interviewed. These interviews will be referred to as the in-depth survey. It was carried out during 1980 and 1981. These surveys are described more in detail in the Data Appendix.

6.4.2 Task Organization

Division of labour

By 1981 the separation of analysts from programmers was still strong. However, according to the CEL 1981 survey some organizations (28%) defined their staff primarily as analyst/programmers, but many of these were small departments and reflected the general lack of specialization associated with small organizations, rather than a trend to recombine former specialisms. When classified by Computer Economics job categories, 19% of individual development staff in the sample were recorded as analyst/programmers (32% were classed as analysts and 49% as programmers).

Loseke and Sonquist note that commonly used job titles may not distinguish actual work functions (1979, p. 165).[3] Nevertheless, the CEL 1981 survey had the advantage of using standardized job titles designed by Computer Economics, and of surveying a population which had many years of experience of filling out survey forms based on those job titles for their salary information.

It is notable that in only 20% of organizations in the CEL 1981 survey did a

)arated organization structure exist between analysis and
'sually (55% of cases) analysts and programmers, or analyst/
_.s were organized on a project team basis (Table 6.2).

Most of those that used a team structure (63%) had teams with a life expectancy
of more than one project. Teams would work on more than one project at a time
and individuals would belong to only one team at a time. These permanent teams
would be responsible for specific areas of the firm's business. About one-third of the
organizations used teams in a different way. Teams would be formed for one
project and then disbanded when the project went live. Staff could belong to more
than one project at a time in these organizations.

The trend towards project teams was noted in the CEL 1972 survey and again in
the NCC 1975 survey. The main reason reported for this move was to provide
better control and coordination of projects, but some respondents also mentioned
the need to motivate junior staff, provide greater job satisfaction and help career
development (Hansen and Penney, 1976, pp. 17–20). By the CEL 1981 survey it is
possible that the proportion using project team structures had stabilized. In the
NCC survey a few installations reported reverting back to having separate
programming departments, reflecting the switch of emphasis from large-scale
development to small maintenance and support jobs. In some of the smaller
organizations project teams were regarded as inflexible and wasteful of manpower
because they committed people to a project in such a way that it became difficult to
reschedule them to other work. One important feature of the spread of computing
has been the diffusion of computers to smaller firms as hardware costs have fallen.
This and the growing availability of packages and external services had meant
that the average size of DP departments has been falling, purely because of the
rapid addition of smaller departments.

By late phase two further divisions of labour among systems developers had
become common. In most departments applications development was separated
from systems software development (78%). Also a number of specialist job titles

TABLE 6.2 Which of the following structures best describes
the organization of your development staff?

	%
Teams of analysts and programmers	36
Separate teams of analysts and teams of programmers	8
Teams of analyst/programmers	19
Matrix organization of analysts and programmers	16
Matrix organization of analyst/programmers	5
Pool of analysts and pool of programmers	6
Pool of analyst/programmers	4
Teams of analysts and pool of programmers	6

Source: Friedman and Cornford (1982b, p. 13).

had become quite common, primarily network controllers, telecommunications specialists and database administrators. However, the separation of systems development from maintenance had not proceeded as far as might have been expected. In the NCC 1975 survey, 'many organizations', it was reported, 'have drawn a dividing line between development work and maintenance of existing systems'. Maintenance has long been predicted to rise to the point where development work would only be undertaken by a small separate group. Certainly the percentage of time spent in maintenance had risen during the 1970s. The CEL 1972 survey reported that 23% of systems and programming staff effort was spent on maintenance. The CEL 1981 survey found 38%. However, by our CEL 1981 survey only 28% of installations reported that development and maintenance were carried out by different personnel. While some installations did a lot of maintenance and this pushed up the average maintenance proportion, most (72%) spent less than 50% of their systems and programming efforts on maintenance. Almost half (40%) reported maintenance accounting for less than 30% of their efforts.

New technology

Interactive programming was used by 93% of the CEL 1981 sample. It is clearly a technique that was regarded by almost all DP managers as a necessity, a clear productivity advance whatever strategy towards staff they were pursuing. On average, installations initiated interactive programming in the mid- to late 1970s. Other techniques which extended the computer systems core and which were diffusing very quickly at the time were database management systems, data dictionaries and, to a lesser extent, report generators. By the time of the survey 59% reported using database management systems, 38% data dictionaries and 68% report generators (Friedman and Cornford, 1982b, p. 15).

Structured methods were well known by 1981, especially for programming. Of the CEL 1981 sample, 66% stated they used a structured programming method and 32% structured analysis. Altogether this represented 70% of respondents. If we accept the interpretation of structured programming suggested by Kraft (1977), as well as the claims made for these methods by their originators and purveyors, then we would expect this spread of structured methods to indicate strong moves towards direct control during phase two. However, during our in-depth interviews a rather different picture emerged.

First, the reasons for adopting structured programming were not simply to deskill programmers. Most DP managers tended to view structured programming as a method of decreasing the long-term problems of maintenance and enhancement of a system. Many said that the introduction of structured programming and revamped standards had occurred because of the development of a major new system. Very few would accept the proposition that structured programming increased productivity in the short run, or that it enabled them to use less-skilled programmers to develop the system. Indeed, many said that structured programming gave slower initial development times and required, if anything, more skilled programmers. Their main quoted reason for introducing structured programming was to make the system easier to understand, enhance and maintain in the future, by people who were not involved in its development. The in-depth interviews also suggested that in areas with a high labour turn-over among programmers and analysts there was a greater tendency to use structured methods. Clearly, DP managers experiencing high labour turnover among programmers had found maintenance a problem when the originators of their systems had left. The use of structured programming was intended to ease this problem in future.

Second, many of the DP managers who said they used formal methodologies in fact used only 'watered down' versions of the methodologies. Many methodologies for systems development specify a large number of milestones for formal reporting. Often managers who said they used a methodology in fact kept to a reduced number of milestones. The Michael Jackson structured design method—the most popular structured methodology in Europe—is rarely used in full.[4] Around half of those using structured programming said they were using modular programming alone. For most of those, modular programming simply meant that large jobs were broken up into smaller programming modules before tasks were assigned. Most structured programming methods specify that in addition to separation into modules these modules should be independent of each other, except for single entry and exit points. Also they should be standardized in that only a limited range of commands or sequence of commands should be used within modules.

Third, many DP managers who said such methodologies were used indicated that these methodologies were available, but not imposed. Staff had been sent on courses to learn the methods, but their use was not required. Also a number of DP managers indicated that methods were introduced by the programmers and analysts themselves. Around a tenth of those using the Jackson method stated that its use was instigated by ordinary development staff. A number of programmers we spoke to considered familiarity with the Jackson method to be a skill that was especially useful when they had to maintain or enhance large programs which they had themselves written in the past.

Our exploration of structured methods revealed the difficulty of interpreting their usage as clear indicators of direct control types of strategies. Usage of these techniques may reduce the creativity and variety of programming work if they are strictly imposed. However, we discovered that this could rarely be inferred with confidence. Another way to approach the task content element of management strategies towards systems development staff is to investigate task size.

Task sizes

In the CEL 1981 survey DP managers were asked if they tried to control the size of individual tasks assigned to development staff. A rather high 76% said yes (20%

said no and 4% did not respond). This may be taken as evidence for direct control. However, when asked what would be regarded as a desirable task size for different job categories most indicated very large tasks and an extremely wide variance was revealed (Table 6.3).

For analysts and analyst/programmers the distribution of opinion concerning desirable task sizes was fairly even, between 1 week and 3 months; for programmers, between 1 week and 1 month.

It is notable that very few DP managers considered task sizes as short as a day or half a day to be desirable. In the mid-1970s Kraft predicted that programming work was becoming like mass production industrial work. Task length for such work may be measured in minutes. Clearly by 1981 management of development staff was a long way from this 'ideal'.

6.4.3 Employment Relations

Although efforts to develop direct control strategies were a major feature of computing during phase two, we have noted that these initiatives were not pursued as vigorously as appeared from the outside. The rising proportion of DP department budgets spent on software (i.e. systems and programming staff) stimulated many to search for new techniques to 'break the software bottleneck' (Friedman and Cornford, 1981). However, shortages in the labour market, particularly for experienced systems analysts and programmers, continued throughout phase two. This allowed computer specialists to resist unpopular management strategies by simply changing jobs.

The British government's Central Computing and Telecommunication Agency (CCTA) produced a report in 1980, which noted the very high levels of labour turnover in government installations among programmers with two to three years' experience. This was largely associated with Civil Service pay scales that did not

TABLE 6.3 Desirable task sizes per category of development staff

Job category	Time						
	1 hour (%)	1/2 day (%)	1 day (%)	1 week (%)	2 weeks (%)	1 month (%)	3 months (%)
Systems analysts	0	0	1	13	17	31	38
Analyst/programmers	0	2	0	19	25	40	14
Programmers	0	1	2	35	32	29	1

Note: The figures are percentages of respondents who attempt to control task sizes, excluding those who did not employ anyone in the job category and those who did not attempt to answer the question. This represented 23% of the sample for systems analysts, 62% for analyst/programmers and 75% for programmers.
Source: CEL 1981 survey; see Data Appendix for details.

allow government departments to follow private-sector salary rises. The CCTA also noted a tendency for long-standing project teams to develop their own autonomy and that these teams did 'not readily respond to essential installation, or departmental, disciplines' (1980, p. 5).

Two different sorts of responsible autonomy types of strategies aimed at retaining staff had emerged by late phase two. One was to pay high salaries and offer good working conditions. For many programmers good working conditions meant access to up-to-date or state-of-the-art technology rather than merely an absence of direct control structures. One of the main reasons for high labour turnover among programmers has been their fear of skill obsolescence, according to Mike Arthur (1977). One of our in-depth respondents mentioned use of Jackson structured programming as an *attraction* of his installation. It was regarded as a technique to be mastered. For many programmers the opportunity to work with the latest version of IBM's operating system or a database management system had been the primary reason for switching jobs.

A second strategy employed by organizations to attract and retain staff was to offer a career structure to their computer specialists. Early in phase two the problem of career prospects for analysts was noted by Mumford. Hansen and Penney noted several techniques that were being developed during phase two to provide a career structure within DP. For programmers the obvious place to go has been into systems analysis—in spite of reports from several managers that 'programmers don't make good analysts' (1976, p. 36), because of their more narrow machine orientation. Hansen and Penney note the rise in use of the analyst/programmer job grade to bridge the gap. They note that few installations provided formal training for systems analysis. By and large the training provided was what the trainees could pick up by working closely with practising analysts. However, 28% of their sample recruited only experienced analysts from outside (21% recruited all analysts from within and the rest mixed external recruitment and internal promotion; p. 29). The CCTA recommended fostering career development of computer specialists who wished to stay with the Civil Service and allowing them to concentrate on development work, while those who had not yet shown a desire to remain (those with less than two years in the service) would concentrate on maintenance work (1980, p. 20).

Table 6.4 shows the average number of days per year spent in training courses during first and subsequent years of employment for different job categories from the CEL 1981 survey. By far the most training was given to programmers in their first year. Analysts in their first year also received rather more training than other job categories. It seems that earlier claims of a lack of training for analysts had been heeded in some departments. However, note the large standard deviations for all categories.

Another career path for programmers was to specialize within programming, particularly on systems programming and telecommunication. This has only been possible for a few programmers. Finally, with the growth in size of DP departments

TABLE 6.4 Days in training courses per year

	Mean no. of days	Std. dev.
DP management	7.1	7.3
Systems analysts first year	16.6	12.3
Systems analysts later years	7.5	5.1
Programmers first year	25.7	23.1
Programmers later years	8.2	5.2
Operators first year	9.4	8.8
Operators later years	4.5	4.1
Data preparation	2.7	7.0
Data control	2.1	3.3
Secretarial	2.2	9.9

Source: CEL 1981 survey; see Data Appendix for survey details.

there has been a lengthening of the grading structure. Almost all organizations in the NCC 1975 survey reported having some kind of staff appraisal and grading system (pp. 34–35).

By our 1981 in-depth survey several DP managers were expressing their concern to design grading structures that were long enough within programming grades to keep their programming staff in programming. Also many installations had specialists that now included database experts as well as network specialists and systems programmers. However, the major development of consequence for programmer careers was the growth in the analyst/programmer job category. As we will see in later chapters, the role of analyst/programmer was becoming an important job category in its own right, rather than merely a transitional role.

Career development for analysts improved somewhat during phase two. This occurred for two rather different reasons. First, the sheer growth in size of DP departments provided a wider range of internal opportunities for analysts. During phase two the status of DP functions rose in many organizations. Hansen and Penney recorded a strong fall in DP departments that were part of finance departments (36% to 19% between 1969 and 1974) and corresponding rises in those that were independent functions or part of management services (pp. 12–18). The proportion of DP managers reporting to finance management fell from 50% to 42%; the corresponding rise was in those reporting directly to the managing director (10% to 17%). These trends were predicted to continue in the future (p. 19).

The second possibility was for analysts to move into line management. This was described as a frustration point by Mumford. Hansen and Penney state that progression into line management was still the exception rather than the rule by 1976, and only likely in the largest organizations (p. 35). They did note that a few large organizations were beginning to include a stint in DP as part of their general orientation of fresh graduates who were hired as management trainees. According to Hansen and Penney this should increase computing awareness among line management and provide good management material for the DP department when trainees chose to make a career in DP (pp. 35–36). However, such experiments were often abandoned during the late 1970s and early 1980s owing to the general reduction in training among British firms. Also there were problems associated with such programs. In our US surveys (see Data Appendix) as well as in Britain the problem of frustration that such programs meant for analysts who worked their way up in DP departments was expressed. Also if the work of systems analysts is regarded as too specialized compared with low-level management work elsewhere in the firm, there are high costs to losing these DP specific skills when trainees move elsewhere. In both countries it would have often been the case during late phase two that the DP department provided the only steady source of new job opportunities. This would force organizations to cease department rotation programs once new staff had been assigned to DP.

Perhaps the most striking problem area for career prospects among analysts and programmers which emerged during phase two was at the top. The 'plight of the data processing manager' became a notable subject (Nolan, 1973). Although DP departments grew and the status of many also increased, changes in technology and changes in management fashion could easily cast the DP manager into the role of the 'has-been'. The skills and temperament appropriate for managing a small installation running batch jobs and developing systems that would mainly replace existing manual systems were likely to be different from the requirements for running a large, high-profile department, developing applications that interacted with important users. Rising user demands for new systems put DP managers into a strong bidding position for organization resources. However, this situation also exposed them to the approbation attached to more visible, more spectacular failures. Late systems and budget overruns became public. The story of the previous DP manager's cloudy departure became a frequent theme of our 1981 in-depth interviews.

6.4.4 Staff Control

Early in phase two Mumford noted that tight staff control required a combination of control procedures. In all organizations in her sample programming work was checked by unit supervisors. This was rarely supplemented by tight working procedures or by detailed specifications. Also checking was rarely done by specialist auditors. According to the CEL 1972 survey 'only' 15% of user organizations had regular checks by specialist auditors (1972, p. EV). This situation had not changed substantially by 1981.

In accord with Mumford's findings, almost all (97%) respondents to the CEL 1981 survey reported some procedure for checking programmers' work other than by the programmers themselves (Table 6.5). Most (85%) required clearance by

TABLE 6.5 Methods for checking programmer work at various stages in the process

Method	Stage			
	Program design (%)	Coding (%)	Testing and debugging (%)	Method not used (%)
Clearance with senior required before further progress	64	35	65	15
Walkthroughs and reviews	46	28	25	44
Clearance from user required before further progress	13	1	41	54
Documentation required before further progress	38	18	44	41
No checking at this stage	13	44	11	3

Source: CEL 1981 survey; see Data Appendix for details.

supervisors at some stage of the work. However, a large proportion (46%) reported requiring clearance by users at some stage. Even more (56%) used structured walkthroughs and review by peer groups in order to check programming work.

The relatively high proportion of organizations where it was standard for users to check programming work by 1981 is notable. The model division of labour from phase one, in which it was only analysts who were expected to communicate with users (and only at the requirements analysis stages), became increasingly unrealistic as the character of computing applications changed, i.e. as user interaction with computer-based systems grew. For the programmer, outsiders checking his or her work could be as onerous as having specialist auditors checking the work. However, in most cases user knowledge of programming procedures and of the detailed possibilities and limitations of programming environments would have made it relatively easy for programmers to mask their own errors. Direct checking by users in many instances could be taken as evidence of responsible autonomy rather than direct control. Users were only competent and only interested in getting the product right, not judging the process of generating that product. Direct exposure to users would have increased programmer responsibility as a spokesperson for the DP department and also it would give programmers more autonomy to move around the organization, beyond the view of their own supervisors. That overwhelming concentration of user checking should have occurred at the testing and debugging stage of programming is also notable. The very few organizations that involved users at earlier stages of programming indicates the dominance of the view that users could have nothing useful to say about detailed program design or coding.

The most favoured supplements to supervisor checking at program design and coding stages were walkthroughs and reviews. In fact walkthroughs were suggested as part of many structured programming methods. Here, too, interpreting use of this practice as a direct control technique is misleading. The most popular and perhaps the most efficient way to learn and to improve programming techniques is to have a more experienced practitioner go over your work with you. Many of the in-depth respondents which used walkthroughs and reviews admitted that they were only standard practice for their less experienced programmers.

The final method of checking work—documentation required before further progress—is closer to a direct control strategy. Many programmers would admit that documentation during or immediately after programming is a key element in their own good housekeeping. However, few programmers will do it unless pushed. There always seems to be pressure to get on with the next job. New work is usually much more interesting than going over old ground. What is notable from Table 6.5 is that 41% of installations did *not* require documentation during or immediately after programming.

The method mentioned by Mumford and Computer Economics as one which would really ensure that checking would substantially control programming work was to have a separate auditing section. Only 10% of the CEL 1981 sample indicated that they had a separate quality assurance function.

Tight working procedures and detailed specifications were essential complements to checking procedures, according to Mumford. Table 6.6 shows the

TABLE 6.6 Standards and methods of enforcement

Q: Do you encourage any of the following design and coding standards at your installations and if so how are they enforced?

	Installation standards (%)	System or program specification (%)	By inspection (%)	Using any method of enforcement (%)
Avoid GOTO statements	32	1	18	43
Control flow limited to sequence, selection and iteration	25	6	10	30
Maximum module size	47	11	17	58
Requirements for commentary within code	79	9	36	91
Formatting conventions on program layout	68	11	31	80
Formatting conventions on output layout	55	26	25	75

Source: CEL 1981 survey; see Data Appendix for details.

proportion of respondents to the CEL 1981 survey that used certain standards and how those standards were enforced.

The table indicates a clear distinction between technical standards (the first two items), which were enforced in a minority of installations, and standards concerning forms (last three items) which were very widely used. Most DP managers who we spoke to admitted that mere inclusion in the installation standards was in fact a very weak form of enforcement. Frequent changes in technology and changes in DP management ('plight of the data processing manager'—see Nolan, 1973) meant written standards were often out of date. The 'book' is often a piece of standard installation decor, a fat load of printout gathering dust on the shelves of senior programmers and analysts. Inclusion in the specifications is a much more serious way of supplementing checking of programmers' work. The high proportion enforcing formatting conventions on output layouts relates to a different characteristic of using the specification as a control mechanism, other than its strength, i.e. flexibility. It is likely that analysts and managers will want to specify particular output layouts for only some jobs— for example, when users have been particularly clear about what they want. Why, one might wonder, are standards not enforced *more often* by inclusion in the specification, the more analyst or programming manager time is substituted for (cheaper) programmer time. However, a desire not to treat programmers 'like babies' is also a factor.

In addition to controlling the flow of work and the way work is done, there are more people-oriented methods for controlling computing staff. Three methods for recording the progress of individual programmers and analysts were investigated in the CEL 1981 survey. All were used by about the same proportion of respondents. They were:

(1) reports by line supervisors through personal contact, 86%;
(2) recording on worksheets, 87%; and
(3) records of performances against estimated targets, 85%.

However, not all of those who recorded the progress of individuals used those records in formal employee appraisals. Sometimes these records were used for charging users. This was common for worksheets in particular. The proportions of respondents who used each of the methods for formal employee appraisals were:

(1) reports by line supervisors through personal contact, 67%;
(2) recording on worksheets, 35%; and
(3) records of performances against estimated targets, 64%.

It is notable that when records of performance against set targets were kept, almost all (90%) said they involved the person carrying out the work in setting targets. It is also notable that the group of organizations where either targets were used for appraisal without the person doing the work being involved in setting the target, or where worksheets were used for appraisals, when worksheets had to be filled out daily or weekly using a unit of time measured in units of one hour or less, was correlated with the group which closely checked the progress of work.

From the American survey of 1977, Loseke and Sonquist found a mixture of strong and light supervision similar to the British surveys:

> We found that though computer workers unanimously value independence, they are not without supervision. About half the nonacademic workers reported that their supervisor reviewed the way their job was performed as well as their output. Fewer than one in three said that only the results of their work were reviewed. As few reported no supervision. (1979, p. 175)

Although Loseke and Sonquist report their results emphasizing how widespread supervision is. In fact they could equally have said that almost a third of the non-academic workers in their sample (BA degree or less) reported no supervision at all and about half reported that the way their job was performed was not reviewed by supervisors.

Loseke and Sonquist reported that about 40% of their sample received supervision less than once a week, about 10% daily or more frequently and about 50% in between (1979, p. 176). They state that 'computer workers themselves generally have few supervisory responsibilities' (p. 176). This was then clarified as slightly more than 25% having some supervisory responsibilities, which appears to us to be rather a high figure. Especially as Loseke and Sonquist further report the following:

> One statement repeatedly heard in the interviews was that computer workers did not want to become managers, they wanted to stay in technical jobs. (1979, p. 176)

This seems to confirm that computer specialists late in phase two still derived considerable satisfaction from the intrinsic task characteristics of their jobs.

6.5 CONCLUSION

During phase two there appears to have been a general rise in concern with staff management issues in DP departments. This led to a rise in certain formal structures and techniques being used. However, two rather separate trends can be discerned. The first is that DP managers seem to have become more conscious of pursuing strategies designed either to retain staff or to make staff more easily replaceable. In a sense, the choice between responsible autonomy or direct control types of strategies became clearer. Techniques for deskilling staff as well as techniques for providing staff with better career prospects became more widely available. Both diffused substantially during phase two. Therefore the range of strategies along the responsible autonomy versus direct control continuum was extended. However, there is also evidence that the mean position was moving in the direct control direction. To this extent we would agree with Kraft and Greenbaum.

In spite of discernible moves towards direct control, the statement made by Kraft (1977, p. 97), that the work of programmers 'is less and less distinguished from that of clerks or, for that matter, assembly line workers' was clearly an extreme exaggeration. Couger and Zawacki (1980, pp. 18–23) found that all three general categories of what they call DP professionals (programmers, programmer/ analysts and analysts) reported levels of satisfaction with their jobs that were not only far above clerical staff, but were also higher than for other professional groups.[5] This result cannot be ascribed to lower aspirations concerning job satisfaction on the part of systems developers, in fact Couger and Zawacki found that programmers, programmer/analysts and analysts expressed *higher* 'growth needs strength' than other professionals (see section 5.6).

ENDNOTES

1. Note the 'problem of tenses' discussed earlier (section 2.3.4).
2. See Friedman (1989) for a further discussion of the strategic dimensions of these sets of policies and for more on the general connections between general managerial strategies and particular policies or policy initiatives by managers.
3. Loseke and Sonquist found that programmer/analysts in the USA were more frequently used in implementation and maintenance jobs, rather than in design work, compared with people labelled as analysts or programmers. (People called analyst/programmers in Europe are normally called programmer/analysts in the USA.) However, their sample was very small—only 12 programmer/analysts. Also they noted that in their whole sample people carrying out implementation and maintenance roles were younger (average ages 27 and 25 respectively) compared with those carrying out design work (average age 30). It may be that the programmer/analyst label was simply used for new staff.
4. Personal communication with M. Jackson (1981).
5. On a seven-point scale 'other professionals' scored 4.88 for general satisfaction with their jobs, compared with 5.10 for analysts, 5.37 for programmer/analysts and 5.30 for programmers. While computer systems developers' general satisfaction with their jobs was higher than other professionals, they were less satisfied with their co-workers and with supervision than other professionals. The results for systems developers were based on 'over 1000' questionnaires. The results for other employees come from other published survey results cited in Couger and Zawacki (1980, pp. 9–82).

Part 3
PHASE THREE: USER NEEDS DOMINATE

'The 1980's could go down as the decade of the user', declared an editorial in the UK computer press in 1986 (*Computer News*, July 17). In an American survey of key information systems issues for the 1980s, the top issue after improved information systems planning was facilitation of end-user computing. Productivity improvement and measurement only ranked fifth (Dickson *et al.*, 1984).

Why has the computer world become so concerned about users in the 1980s? Why have users had to wait until the 1980s to have their decade? What difference is the decade of the user making to systems developers and to the process of computer systems development? How has it affected the movement towards direct control strategies over computer systems developers which we associated with phase two? We attempt to answer these questions in Part Three.

Dealing with user relations requires us to address issues beyond those which have traditionally been found in texts on systems development methods. We must examine the interaction of computer-based systems with those who use them as well as those who are affected by them in an indirect way. There is a huge literature on this subject. It is a sign of this new phase of computer systems development history that the literature aimed at teaching computer systems development methods and the literature on the effects of computer systems on users have been merging.

User relations problems have existed from the outset of business computing. There have always been three types of problems. First, there have been problems with the quality of computer-based systems. Does the system perform as expected by users? Does it provide what users thought they needed? Second, there have been problems with user relations during the process of computer systems development, as well as during the process of systems maintenance and enhancement. Third, there have been problems with the effect of systems on users after they have been implemented. What are the unexpected consequences of the system? Have user requirements changed during the time taken to develop the system? Of course these types of problems are related, but it will be illuminating to discuss them separately here. Towards the end of phase two important changes were occurring in all these areas.

In Chapter 7 changing perceptions of system quality and changing emphasis on different phases of the computer system life cycle will be discussed. A classification of different types of users, which will be helpful in later chapters, will also be presented.

In Chapter 8 the literature on user relations problems will be summarized. User relations problems have been described from many different perspectives. We will show that a change in the balance of this literature has occurred (particularly from the late 1970s) towards a greater proportion of formulations coming from within the computer community. In addition the literature has become more extensive and more integrated from the late 1970s. Increasingly writers expressing one perspective have been referring to work expressing other perspectives. These trends are symptoms of the coming of phase three.

In Chapter 9 an analysis of the generation of user relations problems and an explanation of why they became a primary concern within the computer community in the 1980s will be provided. Three broad sources of user relations problems will be identified and analysed:

(1) the distinctiveness of computer technology and changes in the core computer technology;
(2) changes in computer applications, leading particularly to changes in the types of users interacting with computer systems and with the systems development process;
(3) market relations surrounding what are now known as information systems departments, both in terms of competition faced by their output, and competition for labour inputs.

Chapters 10 and 11 describe strategies for dealing with user relations problems. Early reactions to user relations problems are described in Chapter 10: separating analysts from programmers, developing requirements definition languages and imposing market-like relations (chargeout systems) between information systems departments and user departments. The inadequacies of these early reactions are then summarized. In Chapter 11 the strategies for dealing with user relations problems which have come to characterize phase three are described. Although champions of each of these strategies have made great claims for them, we find that reports of experiences with them are more qualified. Progress is reported, but further problems remain.

This part ends with Chapter 12, in which we return to the issues discussed in Chapter 6. We examine how the late phase-two picture of work in computer installations has been altered during the 1980s. We discuss the extent to which strategies for improving user relations have affected strategies for managing the work of computer systems developers.

Chapter 7

SUCCESSFUL SYSTEMS DEVELOPMENT, THE SYSTEM LIFE CYCLE AND IDENTIFYING USERS

In this chapter we provide a preliminary discussion of three concepts that will be used later in Part Three. The first is that the coming of phase three has meant a change in the criteria for judging the output of information systems departments as a success. Satisfying user demands for effective or useful systems has become of prime importance for a growing proportion of information systems departments.

The second concept is the computer system development life cycle, the set of separately identified steps, or stages or phases[1] that are followed during the development process. Examining changes in the way these life cycle phases are prescribed and followed provides an interesting indicator of the way phase-three concerns have altered the process of computer systems development and the work of computer systems developers. We note that the front and back ends of the life cycle have expanded in phase three.

In order to understand how user relations came to be of prime concern and to analyse the consequences of this newly elevated concern on the systems development process, it is necessary to describe users more accurately. Has concern for relations with *all* users distinguished the 1980s, or has this concern been generated by the appearance of new types of users? Has the change occurred because users are interacting with systems in different ways than before? A number of classifications of users are presented in this chapter. These will contribute to analysis presented in later chapters.

7.1 OUTPUT OF INFORMATION SYSTEMS DEPARTMENTS AND USER RELATIONS

Problems associated with the quality of computer-based systems have always been present. During phase one instances of employees being paid enormous sums because of bugs in payroll systems, or the system simply grinding to a halt, were well known. However, the presumption among computer specialists was that eventually, once hardware reliability had improved sufficiently and the software bugs had been removed, quality systems could emerge. During phase one it became clear that all the bugs could never be removed from systems (at least from the kind of systems that were being developed in the field). Even if in principle all bugs could be removed, the cost of finding them was prohibitive. The perception of a successful or high-quality system quickly became a relative one. Correct programs were for small exercises in university engineering departments or emerging computer science departments. Real-life programs were big and programming solutions aimed for were 'quick and dirty', especially when seemingly inevitable project slippages occurred. Bergland stated the problem in the following graphic terms:

> A correct program is one that accurately implements the specification. A 'correct' program often has limited value since the specifications are in error. Again, correctness cannot be verified by testing. Searching for errors is like searching for mermaids. Just because you haven't seen one doesn't mean they don't exist.
>
> It is also unfortunate that, for most problems, mathematical proofs of correctness are as difficult to produce as a correct program. (1981, p. 17)

Users became embroiled in the systems development process, or at least in the maintenance phase of that process.[2] Parnas put it in the following way:

> People write programs without any expectations that they will be right the first time . . . software is released for use, not when it is known to be correct, but when the rate of discovering new errors slows down to one that management considers acceptable. Users learn to expect errors and are often told how to avoid the bugs until the program is improved. (1985, p. 1330)

This had been the clear message from the Garmisch conference. The software crisis expressed early in phase two was that computer systems were dangerously unreliable and the time and money required to produce them was large and impossible to estimate accurately in advance. The solutions proposed at the Garmisch conference and the techniques developed and diffused during phase two did have an effect. The software crisis was not 'solved', but several aspects of the early phase-two crisis eased. A combination of greater experience with computer systems development in large user organizations, reduced ambitions of systems developers, expanded computer systems core and standardized methods led to the delivery of somewhat more reliable systems within more acceptable cost limitations. However, during phase two a major change in the way users judged systems emerged. With the development of systems that had no clear manual counterpart, what was being delivered by the data processing (DP) departments could no longer be viewed as a product, with fairly stable and easily understood characteristics. No longer was it sufficient that systems came out with few bugs and within budget. They had to be useful systems, useful in terms of allowing users to do their jobs better, or to achieve their overall ambitions.

Developments during the 1960s and early 1970s had left DP departments within user organizations even less well suited to produce successful systems by these new criteria than they had been during phase one. DP departments contained young people with technical orientations. Those with experience were in short supply on labour markets. In consequence many large organizations found that computerization meant creating a substantial department containing employees whose working practices, values and salaries were out of line with those prevailing elsewhere in the organization. Furthermore communication problems developed between computer systems developers and user department managers. In order to limit the disruption to smooth corporate order induced by these two problems, DP departments became increasingly isolated from user departments. Communication with users was limited to systems analysts and DP managers. Many companies moved their DP departments to separate sites. Isolation of DP departments made it *more difficult* for systems developers to understand user needs.

As it became more important to understand and to meet user needs, those needs became more complex and more numerous. Rising user awareness of the possibilities for computer systems led to exploding demands on computer departments during the 1970s. Waiting for computer departments to get around to user-identified projects came to be measured in years. Unfortunately during the late 1970s the timing of systems delivery was becoming more important. Increasingly, systems have been aimed at aiding decisions made by higher-level managers. Higher-level managers are more concerned with the organization's relation to its environment. Normally this changes rapidly and unpredictably. Late computer-based systems relating to such decision-making processes are more likely to be out-of-date systems and therefore of limited value.

Thus the criteria for successful computer-based systems changed during phase two. The quality of the system rather than its cost had become important. Furthermore the quality of the system in terms of its usefulness (its value to users) or its impact on user effectiveness had become of greater concern than its quality in terms of reliability. Producing the right system, rather than producing the system right, became the primary criterion for a successful system. This meant that the important part of the systems development process could not be presumed to begin with the receipt of a clear requirements specification and end with the delivery to users of a reliable system; a system that met the requirements specification. Instead the end points of the development process, the elicitation and specification of requirements and the implementation of systems, had to be given more prominence than in earlier phases. Systems developers needed to take a more active responsibility for the effects of the systems they developed on users and on the organization to ensure that systems led to user satisfaction and contributed to user effectiveness. This in turn had important consequences both for the relations between the DP department and users and also for the internal organization of DP staff.

7.2 THE COMPUTER SYSTEM LIFE CYCLE AND USER RELATIONS

The term 'computer system life cycle' is often used in the computing literature to describe an ordered set of activities, or phases, which combine to make up the conception, development, use and eventual replacement of a new computer-based system. The life cycle entered the computer systems development literature in two ways. First, via the operations research literature as an idealization of how projects ought to be planned, and second, through reports describing what sequence of activities had occurred in individual projects. By phase two the computerization life cycle was being used within the computer systems development literature as a prescriptive device to control projects.

There is no general agreement on precisely which particular set of phases should be distinguished. In fact we shall show that there have been systematic changes in the way the computer system life cycle has been articulated during the late 1970s and 1980s, reflecting the new concerns of phase three. A broadly acceptable phase-two description of the computerization life cycle is shown in Figure 7.1.

The life cycle representation was intended to provide a checklist for when different activities and possibly different people need to be brought into projects, as well as an overall pattern of resource requirements. This was often represented in graphical form as a 'snail curve' such as is shown in Figure 7.2.

The structured approach to computer systems development which diffused during phase two spawned new formulations of the life cycle. Not only were the

STAGE	DESCRIPTION
1. Information analysis	Analysis of user requirements and information needed, and the development of a set of specifications for the project.
2. Feasibility assessment	Development of a general approach to meeting these stated needs together with an assessment of its cost-effectiveness and feasibility (technical, economic and operational) for meeting the needs—this implies a proposal and selection of a project approach
3. Systems analysis and design	Definition of how the system proposed/accepted will operate—this covers system specifications and program specifications (i.e. design of input, processing, output, control and document flows)
4. Procedure and program development	Coding and debugging of programs to carry out the system's operations, and the writing of procedures for using the system
5. Conversion	Final testing of the system and conversion from the old system to the new one
6. Operation and maintenance	Operation of the system and its maintenance to keep it in an operable and up-to-date condition
7. Post-audit	Review and evaluation of the system (and its implementation activities) to audit results achieved against target objectives set, and to examine lessons learned to improve the next project's activities

FIGURE 7.1 Classical life cycle activities. Source: Gordon B. Davis (1975) Computer Data Processing, International Student Edition, p. 198

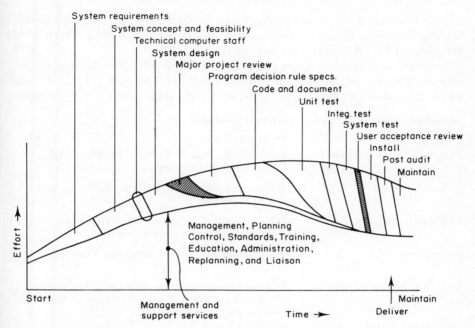

FIGURE 7.2 Classical life cycle in graphical form. Source: Duffy and Assad (1980, p. 42)

phases of the life cycle to represent a resource planning device, but their role as a people control mechanism was enhanced.

Early life cycle models specified *what* was to be done and *when* (inputs, files and outputs) in great detail. Overall project control was the aim. The structured approach added detail about *how* life cycle phases would be carried out (the content of structured programming, design and analysis). Structured design also emphasized ensuring that phases would be completed in their proper order. Each phase of work was to be marked by a milestone involving the production of some visible artifact that could be checked against the prior specification of what was to be produced during that phase. The output from each phase was to be completed and validated before the next phase began, in order to catch errors at an early phase. Sometimes this would involve formally handing over the project to a different set of people. In addition to the physical systems development process occurring in a strict sequence, a parallel or concurrent set of control phases were proposed. Along with the production of the physical detailed design of the system, a separate definition of an acceptable system and test cases upon which the system would be checked were to be prepared. A quality assurance group, separate from the project team, would conduct the final system testing.

By the late 1970s versions of the computerization life cycle as shown in Figure 7.1

came to be called the 'classical' life cycle, to distinguish new versions of the sequence of phases. Figure 7.3 gives a comparison of the 'structured' life cycle with the classical life cycle as summarized by Enger (1981).

Growing emphasis on meeting user needs in the late 1970s stimulated increased effort to discover and to understand those needs. This led to a gradual shift in emphasis from programming to analysis. Furthermore within analysis more

Classical system life cycle stages and products

STAGE	DESCRIPTION
1. Requirements analysis	Evaluate user request. Conduct feasibility study. Define user requirements. Prepare project plan
2. Logical design	Prepare general design specifications. Refine user system requirements
3. Physical design	Prepare detailed design specifications. Define subsystems. Design database structure
4. Program design	Code programs. Unit test programs. Document programs
5. System implementation	Perform subsystem testing. Perform system testing. Train user personnel. Establish conversion controls. Perform data conversion
6. System operation	Operate live system. Maintain new system. Evaluate system

Structured systems life cycle stages and products

1. Requirements analysis (survey)	Evaluate user request. Conduct feasibility study. Define user requirements. Prepare project plan
2. Logical design (analysis)	Transform user requirements. Refine logic structure of system
3. Structured physical design	Identify hierarchy of modules. Identify interfaces between modules. Finalize equipment configuration data. Prepare test plan
4. Top-down implementation	Code modules. Integrate modules
5. Acceptance test generation	Define acceptable system. Generate acceptance test cases
6. Quality assurance	Conduct final system testing. Train user personnel. Establish conversion controls. Perform data conversion
7. System operation	Operate live system. Maintain new system. Evaluate system

FIGURE 7.3 Classical system life cycle stages and products. Source: adapted from Enger (1981, pp. 2–5), with permission of Elsevier Science Publishing Co., Inc.

emphasis came to be placed on operational (rather than technical) feasibility; on organizational (rather than physical) computer system opportunities and constraints. In terms of the process of systems development this meant more effort was required at the front end, at what were traditionally thought of as the early phases of the classical computer system life cycle.

Growing emphasis on meeting user needs also stimulated increased efforts at the back end, at the latter phases, of the life cycle. If the measure of system success is its usefulness to users, then user acceptance of the system and user training also became more important parts of the system life cycle. Another consequence of increased importance attributed to user relations was that the very end of the system life cycle became blurred, or melded in, with the beginning of new system life cycles. This process of computer system regeneration began almost from the outset of business computing.

The practice of regular maintenance came to be accepted as a necessary part of computer procedures during phase one. That is, systems were delivered which only had been tested up to less than perfect standard. Further bugs would be found as part of the operation of the system. Users would become part of the long-run systems development process by acting as guinea pigs, by testing the system and signalling errors. These errors would then be 'corrected' more or less quickly, depending on how serious they were. A usual pattern would be for minor bugs to accumulate until developers got around to a system update. The computer department might notify users about discovered bugs, although the burden of keeping a record of known bugs on hand would more likely fall on user departments. That is, users had to adjust their procedures not only to working with systems that were designed and built in a separate and poorly understood department, but they also had to accept and adjust to flawed computer software. Certain bugs could only be cleared by completely rewriting (and redesigning) the system. Users often had to live with these problems, even if the computer department recognized them to be faults.

Once a computer-based payroll system had been introduced, once the savings this system represented had been realized, once the clerical staff to operate the old manual system had disappeared, then there was no going back to the old manual system. In many organizations it was soon realized that some manual facility had to be retained to deal with exceptional conditions. Gradually, during late phase one and phase two, most of these 'exception' conditions were incorporated into computer-based systems for straightforward applications. These *enhancements* took up an increasing proportion of DP department work. A more important source of work on enhancements was changing requirements. Demands on the earliest systems changed after the initial requirements were specified. For example, computerized payroll systems would have to be altered if changes in the way bonuses and overtime were to be paid occurred. Often changing contexts of the system stimulated enhancements—for example, changes in tax laws affecting payroll calculations. Enhancement demands grew substantially during phase two

STAGE	DESCRIPTION
1. Preliminary analysis	Perceived needs are explored and communicated to the extent that they gain acceptance by users
2. Feasibility analysis (organizational)	Early-stage cost–benefit analysis to determine if information systems are warranted. Is the system proposed in line with organizational objectives as well as technically and financially feasible?
3. Information system planning	Covering a period of up to five years as well as objectives and current information system capabilities to examine if it should include a forecast of developments that might affect the plan, project priorities and detailed resource requirements for the first two years
4. Feasibility analysis (project)	—Economic (can we afford it?) —Technical (can it be done with available technology and skills?) —Operational (will it work in the specific situation in the organization?)
5. Project planning	—Identification of project phases for control purposes —Establishment of work and documentation standards —Delegation of accountability —Appointment of the team, scheduling, budgeting, technical revision and sub-project control
6. Information analysis	—Output analysis —Decision analysis —Process analysis
7. System analysis	—How does the system work and why? —Ensure workable parts of the existing system are carried forward to the new system —Logical design, specification for input and output of the system, decision criteria and processing rules
8. System design (physical design)	Detailed system specification for programming—input, output, layouts, codes, processing steps and decision rules
9. Programming and procedure development	Coding, design and documentation of manual and needed computer procedures
10. Testing	Desk check, program test and debug

FIGURE 7.4 The information system life cycle. Source: adapted from Duffy and Assad (1980, pp. 47–51)

STAGE	DESCRIPTION
11. Conversion	Gathering data for files or databases, training end users, install and check out. Also test system in operational environment, psychological acceptance by end users, ceremonial hand-over
12. Operation	Routines, day-to-day running
13. Maintenance and modification	Correction of errors, incorporation of modification to solve problems, introduce improvements or incorporate system changes
14. Post-audit/review	This should be systematic and ongoing at all stages of management planning and control, standard, training/education, administration, replanning, liaison, communication, conflict resolution, change management, etc. Education of management an ongoing process but especially between stages 1 and 2.

FIGURE 7.4—Contd.

with new computer applications which did not simply replicate existing manual systems.

Enhancements, along with maintenance, represented a further reason, even in the early days of computing, for user contact with DP departments to be continuous, rather than limited to brief encounters at the beginning and end of the systems development process. However, during phase one and phase two these connections were not highly valued.

We may think of the articulation of phases of a computer life cycle as a language for conveying what procedures are required for computerization. Societies develop their language in directions that reflect their priorities.[3] We may chart changing priorities within computer systems development by noting the changing extent to which different parts of system life cycles are articulated.

What distinguished the structured system life cycle from the classical cycle was a more elaborate articulation of the middle phases (see Figure 7.3).[4] What came to distinguish phase-three views of the life cycle from phase-two views was just the opposite tendency, a more elaborate articulation of the beginning and end phases of the cycle; the periods of more intense user contact.

Two examples of phase three articulations of the computer system life cycle are shown in Figures 7.4 and 7.5.[5]

The main reason for such a detailed elaboration of the front end of the information life cycle as shown in Figure 7.4 is to ensure that systems fit in with overall organization plans, priorities and resources. The main reason for such a detailed elaboration of the back end of the DSS development life cycle as shown in Figure 7.5 is that user experience with the system is considered crucial for user acceptance and actual use of the system. During the 1970s more and more

STAGE	DESCRIPTION
1. Planning	User needs assessment and problem diagnosis
2. Application research	Identification of relevant fundamental approaches for addressing user needs and available resources (vendors, systems, studies of related experiences in other organizations and review of relevant research)
3. Analysis	Determination of best approach and specific resources required to implement it, including technical, staff, financial and organizational resources
4. Design	Detailed specifications of system components, structure and features
5. System construction	Technical implementation of the design
6. System testing	Collection of data on system performance to determine whether the system performs in accordance with design specifications
7. Evaluation	Determination of how well the implemented system satisfies users' needs and identification of technical and organizational loose ends
8. Demonstration	Demonstration of the fully operational system capabilities to the user community
9. Orientation	Instruction of top-level managerial users in the basic capabilities of the system
10. Training	Training of direct users in system structure and operation
11. Deployment	Operational deployment of the full system capability for all members of the user community
12. Maintenance	Ongoing support of the system and its user community
13. Adaptation	Planned periodic recycling through the above tasks to respond to changing user needs

FIGURE 7.5 The decision support system (DSS) development life cycle.
Source: adapted by special permission from the MIS Quarterly, Volume 8, Number 2, June 1984. Copyright 1984 by the Society for Information Management and the Management Information Systems Research Center at the University of Minnesota

emphasis was being placed on the front end of the life cycle, but it was only at the end of the 1970s that the back end began to receive more attention. Problems of implementation only became a prime concern in the 1980s.

Both Duffy and Assad, and Meador and Keen note that the phases of the life cycle need not be followed in a linear fashion. Both allow for project teams to return to earlier phases after experience with later phases has accumulated. The cycle would then be followed in an iterative fashion. Changes in the order of phases of life cycles were prescribed in order to ensure user acceptance of systems. This was a particularly important sign of the coming of phase three. Such an iterative process allows user interaction to occur at more than just the beginning and end of the life cycle. This allows the boundaries between the information systems (IS) department and the user department, defined as a provider–receiver barrier, to be lowered (see sections 8.2.6, 8.2.7 and 11.3.2).

7.3 DESCRIBING USER RELATIONS: WHO ARE THE USERS?

The term 'user' is ambiguous. There are several different people who interact with computer systems in different ways. Unfortunately they are all called users. This makes it difficult to explain how relations with users changed during phase two.

The concept of the user was first developed simply to distinguish core computer system builders from others associated with the system once it had been created. Until the 1970s, computer users were usually thought of either as user organizations or as specialists within those organizations. Note the following statement from Walter and Walter (1970):

> The user writes applications programs rather than systems programs. He writes for his specific configuration and, at most, anticipates growth for his installation and plans accordingly. (p. 25)

For hardware manufacturers and others selling parts of the computer systems core, it is still computer specialists in user organizations who would be regarded as the representatives of user organizations. Therefore these computer specialists would be thought of as the computer users.[6]

Within user organizations, during phase one and most of phase two the call for user involvement in system design was seen as a way of ensuring that the system would in fact carry out its intended purpose. User groups were groups of managers who would be exhorted and cajoled into specifying as clearly as possible exactly what the system should do in terms of what the existing manual systems did. A conception of users as managers, who either order the system or who oversee the existing functions that are partially or totally automated by new systems, persists in many companies.

There is an alternative view of who are the users. That is, those who directly work with the system. Sometimes they are distinguished by the term *end users*. They had been almost entirely non-management, non-computer specialist employees (at least until phase three). In the early days of batch production these end users would mainly have been three groups. First, there were low-level data entry or data preparation staff. Second, there were people who manually took output from the computer room and delivered it to user departments. Third, there were low-level staff in 'user departments' who extracted figures from print-outs in order to present results to the final consumer of the system. One example would have been payroll clerks who had made out pay-checks and who later would just distribute, and perhaps monitor, them. Another example were accounts clerks who used output to make up preliminary financial reports. Often final consumers of these systems were outside the organization: customers receiving invoices, tax authorities and shareholders receiving standardized financial information.[7]

In the ICON project we have found a strong cultural pattern in the meaning attributed to the term 'users'. 'Users', meaning end users or the staff of user departments, is much more likely to be intended when Scandinavian IS managers consider user involvement in systems development. US or British IS managers are more likely to think of users as the managers of user departments. This largely reflects the growth in worker influence over a wide range of what are traditionally considered to be management prerogatives in Scandinavia, particularly during the past two decades. However, even when Scandinavians consider user involvement in systems development they still often mean involvement by representatives of end users rather than the end users themselves. A data steward, for example may be a full-time shop steward. It is possible for user involvement by union representatives of end users to result in a lack of 'true' representation of end-user needs and problems. The substitution of user representatives for user managers will not automatically mean *effective* user involvement in system development (Friedman *et al.*, 1984).

A simple classification distinguishing system builders, users and managers or representatives of end users is insufficient. It obscures the fact that computer staff can act as users of systems and that user staff can build systems and process information. The system design process in particular is not completely separate from either system conception or from system operation. This is partly because the system is rarely 'complete'. Systems usually require maintenance and enhancement.

One way to get round this problem is to classify users as those involved with the system at various different phases in its life cycle. This suggests something like the following classification of users:

(1) The patron—fosters the process of computerization or of updating computer systems, particularly at the earliest phases of the life cycle. The patron may be the initiator of the system, the one who perceives the need/opportunity for a new computer system and sets the process in motion. The patron may also act as a kind of godfather to the system and to the systems developers, fighting for resources to be provided and for problems encountered to be overcome at later phases in the life cycle.

(2) The client[8]—the one for whom the system is intended. The person who will use the system in the sense of the one for whom the system's output is ultimately designed.

(3) Design interactors—individuals who are involved in the systems design process at specification or during development of the system.

(4) End users—individuals who are directly involved in manipulation of the system in operation, that is, system interactors, the man/machine interface.

(5) Maintenance/enhancement interactors—individuals who are involved in the further evolution of the system. These may split again into patrons, clients and interactors.

(6) Secondary users—it is important to have a secondary users category distinct from a product interactors category, as not all the individuals who are affected by the system come into direct contact with it. 'Secondary users' is a broad category. It includes the following:

   (a) People who have been displaced by the system. Often these are thought of as system victims. Their work has been automated.

   (b) Others whose work has been affected by the computer system. Some of these will also be adversely affected, such as workers whose jobs have only been partially automated. However, not all of these secondary users are adversely affected by computer systems. Some workers may be 'upskilled'. High-level managers may benefit from the centralization of organization control allowed by certain computer systems, although they had not acted as system patrons or clients.

   (c) People whose non-work life has been affected by systems. Again some of these may be considered victims, such as those whose privacy is invaded or who suffer from adverse military or environmental consequences of computer systems and of computer system failures. Others are positively affected, for example those who benefit from military successes or from improved crime detection.

   (d) User representatives such as official trade union representatives.[9] Certain user department managers will also act as user representatives, sometimes opposed to new systems because of expected adverse effects on their subordinates.

Any of these six categories of 'user' may work in what is formally called the IS department, they may work in the user department or they may simply be associated with the organization within which the system has been developed, either as customers or suppliers. We will refer to these categories of users when we discuss the literature on user relations problems in the next chapter.

There are other classifications of users. The elaboration of different categories of users has become a characteristic of phase three, when user relations have become so prominent. Martin (1982, pp. 100–104) distinguishes three categories of users:

(1) Indirect end users—people who use computers through other people, such as airline passengers booking flights through travel agents.

(2) Direct off-line users—people who specify business information for reports they ultimately receive, such as marketing managers.

(3) Direct on-line users—people who operate terminals, hands on, to gain information.

We would classify Martin's first two categories as system clients, and the third as end users. Rockart and Flannery (1983) subdivide end users into six subcategories:

(1) Non-programming end users—people who only access information through software provided by others. Theirs is a totally menu-driven environment.
(2) Command-level users—people who access data on their own terms. They learn enough about databases to do their daily work. They perform simple inquiries, calculations and generate reports.
(3) End-user programmers—people who use command and procedural languages to develop their own applications, some being used by other end users.
(4) Functional support personnel—people who provide support for end users within their functional areas on an informal basis. They are computer-sophisticated end users. People who are not viewed as computer professionals but who perform tasks that would be expected of computer specialists.
(5) End-user computing support personnel—people located in a central support organization, such as an information centre. They may develop application or 'support' software. They program in end-user languages.
(6) DP programmers—people who operate in a traditional DP organization, but who program in end-user languages.

This classification emphasizes the degree to which users manipulate the system and the degree of computer skill or sophistication users demonstrate. We will return to this classification in Chapter 13.

Another way to classify users is to divide between those who would regard the system as their master and those who would regard it as their slave. Those who are system masters use the system much like a set of tools. They are able to decide when to use a particular part of it, when to avoid the system altogether and even, perhaps, to modify parts of the system. Those who would regard the system as their master (system slaves) are people whose work is predetermined and paced by the system, or who must behave in a fashion predetermined by a computer system in other aspects of their lives (such as in their dealings with government agencies, financial institutions or the medical world).[10]

All the classifications of users specified above distinguish users by their relation to the system. A different way to classify users is in terms of their role in relation to the organization in which the computer is used. This may be done according to vertical or horizontal positions. Users may be classed vertically, in terms of their hierarchical position in the organization:

(1) top managers;
(2) divisional or departmental managers;
(3) foremen or supervisors;
(4) professional or technical staff;

(5) skilled workers; and
(6) semi-skilled or unskilled workers.

This classification may be used to indicate the relative power of users. In Chapter 9 we will show that one main reason for the rise in the power of users has been because more higher-level members of organizations have become end users.

Users may also be classified according to their degree of attachment to the organization, and particularly that part of the organization to which the system is directly aimed. For example:

(1) system clients;
(2) internal users other than clients;
(3) external users with long-term or important connections to the organization, i.e. regular or large customers, suppliers under a subcontracting relation, important shareholders, financiers;
(4) external users with irregular or insignificant connections to the organization, i.e. those who interact with the organization on a one-off basis or whose importance to the organization is minor because they are one of many interacting in this manner, such as the bulk of customers, shareholders and suppliers.

This classification will be of use when we discuss the future of computer systems development in Chapter 13.

ENDNOTES

1. 'Phases' is the term normally used in the literature. Therefore we will use it. The phases of the system development life cycle are not the same as the phases of computerization.
2. They became maintenance/enhancement interactors (see section 7.3).
3. For example, it is well known that Eskimos have many different words for snow.
4. Note that Enger truncates the beginning and end stages of his representation of the classical life cycle, as well as adding further stages to the middle of it, when he demonstrates the structured life cycle.
5. The life cycle representations in these two figures have different names. This reflects the elaboration of computer-based systems. No longer was computer systems development about computerizing a pre-existing manual system. Rather it was about further elaborations of pre-existing computer-based systems, and about creating new systems that had no manual counterpart, or at least no systematic manual counterpart (such as a decision support system).
6. This change began during the late 1970s with the sale of personal computers (PCs) directly to user department managers. The change was substantially accelerated after IBM entered the PC market in 1981. However, most computer equipment is still sold to specialist computer departments in user organizations.
7. Even during phase one there were real-time systems with end users who were skilled employees, such as air traffic controllers, pilots and navigators. However, some early real-time systems were also operated by low-level clerks, such as airline reservation systems.

8. For a clear distinction between clients and users, meaning end users or other interactors, see Knudsen (1984).
9. Data shop stewards in Norway and Sweden are a particularly interesting group of secondary users (see section 8.2.4).
10. The distinction between responsible autonomy and direct control management strategies introduced earlier relates closely to this classification of users. We would expect managers pursuing a responsible autonomy strategy to introduce computer systems in a manner that allows their subordinates to act as system masters. Those pursuing a direct control strategy would introduce computer systems that master or directly control their subordinates. According to some, user relations problems have been generated by a direct control type of philosophy towards end users, held not only by managers of end users but also by computer systems developers (see section 8.2.3).

Chapter 8

THE LITERATURE ON USER RELATIONS PROBLEMS

Expressions of concern over user relations have been expressed for as long as computers have been imaginable. They long predate the coming of phase three. However, we will argue that the impact of these expressions of concern on the practice of systems developers had been negligible before the late 1970s. Unlike the literature relating to software productivity problems discussed in section 5.1, there is no consensus on a single conference or piece of research or author who represented the major turning point in awareness of user relations problems among the computer community.

The user relations problems literature is vast. It appears in sources as disparate as *Communications of the ACM*, trade union pamphlets, medical journals, novels and films. In the next section we present a classification of eight different perspectives on user relations problems. These are primarily divided into two broad categories: user perspectives and computer systems developer perspectives. Vaguely these may be thought of as outsider and insider perspectives. In the following sections each of the eight categories are discussed in turn. The chapter ends with a comparison of these categories and a discussion of the timing and integration of these different perspectives on user relations problems.

8.1 A CLASSIFICATION OF THE USER RELATIONS PROBLEMS LITERATURE

Literature expressing concern over user relations will be reviewed in this section, both from user perspectives and from computer systems developer perspectives. Each of the different perspectives will be discussed in terms of the way representative writers express user relations problems, reasons for these problems and possible solutions. The eight perspectives on user relations discussed are represented schematically in Figure 8.1.

We have separated expressions of concern over user relations between perspectives from the users' point of view and those from systems developers' perspectives. Different *users' perspectives* are distinguished by categories of users defined independently from their use of computers. Members of society defined either as citizens or as employees of organizations may be analysed in terms of their needs and desires, quite separate from their connections with computer-based systems. The issues addressed by the four user perspectives discussed below

189

	Clients and secondary users:	End users and other interactors:
User perspectives	As society	As workers
	As citizens	As managers of end users
Computer systems developer perspectives		Computer systems developers as specialist users
	Requirements specification Problems	Implementation problems
		End user interface problems

FIGURE 8.1 Perspectives on computer user relations problems

concern the effects of computer-based systems on the prior aspirations of these members of society.

Users have been concerned with loss of control over political processes, over organization procedures and over their own work and the work of their subordinates. They have been concerned with the loss of jobs and skills, privacy and democratic rights, worker loyalty and individual productivity, associated with particular computer systems. They have been concerned that computerization will shape individual values and social institutions in the image of the computer itself and that the integration of societies stimulated by improved information technology will magnify the consequences of accident, error and evil design to global proportions. Users have also been concerned with what they have viewed as lost opportunities, a disappointment effect, in that expectations stimulated by the computer community have often been unfulfilled. Benefits from computer-based systems have been slow in coming and unanticipated costs have been high.

Expressions of concern from user perspectives about computer systems, systems developers and the systems development process are multitudinous. One way to acquire an understanding of this literature is to categorize it according to perspectives from different types of users. We have identified four rather different user perspectives (top half of Figure 8.1). The distinction between users as clients and secondary users of computer systems on one hand, and on the other hand end users and other interactors with the systems development process, represents one important cleavage in the literature. The literature expressing client and victim perspectives on user relations may be divided into one line which views users in global or societal term and a second, more specific line, which expresses concern for users as citizens in terms of their democratic rights. Literature expressing end-user and systems development interactor perspectives may be divided into a line which expresses concern from the perspective of end users as workers and a line from the perspective of the managers of end users or from the perspective of the department or organization containing end users.

User relations, as seen from *systems developers' perspectives*, generated certain problems from the outset of computing. One perspective on user relations was very influential during the 1960s and stimulated technical changes in the computerization process long before phase three. This was the perspective of computer systems developers in user organizations as computer users. What computer hardware manufacturers provided to their customers were computer systems made up of both hardware and software. Computer systems developers within user organizations mediated between this computer systems core and end users.

In their interface with end users, analysts and programmers in user organizations are the systems developers, but in their interface with the computer systems core suppliers they are users. Certainly they are more sophisticated than end users, but they are users nonetheless.[1] Complaints about their interface with computer systems core and with its suppliers became particularly vociferous in the late 1960s, with third-generation computer hardware.

Expressions of concern for user relations from the perspective of computer systems developers in user organizations may be divided into three separate lines of literature, relating to three distinct points of contact between users and the computerization process during the classical computer system life cycle. These are:

(1) the requirements specification, which was the traditional beginning of computer systems development;
(2) implementation, the traditional end of the development phases of the life cycle;
(3) the end user interface with the computer system in operation.

The four lines of literature on user relations from computer systems developers' perspectives may also be categorized according to types of users. The first type of user is the systems developers themselves, working in user organizations as systems interactors. User relation problems at the requirements specification phase were normally associated with users as system patrons and clients. Before phase three these have usually been managers of user departments. Problems at the implementation phase and with the user interface in operation were associated with end users. Before phase three these users were normally clerical-level or shop-floor-level employees, at least for commercial systems.

The literature from all eight perspectives discussed below has by no means been entirely negative or apprehensive—although negative attitudes which have been expressed often stem from unfulfilled promises. Each of the perspectives are discussed below as separate lines of literature, but there are overlaps. Those writing from one perspective have often been aware of literature that expresses concern for user relations from other perspectives. However, we will argue that the process of integrating the different lines of literature expressing concern for user relations is very recent. This we take to be an indicator of the transition to phase three.

8.2 PERSPECTIVES ON USER RELATIONS

8.2.1 Computer Systems and Society

Expressions of alarm at the wider effects of the diffusion of computer systems throughout society have usually reflected client and victim perspectives on computer systems. Often this view has been expressed in works of science fiction. Fears about the computer society are reminiscent of fears about the machine society, which have been expressed (often by poets) since the beginning of the Industrial Revolution.

The common fear is that computer-based systems will affect the core of human lives. In some versions people will no longer be involved in productive work, because this will all be automated. Sometimes this theme is expressed in positive terms, that people will be free to do more interesting things and that leisure time will be increased (Toffler, 1980). However, often the vision is that this will lead to violence and other antisocial behaviour because most people will be unable to pursue meaningful or socially useful activities (note the film *Clockwork Orange*, 1971, for example).

In some versions our emotions will be stimulated by purely artificial means, such as by sports or games [2] or by war. [3] Often the fear is not that the computers *per se* will control humanity, but rather that they will allow a small elite of technocrats or a political dictator, a Big Brother, to do so. Apprehensions concerning rule by technocrats were often expressed during the 1960s (Ellul, 1964; Boguslaw, 1965; Galbraith, 1967; Maynaud, 1968).

More recently, as computers have become more widespread, these apprehensions have been expressed somewhat differently. According to Kraemer *et al.* (1981), automation of administration concentrates political power into the hands of those who use the computer system, those who control its usage and those who understand it. The cleavage between the 'haves and the have-nots' of computing intimacy is coming to coincide with the cleavage between the haves and have-nots of political power.

The power of those who are intimate with computer software has also worried those concerned with crime. These fears have grown recently because personal computers and distributed processing in organizations have made computer crime easier (Ball, 1985).

Another strong fear is that the automation of weaponry will lead to nuclear war due to some technical malfunction (*Doctor Strangelove*, 1964; *Fail-Safe*, 1964), or the 'innocent' manipulation of a hacker [4] (*Wargames*, 1983). The earlier fears of push-button wars can be associated with the operationalization of the North American Air Defense (NORAD) system in 1960 (Sackman, 1975). More recently such fears have been regenerated by the use of electronically controlled ('smart') weapons (Walker, 1983) and by the US development of space weaponry known as the strategic defense initiative (or star wars) program (Canan, 1982; Fishlock, 1983; Parnas, 1985).

The basis of these fears is that computers (and especially the joining of computer technology with communications technology) is leading to an integration of human society. This integration is occurring without conscious human control, particularly without any democratic process of control. This leaves the instruments of that integration open to misuse of two sorts.

First, the instruments of integration may be transformed into instruments of control over a wider population and in a deeper or more intimate way than was hitherto possible (the dictatorship scenario). Even if they are used by legitimate political authority, the instruments are so powerful that they will tempt legitimate authority to act in an illegitimate way. A democratically elected government may use the technology in a manner that would be unacceptable to the electorate. This is the stuff of many fictional spy stories.[5]

Second, the technology is not understood well enough and not controlled well enough to prevent accidents or misuse by those who have never been authorized to use it. Minor human error or infringement by unauthorized people for illegitimate purposes can have much more serious consequences because of the sheer numbers of people covered by the technology, as well as the destructive capacity of the instruments controlled by the technology. The global village (McLuhan, 1964) allows certain accidents and misuses of technology to have global consequences.

Another fear is that in a computer-dominated society people will come to behave more mechanically, more rationally, but also more instrumentally. Our emotional facilities will wither for lack of exercise (note the film *Farenheit 451*, 1967). Computerization will encourage public policy to be based on the achievement of quantifiable targets, at the expense of aesthetic desires. The way things are done in general, the means, the 'style' of design, will be sacrificed for quantifiable ends (Cooley, 1976, Bridges, 1977).

Much of the concern here arises from the popularity of trying to describe the functions of the human brain as logical information processors, much like computers. Herbert Simon has been particularly influential in developing such models (Simon, 1957; Newell and Simon, 1972). While Simon and his followers emphasize the limits of human beings as information processors compared with computers, Simon's critics emphasize the inadequacies of computers compared with human beings. Dreyfus (1967; 1972; Dreyfus and Dreyfus, 1986), for example, emphasizes the emotional and physical limitations of computers. Following from this they are concerned about the de-emphasis of these aspects of humanity when computer systems are designed. 'What's wrong with technology is that it's not connected in any way with matters of the spirit and of the heart' (Pirsig, 1974).

Little from this line of concern has fed directly into the computing press or the texts of those who would teach or advise or manage systems developers. One reason for this is that little of this line of literature is based on formal empirical research.[6] Their broad strokes are usually addressed to the general public or to philosophers. Those who view the consequences of computer systems with such trepidation and in such broad terms may advise clients and potential victims to abandon or to sabotage computer systems (Hartmann, 1981), rather than suggest ways to improve user relations with them.[7] However, these writers have influenced contributors to the next three lines of literature.

8.2.2 Computer Systems and the Democratic Rights of Citizens

Demands for more open government have been a regular feature of public policy debate for centuries. Computerization of government records and computer support for the execution of public duties have stimulated additional fears for the democratic rights of citizens. These fears have stimulated specific demands for access to publicly held databanks, for information about prospective government systems and ultimately for direct public participation in systems design.

This line of literature is stronger in the USA than in Great Britain. During the mid-1960s, with the centralization of federal statistics in the USA, concern was expressed that computerized data would stimulate a substantial invasion of privacy (US House of Representatives, 1966; Westin, 1967; Baran, 1968; Miller, 1971). As mentioned above, these fears were also stimulated by spectacular revelations of misuse of information and of invasions of privacy connected with the Watergate scandal and the impeachment of President Nixon.

Since then, examples which generate particular fears of dire consequences from wrong and detrimental information residing in confidential databanks have been publicized. Such information could lead to credit refusal, failure to succeed with job applications or police suspicion. Even non-confidential data can lead to annoyance such as incorrect bills from public authorities (Rule, 1974; Sterling, 1979). In Great Britain official recognition of concern over invasion of privacy came later (Younger, 1972; White Paper, 1975a,b).[8]

A particularly important stimulus to calls for public participation in computer systems design has its roots in protest against plans for urban development during the 1960s. These protests were usually directed against either change of use of buildings or new urban transport systems (Bolan, 1967; Rudofsky, 1969). Contributors to this literature view user involvement in computerization decisions in the same way as citizen participation is viewed by progressives analysing urban planning (Fagence, 1977; Kling, 1982, 1987).

The key concept of democracy joins this line of literature to a very broad stream of political thought which has been particularly important in the USA. For many the key political value in the USA is democracy; that is:

> government by the people: the form of government in which the sovereign power resides in the people and is exercised either directly by them or by officers elected by them. (*Shorter Oxford English Dictionary*)

In the USA many more officers of local government are elected than in most other countries (such as the head of the local police). However, there is still a considerable local bureaucracy that is not elected. Not only are computer systems developers part of this non-elected bureaucracy, but also computer systems *patrons* normally are non-elected officers rather than local politicians. Many computer systems developed in local authorities appear to strengthen the position of local bureaucrats against that of the local politicians (Kling, 1978; Kraemer and Dutton, 1979; Markus, 1979; Danziger *et al.*, 1982). This issue has also aroused concern in Great Britain (Benington, 1976; Turton, 1977).

This line of literature has been particularly stimulated by the Urban Information Systems project (URBIS) carried out from 1973 to 1978 at the University of California, Irvine. The URBIS group produced a substantial literature during the late 1970s and 1980s (see especially Dutton and Kraemer, 1977, 1978; Kraemer *et al.*, 1981; Danziger *et al.*, 1982; King and Kraemer, 1985; Danziger and Kraemer, 1986). The focus of their project was to evaluate the impact of computers on local government services and decision making. In particular they were concerned with who controls the technology and whose interests are served by the technology (Danziger *et al.*, 1982, p. 2).

The researchers concluded that computing was used to reinforce the dominant political coalition in the local governments they studied. This they label reinforcement politics. They warn that the use of computing in local government is 'inherently undemocratic', and that computing has been used

> for internal administrative support and for increasing bureaucratic and social control rather than for service delivery to citizens.

Furthermore,

> computing has rarely been used to enhance citizen participation in government, to inform citizens of their rights (e.g. entitlements and allowances under existing laws) and duties, and to provide new information services to citizens. (Danziger *et al.*, 1982, p. 222)[9]

Their recommendations are that computing should be organized more democratically, to make it more responsive to interests and values other than those of the dominant political coalition. The researchers clearly state that they consider public participation to be a value to be pursued for its own sake, rather than merely a means to greater efficiency.[10] The researchers view participation by end users within the bureaucracy positively. However, although they consider end-user participation in systems design to be a form of democratization, the URBIS team clearly regard this as less important than developing systems which reflect and encourage the wider ideal of citizen's democracy.[11]

8.2.3 Computer Systems and Humanistic or Sociotechnical Management

A group of social scientists and management consultants have argued in favour of employee involvement in certain management decisions for many years. This line

is often known in the USA as the human relations school of
t thought. The human relations approach began with research at the
plant of Western Electric in 1927. It became associated with theorists
at Harvard during the 1930s (Mayo, 1933; Roethlisberger and Dickson, 1939).
The key tenet of the human relations school is that making workers feel that they
belong to the company will lead to increased labour productivity. Positive worker
attitudes towards the company are achievable through psychological techniques.
One way to motivate workers is to involve them in decisions affecting the quality of
their working life, or at least to make them feel that they have participated in these
decisions.

Human relations theorists distinguish the participative and humanistic style of
management they recommend from what they regard as the traditional
authoritarian approach, associated with Frederick Taylor.[12] McGregor (1960)
has labelled these different views of management, rather unimaginatively, as
Theory X (the authoritarian approach) and Theory Y (the human relations
approach).

The most important influence on the computing world derived from the human
relations approach to management is what is known as the sociotechnical systems
approach. The sociotechnical systems approach to management was developed at
the Tavistock Institute of Human Relations in London (Rice, 1963; Trist *et al.*,
1963; Trist, 1981). It has been particularly influential in the Scandinavian
countries. It is based on the idea that there is considerable freedom of choice in
organizational design because technical factors do not completely determine social
factors. It is a major task of management to match social and technical systems
within the organization in the most appropriate way. Also what is appropriate will
depend on the organization's environment; that is, organizations must be viewed
as open systems. It is a basic tenet of the sociotechnical approach that worker
participation in decision making and improvements in the quality of working life
will improve worker satisfaction and this will lead to higher productivity (Emery,
1978). Measuring job satisfaction is a major theme of sociotechnical research. Job
satisfaction measurement of computer specialists in the US is primarily associated
with Couger (Couger and Zawacki, 1980; Couger, 1988).

Adherents to the sociotechnical approach distinguish themselves from the US
human relations approach to management in that they believe that once conflict
has been built into a work situation only structural change can remove it. There is
little that can be achieved by means of a human relations approach, of trying to
change attitudes (Mumford, 1987, pp. 63–64). However the sociotechnical
approach has clearly been influenced by the US human relations school.

The most important proponent for using sociotechnical theory to improve user
relations with computer systems has been Enid Mumford (Kubicek, 1983; Ehn
and Kyng, 1987). Since the late 1960s she has continually argued for user
participation in systems design (Mumford and Ward, 1968; Hedberg and
Mumford, 1975; Mumford and Hensall, 1979; Mumford, 1979, 1983, 1987).

Her influence has been channelled through IFIP (International Federation for Information Processing), which has stimulated collections of articles with titles like *The Human Side of Information Processing* (Bjorn-Andersen, 1980) and *Systems Design for, with and by Users* (Briefs *et al.*, 1983). Also important for spreading the influence of Mumford's approach was an international project into the banking systems carried out in the late 1970s in four countries, which was based on sociotechnical principles (see Bjorn-Andersen *et al.*, 1979). In this Mumford directly addressed her work to 'professional systems designers and managers interested or involved in the design of computer systems' (Mumford, 1979, p. 1).

According to Mumford, major stumbling blocks to computer user job satisfaction are the values which influence systems designers:

> We shall argue that systems are designed in terms of a vision of man and man's needs and abilities which is greatly influenced by the systems designers own values, training and experience ... These models do not typically include human factors such as desire for job satisfaction. (Hedberg and Mumford, 1975, p. 34)

Essentially computer systems developers adhere to Theory X or a direct control type of management strategy. The solution is to change the systems designers' model of man by training, by user (and trade union) involvement in the systems design process, and by increasing user competence and power. Mumford is also aware that systems developers' value systems are influenced by the reward system under which they work. Therefore their values also reflect those of top management. Recommending a new value system on the part of top management ties Mumford's views on computer use and good sociotechnical systems to the general sociotechnical (and human relations) mission of sensitizing all management to sociotechnical problems.

Although the Tavistock Institute is based in London and Mumford works at the Manchester Business School, the influence of the sociotechnical systems approach has been strongest in the Scandinavian countries.[13] There a number of government-supported experiments in sociotechnical systems design have been undertaken under the label of industrial democracy (Emery and Trist, 1969; Emery and Thorsrud, 1976).

Scandinavian projects began with the Norwegian Industrial Democracy Project, jointly supported by the Norwegian Employers' Confederation (NAF) and the Norwegian Federation of Trade Unions (LO) in 1960. The real diffusion of the sociotechnical approach occurred in Sweden in the late 1960s.[14]

Although Swedish projects were initially jointly carried out by the Employers Confederation (SAF) and the Swedish Federation of Trade Unions (LO), the Swedish LO lost its enthusiasm for these projects when it became clear that changes were normally restricted to the shop-floor level. Criticism of the sociotechnical approach in Scandinavia led to what has been called the collective resource approach to systems design, which takes a computer users as workers and as trade unionists perspective (Ehn and Kyng, 1987). However, as Bansler (1987) points out, sociotechnical principles are not always applied in the Scandinavian countries with management's interest in mind. The co-determination law in Sweden allows unions to hire independent consultants to help them to participate. Consultancy companies, that only work for trade unions and which still use sociotechnical principles, have been set up during the 1980s.

The general political and industrial relations climate in continental Europe (particularly in the Scandinavian countries, but also in Germany) has been more supportive of industrial democracy owing to the dominance of social democratic governments since the Second World War and the implementation of laws on the working environment and co-determination in industry.[15] In these countries management and worker organizations at national levels have been more prepared to cooperate on experiments in industrial democracy, including experiments on worker influence on computer systems design.

8.2.4 Computer Systems and Workers

The fourth line of literature comes from trade unionists and radical social scientists who fear that computer systems will result in job losses, deskilling and a general shift in the frontier of control away from labour. These fears long predate computers, as do fears about the general effects of automation on society. They must also be seen against a background of very positive literature on computers and work. Licklider (1960, 1965), for example, viewed the effect of computers on work in terms of the creation of 'man–computer symbiosis' in which the computer is able to liberate man's creative energy in the performance of tasks. The computer would take over the routine aspects of tasks, leaving the creative and conceptual activities to people.[16]

An enormous literature in the form of pamphlets and newspaper articles has been written by rank and file workers, official trade unionists and politicians about the dangers of mechanization. A fairly recent example, specifically addressing the effects of computerization on workers, is Jenkins and Sherman's book, *The Collapse of Work* (1979). In the public's mind the unions have always been set against all new technology. Certainly there has been a strong tendency towards machine breaking and other sabotage of equipment since the earliest years of the Industrial Revolution (Brown, 1977). Luddism is a common pejorative. There have been certain celebrated union actions against computer-based systems in the UK, particularly in the printing industry. However, a much more common stance of unions has been to eschew direct confrontation over new technology. In the USA by the end of the 1930s the main trade unions (represented by the AFL and later the AFL–CIO) had taken a clear decision to concentrate their efforts on struggle over improving the quantitative rewards from work. Issues of worker discretion over task performance and job design, and therefore issues of technical choice, were not subjected to collective bargaining. These would be accepted areas of management prerogative (Cole, 1979, pp. 104–105). There is little evidence of official collective bargaining with trade unions over work design issues in the USA.

This attitude has also prevailed among British trade unionists. They have generally been wary of participation in agreed managerial functions, fearing that participants will be manipulated, that they will become infected with management's perspective and betray the rank and file (Williams, 1987).

However, there has always been a vociferous tendency among British trade unionists and especially among certain Labour Party politicians in favour of various forms of industrial democracy.[17] This grouping had become particularly influential during the first half of the 1970s in Great Britain, matching the high period of Tony Benn's influence in the Labour Party.[18] Although this group's direct influence has waned considerably since then, they have encouraged unions in Britain to take a more proactive stance towards new technology.[19] This culminated in the 1979 report *Employment and Technology*, in which the British Trades Union Congress (TUC) proposed that unions should try to influence the decision-making process concerning computer-based new technology. They recommended that normal company- and plant-level collective bargaining should be extended to include technological development. Standards for 'new technology agreements' were recommended specifically to include safeguards against the feared negative effects of computer-based systems.[20]

Nevertheless, two important effects of these new technology agreements for user relations are:

(1) That disappointment with the results of new technology agreements has led some unions to propose direct participation in systems development (CAITS, 1984; APEX, 1985).
(2) Pushing for the effects of new technology to be put onto the collective bargaining agenda has increased management's awareness of the importance of user relations and has encouraged management and organization theorists to recommend union involvement in systems design (Eason, 1981; Wainwright and Francis, 1984; Francis, 1986).

It is illuminating to compare this line of literature with the second line discussed above, with the perspective on users as citizens. The aim of those writing from the users as citizens perspective appears to be to infuse 'social values' into the design of computer systems, by which they mean the values of 'the public' primarily as client users. The method usually centres on user participation in design. The aim of those writing from the users as workers perspective has been to enmesh the systems development process into already existing collective-bargaining procedures and thereby to protect workers' interests.

The line, concentrating on users as citizens, tends to take a 'pluralist' view of group actions within organizations to develop computer systems. They analyse conflicting interests between groups of users defined by their functional position in the organization. Contributions to the users as workers perspective take a class view of group actions within organizations. They view conflicts of interest within organizations in terms of groups defined by their hierarchical position. For those writing from the users as citizens perspective, computer systems developers represent a separate group with their own interests. However, these technical specialists will usually become aligned with the dominant political coalition within organizations. For those writing from a users as workers perspective, computer systems developers are usually thought of as the representatives of management. Certainly Braverman and Kraft distinguish certain people involved in computer systems development as primarily executors, groups of workers who have been deskilled like any other group. However, the link between computer specialists and users as members of the same class (even as members of the same trade union), pursuing common aims, has rarely been raised either in Great Britain or the USA, although this approach has been developed in the Scandinavian countries.

In the Scandinavian countries a distinctive approach to computer systems design has been developed through a number of large research projects.[21] This has been labelled the collective resource approach to systems design (Bansler, 1987; Ehn, 1988).[22] According to the collective resource approach: 'Good systems design becomes a question of democratization of working life, of influential participation by workers and their trade unions' (Ehn, 1988, p. 24). A key aspect of the collective resource approach is that users as workers should become an integral, but not dominated, part of the systems development process through data shop stewards and other workers being part of systems development teams, with access to sources of independent specialist advice on the implications of various decisions on worker interests. Common education of workers and computer systems developers involved in systems design projects is another important element of the collective resource approach.

8.2.5 Computer Systems Developers as Specialist Users

As mentioned above (section 8.1), to hardware manufacturers and those selling parts of the computer systems core, computer systems developers in user organizations are thought of as users. Management dissatisfaction with software productivity in the 1960s could be interpreted from the point of view of computer systems developers in user organizations as dissatisfaction with the purchased computer systems core. Expectations generated among patrons, clients and end users were disappointed, not only because of a software productivity gap compared with the improvements in hardware, but because the combination of systems software and hardware delivered to user organizations was less sophisticated and less easy to work with than computer specialists in user organizations were led to expect. Many writers from within the computing community complained that soaring software costs and late deliveries to end users within user organizations were a symptom of problems deeper than that of management control over the mediating process. The solution was not simply to try to increase computer systems developer productivity, but also to get hardware suppliers to deliver computers that were easier to work with, more user-oriented.

Many saw user organizations as the victims of competitive strategies of hardware suppliers. This reached something of a crisis point for many large users during the early part of phase two. Demand for computers among large users was already well established by the 1960s. In addition, potential enormous improvements in cost/performance ratios from the coming third generation of computer hardware were well advertised to these users. This allowed hardware suppliers to sell third-generation computers based on technical rather than operational specifications. Detailed specifications would be available from independent sources concerning idealized running speeds and storage capacities, but outer rings of the computer core would be less clearly specified. Performance predictions were extrapolated from internal specifications of new equipment. This did not take into account extra time and storage required for more software control structures, poor quality of object code generated by compilers and, most significant, 'the inability of the user to perceive and to control, let alone optimize, the intricate interrelation between system components and the new systems architecture' (Bouvard, 1970, p. 120).

Many operational problems had to be discovered by users because systems were inadequately tested. Generations of hardware came to be viewed by specialist users as generations of horror (Grosh, 1970), of frustration (Bouvard, 1970) and of trauma (Seidel, 1970):

> Traditionally, software supplied by manufacturers is late, costly, and imperfect. The additional charge that software is needlessly over-complicated is also heard, with increasing volume, as user trauma mounts... Attempting to do too much, too soon— as a result of what might be termed 'marketing fright'—is a common pitfall for software planners. (Seidel, Software Systems Manager, Informatics, 1970, p. 132)

The third generation of computer hardware allowed enormous improvements in internal speeds, storage capacity and machine reliability. The hardware manufacturers' strategy was to create a comprehensive operating system, i.e. to use these improvements as a foundation for a layer of software around the hardware. The idea was, as IBM's Corporate Director of Programming stated at the MIT conference of 1961, to develop machine intelligence as a substitute for human intelligence in programming by attempting to 'cover up all aspects of hardware' with software, with an operating system (Sayre, 1962, p. 265). IBM's massive OS/360 project was the most important example of this strategy.

In trying to shield users from dealing with hardware directly, an interface with systems software was substituted for a hardware interface. This was not a happy experience in computer departments of large user organizations. The systems software interface was difficult to work with for a number of reasons.

First, as with earlier operating systems provided by hardware manufacturers, the interface reflected hardware facilities rather than user requirements. For example, time-sharing facilities were designed to allow sharing of computer power, but in DP departments the need was to share data files.

Second, the operating system for each third-generation computer reflected a particular marketing strategy of hardware manufacturers. This was to make their entire range of computers compatible with each other. This strategy was most notably pursued by IBM with their 360 series.[23] This was clearly done to lock customers into the IBM 'family' of computers, to allow them to trade up computers with a minimum of disruption as long as they stayed within the family. The price of this facility for users was a more difficult entrance into IBM's third-generation family. By using common components and common instruction sets, efficiency and simplicity in relation to any one size of computer in the family was sacrificed. Also the system was too large and complex to be manipulated or adapted any way developers at user installations pleased, in ways other than the standards set by IBM. The consequences of non-standard alterations could not be foreseen.

A third problem was that third-generation operating systems were designed on the presumption that the protection from hardware that they provided would lead to fewer programming errors by users. Therefore they provided poorer debugging facilities and restart and recovery procedures than some second-generation systems software (Bouvard, 1970, p. 121). Another symptom of this attitude was the complex, product-oriented (rather than user-oriented) documentation provided, at least during the first half of phase two. The documentation was designed as a reference work, rather than a teaching aid.[24] Systems developers in user organizations needed a teaching aid because little of their experience working with second-generation systems software was applicable to the new operating systems. In addition it was difficult to convert applications software from second- to third-generation machines.

We should note that OS/360 was a tremendous improvement in the software provided by manufacturers. It did significantly protect computer systems developers at user installations from having to deal with many of the particularities of different types of (IBM) hardware. It offered a wide range of facilities which were available in different operating systems, but none provided them all.

One effect of all this was that most user organizations of any size had to employ specialist systems programmers to deal with the direct interface with the operating system.[25] In the first phase hardware costs were not only the major expense in user organizations, they were also primarily an overhead cost, a fixed cost. The hardware rental charge had to be paid no matter how many applications were being developed or operated. During phase two, not only did software come to absorb a larger proportion of computing costs, but also the proportion of software costs which were overheads rose. Systems software not only occupied a great deal of computer time and storage capacity, it also occupied substantial and expensive programming staff time (Campbell, 1970).

8.2.6 Requirements Specification Problems

During the 1970s the emphasis in developing an engineering type of approach to increasing productivity of computer systems developers gradually shifted from structured programming methods to structured design and then structured analysis methods (Rhodes, 1973; Chapin, 1981; Connor, 1981; Nunamaker and Konsynski, 1981). The value of programming a system in a structured, standardized way could be compromised if the collection of modules that individual programmers were writing did not together reflect a logical, and easily understandable, structured system.[26]

A key corollary of this was that a logical and structured system could only be produced by following a logical and structured procedure. This encouraged an adaptation of views of the system development life cycle from a set of steps that described how a system was produced, to a prescription of how a system should be produced. An important feature of recommended life cycles was that they allowed enough time and care to be taken in specifying system characteristics and overall structures at early phases of the life cycle, before coding took place. Modifications and corrections of errors clearly becomes progressively more difficult and more expensive at later phases in the life cycle. Therefore in order for the overall system to be structured and to minimize late modifications, a clear, unambiguous and correct specification of the system requirements is required:

> Conventional wisdom as I understand it, asserts that before any code is written there must be a set of complete and detailed written specifications of what the system is required to do, and, perhaps in lesser detail, how it is to do it. I have heard people with international reputations in software engineering assert, I might say somewhat stridently, that it is virtually immoral to begin coding without complete specs. (McCracken, 1981, p. 446)

The problem then was how to 'find all the end user's requirements and describe them without any ambiguity' (Dambrine, 1981, p. 342). This could be thought of as two different problems. The first is the elicitation or identification of user requirements. The second is the assurance of the accuracy of the requirements specification. The problem of assurance is to find a system of representation of requirements that will allow both analysts and users to judge that the requirements are correct, that they are consistent, accurate and complete (such a division was made by Naumann *et al.*, 1980). With the dominance of an engineering approach to systems development during the 1960s and 1970s, it was the latter of these two problems that guided work on requirements specification. The problem of elicitation was assumed to be soluble by accurate or efficient methods of representation.[27]

A stream of techniques emerged during the 1960s and 1970s that attempted to create languages, by which analysts could elicit, interpret and judge user requirements unambiguously (a summary of these techniques is presented in section 10.2). Many were computer-aided. They held out the possibility of consistent and accurate definitions of user requirements in a form that could automatically be transformed into programmable system specifications. However, the use of these languages or systems of representation was limited. When used, such systems were rarely used to communicate with users. Rather they remained techniques internal to computer departments, for analysts to communicate among themselves and with programmers and computer managers.

From the mid 1970s, however, more and more conferences and papers began to appear which emphasized continuing poor communication between systems analysts and top managers or end-user managers. For example, the theme of a conference at the University of California at Los Angeles in the mid-1970s was 'Are you going the right thing, or merely doing the thing right?' (referred to in Carlson, 1981, p. 25). Analysis and design errors were revealed to be far more common than coding errors (during the implementation phase and beyond). Some suggested a ratio of almost 2:1. It was also emphasized that the cost of errors was tied to the length of time between when in the life cycle they were made and when they were discovered. It was suggested that more than two-thirds of analysis and design errors were found by users during or after acceptance tests, while only 25% of coding errors were found at that late phase of the life cycle (Bell and Thayer, 1976; Daly, 1977; Connor, 1981).

For some this poor communication problem occurred because analysts were not using the tools available or not using those tools correctly. For example, at a conference in 1980, Chapin (a major exponent of flow charts) deplored the diversity of graphic tools.

> More than fifty graphic tools are available . . . All this diversity degrades the quality of the communication possible with the graphic tools . . . The major forces working for diversity appear to be ignorance, lassitude, and deficiency . . . Employers have been very relaxed about setting and enforcing local standards for their employees to follow. The professional societies in their publications do very little to encourage the use of the standards. (1981, p. 123).

If this is the reason for poor communication, solutions to the problem lie in tougher computer management and better training of analysts. For some the reasons for such a diversity of tools and user relations problems were still symptoms of the basic inadequacy of systems development methods. Whether or not developers were doing the right thing, they were still not doing their thing right. The answer was automation of the systems development process, which would then allow users greater access to the process. Work on computer-aided systems development techniques, which began late in phase one, has continued during phase three. In particular, work on techniques that integrated requirements elicitation, assurance of requirements specifications and translation of accurate specification into working systems were being developed (see section 10.2).

For some, the answer to poor communication with users lay in finding a better requirements definition language, a better form of representing user needs. According to Michael Jackson, for example, the problem with most models for requirements analysis[28] was that these models took as their starting point the need to specify the system function, ignoring the 'real world with which the system is concerned'. According to Jackson, the common complaint of users of DP systems is that the 'the analyst doesn't understand the business'. This springs from a failure to agree on an explicit model of the real world.

> . . . it is not surprising that the delivered system so often fails to meet the user's needs when the user's view of reality differs from that of the system builder. (Jackson, 1981, p. 186)

What is needed, according to Jackson, is a better model of reality outside the computer system (not a model of the computer system itself, which would be used to manage the systems development effort or even one to help guide implementation).[29] Work on such models has continued during the late 1970s and 1980s (see sections 10.2, 11.3.2 and 13.5.1).

For others the whole approach to requirements analysis of the 1960s and 1970s was wrong. The fundamental problem was one of elicitation, not representation. If poor elicitation techniques are the reason for poor communication then, according to some, the path to discovering the right thing to do is interviewing techniques:

> With the advent of truly large scale information systems development we have witnessed within the systems profession a growing recognition of the importance of interpersonal communication skill development, in general, and interviewing skill development in particular. Despite a heightened awareness, the current level of resident expertise is low as a result of many years of prior neglect. (Semprevivo, 1981, p. 119)

For others the elicitation problem could be solved by better education for analysts about user areas and hiring analysts whose personalities and background were more suited to communication with users (for example, the old dictum that good programmers do not necessarily make good analysts, see section 10.1).

For many others the reason for poor communication lies in the system life cycle. One problem with the life cycle concept is that as a narrative tool it does not fit the 'natural' flow of work for a given application. Analysts 'are not permitted contact with the appropriate people or because they are forced to work at a level either too high or too low, their expertise is inappropriate' (Freeman, 1981, p. 323). The second problem with the life cycle, as it is normally used, is that it does not allow for iterative procedures that are a normal part of any good communication process. Good communication is a two-way activity that often requires each party to 'go away and think' about the issues and then return with further information and analysis. The traditional life cycle presumes that requirements specifications can be achieved in a complete and final form at the beginning of the computer systems development process. In a paper entitled 'A Maverick Approach to Systems Analysis and Design' presented in 1980, McCracken declared 'WARNING: Experience has shown that formal detailed specifications are hazardous to the health of your applications development process' (1981, p. 446). Specifications do not improve communication because user requirements are hard to verbalize and they are likely to change between the requirements specification phase and the operationalization phase of the system life cycle.

> Some one has suggested that the plaintive cry of the user is 'I can't tell you what I want, but I'd recognize it if you showed me one!' (p. 447)

If the system life cycle, and particularly its petrification of requirements definition as the first phase, is the reason for poor communication with users, then the solution to the problem lies in prototyping according to a growing number of insiders in the field from the late 1970s (McCracken, 1981; McCracken and Jackson, 1981).[30]

8.2.7 Implementation Problems

The literature on implementation problems from the computer systems developer perspective has traditionally been quite distinct from the literature on requirements specification. Requirements specification issues had become an integral, but distinct, part of the systems analysis literature since phase one, when systems analysis had become a well-defined subject. Implementation issues had rarely been discussed as a distinct subject within the systems analysis literature before the mid-1970s.[31] Generally the implementation literature has had a much shorter history than the literature on requirements specification problems.[32] It was less extensive, at least until the 1980s. It has been more directly influenced by the literature expressing user perspectives discussed above.

Implementation problems literature has also been generated more in Europe than the requirements problems literature. This has been noted by Turner (1981, p. 495). Friedman *et al.* (1984) have attributed this to the strength of trade unions and social democratic governments in northern European countries. In addition far fewer methods and techniques have been developed to deal with implementation problems compared with the enormous flow of requirements-oriented technology.

There is some confusion over the meaning of the term 'implementation' in the literature. Four different meanings of implementation may be found. The definition we will begin with in this section is most commonly used by computer systems developers and those writing from their perspective. For them implementation is a phase in the computer system life cycle. It is traditionally the phase between completion of computer systems development and the operation or live running of the system. It may include a formalized procedure for acceptance of the system. It usually involves passing over documentation to users. It may involve training of users. This is the most narrow definition of implementation.

A second, somewhat broader definition is common in the computer science literature. There implementation is regarded as a process of converting a 'mental' design into a 'real' computer program. It therefore concerns the phases of physical design and program design of the classical system life cycle (Macro and Buxton, 1987, Chapter 8).

A third definition includes the whole process of computer systems development and operation. In this sense, to implement a new computer system is to introduce it into an organization. Whatever effort is required to do so is part of implementation. This meaning of implementation is common in the operations research and management science literature (OR/MS):

> implementation occurs when an organization has serious problems, and a group of 'experts' examine the problems, who attempt through their examination to help the managers of the organization to make the best choice to gain the really important goals of the organization. (Churchman, 1975, p. 23)

Under this definition OR/MS practitioners consider implementation as a process of diffusion of innovations or of models or 'solutions'. In the computer systems context, it would refer to the diffusion of types of systems.

A fourth definition of implementation is that it is a component of organizational change. This definition is the one most likely to be used by those writing from user perspectives. This definition stresses the long-term nature of implementation. It melds into the notion of implications or consequences of the operation of computer systems.

During the late 1970s the latter two definitions began to appear with increasing frequency in textbooks on computer systems development (for example, Wetherbe, 1979), but especially in textbooks concentrating on the development of management information systems (for example, Lucas, 1978) and decision support systems (Keen and Scott Morton, 1978; Sprague and Carlson, 1982). This we take as a measure of the increasing importance attributed to the implementation process and to user relations in general during the late 1970s.

In an early paper Ackoff (1960) suggested that there were three factors that led to implementation failures. First, powerful and enthusiastic patrons within an organization, who had been backing projects, often left or were transferred. This left projects without a power base and lacking continuity. Second, projects lacked top management support. Third, end users often obstructed projects in the interest of their own political power. Similarly an early (and often-cited) study of the implementation of a computer system (Mann and Williams, 1960) concluded that negative reactions by end users reduced the effectiveness of the system. This study included data on user reactions (accounting department clerks) collected during five years after the system was introduced.

According to Ackoff, the underlying problem was that systems developers did not have enough power in organizations. They ought to complain, to insist on formal contracts, never to work for free and to be certain of reporting only to high-level user management. Although this was clearly an early phase-one perspective, there is ample evidence that throughout phases one and two computer systems developers have considered problems of implementation to have been caused by

resistance and lack of top management support to overcome this
re the primary reasons for such problems.[33]

ance was commonly attributed to user pathology, to users' patho-
logical fear of change and especially of new technology. Note the following
quotation from a leading textbook on management information systems of the
1970s:

> Resistance to change is a common phenomenon. In some cases, the resistance is very
> small and the affected persons adjust quickly to the new system. But in extreme cases,
> the reaction can be subversion or destruction of the new system. The reason for this
> resistance is generally that change is threatening. (Davis, 1974, p. 425)[34]

Considering implementation problems to reflect the deficiencies of others led to
two attitudes towards implementation by computer systems developers. The first
was to try to cure this pathology by salesmanship. Users had to be taught what was
good for them. They had to be convinced to do things in a new way. They had to be
counselled not to fear change.[35] The second attitude to user pathology was to
ignore it. Users were viewed as 'troublesome petitioners somewhere at the end of
the line who had to be satisfied with what they got' (Sackman, 1971).

While ignoring the problem seems to have been common practice in the field,
salesmanship was the recommended strategy in the literature. According to Davis
(1974):

> reasons for resistance represent fear of what may happen. The actual event is usually
> less traumatic than thinking about it. In other words, uncertainty is a cause of
> increased resistance. This suggests that methods, which reduce uncertainty will assist
> in reducing resistance ... the way to reduce uncertainty is to increase information.
> (p. 426)

Davis then goes on to recommend the following:

First, that users be encouraged to initiate projects themselves.

Second, that users be included in project groups 'where feasible' (such as feasibility
study and information analysis phases).

Third, that a user advisory group be established to supervise the project from the
user department.

Fourth, that 'informational and feedback' sessions be held, with employees at each
level who will come in contact with the system, before and after both design and
implementation phases of the system life cycle.

Fifth, that systems developers should 'not attempt to install a system which is not
debugged'.

A number of features of this statement of problem and solution are worth noting.
First, the problem is basically the 'fault' of the users. It is due to *their* fear and *their*
resistance. The practice of systems development, the attitudes and education of

systems developers, the very system itself, are not the problems and are not the reasons for resistance.

Second, the solution is time-consuming and therefore expensive. Item four would clearly require considerable systems development resources. Item five is simply wishful thinking in the absolute terms in which it is stated. Large and complex systems are almost never delivered entirely free of bugs. Debugging is costly. Eventually diminishing returns set in. Trying to reduce errors is simply good practice, but methods for reducing bugs are not linked to implementation problems in this statement.

With the problem so defined there is little incentive for systems developers to put forward much effort into the solution. However, the solution suggested would require considerable effort on the part of both users and systems developers.

A third notable feature of the statement is that the solution to the problem is not confined to the implementation phase of the traditional system life cycle. The solution lies in action taken primarily at early phases in the process; at initiation, at feasibility study, at information analysis and at design phases. The solution to the implementation problem is bound up with the requirements specification problem. This points towards future formulations of implementation problems and their solutions. However, a fourth notable feature of this solution is that user communication is not recommended for the 'middle phases' of the system life cycle—coding and testing are not touched.

The overall label that Davis placed on his solution set, user participation and communication, was emphasized more and more in the literature from the mid-1970s. Also the meaning and rationale of participation gradually changed. Participation has come to be seen less and less as one-way communication from developers to users in order to overcome user resistance. Instead researchers have increasingly recommended user involvement as a two-way process, as a mutual learning process (Boland, 1978), in order to improve the effectiveness of delivered systems.[36]

Even in terms of the limited meaning of user participation and communication recommended by Davis in 1974, the practice of implementation seems to have fallen short of the prescription. Mumford reports a 'remarkable' lack of contact between end users and computer specialists, which 'shows alarming deficiencies not only in consultation but in straight forward communication' (1972, p. 144). She cites the following end-user reactions to implementation procedures (p. 144):

> They don't give us much information. They don't tell us what is going to happen. It just happens and then we are told about it.

> They just give you a book to read. There is little explanation of the new things that are happening.

When programmers and analysts were asked what action they would take to overcome resistance to change, answers were generally in terms of salesmanship or coercion, of 'getting the other side to think as we do'. Very few (around 10%) gave answers in terms of involvement, of allowing groups who will be affected by a new computer system to participate in the decisions associated with its creation. Mumford concludes:

> This reluctance in the part of computer men to use a democratic approach may be due to their wish to retain command over the situation in which they are operating. They appear to believe that if they can do this then their system will go in essentially as they have designed it. There will be no need to compromise by having to accept what are to them the misguided and ignorant opinions of the user. (pp. 142–143)

Around the mid-1970s the implementation literature began to expand enormously. One important stream of contributions came from behavioural scientists (especially sociologists, management and organization theorists) writing from user perspectives. These have already been treated in sections 8.2.2–8.2.4. Contributions from psychologists will be discussed in section 8.2.8.

A second important stream came from OR/MS sources. In 1973 a conference in Pittsburgh (entitled *The Implementation of OR/MS Models: Theory, Research and Application*) resulted in what the organizers estimated to be a doubling of the empirical literature on OR/MS implementation (Schulz and Slevin, 1975a). These studies attempted to identify factors associated with successful implementation. Most of the studies referred to models that were computer-based.

They generally confirmed results from earlier studies. User or client resistance was the key factor influencing implementation success (in particular the studies by Schultz and Slevin, 1975b; Manley, 1975; Lucas, 1975; Mitroff, 1975). However, user resistance was normally treated as an intervening variable. The factors treated as independent variables, which influenced user resistance, were extremely varied. They included the following:

(1) characteristics of the development group (the style of its members, its practice and policies, its position in the organization, its age or phase in its life cycle);
(2) characteristics of the users (their task characteristics, their style, their expectations of the system);
(3) characteristics of the interaction of the groups (who initiated the project, user involvement and influence);
(4) characteristics of the organization (its competititve environment, its structure);
(5) top management support and involvement;
(6) quality of the model (how easy is it to learn the model, how well does the user understand it?).[37]

Studies confirming that a wide (and sometimes contradictory) range of factors affect the success of computer systems implementation have appeared since the conference (Lucas, 1981; Bikson and Mankin, 1983; Mohrman and Lawler, 1985).

With little agreement on the precise formulation of factors contributing to implementation success, there have been many different views on what policies are likely to improve implementation. User involvement or participation in more phases of the systems life cycle has been the most common recommendation. As noted above, such a policy was recommended in a standard textbook as early as 1974; however, since then more emphasis has been placed on user *influence* over systems and the systems development process, with user involvement, or participation, being the most obvious way of achieving this aim (see section 11.1 for classifications of user involvement in the 1980s).

One influential researcher working in the implementation area who clearly recommended user-controlled systems design at an early date was Lucas (1974, 1975, 1978). The following statements by Lucas on information systems failure clearly place the blame for user resistance with the systems designers and their procedures:

> users do not understand much of the output they receive; there is duplication of input and output, and changes are frequently made in systems without consulting users. Because of inaccuracies, users often discount all of the information provided by a system. Many users complain of information overload; massive amounts of data are provided which cannot be digested by the decision maker. There are so many complaints about the difficulty of obtaining changes in existing systems. A number of users report that they do not actually use the information provided by an information system. Many feel that computer-based information systems are not worth the time or cost to develop and the organization would be better off without them. (Lucas, 1975, pp. 2–3)

> It is our contention that *the major reason most informative systems have failed is that we have ignored organizational behavior problems in the design and operation of computer-based information systems.* (1975, p. 6; emphasis in original)[38]

The solution for Lucas is what he calls the philosophy of creative systems design (Lucas, 1974). This includes three elements. The first, most important and most radical, according to Lucas, is user-controlled systems design. The computer professional acts as a catalyst to help users construct the system. The systems analysts suggest alternatives for the user to consider. The user determines forms for input, defines processing logic and the file structures for the system, and prepares plans for conversion and implementation. In all this the analyst provides guidance, but not the system. The programming phases are left to specialists.

The second element is that the quality of the information systems should be judged according to user criteria, rather than those of the information systems developers. Technical elegance, in particular, a criterion of interest solely to computer professionals, should not be considered a measure of good quality. Finally, the interface between the user and the system should absorb considerable effort. Users should have the opportunity to work with the new input and output forms and devices before they are made part of the system.

Lucas' recommendations were echoed later with increasing frequency, although before the 1980s his model of creative systems design was clearly prescriptive, and still very much a minority opinion.

User involvement was by no means the only solution suggested for implementation problems. Another solution that has been increasingly suggested since the early 1980s is user development or end-user computing, which specifically includes end-user programming. User development may be thought of as the next logical step along the line of user influence from Lucas' suggestions of user-controlled design. Discussions of user development during the 1980s have been associated with fourth-generation programming languages and with personal computers (PCs). These developments are discussed below (section 9.1). User development would seem to remove the implementation problem as well as all problems of user relations.[39]

One rather different recommendation for solving implementation problems has been to change the emphasis in systems developer education, towards applications, general management and/or social science. The key problems of user relations and resistance may be seen as a reflection of the general lack of mutual understanding between managers and scientists. This view had often been expressed in the OR/MS literature with reference to the lack of understanding between management scientists and general managers (Churchman and Schainblatt, 1965; Wagner, 1971; Grayson, 1973). Similar points have been made in relation to management information systems (Argyris, 1971) and decision support systems (Keen and Scott Morton, 1978). Many well-known figures in the MIS area have suggested that the weak link in implementation is lack of education—education of managers in analytical methods and management scientists in general management (Keen and Scott Morton, 1978, p. 197).

Alter (1981), arguing for certification of systems analysts, stated that knowledge of the functional area for which applications are being developed was

> maybe the most important type of knowledge for an MIS systems analyst. In my experience, systems analysts frequently have to dig themselves out of a hole from day one because they simply don't know the lingo. (p. 525)

Although he recommended that knowledge of functional areas be introduced into formal training programs, for systems analysts he doubted (in 1980) that this would occur. Similarly Keen and Scott Morton stated:

> In general the expectations of graduating OR or MIS specialists have been that their role should be that of a technician, or that any difficulties they encounter with the managers who use the tools they provide come from the managers' inadequacies, not theirs. In the case of DSS this is a particularly damaging view. (1978, p. 209)

Another implementation policy designed to ease user relations is to create specialists in implementation. This policy would parallel the separation of analysts from programmers. Recognizing that the skills required for implementation are different from those required for analysis or programming would be the underlying rationale for such a policy. This policy has not been widely recommended in the literature. However, through the ICON interviews we have casual evidence that certain computer systems developers (often women) take on the role of easing implementation by making it their business to become acquainted with end users and their perspective.

The IBM research laboratory carried out experiments with a decision support system called GADS (geographic data analysis and display system) in the mid-1970s. During this project the IBM group frequently used what has been called an 'integrating agent' (Bennett, 1976, p. 77) or a 'chauffeur' (Carlson *et al.*, 1977)—a skilled intermediary who knew the system in great detail. This integrating agent acted as:

(1) an *exegetist*, who explained the decision support system to the user;
(2) a *crusader*, who 'sold' the system, largely through personal enthusiasm;
(3) a *confidant*, who built up users' self-confidence and acted as advisor; and
(4) a *teacher*, who provided personalized instruction.

Keen and Scott Morton suggest that such an integrating agent will not be easy to find. They believe the required mixture of technical and business experience to be found in a senior manager, rather than a junior staff specialist (1978, p. 207).

Prototyping is another frequently recommended solution to the implementation problem. Prototyping may be thought of as a technique to accommodate greater user involvement in systems development. The idea of prototyping is to build a mock-up of the finished system so that users (and designers) can see what the system will look like or get a feel for the system. One way of thinking about prototyping emphasizes the prototype—the artifact users will see. The more common way to consider prototyping, especially in the late 1970s, was as the outcome of a change in the traditional system life cycle.

There is an interesting twist to the normal prescriptive nature of literature written from computer systems developer perspectives when it comes to discussions of life cycles. The classical rationale for prescribing a strict sequence of steps or life cycle in systems development was to allow resource planning and to control the process. Early in phase two the importance of well-defined stages for control over the systems development process was emphasized as a way to solve the software productivity gap (see section 5.1.1). However, even in the 1960s there was a small sprinkling of protestation in the literature against the strict traditional life cycle. In the real world, especially with large and complex projects, errors, vagueness, misunderstandings, logical inconsistencies generated in one phase are only discovered in later phases. This necessitates an iterative process, rather than the linear, sequential one prescribed by the traditional life cycle.

With the recognition of user relations as a key problem for systems developers, the trickle of literature which stated, perhaps with some regret, that the real world is just not like the traditional life cycle, grew into a stream of prescription based on real-world experiences. The prescriptions should follow and facilitate real-world procedures, because the problem of getting the right system was becoming more important than controlling a process that was leading to a system which would be resisted and/or simply not used.

A clear example of this new emphasis in life cycle criticisms was presented by Bally *et al.* (1977). They distinguish what they call the 'loopy linear' variation to the linear life cycle from the prototype approach (p. 25). What they call the linear life cycle is the traditional approach. They distinguish the steps shown in Figure 8.2.

The loopy linear variation occurs when changes are made in previously 'frozen decisions'. Activities then restart at a phase that was supposed to have been completed. The process is intendedly linear, but loopy in practice. This can occur because of inadequacies at early phases which are only discovered later, but it can also occur because users are not in a static situation. Between the time of requirements analysis and system operation users may have learned new behaviours, or their environment may have changed. Although the latter reasons may be more excusable, they still lead to duplication of effort, frustration and bad relations between developers and users. According to Bally *et al.*, dynamic user situations should be planned for and accommodated.

The alternative is to develop a prototype system on a 'throw-away' basis. Experience in development and with user reaction to the 'implementation of the prototype' is recycled and an improved version is constructed. The new version is again presented and improved, until an acceptable result is achieved.

Prototyping became something of a buzz-word in the computing literature in the early 1980s, particularly in Europe (note the 50 abstracted papers submitted to the Working Conference on Prototyping sponsored by the EEC in 1983; Budde *et al.*, 1984).

The effect of prototyping is to bring together requirements analysis and implementation. This has led to a melding of these two lines of literature. Similarly the user involvement, user development and education strategies may be thought

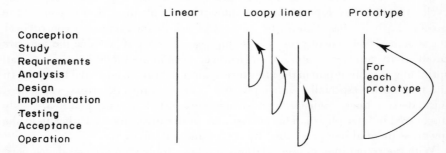

FIGURE 8.2 *Life cycle variations. Note: 'implementation' here means carrying out a system design—what is normally called the coding and documentation stage*

of as general ways of improving user relations. They attack misunderstandings at both requirements analysis and implementation phases, and thereby encourage computer systems developers to regard the two sets of problems as two facets of the same problem. We will examine experiences with prototyping in chapter 11 (section 11.3.2).

Since the late 1970s the literature on implementation has done more than focus attention on the intimate connections between implementation problems and requirements analysis problems, between problems at implementation and phases in the computerization process occurring before implementation. It has also encouraged computer systems developers to pay attention to the consequences of implementation, to organizational change and to the interaction between users and the computer system in operation (Kling, 1980; Keen, 1981; Markus, 1983; Kling and Iacono, 1984).

Most studies of implementation before the late 1970s attempted to identify and measure the influence of factors that led to success or failure. These have been called *factors* studies. They were strongly influenced by the OR/MS perspective on implementation as a diffusion process. From the late 1970s a different approach has become as influential on research into implementation. This is known as the *change process* approach. Influential early explicit adopters of this were Sorensen and Zand (1975), Vertinsky *et al.* (1975), Manley (1975), Boland (1978), and Keen and Scott Morton (1978). These studies have been strongly influenced by behavioural science research on organization change.

One particularly influential theory has been the force field approach to planned organizational change, first proposed by Kurt Lewin (1952) and later popularized by Schein (1961). According to Lewin, individuals and groups in organizations are subjected to both driving forces (stimulating them to change) and restraining forces. The outsider is likely to find an equilibrium-like state with the forces balanced. In order to change this situation a three-stage process is necessary:

(1) Unfreezing the initial equilibrium must be achieved by either increasing driving forces or reducing restraining forces.
(2) The situation needs to be moved in a particular direction by individuals or groups learning new attitudes.
(3) The new situation needs refreezing. Changed attitudes need to be integrated into the force field—a new equilibrium must be established. This means that a permanent change in the balance of forces is necessary if the effort undertaken to unfreeze and move from the old equilibrium is to result in a permanent change in the attitudes and behaviours of the subjects.

In terms of this model one could say that implementation failures arise from a narrow focus on only the middle stage. They ignore unfreezing. This may explain why factors like lack of top management support, or lack of a felt need by end users, have been found to be important influences on implementation failure in the factors literature. More important, they ignore refreezing. Change needs to be institutionalized. Keen and Scott Morton suggest that this may account for

> semisuccesses in computer applications, projects that have an apparently successful outcome but that lose impetus and sink into oblivion when their sponsor or designer leaves the scene. (1978, p. 200)

Although the model is designed to guide outsider consultants or 'experts' attempting to stimulate organizational change, the importance of systems developers (usually part of the user organization, formally at least) not to cast themselves in the role of outside experts in the eyes of the users has been emphasized often in the implementation literature. This could lead to the user involvement policies or to educating developers into the language and knowledge set of the users.

Experience of the wide range of factors that may effect implementation success, and the need to view implementation as a complex process of social change, has led more and more researchers to recognize that no absolutely fixed rules for implementation success can be laid down. It has led them to recommend a contingency approach (DeBrabander and Edstrom, 1977; Edstrom, 1977). Awareness and sensitivity to dimensions such as the political context of the system (if, for example, the system patron is planning to use the system to improve his or her personal status in the organization; see Gibson and Hammond, 1974; Gibson, 1976) may be critical for successful implementation in some cases, but irrelevant in others.[40] This may be a major reason for unsuccessful implementation. It is hard to get people trained in the value of analytical technique to understand and empathize with what Gibson and Hammond call informal social contingencies.

With the more recent shift of emphasis away from ignoring implementation and away from the simple success factor approach to implementation research, and towards viewing implementation as a process whose success depends on environmental contingencies, the implementation literature has not only been drawing on the literatures of social and behavioural sciences and general management theory, but it has also been reflecting new movements in those fields. The systems approach, which strongly influenced sociological research in the 1950s and 1960s, was increasingly criticized in that field during the 1970s (Elger, 1975). Similarly a contingency approach to industrial relations, industrial and social psychology, industrial sociology and organization research became popular in the 1970s, stimulated by work of the 1960s such as that of Burns and Stalker (1961), the Aston group (Pugh *et al.*, 1963–64, 1969) and Fiedler (1964). In general management theory, Mintzberg's contingency approach developed during the 1970s has also been influential (Mintzberg, 1973, 1979). These new directions have, with some lag, come to be reflected in the computer systems development literature, and in particular in the line of literature associated with implementation problems.

It is notable that while the systems development literature did itself have a strong influence on the social science literature of the 1950s and 1960s, largely through the work of Simon, the direction seems to have reversed somewhat during the 1970s and 1980s.

8.2.8 End-user Interface Problems

The end-user interface has only generated a significant critical literature during the 1980s, although a substantial empirical line of literature has existed since the 1940s. The user interface literature has not been well integrated with the computer systems development literature, or the MIS and DSS literature. There are two reasons for this.

First, the interface literature's roots are in what is known as the human factors literature. In this, the man–computer interface is a specialized version of the man–machine interface.[41] The focus here is on how people use equipment, rather than how the systems are created or what the systems are used for. That is, the prescriptive human factors literature traditionally would recommend changes in the design of equipment, rather than changes in the process of design. This literature is dominated by experimental methods. It is presumed that different interface designs can be compared and judged in a laboratory situation, in order to discover which design is 'better'. The interface literature typically draws on the methodologies and models of medical research and experimental psychology, rather than the analytical methods of computer science or the common sociological methods of situational observation, survey and use of official statistics. The separation of the interface literature from the other lines of literature discussed above reflects the traditional separation (and even antagonism) between academic disciplines based on different research methods.

Second, the types of systems and types of end users that have stimulated work on man–computer interfaces have until the 1980s been atypical of the majority of business systems. They have been more associated with scientific and military computer systems. These systems have been on-line (allowing a direct connection to the computer) and real time (allowing interaction with the system via the connection, rather than merely inputting or monitoring output). Many of the large-scale systems of the 1950s were of this sort, particularly military systems and both military and certain civilian air navigation and air traffic control systems.

Such systems have continued to generate studies in these areas in medical schools and university departments of psychology, ergonomics, human factors and computer science, as well as government and military agencies.[42] In the USA the space programme has further stimulated such research. Issues such as the effects of limitations to human memory capacity and of continuous monitoring on the generation of errors, fatigue, and more recently on stress, have been taken up in the psychological and medical literature. Issues such as the effects of readability and other characteristics of VDU displays, posture and noise on work performance and skill acquisition have been carried out in the ergonomics literature. All of these issues have further stimulated particular specialisms within those academic disciplines, such as cognitive science within psychology.

Nevertheless, as noted above, this work remained almost entirely separate from the main body of computer systems development literature until very recently. Spread over so many different academic disciplines and traditions, the man–computer interface literature has also been fragmented: 'more of a catalogue than an integrated body of knowledge' (Eason *et al.*, 1975, p. 91).

Most commercial computer systems development from the late 1950s until the end of the 1970s was of batch systems. Users directly inputting data and directly receiving output were primarily low-level clerks. During this period concern for user relations within the computing world was primarily directed at the requirements end of the life cycle, where users were managers.

One important contributor to the literature during phase two in the USA was James Martin. Martin published *Design of Man–Computer Dialogues* (1973) based on a course given at the IBM Systems Research Institute. He noted in the preface:

> A course on man–computer dialogue design is badly needed elsewhere, especially at the universities, because we are turning out many computer specialists who are inexperienced in this area. (p. ix)

Martin's position was that good design of man–computer dialogues required the shortcomings of both man and computer to be taken into account. Man's limitations concerned his limited capacity to remember and to think logically. Also the wide variations in abilities and experience of different people in their capacities to communicate with computers had to be considered. The computer, on the other hand, is inferior to man in its relative lack of adaptability and lack of ability to explore new directions. Also man is much better at observing a wide variety of visual and audible stimuli and at observing patterns in events and detecting relevance. Man is adept at handling unforeseen occurrences and dealing with events that have a very low probability of occurring:

> This difference in 'thinking' talent—the computer being good for ultrafast sequential logic and the human being capable of slow but highly parallel and associative thinking—is the basis for cooperation between man and machine. (1973, p. 7)

Martin warned that designers and others who think about computer usage should not try to make the computer compete with man in areas where man is superior. Often the worst approach the designer could take, according to Martin, is to attempt to design a dialogue as though man were talking to another man, rather than a computer (at least given the state of the art in 1973).

Considering design methodologies, Martin recommended simulation of the dialogue before programming:

> When a dialogue has been tentatively designed it is desirable to try it out with live operators. (p. 18)

Martin called it simulation, rather than prototyping, but it is a similar technique. However, there is one important difference. Martin was presuming that the real-time systems would be created by outside suppliers and that these suppliers would not have a chance to simulate dialogues with the actual end users. 'The simulation may be performed with persons similar to those who will operate the terminals of the eventual system' (p. 18). Simulation is not associated with end-user involvement, it is a way of the designer acquiring experience of end-user reactions *without* end-user involvement.

Another aspect of the IBM approach as rendered by Martin is what he called 'bullet-proofing'. The programs must be 'made immune to irrational operator behavior'. Operators may accidentally jiggle keys they should not, or even deliberately key invalid messages for fun. Methods for bullet-proofing include simulation exercises, live testing with selected end users, drilling and testing end users and selective logging or monitoring the dialogues (1973, pp. 503–511). Martin did note that bullet proofing works in two ways. Careful testing of the system protects both computer and end user. Invalid or confusing responses from the computer will lead to end-user frustration and errors.[43]

In general the tone of Martin's book was prescriptive and uncritical. Man–computer dialogues are growing in importance. They herald a new computerized society which represents primarily opportunities, rather than dangers (see also Martin and Norman, 1970). In Great Britain the HUSAT research group (Human Sciences and Advanced Technology) at the Department of Ergonomics and Cybernetics, University of Loughborough, began researching man–computer interfaces in 1970. Publications from this group began to appear in the mid-1970s. They reported considerable problems associated with the man–computer interfaces they investigated. These included difficulty of use, boredom, lack of support and lack of task fit (Eason *et al.*, 1975):

> At present it appears that, in designing computer aids, the act of ensuring the computer can fulfil its data handling functions leads to inhibition of man in the performance of his function. (Eason, 1977, p. 56)

In practice, rather than the ideal of a man–computer partnership as prescribed and foreseen by Licklider (see section 8.2.4 above) and Martin, the HUSAT group discovered mismatches.

These were divided into two categories, depending on whether users were willing and able to modify their task behaviour to match the computer system they were using. In circumstances where users had such discretion, tasks were modified in undesirable ways. Eason and Corney (1970) found that waiting time required of managers using a decision support system led them to accept the first solution examined, rather than evaluate a number of possibilities. Tasks routinely involving a set of operations performed in a standard sequence, such as taking airline or hotel bookings, become frozen into a system. This leads clerks to force the task into the sequence required by the computer system even when it is inappropriate (Eason, 1977, p. 58).[44]

When users are unable or unprepared to modify their tasks to match system constraints, different suboptimal procedures may be adopted. These can involve any of the following (Eason, 1977, pp. 58–59):

(1) Compensating work—for example, taking data generated by the computer and making simple calculations or graphs with them because the form of output is inappropriate.
(2) Disuse—such as the creation of manual information systems when computer-based ones are available, but inappropriate.
(3) Partial use—not bothering with some of the available functions.
(4) Distant use—users ask intermediaries to interface directly with the system because intended users are not prepared to expend the effort for direct use. Eason suggests that this is common for managerial users.
(5) Misuse and abuse—'using a computer system often entails being offered choices which are nonsensical in the context of the task being undertaken. When this repeatedly happens to experienced users they may start seeking short cuts; ways in which they may avoid wasting time and go straight to the important issues. This often means using the system in ways which were never intended by the designers and which may damage the integrity of the system.'

Eason recognizes that limiting user discretion in task performance may have been intended in system design to prevent user errors and to improve their performance. However, he questions whether designers, when they take such decisions, have a full understanding of the diversity of tasks the user undertakes. The difficulty of designers foreseeing the extent of this diversity is a major reason for system failure, according to Eason.

Eason also notes that end-user interface problems are particularly difficult to eradicate, because users are often unaware of the consequences of using computer aids. Man–computer interactions lead to the reinforcement of certain habits of mind, of what is known as psychological set, which leads to behavioural rigidity. At the end-user interface similar tasks are often repeated many times. Therefore one would expected people to experience psychological set. One reason for psychological set being encouraged when people interface with computers is that people are stimulated to act quickly. This encourages them to force new problems into existing moulds. They do not have time to stop and think about what they are doing. Chatting to others, working on a variety of tasks, even mechanical breakdowns can provide 'natural' set-breaking opportunities which are lost when work is made more 'efficient' by making it less porous (Eason, 1977; Stewart, 1977). Eason aptly summarized the problem as follows:

If the reason for having man in the man–computer partnership is that he is adaptive, this situation is far from ideal because the computer system is encouraging the user to be non-adaptive. (1977, p. 60)

In spite of considerable, but disparate, early work on end-user interface problems, during the 1980s there has been an atmosphere of new beginnings associated with this field. Note conference titles such as INTERACT '84: First Conference on Human–Computer Interaction (Shackel, 1985). In the introduction to the collection of papers entitled *User Centered System Design: New Perspectives on Human–Computer Interaction* readers are bid to

> Think of this as a book of questions, not a book of answers ... We are at the point of realising just how much bigger the problem is than has usually been acknowledged, but we are not within sight of a grand synthesis of a unifying theory. (Norman and Draper, 1986, p. 2)

Or later in the book one of the contributors states:

> Our intent to consider the users of our systems seriously is clearly a good first instinct, as it is the case in the architectural domain. However, it is clear that we have not solved any problems in this acknowledgement, but instead have just begun to articulate them. (Hooper, 1986, pp. 16–17)

For some researchers a user-centred approach to design interfaces represents a clear break with what they see as the dominant view in the man–machine interaction design community:

> The emphasis within the human–machine interaction community on the need to 'study the user' (Gould and Lewis, 1985) attests to the gulf in understanding that exists between systems designers and users. The need is not simply for more detailed psychological models of how people think and communicate, although such models are of course fundamental to the building of more usable systems, but for a more comprehensive, more enlightened view of people that recognizes their need for variety and challenge in the tasks that they perform. (Bannon, 1986, pp. 25–26)

Essentially Bannon is proposing computer systems that support responsible autonomy strategies towards computer users. The more enlightened view of people suggested is one that does not assume mass idiocy and therefore does not lead to an emphasis on 'idiot-proof' (or 'bullet-proof') systems. Any technology can be used to complement or to replace human capabilities. The human–computer interaction should be designed to complement human capabilities.

This theme is repeated in the other contributions to the Norman and Draper collection. Systems should be designed to be enjoyable to use:

> This means tools that reveal their underlying conceptual model and allow for interaction, tools that emphasize comfort, ease and pleasure of use: for what Illich (1974) has called *convivial tools*. A major factor in this debate is the feeling of control that the user has over the operations that are being performed. (Norman, 1986, p. 49)[45]

This is not easy. One problem is that most systems must be designed to be used by several types of users. What is enjoyable and useful for expert users will often generate very different experiences for novices. Also continuous users and intermittent users will have different requirements. Norman points to the tension between what he calls the 'natural desire to want intelligent tools that can compensate for our inadequacies and the desire to feel in control of the outcome' (1986, p. 54). He refers to Scandinavian researchers (whose work was discussed in section 8.2.4) for the distinction between thinking in terms of systems that lead to the use of computers to reduce the jobs of workers to algorithmic procedures, minimizing the need for skill and control, versus thinking in terms of tools fashioned for the use of skilled workers to create products of high quality (Ehn and Kyng, 1984).

There is a difference between those writing in the end-user interface literature (even recent contributors) and those writing from the perspective of computer users as workers. The interface researchers believe that the tool perspective can be inscribed into the computer system by system designers. Computer systems can be made enjoyable to use. Computer systems can offer more control to workers. Nevertheless this is difficult to achieve largely because there has been little effort put into developing design concepts that can guide such a tool perspective, until very recently.

The Scandinavians and others writing from the user as worker perspective place more emphasis on the organizational context of the end-user interface. If end users have influence over their interaction with computers[46] then whatever conviviality and control interfaces allow end users can be maintained and enhanced. Also there is a greater emphasis on end-user influence in the system design process leading to better interfaces from the user as worker literature.

One design concept that has become popular in the interface literature among those attempting to pursue a tool perspective is that of direct manipulation.[47] According to Schneiderman (1982, p. 251), direct manipulation interfaces have the following properties:

(1) continuous representation of the object of interest;
(2) physical actions of labelled button presses instead of complex syntax;
(3) rapid incremental reversible operations whose impact on the object of interest is immediately visible.

Clearly the notion of direct manipulation owes much to the development of video arcade games, where the only aim of the system is to provide an enjoyable interface.

8.3 TIMING AND INTEGRATION OF THE LINES OF LITERATURE ON USER RELATIONS PROBLEMS

By and large the literature on user relations problems from user perspectives had little direct impact on the practice of computer systems development until the late

1970s. In part this was because the earliest expressions of concern were highly speculative and often intended purely as works of fiction. Optimistic visions and dire warnings of the effects of machines that can think, do our work for us, fly our airships, move us through time, metamorphose us into cogs within those very machines, have been fanning the public imagination long before electronic computers appeared. Fictional accounts of dangers awaiting users of computers, or of a society dependent upon them, continue to appear as ancient myths, in books and, more recently, in films.

In part systems development practice has been indifferent to expressions of concern about user relations problems because, until recently, those expressions have been from outsiders. This literature has been produced by behavioural and social scientists, by workers and worker representatives, and by politicians, as well as by poets and novelists and film makers. These expressions were easier to ignore than expressions of concern coming from within the computer community.

Keen and Scott Morton explain the lack of influence of these lines of literature from user perspectives on management information systems (MIS) specialists in the following way:

> This lack of follow-up may reflect a general sense that the central issues for MIS are technical and that the introduction of the computer into organizations' operations is beneficial and inevitable. (1978, p. 49)

The literature on user relations problems written from computer systems developer perspectives is founded on a concern with computer system failures, in terms of the new criteria discussed in Chapter 7. When the quality of systems in terms of their usefulness to users became a prime criterion for system success, user relations problems could not be ignored by computer systems developers. This generated literature on user relations problems written largely by what Keen and Scott Morton called 'insiders' and was therefore harder to ignore.

During the 1960s two completely separate literatures describing problems with computerization were developing. One was about a software productivity crisis. It was generated by well-known figures working for hardware manufacturers, and certain major user organizations, as well as computer scientists at universities. It was directed to the practice of computer systems development. Also, along with these expressions of concern, varied but definite and detailed solutions to the problems were proposed.

The second was about user relations problems. It was generated by social scientists concerned about the transfer of political power into the hands of technocrats and ruling elites. It was generated by novelists and film makers worried about the consequences of technical malfunctions. It was generated by citizens' groups and certain politicians concerned about invasion of privacy. These expressions of concern related to the consequences of computer systems. Authors were rarely aware of the effect of the systems development *process* on the way computer systems affected users. Their expressions of concern were not accompanied by detailed suggestions for solutions to these problems.

The first line of literature generated considerable new techniques which had substantial impact on computer systems development practice. The second did not.

ENDNOTES

1. In relation to systems software, applications programmers in user organizations may be thought of as end users. End users of computer-based applications may be thought of as secondary users of systems software delivered to the user organization.

2. Kurt Vonnegut Jr's *Player Piano* (1952) is a particularly early and insightful example of this literature. More recent examples can be found in films such as *Rollerball* (1975) and *The Running Man* (1988).

3. George Orwell's *Nineteen Eighty-four* (1944) is the best-known example of this literature.

4. Hackers are people who break into computer systems for kicks.

5. The popularity of these stories may be in part attributable to the real-life revelations of misinformation about the Vietnam war, surveillance of anti-war protesters and dirty tricks campaigns undertaken by the Committee to Re-elect President Nixon (Watergate) and the CIA during the late 1960s and early 1970s.

6. One notable exception is Harold Sackman. As an 'insider' from the Rand Corporation his work is often quoted (Sackman, 1967, 1971, 1975; Sackman and Borko, 1972). Another is Parnas (1985), but his concerns arise from his own experiences of the limitations of software developed for the Strategic Defense Initiative.

7. One line of positive suggestions relating to this line of literature concerns the overall development of what is often called alternative or intermediate technologies (Dickson, 1974; Straussman, 1978). This view is often associated with the problems of transferring advanced industrial technology to third-world countries.

8. '... the idea of easy access to personal information is regarded as objectionable by the vast majority of people ... the computer problem as it affects privacy in Great Britain is one of apprehensions and fears and not so far one of facts and figures. Of these fears about the computer the three which seem to be uppermost in the public mind are its facility to compile 'personal profiles' ... seen by some to facilitate the exercise of power over them ... its capacity to correlate information ... seen by some as infringing the principle that information collected for one purpose should not be available for any other purpose ... and its provision of new opportunities for unauthorized access to personal information ... the fact that computerized information can be tapped via terminals separated by many miles, is seen by some to increase the risk of its falling into the hands of people who should not have it.' (Younger, 1972, cited in Waddell, 1975, pp. 131–132).

9. This same point was made by Adler and Du Feu in Great Britain (1977, pp. 109–117). They did develop a system to improve welfare claimants' knowledge of their entitlements, but the system foundered due primarily to lack of real interest from the welfare bureaucracy.

10. 'But for us the crucial question is not "When does participation encourage efficiency", but rather, "Under what conditions does participatory organization make sense even if it entails some losses in efficiency?" (Danziger *et al.*, 1982, p. 262).

11. 'Clearly "democratization" is not an absolute value, and our democratic bias is not so unqualified that we believe that urban administrations should be democratized in

every conceivable way . . . it is appropriate to ask how and when the democratization of computing might improve the responsiveness of local governments to wider legitimate public interests without reducing the capacity of executives to manage the government . . . Reforms of computing without corresponding reforms of public organizations will not achieve the desired effect of greater democratization.' (Danziger *et al.*, 1982, pp. 234–235).

12. Note, for example, the citing of Argyris (1957), McGregor (1960), Maslow (1964), Likert (1967) and Herzberg (1968), the major works in human relations management of the previous 20 years in Hedberg and Mumford (1975).

13. The sociotechnical tradition was developed in Scandinavia by well-known researchers in each country, such as Bo Hedberg (Sweden), Niels Bjørn-Andersen (Denmark) and Rolf Højer (Norway), who all had contacts with Enid Mumford (Ehn, 1988, p. 268).

14. 'In Sweden "job satisfaction and productivity" have been the slogans and a network of employers/production engineers have taken care of the diffusion. In Norway the slogans were "industrial democracy and participation" . . . but the practical involvement from the individual unions' officials has systematically been lacking' (Qvale, 1976, p. 468).

15 The German Co-determination Acts of 1951 and 1976 and especially the Works Constitution Act of 1972 provided works councils (Betriebsträte) with rights to information about new computer systems as well as certain limited rights to influence the consequences of new systems on working conditions (Hingel, 1983). The important Scandinavian laws were the Danish Law on the Working Environment of 1975, the Norwegian Law on the Working Environment of 1977 and the Swedish Co-determination Law of 1977. These are reviewed and compared regarding the regulation of computer systems in organizations by Mathiassen *et al.* (1983).

16. Interestingly, this literature has developed out of experiences with real-time computer systems used either for sophisticated military applications or to aid powerful and highly skilled workers such as air traffic controllers (Fitts, 1951; Bernotat, 1977; Eason, 1977; see section 8.2.8).

17. This tradition dates back to the nineteenth century (Webb and Webb, 1898) and has been sustained in Great Britain by such organizations as the Fabian Society and the Institute for Workers' Control. In the USA a much smaller grouping exists around the label Quality of Working Life.

18. Benn was Industry Minister at the beginning of the 1974 Callaghan government.

19. The group was influenced by continental European initiatives on industrial democracy, particularly in relation to EEC policies (see Bullock, 1977).

20. Since 1978 hundreds of new technology agreements have been successfully negotiated in Great Britian; most have been signed by white-collar unions (Williams and Steward, 1985; Williams, 1987, p. 82). These have been influenced by agreements negotiated at national as well as local levels in Norway and Sweden during the mid-1970s (Nygaard, 1979; Mathiassen *et al.* 1983). As Williams points out, the British agreements have fallen short of TUC guidelines (Williams 1987, p. 82). In this they have also fallen far short of agreements in Norway and Sweden. Furthermore, agreements in Britain rarely cover direct trade union participation in computer systems design. Rather they normally cover consultation about what new systems are impending and about standards for preserving jobs, skills, health and safety levels, status and demarcation lines. Most agreements have been with clerical unions and, as Williams notes, 'the main objective of the union in these cases appeared to be one of *monitoring*, rather than *modifying* the process of change' (1987, p. 84). The cases where agreements were made with craft unions such as in the engineering or printing industries, such agreements were stronger but narrower, mainly covering safeguards on health and safety

conditions and preserving the work status, wage differentials, autonomy and union organization of the particular craft group (Williams, 1987, pp. 82–83).

21. The collective resource approach has been developed through five large research projects:
    (1) The Norwegian Iron and Metal Workers Union Project (NJMF), run between 1971 and 1973 in cooperation with researchers from the Norwegian Computing Centre (Nygaard, 1978).
    (2) The Demos project (1975–1979) in cooperation with researchers from Stockholm University and the Swedish Centre for Working Life (Arbetslivscentrum) (Ehn, 1988).
    (3) The DUE project (1979–1981) in cooperation with researchers at Arhus University, Denmark (Kyng and Mathiassen, 1982; Kensing, 1983).
    (4) The PAAS project in cooperation with researchers at the Swedish Arbetslivscentrum (Göranzon et al., 1982).
    (5) The UTOPIA project (1981–1985) in cooperation with researchers at the Swedish Arbetslivscentrum (Ehn, 1988).

22. Bansler and Ehn distinguish the collective resource approach from two other approaches that have been influential in the Scandinavian countries. These are the information theory approach, which aims for efficient use of information in organizations, and the sociotechnical approach, which aims for an efficient fit between the technical and the social system of an organization. These two approaches differ from the collective resource approach by viewing organizations as harmonious and by focusing on efficiency, according to Bansler.

23. '... we might characterize the first generation of computers as one or few of a kind machines which left no direct (compatible) descendants; the second generation, as families of computers which were mass-produced, with the more successful members giving rise to compatible issue; and the third generation, as a single family embracing a wide performance spectrum with compatibility across the board' (Campbell, 1970, p. 172).

24. It did 'not acknowledge problems of prerequisites and recursiveness' (Bouvard, 1970, p. 120).

25. This has been a particular feature of IBM installations (Friedman, 1986, pp. 101–102)

26. For example, 'Good programs won't be really useful if the design of the whole system is not good itself. And what is a good system? It is a system which is well structured. A clear structure is necessary for good program specifications' (Dambrine, 1981, p. 343).

27. For example, lists of undesirable features of systems-building features were compiled by Nunamaker (1971) and Konsynski (1976) and later reiterated by them (Nunamaker and Konsynski, 1981). The lists included as problems that requirements are usually not stated explicitly and that users have difficulty in expressing what they need. The solution was systems requirements definition languages and recognition that the problem of definition is important.

28. As evidenced by the entire collection in the issue of *IEEE Transactions on Software Engineering* devoted to requirements analysis (Ross, 1977).

29. Jackson clearly distinguishes a model appropriate for communication to the system's eventual user, with one appropriate for communication with the client for the system.

30. Prototyping is an iterative process in which the systems developer builds up a working model of the eventual system which can be easily changed in the process. This may lead directly to the eventual system or to a basis for writing system specifications (see section 11.3.2).

31. For example, a large conference entitled 'Systems Analysis and Design: A Foundation for the 1980's' was held in 1980 at Georgia State University. Most of the big names in

that field presented papers. Of the 33 papers presented, four were primarily about requirements analysis, and one was primarily about the problem of requirements specifications. Only one was primarily about implementation, although both implementation and requirements specifications were mentioned in most of the papers. Even in the management science literature, until the 1970s the issue of implementation was 'simply overlooked' due to a focus on the 'missionary purpose of developing techniques independent of their effective use' according to Keen and Scott Morton (1978, p. 190).

32. 'In the good times of 1960's, when all aspects of the computer field were growing at a bewildering but exciting pace, the issue of implementation was easily brushed aside' (Keen and Scott Morton, 1978, p. 189).

33. Ginzberg (1975) examines 14 studies of factors associated with successful implementation and finds that of 140 distinct factors identified only 'top management support' appeared in as many as five of these studies.

34. At the end of that passage Davis refers to an earlier influential text on computers and management, Sanders (1970, pp. 320–334).

35. 'The systems designer often describes himself as a salesman who markets a completed product. Training programs and user involvement are thought of as ways to get user acceptance, and not primarily as means to secure user ideas and influence' (Hedberg and Mumford, 1975, p. 43).

36. Remarks about the passage from Davis (1974) in this and the previous few paragraphs are not intended as a criticism of Gordon Davis, rather a commentary on the limitations of the views expressed in his text of 1974. Davis' attitude towards user participation seems to have changed since then, reflecting the general shift to phase three. The section referred to above does not appear in the second edition of this text. Instead of explaining user resistance as simply due to fear about uncertainty, the authors report three theories to explain user resistance (Davis and Olson, 1985, pp. 595–597). That is, it can be due to characteristics of the design of the system, or characteristics of the users, or characteristics of the interaction between the system and the users. In this they follow Markus (1983). They recommend a contingency approach to overcoming user resistance. Strategies such as user involvement or salesmanship (or persuasion) should only be employed after a thorough diagnosis of the organizational setting is undertaken to determine which approach to implementation is appropriate. They recommend a sociotechnical approach to this diagnosis, based on Mumford's work.

37. A figure representing the models of the implementation process used in all of the papers published from the conference may be found in Schultz and Slevin (1975a, pp. 12–13).

38. There is a fine line between the work of Lucas and that of Mumford. Mumford begins with a general theory that deals with the aims of end users as employees, the aims of their managers and how employees ought to be managed, quite separate from computer systems, the sociotechnical approach. Lucas views users as such. He is primarily concerned with improving the way 'we' design computer-based information systems, rather than in job satisfaction or organizational efficiency or effectiveness *per se*. This is clearly a distinction that is not intended to describe a long-run difference between them. Lucas has in fact been influenced by Mumford and refers to her work in very positive terms. It is this very melding of the different perspectives on user relations which we believe was a major symptom of phase three and a major contribution to its coming.

39. User development is one of the factors sustaining the often-repeated prediction of the end of DP departments in user organizations, and the end of programmers as a specialist occupation. These predictions will be discussed in Chapter 13.

40. According to Keen and Scott Morton one distinction between a technician and an

implementor is that the slogan of the technician is 'Have technique, will travel'; that of the implementor is 'It all depends...' (1978, p. 210).

41. During the 1960s a number of researchers drew attention to the human factor issues that were unique to computer systems; Miller (1968) on computer response time, and Nickerson (1969) on computer languages.
42. For example, Jenkins and Glynn (1987) from the US Nuclear Regulatory Commission; Holloway (1986) from the UK Atomic Energy Authority; Quintanar *et al.* (1987), one of whom was based at the Human Factors Division of the US Naval Training Systems Center; and Hart *et al.* (1984) from NASA.
43. Interestingly, Martin calls end users operators, or terminal operators. This label reflects the pre-phase three context of this book. At that time user relations had not yet become a primary concern in the computing literature such that special jargon was *de rigueur*.
44. Bjørn-Andersen *et al.* (1979) reported similar experiences with automated systems in banks in a number of countries.
45. Norman describes what he considers to be the best systems around in the above terms. His list includes *smalltalk, UNIX* and spreadsheets.
46. Through legal protection, through access to independent expertise, through the development of a strong back-up organization such as a network of shop stewards.
47. Sometimes this is called direct engagement (Hutchins *et al.* 1986) or first-personness (Laurel, 1986).

Chapter 9

AGENTS OF CHANGE: GENERATING USER RELATIONS PROBLEMS

There is something about the nature of systems development work which has always encouraged certain negative attitudes between users and systems developers. Their role as change agents put systems developers into potential conflict situations with those whose organization positions and work content were being changed. All categories of users discussed in section 7.3 are likely to find their situations altered by new computer-based systems. With large new systems few could feel themselves in control of the process or certain about the outcome.

However, computer systems developers have not been ordinary change agents. They have been associated with a particular, and generally unfamiliar, technology. Surrounding computer technology has been a particular way of speaking, an insider jargon. Many would also say a particular way of thinking has also infected those who design and program computer systems. This way of thinking relates to the characteristic way that computerization changes systems.

Computer systems, especially early ones, mechanized and automated human systems. This encouraged an engineering view of human relations among systems developers. It encouraged a direct control type of philosophy towards the work of users. In order for a system to be computerized it had to be routinized and standardized, especially in the early years of computing when it was difficult to include a wide range of exception conditions.

Robert Boguslaw called computer systems developers the 'new utopians', because they could be seen as change agents in a broader sense than merely replacing a particular system in an organization with another one. The sorts of systems they were designing were systematically different from what they replaced. These general differences between computer-based systems and manual systems encouraged in computer systems developers a general view of how society should change. As Boguslaw put it:

> ... the new utopians are concerned with non-people and with people substitutes ...
> Impatience with 'human error' has become a unifying imperative among the new utopians. The theoretical and practical solutions they seek call increasingly for decreases in the number and in the scope of responsibility of human beings within the operating structures of their new machined systems. (1965, p. 2)

We believe this view to be exaggerated in that it characterizes certain computer-based systems, rather than all of them.[1]

Nevertheless there is evidence that many computer systems developers did display such attitudes when dealing with users. Early in phase two Mumford found a strong clash of values between computer specialists and users in all three user firms in her sample. According to Mumford, 'The real clash of values in our user firms arose because of an unwillingness to recognize the importance of the human factors operating in user areas' (1972, p. 146).

Most of both analysts and programmers in Mumford's user firms, when asked 'What action would you take to overcome resistance to change among users?', gave answers that suggested coercion or withdrawal, rather than involving or educating the users. In fact only 4% of specialists in user firms said they would involve users in planning and decision making (only 9% in manufacturing and 20% in computer service firms where the users were customers; p. 142). According to Mumford, individuals who had worked in a number of non-DP jobs in the user organization were most aware of the importance of establishing good human relations. Those with a university degree in science were more likely 'to describe coercive and manipulative methods' (p. 147).

There is evidence that, however sympathetic to users recruits to computer departments may have been when they entered the computer department, once there for any length of time they come to identify with computer specialists rather than users. Referring to data from her earlier study of bank clerks (Mumford and Banks, 1967) as well as data published in 1972, Mumford notes that she was struck 'very forcibly' by the 'speed with which recruits to data processing were indoctrinated with, and accepted, EDP group values', even if they entered DP from conventional clerical activities in line departments. This was true even of those only temporarily placed in the EDP group to act as link men:

> ... many of these became so involved with technical values during their stay that they were incapable of performing this linking role and became totally identified with the values of the computer personnel. (1972, p. 199)

Thus policies such as separating analysts from programmers, or establishing other linking roles for individuals to specialize in lateral relations between computer departments and users, were not particularly successful at breaking down the technocratic isolation of computer systems developers. However, until the late 1970s user relations problems were viewed as a minor concern, especially from within computer departments.

Towards the end of phase two, changes in computer systems core technology, in types of computer applications and in market relations surrounding computer departments led to the quality of relations with users becoming the critical issue by which computer systems and computer systems development procedures would be judged (see Figure 9.1). The ways that each of these three agents of change contributed to user relations problems becoming the key issue of phase three will be discussed in the following three sections.

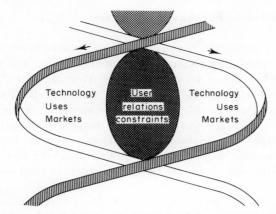

FIGURE 9.1 *Phase three: user relations constraints*

9.1 COMPUTER SYSTEMS CORE TECHNOLOGY

Three key technological changes that seemed to have the potential to reduce the technological isolation of computer departments occurred towards the end of phase two. The first was the development of personal computers. This lowered the entry cost in terms of computer hardware to a level that most user *departments* could afford. It threatened to alter the balance of power between central DP departments and user departments significantly.[2] Go-it-alone users became a common headache for DP managers late in phase two, although more from frustrations that users only went it alone until the inadequacy of PC-based software sent them back to the DP department for help.

The second development followed from the spread of on-line systems in the early 1970s. Initially on-line facilities in user departments were merely for data capture and simple display. During the late 1970s growing networks came to link intelligent terminals in user departments.

The third development was in the software field. More sophisticated operating systems came to support real-time systems and fourth-generation languages. These were often linked to widening databases via database management systems. In particular, report generators and other so-called user-friendly languages came to be used within DP departments. Many of these systems were sold on the basis of allowing user programming or what is now called end-user computing.

These three technical changes might have been expected to lead to an easing of tensions between systems developers and users if the problem between them was simply a lack of computer sophistication on the part of users. However, rather than encouraging users to be less insecure about computerization and more sympathetic to the problems of systems developers, they increased users' expectations of systems developers and increased their power to force systems developers to treat those expectations more seriously.

9.1.1 The Diffusion of Personal Computers

The continuing development of chip technology eventually led to the personal computer (often called a microcomputer or simply a PC) entering the market in 1976. Early in 1976 Steven Jobs and Stephen Wozniak sold their first Apple computer (Apple I) through the Byte Shop in 'Silicon Valley', California. The story of this business, which began in Steven Jobs' garage and came to be a billion-dollar operation within eight years, has now become part of computer lore.[3] In 1977 the Apple (Apple II) was shown at a San Francisco computer fair. By the end of that year $2.5 million worth of Apple computers had been sold. By 1980 Apple sales were over $100 million and by 1982 they were over $500 million (Forester, 1987, p. 132).

Apple's success encouraged competitors. At first competitors were both small companies and new entrants into the computing field such as Commodore and Tandy/Radio Shack. In 1981 this changed dramatically with the launch of IBM's PC. (The IBM PC was launched in Europe in 1982.) Many other firms, including several well-established giants in the IT field, also entered around this time.

By the end of 1983 it was clear that IBM was winning the competitive battle. *Business Week*, in October 1983, announced that IBM had by far the largest share of the PC market, with 26%, in spite of being a comparative latecomer. At that time there were around 150 PC manufacturers in the USA.

As with earlier, larger computers, the personal computer required software to be of use. In the first few years the personal computer was primarily a hobbyist's toy and most personal computers were bought by enthusiasts. During this period thousands of programmers wrote software for the Apple using BASIC. The most important of these has been Microsoft, which developed BASIC and wrote the main standardized operating systems for personal computers (MS-DOS for IBM and MSX for Japanese personal computers).

IBM's success in the PC market came from a meld of IBM's traditional marketing policies and from IBM's wholehearted embrace of the new wide-open policy of encouraging outsiders to write software for PCs. IBM concentrated on the business market, where its distribution network was well established. They sold directly to user departments as well as through central DP departments. Unlike their policy on software for their mainframes, IBM encouraged outsiders to write software for the IBM PC soon after its launch. This has given a great stimulus to the whole software industry. Although IBM has come to dominate the hardware side of the PC market, no one dominates the software side. In 1983 IBM and Tandy both had 9% shares of the business software package market. They were followed closely by many other software vendors, including Apple and Commodore, as well as software specialists such as Microsoft. However, most software for PCs is still custom-made and produced at the traditional site of programming effort—large user organizations.

In the UK after 1980 the penetration of PCs into the home market has been greater than in the USA. By 1982 it was estimated that 6% of UK households had a PC, about twice as high as in the USA (Forester, 1987, p. 140). In Great Britain by the time of the NCC 1982/83 survey, 82% of DP managers reported that there were stand-alone personal computers in user areas within their organization.[4] By the 1985 survey the proportion was 90%.

There are two important characteristics of PCs, other than their cost. First, they were initially developed by new companies. Many were therefore incompatible with each other. The rapid and rather chaotic development of PCs meant that at any one point in time the PC to buy was quite different from the one to buy two months before, and it was sure to be different from the one to buy a few months later. Users often bought PCs on their own and at different times. Therefore many organizations in the early 1980s possessed an odd collection of incompatible PCs dotted around user departments.

The second characteristic of PCs, at least until the mid-1980s, had been their lack of reliable and useful software. PCs were aimed initially at the home market. The most developed software available at first were video arcade games. User department staff soon learned that the packages available were too rigid or too restrictive for their purpose. Some turned to learning BASIC to program for themselves. More turned to their organization's own DP department for help, sooner or later. During our interviews with DP managers in 1981 in the UK, and especially in 1983 in the USA, many expressed their annoyance with these requests. From the DP manager perspective, this user effort was extremely wasteful. Users were all 'reinventing the wheel'. Their different equipment meant that they could not pass these discoveries around the organization, even if they wanted to. Panic requests to salvage crashed PC systems were time-consuming.

Some DP managers allocated staff for user PC support. Some allocated staff to write systems for users' PCs. Many washed their hands of the matter or acted only as purchasing agents for the hardware.

9.1.2 Local Area Networks Spread

At the same time as users were gaining access to powerful but rather empty hardware boxes, often independent of the DP department, the equipment that DP departments had been distributing to user departments was being upgraded. According to the CEL 1972 survey, 19% of organizations supported a network of terminals in user areas. Most of these were only for data entry. However, plans to increase the number of terminals and to upgrade the use of terminals to include use for inquiries and remote job entry were expressed by between one-third and one-half of the sample. According to Computer Economics:

> These figures clearly indicate . . . that the main user requirements over the next three years is increased sophistication of the input/output level of computing applications, rather than the increase in processing speed or power. (p. 29; here it is user organizations, rather than user departments within organizations, that are being referred to)

According to the NCC 1975 survey, 66% of user organizations reported supporting a network of terminals in 1974, with 32% including 'intelligent' terminals. This was predicted to rise to 84% with terminals and 67% with intelligent terminals by 1977 (Hansen and Penney, 1976, p. 11). By the time of our CEL 1981 survey, 94% of organizations supported a network of remote user terminals.[5] The number of terminals as a proportion of employees in the organization has also been rising rapidly during the 1970s and 1980s, as has the proportion of 'intelligent' terminals.[6] According to our NCC 1984 survey, 75.4% reported providing systems allowing real-time file update with on-line inquiry in user areas.

Most large organizations had some sort of network of terminals, but in most of these organizations many devices were either connected to separate sub-networks or completely unconnected. As mentioned above, 90% of respondents to the NCC 1985 survey stated that there were PCs in user areas that were not linked to a central computer. To many progress on local area networks (LANs) has been slow. This is because the cost of networking has been high, due primarily to lack of standardization. Lack of standardization has been of two types. First, there are many LAN systems available based on very different techniques. For example, some systems run from a central control unit, usually a mainframe computer, with different devices coming off it in a star-shaped configuration. Other systems, called 'ring' or 'bus' systems, have no central core. Devices are joined together in a circular configuration. Along with these different types of configurations, three different types of cable are being used in different systems (twisted pair, coaxial and optical fibre).

The second problem is that the devices which organizations have wanted to join together were incompatible. During the late 1970s and early 1980s purchases of different manufacturers' PCs meant purchasing equipment that could not communicate with each other. The software required to make these systems compatible has been very difficult to develop. The compatibility problem eased considerably only after 1983, when IBM achieved a dominant position in the business sector of the PC market. Since then IBM has become the standard, and all major vendors (except for Apple) have strived for 'IBM compatibility'. In the NCC 1985 survey 78% of installations reporting PCs in user areas stated that there was now a standard model or models of PC adopted. Of these 41% cited IBM PCs.[7]

The diffusion of local area networks was rapid during the 1970s in terms of diffusion of some sort of network of terminals to most substantial user organizations. Diffusion in terms of connecting most terminals and PCs to large LANs within those organizations has had to wait until the 1980s and 1990s. Nearly half of the NCC 1986 survey sample (46%) reported having PCs attached to LANs. This technology was particularly widespread in the education and research sector (72%), and in relatively large organizations. The proportion is expected to grow rapidly, with 81% of the total sample expecting to have some PCs attached to LANs by the 1990s. The proportion of attached PCs within organizations was predicted to rise from 25% in 1986 to 60% in 1991.[8]

What began as a simple system for data capture from user areas gradually came to embroil users into computer systems. What was beginning to be computerized early in phase two was the first (and possibly the last) large-scale clerical task within DP departments, i.e. data entry. It was just the sort of function which typified phase one computer applications. It was rather simple work, carried out by individuals who were unskilled and poorly paid, but who represented a large cost because of their sheer numbers. During the brief period when the network was merely for data entry, users operated terminals as passive providers of information. The technology was rapidly developed to allow users to inquire of the system and to make reports. These systems were provided from the centre, rather than being developed on the initiatives of individual users, such as was stimulated by the diffusion of PCs.

9.1.3 Software Developments Expand the Computer Systems Core

Three interrelated software developments during phase two pushed both computer specialists and the computer systems core itself deeper into user departments. These were: first, advanced operating systems which more effectively separated different users and which supported real-time systems and systems development; second, database techniques; and third, fourth-generation languages, particularly report generators. All of these technical developments occurred during the 1960s and early 1970s, but their major diffusion was not until the late 1970s. In section 5.4 these technical developments were discussed in terms of their effect on task content and control structures of computer systems developers. By and large they automated many of those programmer tasks that were closest to the computer systems core. By so doing they increased the possibilities for technically sophisticated users to take over more of the mediating functions that remained.

While the hardware was spreading out from the computer systems core via terminals, as well as chaotically entering user departments on their own initiatives, software elements of the core were developing to support this spread of hardware. An early key to this was the development of operating systems that allowed different users into what were in effect separate sections of the computer. These sections could be thought of as segments of concentric bands around the core of the system. At the outer edge users could work with a segment of file space and have access to CPU power without affecting any other segment. This reduced the need for users to be carefully supervised. At worst they could only ruin their own work. Certain users with passwords which gave them access to segments of inner concentric bands could affect all or most outer segments. This separation of inner and outer segment users at first distinguished users within DP departments—inner bands for systems programmers, outer bands for applications programmers.

The intention behind these sophisticated operating systems was to ensure that multiple users would not corrupt each other's work. This desire also affected software developed to allow common usage of large databases during phase two. Accumulated applications had led to the scattering of data files around the operations room, each associated with different systems and different development staff, in a manner similar to the spread of PCs in user departments. It was difficult to use these data for anything other than the original purpose for collecting it. Multiple usage was hampered by different formats, different structures, different access procedures and especially the lack of a general way to identify the character and location of the data. Database management systems and data dictionaries were beginning to alleviate these problems late in phase two.

Database systems were not mentioned in the CEL 1972 survey. The NCC 1975 survey reported that 32% of organizations were using database techniques in 1974, but Hansen and Penney specifically pointed out that this figure included several organizations that were evaluating, rather than actually using, database techniques. By the CEL 1981 survey, 59% said they were using a database management system. Most had introduced it since 1977. Also 38% said they used a data dictionary, almost all introduced from 1978.

The use of database management systems (DBMS) grew very rapidly late in phase two. There is some evidence that the diffusion of DBMS had stabilized during the early 1980s. In our NCC 1985 survey 60% said they had a DBMS. In part the lack of change compared with the CEL 1981 survey is due to the greater proportion of small installations in the 1985 sample. Usage of both DBMS and data dictionaries was strongly correlated with installation size.[9] Most organizations use the database product developed by the manufacturer of their main computer.

The third set of software improvements which were diffusing rapidly late in phase two were generators. Generators are of three types. Most are methods for programming a computer which are part of a piece of software designed for a specific application or class of computer applications. For example, a statistical package or a financial package will have associated with it a quasi-language which may be used to generate particular statistical analyses or spreadsheets. In a sense these may be thought of as top-down languages. The uses to which the generator may be put are predefined by the type of application package. Different analyses and reports can be generated, but only within the specific application area covered by the package. This means that most are very easy to use, and the developers of these systems aimed them at end users. This has been particularly successful for statistical and financial packages.

A second type of generator is not tied to a particular application package. Rather it is intended as a general productivity aid associated with a database. These are commonly known as fourth-generation languages or 4GLs. Usage of these generators was growing very quickly by the end of phase two in the UK. Generators were not mentioned in the NCC 1975 survey. In the 1981 Urwick/

Computing survey 82% of DP managers said that they were using report generators. Evidence from our 1981 Urwick/Computing survey showed that in 1981 it was often specialists in DP departments who were the end users of these generators. This was reconfirmed in the NCC 1986 survey. DP managers expressed a strong desire that report generators be designed to be used with a minimum of skill, so that user department staff might be persuaded to deal with their own needs for ad hoc reports:

> Increasingly vendors of report generation systems have responded to this type of demand by deskilling the use of report generators to make them more accessible to users. (Friedman and Cornford, 1982a, p. 161)

However, from the NCC 1986 survey it was concluded that:

> most seem to be viewed as tools for IT professionals to use in cutting down development times or creating prototypes. There was relatively little evidence of these products being used by end-users to develop systems. (Cornford, 1987, p. 31)

The third type of generators—program generators and specific function generators (such as test-data generators and documentation generators)—are more specifically aimed at improving specialist programmer productivity. Many have been around for a long time. Program generators allow programs to be written using abbreviated forms to designate blocks of code that are frequently used, such as file descriptions and simple routines. They are languages in that they allow general communication with the computer. These generators can vary widely in their sophistication and thus in their effects on the development process. Sometimes this sort of generator is called a preprocessor or a compiler. In fact all computer languages are in essence the outward expression of a compiler. A compiler translates statements in one language (the source code) into a language the computer can more directly understand (the object code). What distinguished program generators developed late in phase two is that in order to make their source code very simple they translate a single statement of command in source code into a significantly larger number of statements of object code than third-generation languages such as COBOL. We found that 41% of the 1981 Urwick/Computing sample were using some form of program generator. Test-data generators were being used by 42% of the sample and 25% were using documentation generators.

Many DP department managers expressed disappointment in generators. Just over half the sample using report generators provided them as tools for users to assist them in producing their own reports. Several said that providing them for users did *not* mean they were used. The DP department was still processing requests for ad hoc reports.

The learning barrier was still too high for users. Very few offered program generators to users, although it was seen as a major area for expansion in the future. Internal usage of program generators also had some drawbacks. Certain generators imposed their own style and quirks. This could be serious, leading to constraints on the applications generated. It meant that users had to accept formats imposed by the generator. Program generators, and especially report generators, were of no use if the user requests were special.

Figure 9.2 shows how changes in the computer systems core towards the end of phase two affected user relations.[10] Hardware connections between central

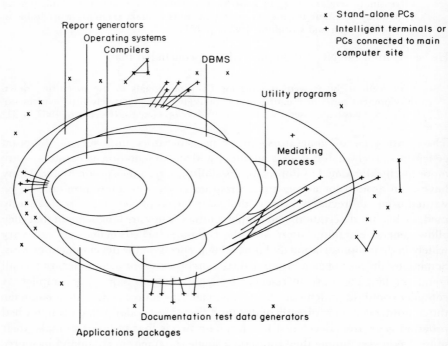

FIGURE 9.2 Phase two changes in computer core and users

computer systems core and users for purposes of systems development (rather than merely input and output), and the purchase of computer systems core directly by users, were distinguishing features of late phase two and early phase three. The model illustrated in Figure 9.2 gives the impression that these changes were built on a base of a single department in which the mediating process had been centralized. Some organizations were experimenting with decentralized or distributed DP throughout phase two (see section 10.3). However, even if the mediating process had been broken up into separate units, each of these would have developed linkages similar to those depicted in Figure 9.2 during the late 1970s and early 1980s.

9.2 CHANGES IN COMPUTER APPLICATIONS

Towards the end of phase two the way computers were being used was changing. Three changes were particularly noticeable. All were continuations of trends established towards the end of phase one.

First, the sort of applications were changing. By late phase two the basic data-crunching applications based on manual systems had been computerized in most medium- to large-sized organizations. New applications came to rely more and more on existing databases stored in computer-readable form. In terms of the hierarchy of applications introduced in Chapter 2, many new applications being developed in medium and large organizations by late phase two were beginning to support management control functions and strategic decisions. Also, by late phase two many organizations had experienced initial attempts at integrating their systems and the development of multi-purpose management information systems. These were the large-scale projects that were regularly failing during phase two— regularly late and/or over budget. Late in phase two the focus was shifting towards smaller jobs that relied on the existing, more or less integrated, base of systems and data. These jobs were often generated by users, who were developing clearer ideas of systems capabilities and of what they wanted in terms of those capabilities.

New administrative systems related less to operational tasks of the firm and more to information. That is, new activities were being generated by the system. Although the organization may have thought of trying to control inventory levels in the sense of establishing general rule of thumb quantities of buffer stocks to hold, to tie ordering for inventories with sales forecasts in order to minimize those buffers would rarely have been attempted before all the base systems had been computerized.

Second, the relationship between users and computer systems was changing. The first on-line systems, implemented early in phase two, facilitated data capture direct from users and supplied output directly to them. By late phase two these facilities were increasingly supporting end-user interrogation of systems. By 1984, according to our NCC survey for that year, almost 60% of user organizations in the UK provided some sort of on-line inquiry facility for users. The turnaround time, both for user requests for information, and between user requests for systems and operation of those systems, had fallen dramatically during phase two. In fact more users were becoming part of the system. They interacted directly with the system as part of their jobs, rather than either being replaced by the system or simply using the results of the system to do their jobs. This meant that end users increasingly became maintenance and design interactors.

Third, the types of users had been changing. Before computer development in business organizations the distinctions between different types of users outlined in section 7.3 were not necessary. Only one or two people would have filled all the roles listed. This situation has continued in scientific settings such as universities and research laboratories.

A good example would be a PhD student carrying out work in some area of numerical analysis. It is likely that this user would be the patron in that he or she would initiate the systems development process, and would try to secure availability of machine time and file space for the system. Similarly, if the purpose of the computer system is to test some hypothesis already developed by the student, the system is not in itself the student's PhD, rather the system is required in order for the PhD to be completed. Therefore the student would have been the system client. If the student works alone, he or she will be the only one designing and maintaining the system; and thus the only design and maintenance interactor, and the only end user. If the system fails or it turns out that the student should have used some other method of developing the hypotheses, then this student will be the major system victim. In this example only one other person may have taken on a user role—the student's supervisor, who may have been the patron, advising the student to carry out the work and helping the student with resources and skill development. The supervisor may also be system client, if the student was working on a larger project developed by the supervisor.

The main difference between such a PhD student working during phase one compared with a PhD student in later phases would have been the availability of more support for the computing work. In universities and other places of scientific computing today, clients of the system are still often expected to be design interactors as well as end users. Those who support the system will also expect these users to be maintenance/enhancement interactors.

What distinguished business from scientific users was that business system patrons and clients had no computing skills and no intention of acquiring these skills. DP departments were born. A clear separation emerged between design interactors and other users. Certain of the latter categories became known as *the users*. At first the term referred either to patrons or clients, generally top managers and either finance or personnel department managers for early administrative computer-based systems. Soon it became clear that new computer-based systems could not eliminate all the low-level clerical staff previously carrying out the manual system. 'Raw' output of the computer system could rarely be taken directly to department or top managers by a low-level clerk from within the new DP department. Reading raw output, translating it into a form acceptable to patrons and clients, *and* carrying out certain checks on the results, were further aspects of the mediating process which came to be done by staff outside the DP department. Such staff were familiar with the purpose of the system and they could be made to acquire the skills of reading the raw output and interpreting it for certain basic purposes.[11]

Therefore a division of labour also occurred in user departments, between patrons and clients on one hand and end users on the other. Furthermore, many of these end users also became involved as maintenance/enhancement interactors.

By early phase two, experiences of maintenance requirements and the awareness of enhancement possibilities would have more firmly rested in middle-management hands. A specialization of user roles that matched the hierarchical division of labour in user departments had emerged by early phase two. Top managers and user department managers had become specialist patrons and clients. Middle managers had become specialist enhancement interactors (and maintenance interactors to a lesser extent). Low-level clerical staff had become specialist end users and main secondary users who were victims of the system.

During phase one the DP department had become an isolated citadel of technical expertise in many respects. Most interaction was between DP managers or systems analysts, and user department managers or their assistants. A certain interaction did occur between programmers and various users, but during phase one and early in phase two this led to 'problems' with users. Therefore a clear separation of roles between analysts and programmers was recommended. Analysts were to concentrate their efforts on the outer border of the mediating process—the border with users and uses. They alone would deal with users. Programmers would be occupied entirely within the mediating process, or they would deal with the inner border—the border with the computer systems core.

This division of labour within DP departments was based on the hierarchical division of labour among users described above. The really important users were the clients (or patrons). The model was based on a large job ordered by a user department manager that would, once delivered, no longer require DP department involvement. It was assumed that implementation was a straight-forward exercise, perhaps requiring a demonstration and an instruction manual. It was assumed that the analyst could get a clear idea of client requirements during the initial period of analysis. At most a steering group would be required, although this was often mainly to monitor progress with systems development.

Changes in the nature of systems development projects during phase two made this model increasingly inappropriate. Changes in the types of systems (towards those concerning management control or strategy which meant dealing with less stable and less predictable entities) meant changes in the relation between end users and computer systems. End users became more important. Technological changes allowed them to communicate directly with the system, rather than simply to provide input or to reprocess output manually for system clients. This stimulated end-user knowledge of systems and made them more likely to take on the role of maintenance interactors, or even enhancement interactors. This could then lead to end users becoming clients for small enhancement projects. The rationale for only allowing high-level systems analysts to deal with users began to disappear. The users to be dealt with at design phases were no longer exclusively high-level user managers with no knowledge of computers. However, the growth of knowledgeable users did not only occur through the upgrading of end users into both clients and design interactors for enhancement projects. Clients and patrons were also becoming more knowledgeable and, most important, systems developed towards the end of phase two were increasingly designed with the aim of high-level managers taking on the role of the end user.

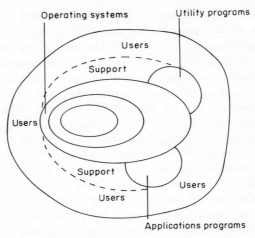

(a) Scientific

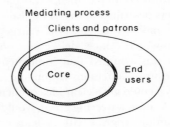

(b) Business in phase one and early phase two

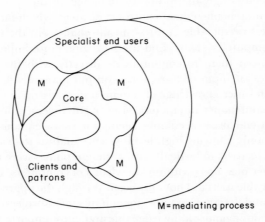

(c) New relations towards the end of phase two

FIGURE 9.3 Changes in the nature of user relations

Middle and top managers were to be the end users for new simulation systems, forecasting systems and communications systems (electronic mail and diary systems). Administrative DP departments became management information systems departments (or divisions). The emphasis of management information systems began to focus on decision support for managers. Whether it was an intelligent terminal or a personal computer, the hands on the keyboard would increasingly be those of a manager, at least for part of the time. If successful this would mean a reduction in clerical-level end users.

Therefore by the end of phase two there was a clear movement towards integration of the user roles, towards something like the computer-skilled pre-business user, the PhD student, described at the beginning of this section.

Figure 9.3 shows the different character of the interface with users between scientific and business computing in phase one. It also shows how the user interface in business computing was changing towards the end of phase two. Some users in scientific settings dealt directly with the computer systems core at the systems programming level. Most worked through utilities that allowed higher-level interaction (such as through statistical packages). However, almost all relied on mediators, usually called programming support or system support, to sort out problems with purchased software and operating systems. Such specialists also were able to provide introductions to the systems environment to novice users. These conditions were being replicated, to some extent, in the business computing area towards the end of phase two. This was stimulated by changes among users as well as by extensions of the computer systems core. This pattern will be discussed further in Chapter 13.

9.3 MARKET DEVELOPMENTS

9.3.1 Changing Market Relations for Output from DP Departments

So far we have discussed the output of a typical DP department in terms of whether it is judged more on quality or on cost and timeliness. We have also discussed who the product is for. Who are the users? During phase two important changes were also occurring concerning who would supply systems. This had important consequences for competitive pressures faced by DP departments.

As noted in section 5.2.1, by early phase two the typical configuration in user organizations was for there to be a centralized DP department with a *monopoly* in computer systems supply to user departments. During phase two, with the emphasis of system quality on cost and timeliness, the relation between DP departments as suppliers of systems and user departments as clients, became somewhat more market-like. By the CEL 1981 survey, 60% of the user organizations said they charged users for DP services; 84% of these (50% of the total sample) charged for systems analysis and programming. Only 5% of the sample stated that the computing function was organized as a profit centre, but a further 10% were organized as a separate service company. Most (80%) stated that the DP department was organized as a cost centre. Also a rapidly growing, but still small, proportion of software used was being purchased from external software suppliers. *Datamation*, which estimated that US firms spent only 2% of their computer budgets on external software in 1978, estimated the figure to be 10% by 1982 (cited in OECD, 1985, p. 52).

Computer systems development associated with user organizations may be classified according to the degree of protection from direct competitive pressures the organization provides. This classification scheme can apply to any function within an organization (such as research and development, security or catering). There are three dimensions to this protection:

(1) The degree to which activities are embedded within the organization. Degree of 'embeddedness' within the organization refers to the extent to which the service provided is protected from external market pressures, from alternative suppliers outside the organization.
(2) The number of sources within an organization which supply the service, or substitute services. That is, the extent to which the service is protected from internal market pressures.
(3) The degree of competition faced by the organization in what we will call its primary product markets; that is, the main markets in which the organization as a whole competes. This will affect the degree to which a service or subsidiary activity within the organization is protected from budget cuts—direct threats to its resource base, as opposed to threats to its resource base coming from competition against its own output (or sales).

Figure 9.4 demonstrates different financial positions for DP ordered on a scale indicating degree of protection from market pressures. These positions primarily reflect the first dimension of market protection: degree of embeddedness.

Competing DP departments within organizations are rare (except perhaps for competition between parent company central DP departments and subsidiary company local DP departments). Most recently the main internal competition has come from the users themselves, from go-it-alone users. In the past the degree of competition in primary product markets has been related to threats to the resource base for DP in a manner rather different from other services. Although services such as research and development, security or catering may be regarded as essential for the running of an organization, in times of great financial stress to the organization such services are likely to be cut. Their contribution is directed to long-run sub-goals of the organization (stream of product improvements, happy workers). It is possible to meet short-run output targets without these services, or at least with greatly reduced levels. Cutting them would therefore result in straightforward short-run cost reductions.

Developing new computer systems, at least during phases one and two,

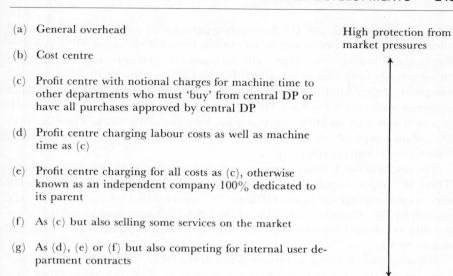

(a) General overhead

(b) Cost centre

(c) Profit centre with notional charges for machine time to other departments who must 'buy' from central DP or have all purchases approved by central DP

(d) Profit centre charging labour costs as well as machine time as (c)

(e) Profit centre charging for all costs as (c), otherwise known as an independent company 100% dedicated to its parent

(f) As (c) but also selling some services on the market

(g) As (d), (e) or (f) but also competing for internal user department contracts

(h) A software house or service bureau

High protection from market pressures

No protection from market pressures

FIGURE 9.4 Degree of protection from market pressures

contributed directly to cost reduction elsewhere in the organization, due to redundancies among employees previously working with manual systems. Cutting costs in the DP department would therefore mean forgoing greater cost reductions in user departments. Top managers frequently faced this dilemma.

Our in-depth surveys in the UK coincided with the worst years of the depression in the UK economy since the 1930s (1980–1982). At that time large-scale cost-cutting exercises were being carried out in most organizations we visited. However, most either waived the standard cut being applied to all other departments or expanded DP department budgets in order to speed up cost cuts elsewhere.[12] In extreme cases, the expected relationship between worsening competitive pressures in primary product markets and increasing pressure on service department budgets was reversed when it came to computer systems development. Thus, the most clear-cut connection to market pressures has been via the embeddedness relationship. Even though top managers may be anxious to implement new computer-based systems in hard times as well as in good times, these systems do not have to come from internal DP departments.

Protection from competition from outside suppliers, particularly for internal user departments jobs (level (g)), the burying of the costs for individual delivered systems within the DP department budget (level (c)), and the burying of the entire computing budget within general overheads (level (a)) are the important milestones for protection from market pressures. This protection was being removed in a growing number of user organizations during phase two. In our

CEL 1981 survey, 61% of DP managers reported that user departments within their organization directly employed outside firms for obtaining DP services or hardware. However, most of these DP managers (71%) reported that the decision to use outside firms had to be ratified by the DP department. Only 18% of the sample reported that users sometimes pursued external solutions without requiring ratification from the DP department. Similarly 17.5% of the sample reported that internal DP had actually bid for some of this work. Therefore over 80% of the sample of user organization DP departments were effectively protected from external market competition.

The results of our US survey were surprisingly similar to those in Great Britain. There 58% reported that user departments directly employed outside firms for DP services or computer hardware. Of these 63% reported that this decision had to be ratified by DP. Therefore only 21% of the USA 1983 sample reported that users sometimes pursued external solutions without requiring ratification by the DP department.

We went into this issue in further detail in the NCC 1984 survey. The figures were remarkably similar to the 1981 survey in spite of the different sample base and the separation by three years. In that survey 56% of the organizations reported that user departments directly employed outside firms, 22% of the sample reported that in addition DP did not have to ratify this, although only 16% reported that the DP department had bid for some of this work.[13] In that survey we also asked DP managers why they thought users used outside resources. The results are shown in Table 9.1.

The most frequent reason for users turning to external suppliers was that the bought-in solution was cheaper than could be provided by internal DP departments.[14] The two most common reasons listed under 'other' were 'specialist software needed' and 'specialist hardware requiring specialist development'. The latter was most often due to the purchase of PCs or was associated with CAD/CAM. Rather than looking at external development as arising out of a deficiency

TABLE 9.1 DP managers' opinions of why users have opted for external DP solutions

Q: Why have users used outside resources?	%
DP felt application was not viable	6.5
DP's delivery date was too long	35.2
Bought-in solution was cheaper	39.4
DP did not have the required skills	31.0
DP lacked hardware resources	37.5
Other	33.8

Source: NCC 1984 survey.

in internal DP, 'other' was ticked because DP managers had *chosen* not to acquire these specialist skills. One DP manager actually gave as a reason 'why reinvent the wheel?'. Another common reason was lack of staff (sometimes another way of saying lack of skills, but also sometimes another way of saying lack of finance). The last of the fairly common reasons given (more than 15% of the reasons) was some euphemism for bad DP–user relations: 'users think they know best' or 'users believe hardware supported by internal DP is not suitable'.[15]

Many of the reasons most commonly given for users to try external solutions to satisfy their needs appear to imply a deficiency in internal DP and may therefore indicate the presence of competitive pressures on internal DP. However, most of these reasons were not perceived as problems by DP managers. For example, internal DP's lack of required skills was more likely to indicate the problem of DP acquiring appropriate staff on the labour market, rather than incompetence on the part of existing DP staff. Although top management policy decisions were rarely mentioned as the direct reason for users going outside the organization, reasons such as lack of hardware resources (in fact all of the common reasons given) could be traced back to a long-run decision not to reinvent the wheel. Clearly user demands had become so great and *so varied* by the 1980s, and the external market for software services and products had developed sufficiently, for there to be cost disadvantages to trying to satisfy all user department needs internally.

In the 1981 Urwick/Computing survey DP managers were asked what they regarded as their main problems (Table 9.2). The only one that really stands out is failure to meet project deadlines. Rather surprisingly, staying within budgets was the major concern of very few. This is in spite of the great concern with financial controls over DP, which was so notable throughout the 1970s.

The major market change that distinguishes early phase three from early phase two is the presence of a well-developed external market for software products and

TABLE 9.2 Major issues facing DP managers

Q: What is the major issue facing you at present?

	%
Meeting project deadlines	53.6
Maintaining existing programmes	13.7
Evaluating present technology	13.7
Evaluating future technology	12.8
'Go-it-alone' users	11.6
Meeting project cost targets	7.7
Staff recruitment	7.4
Staff retention	4.2

Source: 1981 Urwick/Computing survey (Friedman and Cornford, 1981, p. 6).

computer services directly supplying user departments in the majority of medium- to large-sized organizations.

During phase two growth of the computer services sector, particularly of software houses from the early 1970s (after unbundling),[16] meant that more credible alternatives to internally generated DP systems were becoming available. However, it appears that direct competition between external suppliers and internal DP departments was limited. In the great majority of cases internal departments maintained a quasi-monopoly position to supply users inside the organization. The internal user market has become segmented. Internal and external suppliers came to coexist as non-competing groups in around 40% of organizations.[17] Internal DP departments were sole suppliers in a further 40% of organizations. These figures roughly correspond to the situation both in Great Britain and in the USA in the early 1980s according to our CEL 1981 and USA 1983 surveys.[18]

Why have internal DP departments maintained monopoly or quasi-monopoly positions in spite of the rapidly emerging software industry? The answer lies in our earlier discussion of changing uses, users and relations between computer systems developers and users. These changes meant that more intimate knowledge of user needs and sensitivity to how those needs might develop was required of systems developers. This moved the balance towards internal solutions for many of the latest applications, even if older applications could increasingly be well satisfied by packages, by service bureaus or by custom-made software from external suppliers. However, this same set of changes also meant that a new potential rival supplier of computer services has been emerging—the computer-skilled user.

As we noted earlier, the death knell of DP departments had often been rung in the past. Users would no longer be requiring a mediator with the computer in business settings once new, easy-to-use languages had been developed. By 1981 only 11.6% of British DP managers considered 'go-it-alone' users to be a major issue facing them (Table 9.2). Most of these were concerned about *extra work* required of them when user-developed systems crashed, rather than loss of their 'market'. Concern with go-it-alone users was part of a much wider set of problems that were emerging at the end of phase two. This was with meeting the growing volume of increasingly varied and sophisticated user demands. High concern with meeting project deadlines rather than meeting project cost targets reflects the new situation.

Timeliness rather than cost had become the major measure of DP department success. As we will show in Chapters 11 and 12, responses to this and other user demands stimulated a wide variety of new strategies, both within DP departments and between DP departments and user departments.

9.3.2 Labour Markets

The labour shortage that created problems of recruitment, discipline and labour turnover, and which thereby contributed substantially to the software productivity problem of phase two, continued throughout the 1970s and 1980s. We will consider demand and supply factors.

On the demand side the growth of computerization has continued unabated. Stimulated by further improvements in cost/performance ratios and lower entry costs with the coming of PCs, successively smaller organizations have been able to acquire computer systems. Successively more complex systems have also become feasible. With the accumulation of large organization-specific databases and the development of sophisticated software to allow easier access to those databases, more systems that support the competitive position of organizations were being developed. With the accumulation of more operational systems, maintenance requirements have grown. With the rise in computer literacy among users, their demands for new applications have also grown.

Growth of computerization stimulated growth in demand for computer-skilled staff. Although the demand for people to carry out certain tasks has been affected by automation (improved operating systems, database management systems, generators, application packages), many traditional activities are still carried out in DP departments. Some new applications are not appropriately carried out using automated methods. Maintenance of old systems requires traditional skills. Also automation has very rarely provided the solutions to all of a large organization's needs. Even where automated methods are pursued, there is still a need for programming and analysis skills. For example, most large organizations that buy packages 'customize' them to suit their hardware configuration, their software environment or their application needs.

Demand for computer staff has been changing as well as growing. The 'location' of the mediating process in our model of the computerization process has been changing substantially as a result of the changes in applications and technology. This is shown in Figure 9.5. It has been moving further into user functions at its outer edge, reflecting the new types of applications. It has been moving further away from hardware aspects of individual computers, although it has been embracing communication or networking tasks among pieces of equipment during

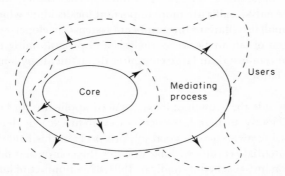

FIGURE 9.5 Changing 'location' of the mediating process

the 1980s (not only between computers but also between computers and other office machinery).

This has stimulated demand for network specialists. Not only has the typical configuration of hardware come to embrace more disparate pieces of equipment, due to the spread of PCs and the coming of office automation, but also typical computer systems development environments have come to be composed of a more disparate collection of software. In part this software heterogeneity simply reflects the heterogeneous collection of hardware to be operated. In part it reflects the availability of powerful packages specific to a particular application area, i.e. of 4GLs. In part it reflects different levels of computer literacy among systems developers, many of whom would be thought of as end users. Although we found that 89% of our CEL 1981 sample of user organization installations used COBOL, only 16% of the sample used only one language.[19] More than half the sample (55%) used three or more languages. Most used some form of report generator, database language or other utility.[20]

During the 1980s the use of these language-like packages and tools, as well as use of specific application packages, diffused even more widely. Demand for systems programmers to service this growing collection of packages and languages has therefore been growing rapidly. Demand for applications programmers has continued to grow, but the demand for systems programmers and network specialists has grown more quickly, particularly during the 1980s.

Since the late 1970s the greatest growth in demand has been for analysts and for computer systems developers who are able to analyse, design and program computer systems (for what are called analyst/programmers in Europe and programmer/analysts in the USA). This has occurred for a number of reasons:

(1) The shifting of the mediating process towards users. Within analysis there has been a growing demand for business analysts. Individuals carrying out programming work must also be able to work with users.
(2) Rapid growth in the number of small computer departments situated in small organizations. In smaller organizations there is more likely to be a higher proportion of systems bought in from outside rather than developed internally. Analysis skills are more important for deciding which packages to use. With small installations the number of systems developers will not justify a strict division of labour between analysis and programming functions.
(3) Attempts to retain staff in large computer departments by lengthening their promotion ladder.

On the supply side the growth of inexperienced applicants for computing jobs has grown sufficiently to match, sometimes even to exceed, demand for new entrants. Increasing awareness of good job prospects in this field[21] has meant a sufficiency of potential recruits wishing to enter the computing field.

When the economy reached its nadir in 1981/82, a number of large computing organizations cut their intake of recruits or refrained from recruiting at all. At that time several DP managers told us that they were regularly receiving large numbers of job inquiries from inexperienced people. Since then the demand for new recruits has increased substantially, but so has supply. Growth in supply has occurred in part because of short training programmes sponsored by the British Manpower Services Commission. It has also increased owing to an enormous increase in the number of information technology 'conversion' courses being put on by higher education institutions in Great Britain. These, in turn, have been stimulated by government policy favouring new posts in information technology and new research in this area at a time of general cuts in government support for higher education.

Of 437 difficult-to-fill posts reported in the NCC 1986 survey, only three were for junior or trainee programmers (compared with 108 for higher-level programmers). The NCC 1987 survey concentrated on shortages of IT skills, so great had this issue become to the community of user organizations. However, the general conclusion from the survey was:

> Few of the respondents expressed difficulties in recruiting trainees with appropriate educational qualifications. This implies that the shortage is entirely of staff with appropriate IT skills and experience. (Buckroyd and Cornford, 1988, p. 16)

Clearly supply is still a problem. As noted in Chapter 5, the fundamental labour supply problem in the computing field is the difficulty of acquiring appropriate skills *off the job*, in training institutions. This problem was not substantially alleviated by productivity tools developed during phase two. One reason for this is that these productivity tools were not universally applicable. Their value was contingent upon the programming environment in which they were introduced. In most installations they were not used in full and not imposed for all computer systems developers. Eighteen months to two years of experience still seems to be essential for programmers to be considered fit additions to a computer installation. This is clear from a perusal of job advertisements. According to the NCC 1986 survey the highest rates of labour turnover among development staff were for programmers and analyst/programmers who had completed this period of on-the-job training (Cornford, 1987, p. 39).

Perceived shortages of over 10% of staff in post were reported across all development staff categories in the NCC 1986 survey, except for DP management.[22] The problem has been exacerbated by a reluctance to train new staff, particularly on the part of the rapidly growing group of smaller organizations.

A similar pattern emerged in the USA by the early 1970s. Labour shortages continue to exist, but only for experienced computer-skilled staff. According to Couger and Zawacki (1980, pp. 2–4) two of five reasons for the inability of DP departments in the USA to clear the backlog of new system requests were a shortage of qualified personnel and labour turnover.[23]

Unlike the substantial changes taking place in technology, types of application and markets for computer services towards the end of phase two, the conditions of markets for experienced computer systems developers had not changed substantially. There were still severe shortages and high labour turnover for all categories of development staff. Although the market was undoubtedly wider, it was still tight.

9.4 CONCLUSIONS

The most important agent of change stimulating the transition from phase one to phase two was the dramatic improvement in the cost/performance ratio of computer systems core. Arguably changes in the character of computer uses and computer users was the most important stimulant of the transition from phase two to phase three. This transition was also stimulated by the infiltration of computer systems core directly into user departments via PCs, intelligent terminals and software that was aimed at end users. It was also stimulated by deterioration of the monopoly position that DP departments held in user organizations. However, these latter two factors must not be thought of purely as autonomous external agents. Certainly the availability of computer systems core at prices user department managers could afford, and the development of an external market for computer software and services, contributed to the change in power relations between computer systems developers and computer users. This stimulated greater concern about user relations among systems developers. However, the extent to which users could go it alone or rely on external solutions has continued to depend on DP department management. DP departments have been relied upon to support users in their dealings with outside suppliers of software and hardware and with their own systems development efforts. Also direct user purchases of external computer services by and large must be ratified by DP department management.

DP department managers and systems developers have rarely been worried about redundancy or not having enough work. Acute shortages of experienced computer systems developers have continued. Rather the introduction of market-like relations with users and the spread of computer systems core into the user domain has been used as positive strategies to alleviate the more fundamental increase in volume and power of user demands for timely and appropriate systems from DP departments. In the following two chapters strategies to alleviate user relations problems will be examined in detail.

ENDNOTES

1. Boguslaw's view was a more accurate description of the main types of DP computer systems being introduced during phases one and two. We would argue that his description was also more accurate than that of others writing in the 1960s who saw new

computer systems as establishing a complementary man–machine partnership, such as Licklider (1960, 1965). During the early phases a small number of real-time systems were introduced which did complement human skills (such as navigation aids and air traffic control systems). The balance of systems developed during phase three indicates more support for Licklider's interpretation and less for Boguslaw.

2. Some minicomputers available in the mid-1970s were 'simple' enough for user department staff to be able to operate them without specialist computer systems developers, but non-specialists were not able to develop systems on them without considerable training.

3. See Freiberger and Swaine (1984) for a romantic rendition of the lore, and Moritz (1984) for a more sober view.

4. Also 14% of these admitted that they did not know how many there were.

5. In later surveys similar proportions were reported (NCC 1985 survey: 95%). Note that differences in sample sizes mean that these figures are not strictly compatible.

6. Finance and education were sectors that stood out as having a high proportion of terminals per 100 employees.

7. ICL PCs and ACT PCs were each cited by 12%, DEC by 6% and Apple by 5%.

8. In addition to LANs, there has been substantial growth in the use of WANs (private wide-area networks). In the NCC 1986 survey, 53% reported using them and the forecast use by 1991 was 68%. Spectacular growth was predicted for use of VANs (value-added networks). These are primarily connections to external databases, providing information on such topics as credit ratings, news services and technical, legal and marketing information. Use of VANs was predicted to rise from 44% to 78% between 1986 and 1991.

9. Only 45% of small installations had a DBMS compared with 68% of medium-sized ones and 87% of large ones in the NCC 1985 survey.

10. Figure 5.4 showed how changes in the computer core during phase two affected the mediating process.

11. The ideal of a phase-one system was total automation of an operational department's tasks. The output of such a department should be produced in a form ready for distribution without human intervention. For example, pay cheques and invoices. Even if no manual checks on the output were made, it would have been rare for department managers to receive records of the direct output in the form of computer printouts, without the help of some interpretation.

12. Some companies applied their standard formula for cost cutting to DP departments. For example, a policy of 'cut all staff budgets by 10%' would be imposed regardless of the effect on user department costs. Others maintained a fiction of equal treatment for all departments, but allowed cuts to be made in data preparation staff, who would have been formally part of the DP department, rather than systems development staff. Many departments had plans to cut data preparation anyway and they were allowed to include these plans in the required cuts.

13. Interestingly substantial changes in these proportions were reported in our NCC 1985 survey. Fewer reported that decisions by users to obtain facilities from outside sources had to be ratified by DP (55%) and 34% reported that they competed directly against outside suppliers. It may be that the change between these two years (which was confirmed by a matched sample of respondents to both surveys) reflects a decomposition of large organizations occurring in the UK after the general economic recovery began in 1983.

14. Not surprisingly, this was correlated with the size of the DP department. Large installations (more than 30 analysts and programmers) stood out, with almost half (48%) stating that the bought-in solution was cheaper. 'Long delivery dates' was also

correlated with size, but the main difference occurred for very small installations (less than ten analysts and programmers), where only 27% indicated this reason. Lack of hardware resources was the reason favoured by very small installations (45%).

15. The remaining reasons mainly concerned relations among partners in merged firms, relations with suppliers or top management policy decisions.

16. In 1969 the US Department of Justice required IBM to invoice its hardware and software separately, i.e. to unbundle it. Until that year IBM, along with all other hardware manufacturers, included software normally supplied with the hardware in the price of the hardware. It was not invoiced separately. Within a few years after 1969 other hardware manufacturers also came to market their software separately. Unbundling is generally regarded as the key event for the foundation of the software industry (OECD, 1985, pp. 55–56). Note that in the UK it is common to label firms supplying software along with those only providing computer services (service bureaus) as the computer services industry.

17. In around 60% users were supplied directly by outsiders, but in one-third of these there was also direct competition between internal computer departments and external suppliers.

18. According to Informatics (one of the largest software houses in the world), between 10% and 15% of all instructions executed on US computers were software purchased from outside suppliers. OECD cites an IBM source confirming the same picture for the USA at the beginning of the 1980s (OECD, 1985, p. 49).

19. For 75% of the sample COBOL was their first language.

20. A grey area exists between what might be called a language and what is 'merely' a software tool. To some extent this depends on how the tool/language is used. For example, tool/languages such as Filetab, Mantis and Mark IV may be used as general programming languages or as report generators or prototyping systems. In our surveys these (and many others) were listed by respondents under both languages and under report-generating or program-generating packages.

21. In contrast with dwindling opportunities in other areas of the British economy, which were markedly slowing down from the mid-1970s.

22. Job categories were systems analysts, analyst/programmers, programmers, systems programmers/technical support and network staff. Shortages reported for DP managers were only 1% of staff in post. Shortages reported for operators and data preparation staff were 2% and 3% of staff in post.

23. The other three reasons were from the demand side of the labour market: increasing complexity and quantity of systems demanded, and increasing maintenance requirements.

Chapter 10

EARLY REACTIONS TO USER RELATIONS PROBLEMS

As emphasized earlier, user relations problems have existed from the outset of computing. In early years the problem was conceived of as one of translating user requirements, which were imprecise and incomplete, into clear systems and programming specifications. A secondary problem was also evident to some during the early years. This was how to implement the completed system, given that the translation of requirements into systems would have been imperfect and that requirements themselves were likely to have been misunderstood by users and by computer staff.

During phase one and most of phase two this problem was not perceived as critical. Most major systems replicated existing manual systems. The job of systems analysis could be carried out from existing manual systems descriptions and fairly perfunctory liaison with the client. However, this contact with the client quickly became the focus of the user relations problem.

The problem was often considered to be one of conflicting ideologies associated in part with an age gap. Computer department staff were paid high salaries at a young age. This upset established differentials. A greater problem was the ideological one. DP staff were change agents. Increasingly they viewed established traditions and procedures with a critical eye. The applications undertaken may have begun largely as *replacements* of existing manual systems. However, greater experience with computerized solutions led to greater expectations of *enhancements*. This could lead to conflicts between clients and young computer specialists, who were regarded as outsiders, overpaid upstarts who only saw the formal side of systems, who did not understand how things really got done.

In this chapter, three strategies for dealing with user relations problems associated with the period before phase three will be discussed. The first, separating analysts from programmers, was well established in the computing field during phase one. It was a policy strongly recommended by IBM. The second, developing techniques that would allow analysts to specify user requirements accurately, has absorbed a great deal of academic and consultancy effort since phase one. In spite of an enormous and well-regarded literature on this subject, and in spite of a flood of techniques to emerge for this purpose during phases two and three, few computer installations have invested substantially in introducing[1] and ensuring use of these techniques.[2] The third strategy, creating market-like relations between computer departments and users, is a strategy that also has a long history in the computing field. Although often recommended and important for controlling DP costs, we would argue that attempts to create financial arms-length relations between computer systems developers and users has exacerbated user relations problems.[3]

10.1 SEPARATING ANALYSTS FROM PROGRAMMERS

Clearly, even in phase one this problem was recognized. In fact the division of labour between analysts and programmers was in part an attempt to deal with this problem by isolating it. By the end of phase one the division of labour between analysts and programmers was well established in DP departments. Analysts were primarily concerned with early phases of systems development and with user relations, and programmers primarily with later phases of systems development. Programmers worked more closely with hardware. Programmers in user organizations in Mumford's survey had very weak links with user departments. An overwhelming 90% said they needed human relations skills only in dealing with staff in their own department (compared with 67% in manufacturing and 57% in computer service firms who did not develop such skills outside their own department; p. 167). In fact, when asked which groups DP department staff had most contact with, 95% of analysts in Mumford's user organizations said user department staff, compared with only 25% of programmers.

Mumford (1972) emphasized *similarities* in technocratic values among analysts and programmers, although granting that the 'problem' (as she saw it) applied more strongly to programmers. Hebden emphasized *differences* in perspectives between analysts and programmers. Analysts identified more closely with organization members outside DP. They derived social satisfaction from negotiating with line management to get a 'system to go live' (Hebden, 1975, p. 122). Programmers identified more closely with DP specialists, even if they were outside the organization, and were more concerned with technical success, in getting the computer to respond.

The following picture emerges of user relations early in phase two. First, there was a strong division of labour whereby contact with users was primarily confined to a specialists group, the analysts. Programmers had little contact or sympathy with users. Second, the analysts too were ideologically separated from the users. Their contact appears to have been primarily with system clients, rather than end users; that is, with user department managers rather than the clerical staff who would become the actual man end of the man–machine interface with the new system in operation. Third, to the ordinary staff of the user department the DP department was an unknown place. 'There was almost total ignorance concerning the computer department', Mumford reports of ordinary clerical workers. Comments such as 'they don't give us much information', 'they don't tell us about changes in time' or 'they just give you a book to read' were given in all of the user organizations in Mumford's survey (1972, p. 144).

Clearly the image of citadel DP had been established during phase one. In order to reduce tension between DP staff and user staff, a specialist—the analyst—was established to carry out the liaison work. However, it is also clear from Mumford's study that this did not solve the user relations problem.

10.2 SYSTEMS ANALYSIS TECHNIQUES: REQUIREMENTS DEFINITION LANGUAGES[4]

Separating analysis from programming work and creating specialist analysis and specialist programmers was regarded by many as only a precondition for increased effectiveness of analysis and increased productivity of programming work. New techniques specifically aimed at improving the performance of each of these specialists were required. In Chapter 5 we concentrated on techniques developed during phase two to improve programmer productivity and systems design. During phase two a stream of techniques designed to improve the job of systems analysis were also developed.

As noted in section 8.2.6, the analysis of user requirements may be thought of as both a problem of elicitation of user requirements and one of assurance of the accuracy of the specification of those requirements. Before phase three the desire for assurance dominated the development of systems analysis techniques. The aim was to create structured systems of representation that would allow and encourage analysts to specify user requirements unambiguously, in a manner that could be transparent to other analysts, to programmers and to managers. To create such a system of representation was, in effect, to create a language. These systems have often been labelled requirements definition languages.

Requirements definition languages may be distinguished from programming languages which focus on the procedural aspects of *how* to build parts of an information system. Requirements definition languages focus on defining *what* is required for building parts of an information system.

Early attempts to develop requirements definition languages long predate the computer era.[5] The roots of systems analysis techniques for analysing information flows lie in the process flow chart, an industrial engineering technique for representing the flow of materials developed by Taylor and the Gilbreths in the early 1900s (Couger, 1973). Process flow charts displayed how materials moved and indicated points when they were transformed. Later flow charts were used to show the flow of forms, including the transformation of data or data processing. Eventually, with the development of data processing machines, these process flow charts for forms, or data processing flow charts, included transformations using mechanical devices such as card punchers, tabulators and sorters.

As with the computer system life cycle discussed in Chapter 7, process flow charts could be used to describe a process, or to prescribe how a process should occur and facilitate monitoring that the process did in fact proceed as prescribed. Flow charts were used in both ways. As description they were used to plan what resources were required and when. As prescription they were used to represent how long each step in the process should take and the precise manner in which it should occur. In this latter way they could act as a method for standardizing and controlling work.

The intention behind the work of Taylor and the Gilbreths was to allow management to gain direct control over both materials flow and the work of their employees. Their techniques represented a major contribution to the formulation of direct control strategies, particularly when work was divided into very fine parts. The process flow chart could indicate any number of separate processes. It was a key tenet of Taylor and the Gilbreths that the way work was traditionally broken up into separate processes was inadequate. 'Ordinary management' was what Taylor disdainfully called the practice of overseeing work patterns that had developed historically. With what Taylor called 'scientific management' work assignments were based on a structure of separate tasks defined by management. Each individual task was to be simple and short. Regarding each scientifically determined task as a separate process would lead to a much finer division of labour and a much more detailed process flow chart than one which described a traditional work pattern.

It is important to recognize that use of flow charts does not have to accompany a direct control strategy over employees. The process flow chart was primarily for charting the flow of materials and later for the flow of forms. It is possible for flow charts to depict flows between highly skilled individuals or groups or workers who have considerable discretion over how the materials are transformed, and who are not closely supervised. However, the value of charting flows of materials is considerably increased when the path of materials flow is complex. This occurs when individual transformation tasks are a small part of the whole process; when the work has been divided into many small and interlocking processes; and when the work of any one individual in the overall process is simple, and therefore is likely to require little skill. Traditional industrial processes with which Taylor was dealing were carried out by craftsmen who performed a large number of tasks before worked-up materials were transferred elsewhere. Process flow charts were an important technique of scientific management because the purpose of analysis of the labour process was to redesign it along lines whereby the work of individuals would be simplified, but coordination of the work of all the individuals would become more complex.

The emphasis of these early industrial engineers was to establish a clear set of techniques that would allow work processes to be standardized and controlled. This guided the process of information gathering. Observation of existing systems was concentrated on visible aspects of work that could most easily be formalized and then standardized. The dominance of assurance over elicitation in modern systems analysis techniques has its roots in the approach of these early industrial engineers.

In this early period, before computers, it was the new systematic and standardized distribution of work tasks that guided information gathering from those directly involved in the pre-existing system. This new distribution of work tasks was not created at the behest of those performing the old work tasks. The 'end users' were not clients of the new distribution. Elicitation of requirements for the new system from those directly performing work tasks was irrelevant. Rather they were to be observed, to be studied. The direct managers of these 'end users' also were not clients of the new system. Erratic and informal methods used by foremen and supervisors to coerce, cajole and exhort their subordinates were also to be redesigned. The purpose of the new system was not to provide a structure of support for this level of management. In many cases their jobs were to disappear (Littler, 1982, p. 181).

The clients of the system were top managers. However, elicitation of their requirements was also largely ignored. Taylor believed that ordinary managers did not understand what productivity gains could be had from a scientific approach. They were to be taught what was best for them. According to some, the missionary zeal of early industrial engineers re-emerged with computers. Systems analysts and designers were the 'new utopians', according to Boguslaw (1965).

Scientific management techniques were not welcomed by those whose work was being redesigned. Timings for the steps were gathered at first by simple observation using a stop-watch, and later by experimental methods, by timing task performance in laboratory conditions. The use of laboratory methods was partly stimulated by a desire to make more detailed timings and more accurate measures of what speeds were possible. It was also stimulated by resistance among employees to work measurement and to an early version of systems analysts: work study engineers. In fact resistance to scientific management was enormous, from foremen and supervisors as well as from organized labour,[6] but this resistance was largely confined to the industrial sphere. In offices resistance was not significant for two reasons. First, office employees were not organized. Second, data processing was such a new activity that there were no traditional craft methods of organizing work which were being destroyed by systematic design.[7] Systematic design was in fact the traditional method for organizing large-scale paperwork functions between the world wars. This made it relatively easy to computerize data processing compared with industrial processes.

During much of phase one the pre-Second World War type of data processing flow chart, developed for tabulating operations, was used for analysis of computer-based systems in most installations (Couger, 1973, pp. 46–47). However, some new techniques were developed. These involved:

(1) algebraic set representations (Young and Kent, 1958) or what the CODASYL development committee[8] called information algebra (CODASYL, 1962); or

(2) techniques that moved towards formal and consistent annotation of flow charts and other types of directed graphs in a manner suitable for computer-based systems.

Information algebra was developed by the Language Structure Group (LSG) of the CODASYL Committee from 1959. Their aim was to produce a structure for a problem definition language that was machine-independent. Information algebra was based on *relations* among data properties, rather than *procedures* for transferring or transforming data. A system for specifying relationships and rules of association would not require dealing with the details of how data were treated within particular machine environments. The LSG did not produce a requirements definition language or an algorithm for translating information algebra statements into machine-language problems. They expected that these steps would be taken by others based on their work. Couger notes that these expectations were fulfilled, and that the significance of information algebra was that it provided a theoretical basis for automating the step from requirements specification to systems specification (1973, p. 47).

Two of the earliest directed graphs systems, developed during what Couger calls the first generation of systems analysis techniques (1950–1960), were information process charts or IPC (Grad and Canning, 1969) and NCR's system charting technique called MAP (1961).[9] Neither of these systems was widely used (Couger, 1973).

During the 1960s and early 1970s several more systems using directed graphs were developed.[10] As noted above, use of flow charts had already been widespread, but they had been used as a step towards producing program specifications rather than for communicating with users. System charts as defined by the ANS standard have been less widely used (although listing inputs and outputs in tabular form has been common since the 1950s). In part this is because they are too simple. They convey too little information by themselves and must be supplemented with considerable annotation (Chapin, 1981). The simplicity of both these graphical methods (in that as languages they contain too few different terms, or shapes) means that their use to describe a complex system appears too complex, especially to users. As with flow charts, the use of systems charts has remained confined to communication within computer departments, and often only as a rough aid for analysts' own use alone.

In Accurately Defined Systems—ADS, an approach that was developed at National Cash Register from 1962 (NCR, 1968)—different forms defining inputs, outputs, processes and data are linked using directed graphs. An advantage of ADS was the coordination of its overall organization. Another directed graph approach (which also used matrix algebra) was developed by Langfors (1963) and later taken up by Nunamaker (1971) and Konsynski (1976).

Coinciding with their launch of the 360 series, IBM produced TAG (Time Automated Grid), a forms-oriented method for systems definition. The method starts with identification of output and works backward towards the data elements required to produce the output. The availability of data elements for processing is identified on a time grid (Kelly, 1970, pp. 367–402; IBM, 1971). TAG was an automated procedure. The forms the analyst would fill out could be run through the computer using programs that would provide a set of reports to identify redundant data items, to design files, to define sorting requirements, etc. Another early phase-two automated procedure was AUTOSATE. This was developed at Rand in 1964 and 1965 (Gatto, 1964).

Other early phase-two tools were SYSTEMATICS, which relied on a decision table approach to specification (Grindley, 1966) and PSL (Problem Statement Language), which was based on statements rather than forms. PSL was an attempt to incorporate the best features of all the languages discussed above; it records user requirements in a machine-readable form that can be analysed by a software package called PSA (Problem Statement Analyzer). Numerous versions of PSL were developed throughout phase two based on the initial work by Teichroew from 1966 at the University of Michigan (see Teichroew and Sayani, 1971; Nunamaker and Konsynski, 1981).[11]

Couger considers TAG, SYSTEMATICS and PSL/PSA to be third-generation techniques.[12] According to Couger and Knapp:

> Second generation techniques were manual techniques designed to facilitate analysis of the existing system and to develop an improved system. Third generation techniques began to employ the computer as an aid in system analysis. (1974, p. 42)

Although many third-generation systems were developed in the mid-1960s, by the mid-1970s none of these third-generation systems were widely used. Couger and Knapp report that in 1973 less than 100 of the 50 000 US computer installations were using third-generation techniques (1974, p. 83). The proportion of installations using such techniques in Great Britain and in the rest of Europe would have been even smaller.

These early approaches were not widely used, in part because they were complex and limited to certain classes of problems, but also because the user requirements specification problem was not regarded as compelling at that time. IBM withdrew support for TAG during the late 1960s, and AUTOSATE was never well supported. Users could not look to the suppliers for training, program corrections or documentation of program changes (Davis, 1974, pp. 423–424). Also structured programming and design methods were not yet available to back up these early attempts at requirements definition languages. From the mid-1970s both the pace of technical development and the diffusion of structured methods and of requirement definition languages quickened.

Use of graphical techniques for representing user requirements was stimulated by their inclusion in various structured analysis and design methodologies during the 1970s. Some of the more commonly used ones in the USA are data flow diagrams (DFD) and bubble charts. These are special versions of the system chart. They have been recommended for use in the structured analysis methodologies associated with Gane and Sarson (1971) and Yourdon (Yourdon and Constantine, 1975; DeMarco, 1978).[13]

In 1973 IBM developed HIPO charts (Hierarchy, Input, Processing and Output) as both a design aid and a documentation tool (IBM, 1973; Katzen, 1976).[14] HIPO charts stress a hierarchical definition of processes and subprocesses. The use of HIPO charts became fairly common in computer departments during the late 1970s. Another system developed at IBM was Business Definition Language, BDL (DeJong, 1976). BDL was intended as a successor to TAG. It was based on the expression of graphical relationships of elements in the system. The idea was, as with PSL, that BDL could be used by the users themselves.

Although graphical techniques have become widely used by systems analysts and designers, their usage has not improved communication with users. Even in their role as generators of documentation for users they have been found wanting:

> ...most graphical tools are harder to use than are narrative text tools... The narrative tools can be practiced with little special training, while the use of the graphical tools normally requires special training ... because the typical receiver in the user group is not technically trained in the use of graphical tools, but knows narrative text forms of documentation, the graphic tools are often an expensive choice. The personnel in the user group often refer to the documentation of the information system for guidance about what to do when some situation arises. They want specific directions, not a general explication of relationships. The emphasis given in most of the graphics tools is not the emphasis helpful to most user personnel. (Chapin, 1981, p. 129)

Rather than eliciting user information about their requirements, such techniques contributed to the continuing technical wedge between users and computer systems developers. They assume that the major problems of requirement specification are that users are inconsistent and incomplete in the way they state their requirements. The analyst must therefore express those requirements in a language that will make inconsistencies apparent, and identify gaps.[15]

Emphasis on techniques for the *elicitation* of user requirements, in forms that were intended to reflect users' own ways of thinking rather than representing requirements based on models of computer systems, exhibits a curious time pattern. During the late 1950s and the early 1960s IBM developed SOP (Study Organization Plan). This plan for overall systems planning centred on the organization chart. It was based on the assumption that new computer systems could be best elicited by reference to organization charts, which related the planning of information system application systems to the organizational units.[16] SOP was extremely successful and was used throughout the 1970s. However, the SOP system was really best geared to handling the automation of existing manual systems. It organized the elicitation of needs in terms of the existing organization structure, while more and more applications desired during phase two crossed organization boundaries.

Although SOP had a greater emphasis of elicitation than the requirements definition languages discussed above, this feature was still limited to a very simple and rigid model of user needs. It presumed that organizations operated as might be described in an organization chart. This represented a model of how organizations ought to behave. It concentrated on formal, rational and also on static aspects of information systems. In this sense it, like the requirements definition languages based more tightly on the model of the computer systems, emphasized what users ought to require, rather than eliciting requirements in users' own terms. However, to the extent that organizations behaved in this way, SOP was appropriate. Also SOP was appropriate for organizations in which top managers wished to use the development of computer-based systems in order to rationalize their operations, to force the organization to behave more like this rational ideal.

It was not until 1979 that IBM released a new version of SOP called BSP (Business Systems Planning; IBM, 1978).[17] Some further techniques aimed at elicitation were developed during the late 1970s, notably Business Information Analysis and Integration Technique or BIAIT, developed by Burnstine (see Carlson, 1979),[18] and critical success factors (Rockart, 1979).[19] However, these methods have not been particularly successful. Davis provides a useful summary of these techniques, but he begins with the following rather negative assessment:

> Correct and complete information requirements are key ingredients in planning organizational information systems and in implementing information systems applications. Yet there has been relatively little research on information requirements determination, and there are relatively few practical, well-formulated procedures for obtaining complete, correct information requirements. (Davis, 1982, p. 4)

10.3 MARKET-LIKE SOLUTIONS: CHARGEOUT SYSTEMS

A strategy concerning the *form* of DP–user department contact has been pursued with increasing vigour since the beginning of phase two. This is the creation of clearer financial ties between the departments.

In phase one the computer was placed in the department for which the first computer application was being developed. Usually this was the accounts or finance department. However, during phase one this hardware represented a very large purchase. It had to be utilized as efficiently and as much as possible to make it pay for itself. This led computer managers to seek out applications for computerization from other departments. As software costs began to grow rapidly (absolutely, and even more so relative to hardware), they could no longer be borne by the initial user department. This led to the emergence of the independent DP department.

As user demands for enhancements and new systems grew, the DP department began to fall behind. Systems arrived late. Budgets overran. If success for DP was to get systems out on time and within budget, an obvious way to control against failure was to tighten the financial strings round that department. In many organizations the DP department had become a simple overhead. Its budget was attributed as a whole either to the finance department or increasingly to management services. From senior management's perspective this became a serious problem once the overhead item changed from being primarily for equipment, supposedly an infrequent expense, to an item primarily composed of salaries, a recurring expense and one that was growing quickly.

This led relations between DP departments and users to be defined more and more in financial terms. If DP services were being charged out to others, DP managers would be encouraged to view their staff time in cost terms. This is one of the reasons for the proliferation of standardization and structured methods during phase two.

The stimulus for accountability of DP has been presented purely in terms of the growing importance of software costs, both as an absolute amount and in terms of the variable cost as a share in total system costs. In fact the problem of satisfying users' needs/wants had already emerged as a major problem. The productivity problem had made itself apparent in many organizations originally as a failure to meet target dates and costs. This arose out of early misspecifications of user problems which then had to be corrected. This type of problem was exacerbated by changing user environments combined with long lead times in development of systems. What might appear to be a minor change in the system to a user could well be a major change to the system itself. Thus the inability to specify or predict users' needs accurately was partly responsible for the appearance of the productivity problem and recriminations between DP and users regarding the blame for failed, late or inadequate systems.

The setting up of accounting controls over the DP department established a much stronger client–provider relationship between the users and DP. The controls were designed partly to solve the productivity problem as reflected in rapidly rising costs and missed deadlines. They were also set up to deal with interdepartmental problems (including resource allocation between departments) and to attempt to deal with the specification problem. In most places this simply meant setting up cost centres and making the DP manager responsible for a budget.

In some places these cost centres were considered inadequate because they required the DP manager or some committee to make difficult decisions on establishing priorities. In order to reduce tension between DP and the users, to force the users to be more careful about establishing priorities themselves and to make the users more aware of the costs involved in changing specifications, several organizations established a *profit centre* relationship between DP and the users. Many emphasized that it was the users who were the owners of the system, and a contractual or market relation was established with the expectation that the market would allocate resources efficiently.

In some cases chargeout systems were imposed on DP departments and user departments. However, sometimes they were positively encouraged by DP managers. Delays and budget overruns for computer-based systems led to the danger of blame being pointed at the DP department and the DP manager in particular. However, it was becoming common currency around computer departments that the lack of clear specifications from the users was the main problem hindering successful systems. Delays and budget overruns were generated by the users changing their minds, or by users who did not know their own minds. The solution seemed to be to make the users more responsible for this process. This led DP managers to approve the proliferation of chargeout systems and the ideology that users should consider themselves as system owners. To them this was a way of shifting responsibility for systems development failure, at least in part, on to users.

This concentration on efficiency of resource allocation would mean that the 'customers' would get what they needed at the best possible price. What subsequently happened was that user departments then found it easier to go to outside suppliers of DP.

10.4 INADEQUACIES OF EARLY REACTIONS

The phase-two types of solutions to user relations problems described above were inadequate. They did not clearly fail, but by themselves they were clearly inadequate to stem rising concern with user relations. Each of the 'solutions' was inadequate for very different reasons.

With requirements definition languages the problem was simply low diffusion, up to the early 1980s. Three aspects of these languages contributed to the problem. First, most have been based on a model of information requirements which presumes that what is missing from a complete and accurate specification of requirements can be discovered through logical analysis on the part of computer systems developers. Implicitly they assume that those requirements are invariant. Implicitly they presume that all requirements can be expressed in a standardized way.

Second, they emphasize connections with the design characteristics of computer systems, rather than characteristics of user problems. They represent user requirements in a form that is intended to be transparent to computer systems developers, some even to existing computer systems ('machine-readable languages'), rather than the user. To the user they were an attempt to entice or to bludgeon them into thinking like computer specialists. As noted above, elicitation techniques had been rather neglected until the 1980s. The SOP system was based on computer systems that were automating existing *manual* systems.

Third, the chief reason for designing these languages with an emphasis on their connection to characteristics of computer systems core, rather than characteristics of user problems, was that they became caught up in the automation dream. The logic behind the development of these tools, at least from the third-generation tools (those developed in the 1970s), was to use the computer to cover all the life cycle phases, from accurately represented user requirements to completed system.

There were several problems with chargeout systems. One clear disadvantage was that computer departments still had a quasi-monopoly position as internal suppliers. The link between markets and efficient resource allocation rests on the assumption of competition in markets. Competition both among customers and among suppliers is required. Second, there were good reasons for users changing specifications beyond a lack of appreciation of the costs of change. If an advantage to be gained from chargeout systems was to make users more careful and more accurate in their requests, the growing need for systems that deal with dynamic situations would reduce this advantage. Establishing market-like relations is not a costless exercise. If the relation between DP and users was to be financial, then this would encourage both parties to specify requirements in greater detail. With changing requirements and requests for small jobs this would increase paperwork and contribute to delays.

The third problem with this method was related to the nature of the systems that were being created. They were no longer restricted to one user department or function, but extended across many. Also increasingly they could not be justified in simple cost-saving terms. As John King noted:

> The true costs of computing are driven by decisions about new applications, which in turn are made because of business considerations in the real market-place outside the organization, not for some pseudomarket within. (1988, p. 66)

The fourth problem was that by creating market-type links between DP and users, the separation of DP as an organization from the users was formalized, in that they had financially competing interests. Ever since DP began to work on projects for different user departments there has been some procedure for communicating the desire for work to be done and for ensuring that the results are delivered correctly and on time. At first DP identified opportunities and took entire responsibility for delivery. Gradually top management intervened because DP failed to fulfil its promises. Around this time two sorts of things were happening. First, top management introduced accounting procedures, cost centres or profit centres for DP. Second, users began to identify opportunities and to request systems from DP. Both of these developments encouraged more formal procedures for monitoring results. Sometimes the pressure for such procedures was initiated by DP. This seems likely to have occurred when DP became a cost centre. In order to stay within budget DP required a clear specification that did not change and some procedure for learning about future requests in advance. The kinds of formal procedures that DP pushed for concentrated on prioritizing work, such as DP resource committees. Another way of dealing with the same issue from DP's point of view would have been to change into a profit centre. So in some ways a profit centre could be regarded as a backward step in terms of personal organization relations between DP and users. On the other hand, when profit centres were set up this would also encourage users to demand greater opportunities to monitor results and emphasize formal signing off, especially at milestones within systems development.

When DP became answerable for costs in terms of a budget, DP managers were stimulated to adopt more formal procedures for signing off by users for a number of reasons. First, in order to remain within budget it was necessary for DP to know what would be required during a project. The formal sign-off established the work that could be expected of the DP department within budgets. Any changes or extras became the responsibility of the user. In other words it was a let out for DP. Second, it was hoped that formal user involvement during the project would actually improve the initial specification and the identification of specification errors or changes at an earlier stage in the development process.

In phase two the relationship between DP and the users was seen very much from the perspective of the productivity problem. Formal sign-off methods that were introduced were intended to rationalize the problem and to identify the sources of productivity problems, particularly *vis-à-vis* users and DP. These solutions may have served to reduce the level of recrimination and to identify the source of cost overruns, but they did not go very far towards solving the technical problems involved in correctly specifying the system to DP.

Setting up a financial relation between user departments and the DP department in a situation where the demand from user departments was high, and at a time when the DP department seemed to be the only feasible supplier, was not conducive to focusing attention on the quality of the product. The situation of strong user demand and virtually monopolistic supply on the part of the DP department, meant that establishing a financial link between the two in order to stimulate market discipline, was not likely to succeed. Furthermore, this financial link tended to *substitute* for an organizational link. As Computer Economics pointed out:

> The picture is that of the user organisation department accepting the feasibility report, and then tending to become decreasingly involved as the development stage proceeds. If the feasibility report were an exact specification of the product to be delivered to the user on completion, lack of user management involvement would be of less concern. However, with most application fundamental decisions are made during the development stage which will critically affect future operations. (1972, p. 23)

The strategy of separating analysts from programmers emerged in phase one as a simple expression of clear differentiation of work tasks between programming and analysis. When the analyst role was conceived as the answer to the problem, it was the problem of a perceived inadequacy on the part of many computer specialists in communicating with clients. The problem was not that clients were difficult or that they had problems which were particularly difficult to deal with; rather it was that computer specialists were thought of as a breed apart—odd ones in the corporate world who were contemptuous or unaware of people problems, much better at communicating with machines.

Similarly tying the DP–user department relation with financial strings was primarily conceived as a way of controlling exploding DP budgets, rather than as a tool for improving specification of user need and implementation of really useful computer-based systems.[20] Both these strategies *could* result in clearer and more accurate specification of user needs, as well as faster and more sensitive implementation. However, it was not until phase two that strategies which were intended to deal with these problems had come on to the agenda in the computing press and in the more progressive parts of the computing world (academic world, IBM, certain major user organizations). It was not until phase three, until the 1980s, that these became the premier items on this agenda, or that such strategies were being diffused into the real world of DP departments. By that time these early strategies had been superseded.

They were superseded by strategies described in the next chapter because they addressed the user relations problem from the perspective of the common computing environment of phase two, an environment that was being displaced during the 1980s. Their relevance to user relations problems was primarily in the context of developing large and stable systems, in centralized DP departments, for users who lacked the ability and desire to develop systems themselves.

As we shall see in Chapter 12, chargeout systems have continued to operate, systems analysts are still separated from programmers and work on requirements definition languages has continued during the 1980s. In part this is because many organizations still operate primarily in a phase-two environment. More important, sections of most large organizations still operate in a phase-two environment. Even where distributed processing is common and where processing has been decentralized, a central DP function has been retained. Large systems requiring substantial systems analysis are still developed along with smaller projects. Many users would prefer to let the 'experts' develop systems for them. Even users who would prefer to develop their own small systems would rather leave primary responsibility for large systems development to a specialist group. In part the retention of these policies is also due simply to inertia. Just as the diffusion of new techniques takes time, so does the scrapping of old ones.

ENDNOTES

1. Although recently such techniques have been widely publicized, see Chapter 13 on CASE (computer-aided systems engineering) techniques (section 13.5).
2. In the ICON surveys the difference found in most countries between formal availability and actual usage of techniques and methods was striking. Hørlück (1985, p. 9) found a ratio of availability to usage on a range of techniques to be around 4:1.
3. This strategy will also be discussed again in section 13.5.
4. The analyst's job consists of two rather different activities: first, analysis of existing systems and of user requirements; second, design of a system to meet those requirements. There may be considerable overlap between these two functions. We will concentrate on the front end of the analyst's job—techniques for analysing user requirements.

5. For useful summaries of requirement definition languages see Couger and Knapp (1974), Taggart and Tharp (1977), Cooper and Swanson (1979), Nunamaker and Konsynski (1981) and Couger *et al.* (1982).
6. Nelson concludes from a survey of 29 Taylorized plants that Taylor's followers 'encountered more opposition from the managers than the workers' (1974, p. 496). There were several famous strikes over the introduction of Taylorist schemes (notably the Watertown Arsenal strike which led the House of Representatives' investigation of Taylorism in 1912; Aitken, 1960).
7. Nineteenth-century clerks were a craft-like occupation, but the explosion of paperwork accompanying the tremendous growth in firm size among larger firms at the turn of the century, and the positions of responsibility that the old style of clerks enjoyed, meant that most were easily absorbed into management. The direct users of the new paperwork systems were new employees. Almost all nineteenth-century clerks were men. Most of the new DP employees were women (Braverman, 1974).
8. COnference on DAta SYstems Languages of the ACM based in New York.
9. See Table 2.2 for a summary on Couger's generations of systems development techniques.
10. During the 1960s a committee drawn from computer manufacturers and a few major user organizations worked on establishing standard flow-chart symbols. In 1963 their standard for flow charts was published as an American standard through the American Standards Association. This was revised several times and in 1970 two types of chart were defined in the ANS (American National Standards) standard × 3.5–1970: the flow chart, representing sequences of processes over time that the computer is to carry out on data; and the system chart, representing changes in data through time. The flow-chart standard specified symbols (graphic outlines or boxes) for data-carrying media, equipment types and types of processing actions, as well as other details (Chapin, 1971).
11. PSL emerged from a very ambitious software project called ISDOS (Information System Design and Optimization System). The ambition of this project was to automate the whole system-building process (see section 13.5.1).
12. As well as the Hoskyns system, Decision Table Preprocessors and SODA (Systems Optimization and Design Algorithms) (Nunamaker, 1971).
13. Other graphical techniques associated with structural methods (mainly structured design, rather than analysis) are structure charts (Meyers, 1975), Nassi–Schneiderman charts (Nassi and Schneiderman, 1973) and Chapin charts (Chapin, 1974). In Europe the Jackson chart and, to a much lesser extent, Warnier diagrams, became more popular along with their structured methodologies during the late 1970s (Jackson, 1975; Warnier, 1974). For a brief description of these different graphical techniques see Chapin (1981). Structured methods are discussed in section 5.5.
14. The method of generating HIPO charts involves, first, identifying functions of the system (the Visual Table of Contents, VTOC). Second, an Overview diagram is prepared by proceeding from a list of outputs backward to inputs and processes required to produce each output (as with the TAG system). Third, after a review of the VTOC and its supporting Overview diagrams, Detailed diagrams and Extended Descriptions are produced for each box in the VTOC processes and data in more detail are outlined and rearranged in several steps to refine their logic and simplify the Detailed diagram. Fourth, after a further review, the whole system can be further refined, emphasizing how the processes should be carried out in order for the HIPO charts to be used as part of the program specification.
15. DeMarco lists six major problems of analysis. First on the list is communication problems. Communication problems are, in turn, due to the natural difficulty of

describing procedure, the use of inappropriate methods (narrative, rather than graphical techniques), the lack of a common language between analyst and user, and the lack of any usable early model for the system (1978, pp. 10–11). Elicitation problems may be implied in this list, but they are not explicitly stated. Similarly techniques for elicitation are not emphasized in DeMarco's proposed structured analysis methods.

16. Six IBM manuals published between 1960 and 1963 describe SOP (see Gland *et al.*, 1968).

17. BSP is based on business processes, i.e. groups of decisions and activities required to manage each of the resources of the organization. It is based on the assumption that these processes remain relatively constant.

18. BIAIT uses an order (received by the organization to supply a space, a skill or a thing) as the basis for eliciting user responses. It is highly directive. Business Information Characterization Study (BICS) is a further method, which is essentially a combination of BIAIT and BSP (see Kerner, 1979).

19. Users are asked to define factors that are critical to success in performing their functions or in making decisions. This is not a very difficult process.

20. There are other reasons for introducing chargeout systems. The main one is to provide detailed information about the allocation of computing resources and about demand for these resources. This information may be used to identify the need for new equipment and systems as well as allowing better estimation of user department overall costs. In large organizations this form of accounting information is widely used. Chargeout systems have been retained in spite of growing recognition of their inadequacy for solving the key computing problems of phase three or phase two, largely for these general policy reasons (see King, 1988).

Chapter 11

PHASE THREE STRATEGIES FOR DEALING WITH USER RELATIONS PROBLEMS

In this chapter we consider five strategies commonly pursued during the 1980s for dealing with user relations problems:

(1) user involvement in systems development;
(2) end-user computing;
(3) changing information centres or decentralization;
(4) prototyping or evolutionary systems development; and
(5) changing the recruitment and skill base of systems developers.

These are not inherently competing strategies, although some of them (notably the first four) have proponents who claim them to be *the* answer to user relations problems. We note that under the umbrella of each of these labels lies a wide range of different policies. This reflects the bottom-up manner in which these strategies have developed. They have usually entered the literature via reports of actual procedures followed at different installations. Many were informally pursued, often in conflict with prescribed standards. User relations strategies have not generally been marketed as 'methodologies' with such enthusiasm as the structured methodologies of phase two. Different activities that might come under each label are only gradually being elaborated in the literature.

In the following sections each overall strategy will be defined and variants of the strategy will be outlined. Claims for the value of the strategy will be discussed and an indication of the extent to which DP or information systems departments are pursuing each strategy will be presented.

We contend that no strategy represents the 'one best way' to improve user relations. Reports of pitfalls into which practitioners have fallen while pursuing each strategy are discussed at the end of each of the following sections. The chapter ends with a brief comparison of these strategies.

11.1 USER INVOLVEMENT: THE NEW PANACEA?

It would be easy to conclude from a wide section of the literature on user relations problems that the 1980s ('the decade of the user') would mark the coming of the era of user involvement. Writers contributing to most of the lines of literature discussed in Chapter 8 have been coalescing around this recommendation for solving user relations problems.

Those writing from *users'* perspectives have been more united in their recommendation of user involvement. The URBIS group viewed end user, and especially public or client, participation in systems development carried out for government agencies as a key form of democracy. It was a goal to be pursued in its own right. Writers in the human relations, and especially the sociotechnical, school of management, view involvement by all types of users as important contributors to job satisfaction among employees. Increased job satisfaction will improve motivation and productivity. For these writers user involvement in computer systems development should be viewed as a component of a general (responsible autonomy) type of management strategy. Fundamental to that strategy is employee participation in decisions that affect their working situation. Particularly in the Scandinavian countries, many employee representatives and researchers have come to view end-user and secondary-user involvement in computer systems development as an important adjunct to traditional collective-bargaining procedures.

Among those expressing computer systems developers' perspectives, writers focusing on implementation problems have been most united in their recommendation of user involvement. Most writing in this area see user involvement as one among several strategies for achieving implementation success, but it is regarded as the critical strategy. Even in the line of literature which focuses on requirements specification techniques, contributions emphasizing techniques to prolong user participation were receiving more attention by the end of the 1970s. The traditional approach in this field was to try to develop languages that would allow analysts to extract consistent and accurate user requirements in a form that could easily be made computer-readable. Emphasis on the process of elicitation, rather than ease of translating user requirements, implies prolonging the period of user participation in the systems development process.

Defining user involvement strategies

Like most popular concepts, user involvement has come to mean several different things. In section 8.2.7 we described the limited sense in which user participation was viewed by most in the mid-1970s. During the 1980s several detailed classifications of user involvement or participation in computer systems development have been proposed. These tend to focus on the degree of user influence on computer systems development in order to highlight the limitations of earlier views.[1]

In Great Britain, Frank Land (1982) proposed the following classification of approaches to user participation:

(1) Consultative participation—users provide input to the systems design process, but most decisions are left to the computer systems developers. This is the sort of participation proposed by Davis (1974).

(2) Democratic participation—all participants, users and specialist developers, have an equal voice in decisions, but implementation of those decisions is left to some other group, such as senior management.
(3) Responsible participation—all users are involved with both development and implementation on a continuous basis. All participants in the process are fully responsible for its implementation.

In the USA, Ives and Olson (1984, p. 590) also made a distinction between strong and weak user involvement. They proposed the following classification:

(1) Involvement by weak control—users have 'sign-off' responsibility at each phase of the systems development process.
(2) 'Involvement by doing'—user as a design team member or as the official 'liaison' with the information systems development group.
(3) Involvement by strong control—users pay directly for new development out of their own budgets, or the user's overall organizational performance evaluation is dependent on the outcome of the development work.

Ives and Olson also consider weaker forms of involvement: symbolic involvement, where user input is requested but ignored; and involvement by advice, where user advice is solicited through interviews or questionnaires. Unfortunately, all of the three higher degrees of involvement categories can, in practice, allow no more user influence than merely symbolic involvement. Often end-user participation in systems development (Ives and Olson's involvement by doing) will be tried as a reaction to the inadequacy of 'strong control' structures, such as having users pay directly for new development out of their own budgets. Setting up a customer–supplier relation with the DP department need not contribute significantly to user influence. As noted earlier (section 10.3), the financial relation may well drive a wedge between the interests of the two departments, making it more likely that they will pursue subunit goals at the expense of overall organization effectiveness (Cyert and March, 1963). The IS department will generally retain a monopoly or near-monopoly position for the provision of major information systems to user departments (see section 9.3).

Involvement by doing may also be ineffective. Users may not have the technical ability to suggest alternative solutions to problems. They may be taken in by computer specialists dressing up their own preferences as technical imperatives. The problem of 'captive' users with inadequate technical backgrounds participating in development teams has been noted by Ehn and Sandberg (1979) and Kyng and Mathiassen (1982).

Ives and Olson do not specify how many members of the design team would be users under involvement by doing. Clearly if only a few users are included, and especially if they are not accorded at least an equal voice in the team, this category may in reality amount to no more than Land's most primitive category of consultative participation.

Generally European views of user involvement are more likely to embrace an appreciation of the distinction between consultative participation and 'real' influence over computer systems design. The Europeans (or rather the Scandinavians) seem to be more likely to consider power relations between users and systems designers in their definitions.[2] American analyses are more likely to focus on personality conflicts and differences in cognitive styles between users and computer systems developers (see Zmud, 1979; Taylor and Benbasat, 1980; Gingras and McLean, 1982; Dagwell and Weber, 1983; White, 1984; Paddock and Swanson, 1986–87).

Incidence of user involvement

In our CEL 1981 survey we asked a number of questions about user department relations that were very similar to those asked in the CEL 1972 survey. Table 11.1 shows that growth has occurred mainly in the forms of involvement that were less common in 1972. In those places where users were involved in the development process, that involvement has deepened. Nevertheless the first four types of involvement may be thought of as formal, even symbolic. Detailed involvement in project management still only normally occurred in about one-quarter of the sample by 1981.

In the NCC 1984 survey we asked several, somewhat different, questions about formal and detailed user involvement (Table 11.2). Note that the sample was

TABLE 11.1 User involvement 'by doing' strategies 1972 and 1981

1981 Question: To what extent is user management normally involved in the development of new applications?

1972 Question: Is user department management involved in the development of new applications in its area?

	1972	1981		
	Yes (%)	Always or usually (%)	Sometimes (%)	Never (%)
Identify opportunities	69	68	32	0
Specify payoffs	45	68	29	3
Accountable for results	33	56	30	14
Project steering committee[a]	63	74	19	7
Detailed project management	16	26	28	46

Note: The 1972 sample were offered the option 'users not normally involved', which 5% of the sample affirmed. We therefore assumed that a 'yes' to the 1972 question was roughly equivalent to always or usually in 1981. This is most likely to provide an *underestimate* of the 1981 response compared with 1972.
[a] In 1981 we specifically asked about project steering committees; in 1972 the question was: Is progress on projects under development regularly and formally reported to user management?
Sources: Peat, Marwick, Mitchell and Computer Economics, 1972; CEL 1981 Survey.

TABLE 11.2 User involvement in development process, 1984 survey

Q: Are users involved in the following aspects of the development of new systems?

	Always (%)	Usually (%)	Sometimes (%)	Never (%)
Users identify opportunities	9	53	37	1
Users sign off outline specification	44	36	13	7
Users sign off detailed specification	33	28	26	13
Users represented at project meetings	49	35	15	2

Q: Are users involved in the following detail aspects of the development of new systems?

	Always (%)	Usually (%)	Sometimes (%)	Never (%)
Users provide project management	6	11	37	47
Users provide systems analysis	0	2	30	69
Users provide programming staff	0	1	8	91

Source: NCC 1984 survey.

different from the 1981 survey. However, the 1984 sample was probably a better reflection of the population because it included more small departments as well as being a larger sample (see Data Appendix). Again the rather low proportion of IS managers reporting detail involvement is significant, even though formal involvement was very high—between 60% and 84% for each of the measures.

However influential proponents of user influence may have been in academic circles, *they* were clear that, at least until the early 1980s, user involvement strategies have been sporadic and perfunctory. Advocates of substantial user influence throughout the systems development process still consider themselves to be crusaders, fighting against the deadweight of conventional wisdom.

Many of those who championed the cause of user involvement met at a conference in August 1985 at Aarhus, Denmark. At the conference, Floyd (1987) developed the idea of two broad approaches to software production: product-oriented and process-oriented. The first was the majority approach in the computing world. The second, the minority approach, was the one Floyd preferred. It was also clearly the approach preferred by conference participants. With the product-oriented approach the software developer is regarded as outside the system environment. A strict separation is made between development and use of the system. With the process-oriented view the system is regarded as dynamic and evolving, in interaction with its environment. Development and use influence one another. Floyd characterizes the relation between these approaches as a paradigm change, with the product-oriented approach as the 'ruling paradigm'. According to Floyd, existing systems development methods embody primarily a product orientation.

Evaluation of experiences with user involvement

Experience with detailed involvement via user participation schemes during the late 1970s and 1980s has been reported widely in the literature. Reviewing this literature leads to the conclusion that user involvement has *not* been the great panacea, although it has led to certain positive results. As Kubicek wrote:

> During the last ten years or so, increasing consent on the fact that user participation should be an integral component of system design has emerged. Noteworthy agreement on the meaning and implication of user participation, however, has not been reached. In fact, disagreement on the raison d'être of user participation, its implementation and its results have apparently increased. (Kubicek, 1983, p. 3)

Certain cases of success have been reported, particularly for user involvement in the development of decision support systems (Sprague and Carlson, 1982; Bahl and Hunt, 1985; Kasper, 1985). Involvement in development can lead to increased user satisfaction with the system, increased use of the system and increased effectiveness of users, in their own view (see Baroudi and Olson, 1986, for example). However, rather important negative sides to major user involvement efforts have also been reported. For example, Hirschheim (1983) reported that in 20 organizations where participative systems design projects were tried it was preferred over any other approach, particularly by users. Most thought it led to higher-quality systems. However, he also reported that very few of these organizations chose to use participative systems design again.

Problems with user involvement schemes are numerous and complex. It will be useful to classify these problems into two groups. First, there are problems specific to the perspective of one of the groups of actors associated with these schemes; that is, the users, the systems developers or top managers. Second, there are general problems with user involvement schemes that may be associated with the primitive state of technology in this area.

The main complaint from *users' perspectives* is that involvement and influence are not the same, even though they may have been led to believe that involvement would lead to influence. This problem has been noted by many (Adams, 1975; Kraft, 1979; Lanzara, 1983; Mambrey and Schmidt-Belz, 1983). Often users have found that they have either been bewildered by jargon and cowed into quiescence (the hostage model) or that systems developers have tried to indoctrinate them into their way of thinking (Hedberg, 1975; Schneider and Ciborra, 1983). The solution to these problems seems to be try to develop user expertise, through training, through repeated experiences or through access to independent advice (see Ehn, 1988). However, the obstacles to these solutions are formidable. Training is costly and there is the danger that well-trained users will lose their perspective as users. Lack of repetition of participation schemes as reported by Hirschheim and lack of independent, user-oriented experts suggest that user expertise in involvement will not develop rapidly.[3]

What distinguishes the 1980s is the appearance of critical reports of experiences with user involvement from the *perspective of computer systems developers* who have been committed to these schemes. Systems developers have been disappointed in users. They have found users unappreciative of their efforts:

> The requirements of the users were sometimes regarded as being very simple and the designers shrinked from realising such 'primitive, short-sighted and obsolete solutions' ... After lengthy, troublesome preparations [systems designers] were confronted with disinterest, acceptance of the work as being trivial or criticism of marginal details. (Mambrey and Schmidt-Belz, 1983, p. 67)

System designers complained that users displayed 'typical consumer behaviour', that they preferred to view the systems designers as the experts who would solve their problems. They preferred to make their views known after the development process, rather than before or during the process. They wanted to be confronted with a detailed plan which they could discuss, rather than be involved in the planning (Mambrey and Schmidt-Belz, 1983). Many end users preferred others to participate for them (Wagner, 1980; Oppermann and Tepper, 1983; Hogue, 1987).

Fundamental to the problems systems developers have had with user involvement schemes has been the isolation of these schemes from users' general working situation. Systems developers are concerned with successful systems. They conceive of user involvement as a way to achieve better-quality systems, systems that will really be used, systems that will satisfy user needs, systems that will thereby enhance their own standing. Users are concerned with their overall working situation, with their jobs, with both the complete range of tasks they perform and with their relations within the overall organization. Relations with a particular new computer-based system are only a small component of these concerns. The achievement of real influence over a new system can be embedded in an overall working situation where users have little influence over their tasks and their relations within the organization. Focusing on involvement in a new system has frequently led to 'a continued and unmotivating situation, ending up with bored and disappointed end users and frustrated systems designers' (Høyer, 1979, p. 53).

Another related problem for systems developers has been that they have become embroiled in political conflicts between different user groups. This is a specific instance of a more general problem for systems developers. User involvement, especially if it means participative design, will require a much greater level of communication and a much greater level of knowledge of user situations than systems developers possess. This implies a serious skills gap in IS departments (see section 11.3 below).

Problems with user involvement projects from *top managers' perspective* are diverse. A commonly expressed problem is the imbalance in tangibility between costs and benefits. User involvement schemes are time-consuming; they may result in a system that is more sophisticated and expensive. These costs are measurable and must be paid in the short run. The benefits are more likely to be intangible and realizable only in the long run. Realization of benefits such as a more positive attitude towards the system by users, greater system use and more flexibility in working procedures will also depend on other factors in the future (such as labour turnover among users and other future events in labour relations). The imbalance between costs and benefits makes such schemes difficult to evaluate. Hirschheim (1983) reports that formal evaluation of participative systems design schemes rarely occurs.[4]

A second problem is that user involvement does not necessarily lead to what top managers would view as better-quality systems. Particularly when there are several different user groups involved in systems design, conflicts of interest among these groups may lead to compromises that threaten the value of the system. Furthermore, systems which succeed in satisfying user groups may still be suboptimal solutions for the organization as a whole. Users in their role as members of sections of an organization can aim for systems that will increase their power in relation to other sections, or in relation to clients and customers of the organization. Users in their role as workers can aim for a degree of control over their working situation that can make it difficult for managers to alter working procedures or to discipline individual workers.

We can relate these problems for top managers with the user involvement strategy to the types of strategies for managing computer systems developers we introducer earlier. A strong user involvement strategy for dealing with user relations problems—one which allows users real influence over the systems development process—implies a responsible autonomy strategy for managing users. This may simply be anathema to the general strategy top managers are pursuing in relation to their employees. This point was made by Hirschheim:

> Organisations have evolved in a Weberian fashion embracing the ideals of Taylorism. This has led to organisations that are highly bureaucratic and rational and not amenable to change ... One of the respondents felt participative design, although a very valuable approach, was doomed to failure because it was 'too foreign to most managers in organisations'. (1983, p. 324)

Similarly Hedberg and Mumford (1975) noted that computer systems developer indifference to user involvement may, in part, be attributed to top management's encouragement to act in a direct control fashion. User participation schemes may occur in isolation from other organization factors, because they are a responsible autonomy type of strategy. Top managers may be swept into approving or tolerating such schemes by the literature, which represents user involvement as the key way to solve user relations problems. However, if top managers are committed to using direct control strategies for managing users in their role as employees, such schemes can reduce the effectiveness of the overall management strategies. Users may withhold cooperation in these schemes as a bargaining counter in negotiations (over better working conditions in other areas, or higher salaries) because their general motivation levels are low, or because they have not been accustomed to valuing intrinsic benefits from work that may arise from working with better information systems or from the process of participation.

The second category of problems with the user involvement strategy relates to the primitive state of technology in this field. There are two reasons for the technology being primitive. The first is that concern with user relations and substantial experiments with strong user involvement schemes are still relatively recent phenomena. New techniques to support user participation, notably prototyping methods, elicitation techniques and the use of outside consultants to support users from their own perspectives and interests, are still regarded as radical and experimental. A second reason for the technology being primitive is that the user involvement strategy for solving user relations problems is very specific to the organization and to the type of system being developed (Dagwell and Weber, 1983). More than any of the other strategies discussed in this chapter, user involvement embroils the systems development process and computer systems developers in the political, industrial relations and communications details of the organization. Techniques for effective user involvement may have to embrace a wide range of skills associated with disparate disciplines and technical bases, but not necessarily. For example, in some organizations and with certain sorts of systems, techniques that allow political relations between departments to be dealt with are critical, but in other circumstances such techniques may be irrelevant, or even harmful (if a policy of letting sleeping dogs lie is appropriate). These considerations have encouraged writers on implementation problems to suggest elaborate contingency approaches to systems development (see section 8.2.7).

In addition to user involvement strategies being very sensitive to organization and system characteristics, they have been found to be dependent on the personalities of the particular systems developers (Scharer, 1982; Paddock and Swanson, 1986–87), the users (Markus, 1983) and the view each group has of the other (Gingras and McLean, 1982). The essence of technological development is the development of ways of doing things that are easily communicable to others and portable to new situations. The lack of portability of user involvement techniques, not only between organizations but also to new situations within a single organization, has hampered the user involvement strategy.[5]

11.2 END-USER COMPUTING: THE DREAM COME TRUE?

As already noted, the dream of users developing their own systems, of clients being both design interactors and end users, is an old one. It has often been expressed as a strategy to remove the need for departments of specialist programmers and analysts altogether. During phase three that dream of end-user computing is being increasingly realized, but it is coming piecemeal, for only limited types of systems or limited parts of the development process. The consequential disappearance of separate IS departments has not occurred.

In the information systems management literature,[6] end-user computing has been the hot issue for the past five years. It has been the fastest growing activity in information systems (Sprague and McNurlin, 1986; Magal and Carr, 1988). It is expected by some to become the dominant form of computing in the 1990s (Watson and Carr, 1987, p. 94).

Unfortunately this has led to the usual hyperbole and the problem of tenses. Because end-user computing has not been a hot issue in this literature before the 1980s, there is a presumption that it was not an issue within DP departments before the 1980s. For example:

> End-user computing (EUC) has risen rapidly to prominence as an important set of activities in many organisations. From having practically no importance prior to 1980, this practice has grown to become a key component of many firms' activities today. (Munro *et al.*, 1987–88, p. 6)

Because it has become such a common issue in the literature during the 1980s, there is a presumption that end-user computing has 'changed the landscape of organizational systems' (Zwass, 1987–88, p. 3).

The 1980s literature on end-user computing is somewhat different from the literature reviewed in Chapter 8. The literature reviewed in Chapter 8 was motivated by experiences of user relations problems. The more recent literature reviewed in this chapter has been motivated by experiences with actual growth of what may be regarded as solutions to, or rather strategies for dealing with, user demands and user relations problems.[7]

By end-user computing we mean the provision of a programming environment, normally by the information systems (IS) department, which allows users to tailor a system to their own needs using some form of programming syntax, having little or no interaction with IS during the process. The weakest form may be to provide an interface to a system that allows users to specify reports and report formats. A stronger form would be to provide a database inquiry system. Higher forms would be the provision of program generators or specialized tools, and high-level programming languages.

The purpose is to provide increasing degrees of flexibility in computer use to the user. This can be looked upon as a process of growing from a base of minor parameter setting or minimal flexibility to the point where the user is provided with a language that has a limited, but high-quality, vocabulary. That is, with few statements, which are easy to specify, substantial and detailed results may be obtained. The vocabulary allows good control over the limited functions for which it was designed.

Three technical catalysts stimulated end-user computing (see Chapter 9). The first was the spread of on-line systems that occurred early in phase two. From the beginnings of computerized systems there have been high-technique users, such as actuaries, production engineers, and scientists in research and development departments, who would not only have demanded their own facility but who also would have been prepared to develop them using the existing internal computer department tools. Since the onset of on-line systems there was a very rapid growth in demand for new systems based on existing on-line systems.

The second catalyst was the development of software tools that would allow users to carry out their own requests (see section 9.1.3). The provision of such tools partly represents a solution to the phase-two problem of how to overcome the backlog of user requests by transforming it into the phase-three problem of how to respond to user needs for flexible and changing information.[8]

The third catalyst was the spread of PCs (see section 9.1.1). This stimulated user interest in developing their own applications. It also stimulated further development of packages for non-computer specialist users, especially spreadsheet and word-processing packages.

Recent growth in end-user computing has occurred because of an increase in the number of users prepared and capable of taking some form of technical plunge, as well as because of the extent to which cheap hardware and high-level software tools have been available to make this plunge easier.

End-user computing has been stimulated by social as well as technical catalysts. General computer literacy has increased substantially during the 1980s. In part this is due to a contagion effect. More neighbours at work and at home ostensibly working with computers and speaking computerese stimulates interest in computers. Greater accessibility of computer training owing to government and private efforts has also contributed to rising computer literacy (Watson and Carr, 1987).

More specifically the rise of end-user computing may be seen as the result of several trends observable during phase two. One trend was the move towards what computer systems developers saw as 'go-it-alone' users. With the growth of software houses, service bureaus and external consultancies during the 1970s, users frustrated by delays with internally generated systems were finding a range of alternatives available on the open market. Service bureaus in particular were gradually upgrading their products. They were moving from providing data preparation and running traditional DP services, such as payroll systems, into providing both better inquiry and individualized enhancement facilities on traditional systems, as well as new forecasting, simulation and other decision support systems. During the 1980s service bureaus have been supplying users with terminals connected to their own mainframes on a time-share basis and providing tools that allow users to carry out their own ad hoc inquiries and simple applications. Service bureaus have been pushed into this marketing strategy because of declining markets during the 1970s, with their traditional business being taken over by internal DP departments. Many user departments equipping themselves with their own PCs have been internalizing work done by external service bureaus, rather than work done by internal IS departments, and thereby saving on external costs.

The reasons for users going it alone have not disappeared. There are still long waiting times for new applications. Estimates ranging from several months to as much as five years have recently been noted (Head, 1985; Burch and Grudnitski, 1986).[9] However, new reasons for going it alone relate to desires that can best be satisfied by connections with the organization's own database: desires to make queries, analyse data and generate reports based on data held in the organization. This has encouraged users to deal with waiting time frustration by developing their own systems on their own PCs or intelligent terminals, rather than going for external services.

A second trend has been the decentralization of computing to user departments because the character of systems required to support certain functions is so different from standard DP applications. These systems could best be developed and supported either by a computer specialist with a good knowledge of these functions or by particular computer-sophisticated users. From phase one such activities, such as computer support for production control, and technical calculations, were often housed away from the central DP department. They may be thought of as a form of end-user computing. Now, with the development of more systems aimed specifically at management functions, we may think of the collection of these management support systems as a new separable form of computerization, much like support for production engineers. The growth of end-user computing appears to be so great because this new group of users being supported by specialized systems is much more visible and powerful than earlier groups.

We may think of the end-user computing strategy purely as providing degrees of flexibility in computing to users. Then we have the following scale:

—Systems where choice is built into the system, but is not available to users.
—Systems where choices can be programmed, stored and reused.
—Increasing control over the choice of parameters.
—Increasing control over operations.
—Total control over operations and parameters.

The strategies we measured were whether users are provided with software tools either for making ad hoc inquiries or for building their own applications. The proportion of the NCC 1985 sample saying yes was 29.6% for applications building, and 62.9% for ad hoc inquiry processing. The same question was asked in the NCC 1984 survey. We extracted results for the 127 installations that participated in both surveys. This matched sample revealed an additional 7.0% providing tools for applications building and an additional 6.6% for ad hoc inquiries in 1985. A similar rise occurred between the 1982/83 and 1984 surveys.[10]

Experiences with end-user computing, as with user involvement schemes, have not been judged an unqualified success. While end-user computing clearly allows users to circumvent the applications backlog and to avoid having to communicate their vague and changing requirements to specialist computer systems developers, it can lead users to spend more time than they expected or desired on computer-related activities. It can also leave users with inferior systems (Alavi and Weiss, 1985–86). Although users have a better idea of what they want than computer specialists, they are likely to be much less able to get what they want, even if they are using fourth-generation languages. For example, users will be less aware of the importance of tight controls on input and the importance of validation routines (Christoff, 1985; Hørlück, 1986). Also users will be less likely to test their work sufficiently and may develop habits of taking short cuts that will make their work more difficult to maintain (Alavi and Weiss, 1985–86).

The greatest dangers of end-user computing are those seen from the perspective of the organization as a whole. Uncontrolled end users can clearly lead to wasted resources. If users develop applications in isolation from each other it is likely that several will 'reinvent the wheel'—duplicate efforts already expended (Hørlück, 1986; Friedman *et al.*, 1988). The problem of maintenance gaps when key computer specialists leave also applies to systems developed by end-user programmers (Hørlück, 1986).[11] One particularly worrisome effect of duplicated efforts is that the validity of the organization's database can be compromised. ICON interviewers in the USA were told a tale by one computer manager about a bank that lent a particular customer several times more than his overall credit limit. Loans were approved at several different branches of the bank using PC-based credit approval systems, independent of the bank's overall database.

Another organization-wide problem with end-user computing is that, unless standards on documentation and structure are followed, systems developed by one set of users will be difficult for others to use (Alavi and Weiss, 1985–86; O'Donnell and March, 1987). According to Necco *et al.* (1987, p. 100), 'when end-users develop CBIS they can repeat all the mistakes made in traditional MIS development'.

Several prescriptions concerning top management control of end-user computing based on a Nolan-type growth stages model have appeared recently (O'Donnell and March, 1987; Munro *et al.*, 1987–88; Alavi *et al.*, 1987–88; Huff *et al.*, 1988). For them the solution to top management's problems lies in an explicit organizational strategy that is sensitive to the stages of end-user computing growth. This strategy would mirror Nolan's recommendations of control versus slack (or rather control versus productivity, as O'Donnell and March would prefer to call it).

11.3 CHANGES WITHIN INFORMATION SYSTEMS DEPARTMENTS

User involvement and end-user computing are not the only strategies that are being pursued in order to meet user demands. Both of these strategies concentrate on improvements to the IS–user relationship derived from action taken primarily by the users. Clearly it is possible to improve the relationship if changes are made by the other partner—the IS department staff.

We can distinguish three broad types of phase-three strategies within IS departments: first, those aimed at altering the organization of work in IS departments; second, those aimed at altering the systems design process in order for user involvement to be accommodated and made more effective; and third, those aimed at altering computer specialists as individuals.

11.3.1 Changing the Organization Structure of IS: Information Centres and Decentralization

There are two developments in internal IS organization structures that are being stimulated by user relations problems. First, groups of IS specialists are being specifically assigned to user support. Second, the overall structure of IS is sometimes being redesigned to mirror user department functions.

User support teams and the information centre

User support can mean two rather different sets of activities. First, it can mean post-development support, such as dealing with implementation problems, ad hoc inquiries, minor maintenance and enhancement, user training, user liaison and public relations. Second, it can mean providing a consultancy service to assist users' own development of systems, or their purchase of systems from external suppliers. This second set of activities is what has come to be known as the information centre although, as we shall see, information centre staff often carry out the first set of activities.

Post-development support has always been a feature of IS. During phase one this was a function of computer department management. If a department secretary existed, she could have dealt with inquiries.• The technical aspects of these inquiries and the jobs that were generated by them would be delegated directly by computer management to the technical staff. An alternative phase-one pattern might have occurred when the computer department manager was a technical specialist (probably from a hardware manufacturer). Then someone at a fairly senior position (analyst or assistant computer manager) would be drafted in from a user department. He or she would be able to answer ad hoc inquiries and smooth over implementation problems because of his or her user department experience. There was little activity in this area during phase one. End users were less demanding and less involved in the system on a day-to-day basis (at least for the usual batch systems carried out in the business sector). Therefore they rarely formulated questions for the computer department. The important user liaison was with the client or patron; that is, it was between managers.

In phase two there was a shift towards the initiative for systems coming from users. At the same time the DP manager's job increasingly involved the internal management of DP staff as departments grew. The need for more intimate user liaison grew because of the growing number of implemented systems and the growing diversity of users and of systems. On the other hand, the supply of this support from senior DP staff was declining because DP was no longer actively seeking new applications and because the task requirements of senior DP staff were growing in other directions. Analysts were becoming more concerned with systems analysis and design at early phases of development, rather than at the implementation phases (see sections 8.2.6 and 8.2.7).

The task of user liaison was given to relatively junior members of staff, often trainee programmers. They would be expected to deal with the simplest problems by themselves or to learn who could give the answer. This would be considered part of the training of new programmers, to learn how the DP department was organized. Problems with this procedure were that trainees would be inefficient because they were new. Also, when a request involved a substantial piece of work, it was likely to throw up maintenance problems because of the loose structure of existing systems. In many of the departments we visited in 1980 and 1981 we found that the problems involved in dealing with user inquiries were not treated with a high priority, nor were they clearly understood. Rather it was a complement to the accounting forms of the relations between DP and users that were set up during phase two. An alternative to this scenario was for calls to be diverted directly to the maintenance team. This, in many cases, caused problems because the user would be essentially dealing with a technical person (programmer) whose training and aptitude were often antagonistic to dealing with users.

During phase two the types of inquiries to DP changed and multiplied considerably. First, because of increasing numbers of on-line or interactive systems, there were low-level users in user departments who interfaced with the systems and thus required some form of personal servicing from DP. Second, because of changes in the types of systems described in Chapter 9, more requests for ad hoc information or enhancements came directly from managers in their new role as end users.

The implementation of on-line systems also threw up new problems during phase two. In phase one the implementation of operational systems usually stimulated redundancies or job changes among clerical staff. In phase two low-level users who interacted with the system needed to understand a certain amount about the system and also to cooperate in the process of reporting and ironing out flaws. The analyst was not necessarily the best person for liaising with low-level end users in this way. In phase two user training was largely a matter for the analysts to produce instructions for using the system and the user department to carry out the training according to those instructions.

Now, in phase three there has been a rise in the number of post-implementation requests from end users. Also the complexity of the implementation process has increased because users are working on-line and because there is likely to be a degree of end-user programming. As users are carrying out a non-predefined 'programming-like' interaction with the computer, there is a greater element of learning by doing and more opportunities for user-induced errors. Systems errors become more visible to users and are thus more likely to be reported. Finally, users have been requesting more training and better quality of training in consequence of their higher level of computer awareness.

The enormous backlog of work for IS departments or divisions, which has been building up during the 1980s, is largely made up of requests for reports, queries and data analysis (King, 1984; Watson and Carr, 1987; Necco *et al.*, 1987). James Martin estimates that:

> About 70% of the immediate needs of typical end users can be satisfied with query languages and report generators, if an appropriate data base exists or can be created. (1982, p. 38)

Individually these are small jobs. To traditional computer systems developers they are much less interesting technically than requests for new applications.

The second type of separate user support function within IS is for the IS department to act as a consultancy service for users. This appears to be the dream of end-user computing coming true. That is, IS would disappear as a centre employing large numbers of computer specialists, although it may continue in a consultancy role. The primary function of IS would be 'to help users to help themselves'. We have found little evidence of this (so far). Rather consultancy work has become a new function *added on* to the existing workload in IS. In many organizations this consulting function has been labelled the information centre.

The information centre was the creation of IBM Canada in the early to mid-1970s.[12] The number of organizations setting up information centres was growing rapidly by the early 1980s (Wetherbe and Leitheiser, 1985; Christy and White, 1987; Munro *et al.*, 1987–88; Magal and Carr, 1988). Officially the 'mission' of the information centre is to provide users with services that will help them to help themselves (usually meaning end-user computing). In fact information centres have become a catch-all, most of them providing both sets of user-support activities described above.[13]

It is important to recognize that the phenomenal growth of information centres reported in the literature during the 1980s has occurred in part because of growing familiarity with the information centre label. User support functions were requiring increasing efforts during the late 1970s and early 1980s.[14] Much of this work was being carried out informally by analysts, programmers and IS managers during phase two. Formal responsibility for this work was often delegated to low-level staff such as trainee programmers. Growing recognition of the importance of providing user support has encouraged IS managers and top managers to give this support a higher profile by calling it an information centre. Nevertheless the activity has usually been upgraded and better resourced in consequence of being constituted formally as an information centre.

In addition to traditional user support, most information centres perform two further functions. First, they carry out systems development work. This has been noted, with some surprise, by most studies. The major reason for users going to information centres rather than to traditional DP or IS is for faster turnaround time on requests for development work. As has been pointed out, one of the problems with information centres is that they can become reflections of existing IS facilities because users are unwilling to help themselves and do not wish to acquire the necessary expertise (Wetherbe and Leitheiser, 1985; Horwitt, 1985). This can be encouraged by information centre managers who 'use completed computing applications as the principal indicators of their centers' success' (Wetherbe and Leitheiser, 1985, p. 9). Also IS managers were happy for the information centre to take on development work connected with end-user computing. As mentioned earlier (section 9.1.1), IS managers in the mid-1980s were sometimes resentful of having to carry out this work, seeing it as having to clean up a mess created by uncoordinated user initiatives, largely connected with purchasing PCs.

A second activity additional to traditional user support carried out by information centres has been the control of equipment purchase and the development of standards for end-user computing. These are clearly new functions associated with the 1980s spread of PCs into user departments (although these functions were carried out in scientific and education establishments in earlier phases). This set of activities has attracted a great deal of attention in the literature. Several commentators have noted the potential conflict between the helping-hand role of the information centre and its management and control role towards end-user computing. Clearly there are great advantages to centrally controlled purchasing and strictly enforced standards.

Central administration of user purchases and use of PCs can have major advantages. Users were often unpleasantly surprised to discover, post-implementation, about the low capacity of PC systems and the paucity of support from suppliers. The task of defining system requirements in terms of hardware and software is, after all, a skilled task within IS. Why should users assume that they could do it, or that all vendors were honest or thorough in their appraisals? Similarly the standards and procedures which are now second nature within IS, such as backups and error checks, were not well known in user departments.

Economies which could be achieved by central purchasing include: (a) bulk discounts; (b) compatibility between PCs and the existing network of terminals; (c) group purchasing of software; and (d) training/learning savings within IS (if IS would support PCs) and among users (if users move from one department to another). Evaluation of different PCs, especially in the early days before the widespread literature on comparability of specifications had developed, was a particularly time-consuming task.

Given that IS had developed a body of consulting knowledge on the capabilities of PCs, then IS would be able to give advice on the suitability of PC-based, versus mainframe-based, versus service bureau-based solutions. When IS acts as a consultant to all user departments they can coordinate and act as a clearing house for development efforts, programs and expertise in diverse user areas. They can stop the reinvention of the wheel.

In spite of these advantages information centres have generated certain problems. Too much control can stifle end-user enthusiasm and creativity. If the information centre looks too much like an easy option for getting development work carried out by avoiding IS's controls and delays, the information centre can become just as swamped as IS, in addition to leading to poor-quality development work. Other problems encountered have been the difficulty of keeping up with the speed of technical change in this area and the difficulty of providing advanced training for more computer-sophisticated users when the size of the typical information centre is rather small.[15]

Mirroring users and decentralization

During phase one computer systems development was clearly a technical function. The division of labour between analysts and programmers emphasized this. Programmers mainly had technical knowledge. Analysts came from methods, work study or operations research departments and backgrounds. Also at first, computer systems development was most likely to be situated within a user department, usually finance. They developed systems for only one user department.

Two important changes occurred during phase one and early phase two. First, computer systems development gradually developed a wider client base within organizations and in consequence became a separate department. Second, analysts become more technically proficient as more and more of them had programming backgrounds. Also more complex systems meant outline or requirements specifications were no longer a sufficient basis to begin programming work. They had to be transformed into more technically oriented systems specifications. These in turn had to be broken into more detailed program or module specifications. Whether it should be technically oriented analysts or programmers with design and analysis skills who carried out this work was not clear, and the relative advantages of each could change with changes in the nature of the task and the availability of personnel during any project, as well as between projects. During phase two there were two developments within DP which reflected this situation. First was the move to reintegrate analysis and programming into project teams early in phase two (section 6.2.1). Second was the reintegration of analysis and programming within a single individual, the analyst/programmer, late in phase two and during phase three (see section 11.3.3 below).

These developments occurred partly to remedy some of the diseconomies of specialization and partly to develop clear career paths. However, they also were important for user relations. They facilitated communication with users by those doing the programming work. They also gave users a specific target within DP who was accountable at a detailed level for their project alone: the project leader. The next step in this process was to make project teams permanently associated with a user department. This standing team would be responsible for all systems associated with a particular user. It would carry out maintenance and enhancement of existing systems as well as develop new systems for that set of users. One-third (33·9%) of NCC 1984 survey respondents reported that they used a team structure and that teams within DP were permanently assigned to user areas.[16]

If this trend were to continue, we may expect in future to find decentralized DP or information systems functions (perhaps instead of end-user computing). Early in phase two signs of this trend could be seen in high-tech firms. Many firms bought minicomputers to carry out technical, as opposed to administrative, computing. These minis were often located in the user area concerned. Now many different hardware configurations are possible.

11.3.2 Changing the Systems Development Process: From Waterfall to Whirlpool Methods and Prototyping

Waterfall and whirlpool models

There are enormous differences in the way systems development proceeds in different computer installations. Nevertheless during phase two the software engineering approach received considerable attention. Towards the end of phase two the emphasis was shifting from structured programming to structured design and analysis. Often these were called 'methodologies' rather than methods. Like the distinction between technologies and techniques, the advent of the term 'structured methodologies' may be thought to indicate the structuring of the overall systems development process. However, in the literature the term 'methodology' is often used interchangeably with 'method' or 'technique'.[17] Nevertheless considerable research effort has gone into putting structured analysis, design and programming together into coordinated development environments. On the ground the pattern of structured methods use is complex. During the 1970s they were diffusing rapidly, especially to larger installations. Penetration of these methods seems to have continued within large installations during the 1980s in terms of more phases of the life cycle being supported by these methods. However, most installations have adopted methods piecemeal, or 'bottom up'. Often the use of methods is not imposed on developers and several competing methods are supported in individual organizations (see Hørlück, 1985; Friedman, 1986). Furthermore, structured methods are rarely used in smaller installations. Also the size distribution of installations has been continually changing in favour of smaller-sized installations, owing to entry of small installations, reflecting continuing reductions in the real cost of computer systems core (see sections 6.4.2 and 12.1.2).

One intention of these methods was to improve the product of the systems development process, i.e. to produce systems whose structure parallels the structure of the problem. The system structure should have a simple logic. It was assumed that this structure would mean that assurance of reliability would be easy and that the system would also be easily modifiable.[18] In order to produce systems with these clearly desirable characteristics, structured methods generally recommend that systems development proceed through an 'orderly and manageable process' (Colter, 1982, p. 75). That is, changes in the systems development process are required both to ensure that the required structure is adhered to (such as design reviews and other controls at specific milestones) and to make it easier to produce the desired structure (such as program libraries).

As noted in section 7.3, the effect of structured methods on the computer system life cycle was twofold. First, the structured system life cycle was distinguished by a greater elaboration of its middle phases. This was largely due to greater attention to specifying the logic structure of the system, to modularization and to quality assurance. Second, structured methodologies encouraged systems developers to follow a pre-specified set of phases in strict order. They emphasized the production of 'deliverables' or the performance of formal ceremonies (such as meetings or sign-offs) at milestones marking the end of each phase. One phase of the life cycle was supposed to have been completed before the next phase began. Within phases feedback loops were recommended. Progress was to be checked with superiors or through walkthroughs with peers. This could lead to alterations, which would require redoing that phase once again. One of the intentions behind feedback loops within phases was to avoid errors that would necessitate returning to earlier phases. In practice the life cycle rarely proceeded in this way. However, the ideal of systems development proceeding in a linear path through the life cycle—a one-way flow based on a 'waterfall' model of the life cycle—remained (see Figure 11.1).[19]

As noted in Chapter 5, even at the dawn of structured methods in the late 1960s

Initiation
  Requirements specification
    Systems specification
      Program specification
        Module specification
          Flow charts
            Coding
              Testing
              Debugging
                Implementation
                  Operation
                    Maintenance

FIGURE 11.1 The waterfall method of systems development. Source: Boehm (1981, Chapter 4)

voices were raised against the waterfall approach to systems development. Du g
the 1970s the bulk of recommendations concerning the life cycle sequence
emphasized the one-way or linear flow. However, by the early 1980s the
breakdown of the waterfall by introducing feedback loops, i.e. iterative procedures
covering earlier phases of the life cycle, or what may be thought of as whirlpools,
were not only being recognized as common practice, they were also being
recommended as a solution to user relations problems.

This procedure achieved a degree of legitimacy when it was given a label. The
commonly accepted label is prototyping, although some have preferred to call it
'versioning', incremental systems development or evolutionary systems development. Prototyping, like user involvement and end-user computing, has become a
generic term covering a wide range of different activities and procedures.

Defining prototyping

There are many different definitions of prototyping in the literature. Let us begin
with a fairly well-known definition. Floyd (1984, p. 2) defines prototyping as 'a
process which provides an early and practical demonstration of the relevant parts
of software on a computer'.[20]

This definition would normally be narrowed to specify that the demonstration
should be for users. Riddle (1984, p. 20), for example, defines prototyping as a class
of software modelling, meaning abstract descriptions of software systems, used for
answering questions about the system, where the questions of interest stem from
the interests of users. Some would prefer to narrow the definition even further.
They would specify that a prototype must be intended to be thrown away (Budde
and Sylla, 1984, p. 32; Monckmeyer and Spitta, 1984, p. 124).[21] On the other
hand, some have defined prototyping more generally than Floyd. For example, in
Ortner and Wendler's view (1984, p. 244) prototyping seems to include any
communication with users based on advanced knowledge of what a system might
look like. They distinguish three types of prototyping, which they consider to be
steps of an overall methodology. These steps are:

(1) Semantic prototyping, user-oriented consideration of the meaning of the data
    and their processing.
(2) Logical prototyping on a formal data model considering the structure of the
    data and the users' view of it.
(3) Physical prototyping considering the performance of the system.

The first and possibly the second step need not involve a demonstration for users on
a computer.

Another common distinction is between horizontal prototyping and vertical
prototyping. With horizontal prototyping a mock-up of all user interfaces is
produced. Users can see what the system will look like, but the detailed actual

functions will not be developed. Users' ability to really work with the system, as opposed to 'trying out' the interface, will be very limited. This is sometimes called 'full functional simulation' (Floyd, 1984, p. 8). With vertical prototyping a narrow set of functions is developed completely. Users are given enough of a system to work with and, based on their experience with the system, further functions are added.

The value of prototyping

The value of prototyping according to its proponents is that it stimulates an early dialogue with users. This encourages users to clarify their ideas about what they require by presenting them with a tangible means to simulate what it will be like to work with the system. It encourages systems developers to talk about the intended system with users in a concrete manner, in a manner which users find easier to understand. This improved communication encourages mutual learning, which leads to a better-quality system.

In addition, some have claimed that prototyping can reduce the time required for systems development and thereby reduce costs (Livesey, 1984; Monckmeyer and Spitta, 1984; Tavolato and Vincena, 1984). First, by improving early communication with users, the time required to achieve a stable requirements specification can be reduced. Second, it has been suggested that by using the tools necessary for prototyping, the development time after requirements specification

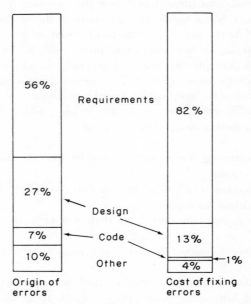

FIGURE 11.2 Origin and cost of fixing errors by phase of the life cycle

would be reduced (Livesey, 1984, p. 93). Third, prototyping reduces the chances of discovering errors of requirements specification at a very late phase in the development process, when substantial resources would have been committed to a 'wrong' design. Often these errors are discovered after the officially alotted systems development process and so the cost of fixing them is attributed to maintenance.

According to DeMarco (1978), after implementation 56% of software errors may be attributed to errors of requirements specification, compared with only 27% due to design errors and 7% due to coding errors (see Figure 11.2). However, the cost of fixing errors committed during requirements analysis is much greater than errors committed later. DeMarco estimates that 82% of the *cost of errors* may be attributed to errors of requirements specification (compared with only 13% due to design errors and 1% to coding errors). Even if prototyping does not reduce the number of requirements analysis errors, at least it reduces the cost of these errors by bringing them to light at an early phase.

According to Jörgensen (1984), these are merely the short-term benefits to be had from prototyping. In the long run prototyping will lead to improved systems design because prototyping allows designers to be confronted with the consequences of their designs on users. 'What is natural to a systems designer is not necessarily natural to a user' (1984, p. 286). Jörgensen cites designers of user interfaces expressing this hypothesis:

> Initially we thought it's very important to have a nice structured hierarchy of menus. After we did some user testing on it we realized that it's a good starting point, but I think that a successful set of menus is one that doesn't stick to a hierarchy. The user wants to go from one path in the tree to another, so why not let him? ... In a hierarchical structure it seems unnatural to jump from one branch to another ... the hierarchical structure pervades our thinking. (1984, p. 286)

In the literature of the 1980s prototyping has been considered to be a new and experimental technique.[22] Nevertheless on the ground, in an extremely high proportion of computer installations, a minimal form of prototyping has been practised from the early 1980s.

In our NCC 1984 survey we asked respondents if they produced prototypes of screen designs and input and output forms for users to inspect or 'try out' as part of the development process. Almost all respondents (96%) reported that they did at least sometimes; 27% said they always did and 44% said usually. This pattern was not substantially different for different sizes of installations or different industries.

Problems with prototyping

Experiences with prototyping have revealed several problems with the approach. These problems may be roughly grouped into three types. First, prototyping may be criticized because its effects are somehow limited. Therefore it is not powerful enough to achieve the main intended results, the sort of communication between users and systems developers and mutual learning that results in better-quality systems. Second, the prototyping process may in itself lead to errors. It may contribute to poor quality systems. Third, prototyping may, in a sense, work too well. It may orient the system's development process in favour of end users to the detriment of efficient resource allocation and/or the long-term strategic aims of top managers.[23]

(1) Prototyping is too limited.
One aspect of the argument that prototyping (by itself) may be too limited is that old habits die hard. Floyd (1984, p. 14) points out that prototyping allows early, but not automatic user participation. Jörgensen (1984) points to the danger of prototyping taking the role played by written specifications in traditional systems development. 'The fundamental idea of prototypes is to iterate the design, not to FREEZE it' (p. 287). Designers must allow users to influence both the modification of prototypes and the further modification of new versions.

For prototypes to fulfil their role of reducing the cost of modifications, they must be available early. This requires a range of tools to be available to designers and to be used (such as fourth-generation languages, database management systems and a good program library). Finally, the technique of prototyping may be inadequate by itself because systems development usually involves organizational and social change. However, the system being developed forms only a part of users' working environment. User dissatisfaction in their role as employees and members of particular departments may not be within the power of systems designers to relieve. Users may then regard their role in the prototyping process as irrelevant to their condition and not take it seriously. On the other hand, systems designers, in their enthusiasm, may give the impression that the systems development process will provide users with benefits that cannot be delivered. These problems parallel those already discussed in relation to user involvement schemes.

(2) The prototyping process leads to errors.
Systematic errors generated by prototyping relate to the difference between operating a prototype and operating the final system. In the artificial context of the prototype, users are less likely to envision needed functions and short cuts; that is, to envision the requirements of experienced users rather than novice users (Jörgensen, 1984). As Naur (1984) pointed out, the prototyping approach relies on learning by example and demonstration, rather than using abstract general methods of description.

'In using examples and demonstrations for explaining the characteristics of a software system it should not be overlooked that the success depends on the user making the right generalization from the special cases shown to the examples' (p. 240).

Because the prototype only provides part of the system it can lead to what Iivari (1984, p. 270) called creeping inefficiency. This occurs when prototyping 'proceeds strictly sequentially and decisions to confirm or terminate are based on marginal considerations'. To really improve the system someone has to stand back and think about it, perhaps along radically new lines. Prototyping can lead to the structuring of discussions on peripheral issues. The prototype may be fundamentally inadequate in that it incorporates an unsuitable model, perhaps because it may have initially been produced by systems designers with an exclusively IS-oriented viewpoint (Floyd, 1984, p. 15).

(3) Prototyping tips the balance of power too far towards users.
The opposite problem with prototyping is that users may not be good designers. Jörgensen (1984, p. 287) reports a case where two systems were developed for carrying out the same task. The first was developed from users' conceptions of the task domain; the second from a concept derived from systems analysis carried out by computer specialists. Users preferred the second system. It was based on far more clear-cut concepts and it was therefore easier to use.

How specifically can prototyping lead to problems if it becomes, in a sense, too successful? First, there is the cost of many iterations, which may continue indefinitely in highly unstable user environments (Naumann and Jenkins, 1982, p. 33). Prototyping is normally thought to involve trading efficiency for better quality. It may not be possible to give all users complete satisfaction of all their requirements within a reasonable budget. Also, Floyd (1984, p. 15) has suggested that prototyping may (like other procedures) be misused to manipulate users into cooperating with systems whose effect will be deskilling or lead to redundancies.

Relation between waterfall and prototyping life cycles

As noted earlier, strictly linear or waterfall life cycles have rarely been followed. Changes in general specifications often occurred once it was discovered, as a result of more detailed work, that the original ideas were unworkable or too awkward or expensive (the loopy linear pattern). Systems development is a creative process. To expect it to follow this waterfall procedure precisely is like expecting a novel writer to know precisely the plot and characterization of his or her novel before it is written, and not to change ideas in the process of writing.

In Figure 8.2 we illustrated the difference in sequencing between linear (or waterfall) and prototyping life cycle approaches to systems development. There are two opinions about the compatibility between these two approaches. The majority of those who write about prototyping emphasize its incompatibility with the waterfall life cycle. They see prototyping as a new and different systems development paradigm (Bally *et al.*, 1977; Earl, 1978; Keus, 1982; Mathiassen, 1984). They see the heart of prototyping to be improvements in system quality derived from the learning process, which is stimulated through dialogue with users. Therefore the systems development effort becomes more focused on organizational change and on social and communication aspects of systems development. These activities are more open-ended. They cannot be controlled easily by stating precisely in advance how long each step in the process will take.

The alternative view is that prototyping is merely a new technique for systems development. It represents an extension of structured methods. The competence required is within engineering and the result of the development effort is purely technical. The structured life cycle included certain intentional feedback loops to allow for testing, and subsequent correction of modules. Prototyping is simply another way of testing out parts of the system with users at an early phase in order to ensure correct specification of requirements.

To some extent the division between those who believe that prototyping is incompatible with waterfall life cycle and those who believe it is not may be due to consideration of the different types of prototyping discussed above. Three approaches to prototyping are discussed below: one incompatible with the traditional waterfall life cycle; one which can be incorporated into the waterfall life cycle; and one which may be regarded as complementary to the traditional model.

One type of prototyping, which may be called iterative horizontal prototyping, aims to present users with a simulation of the user interface in its intended final form, with a view to revising it more than once. At first the rest of the system may be only a mock-up. The user sees what it is like to work with the system, but there would be little validation of input and there may be no real data behind the software at all. The prototype will be built by techniques that allow easy implementation and modification, rather than efficiency. Facilities for handling errors or exception conditions are also likely to be left off. This form of prototyping is intended to lead to a final system. It is closest to what may be called versioning or evolutionary prototyping. This is inconsistent with the traditional life cycle approach.

With a second type of prototyping the prototype is intended as a one-off exercise. The prototype is more likely to be thrown away. Often with this type of prototyping the aim is to present only a few functions—vertical prototyping. It may be used to test a hypothesis about the system, such as whether the proposed section of the system will produce results to a required level of accuracy or resource absorption. Sometimes this may be called partial functional simulation. However, horizontal prototyping may also fit into this type as long as the prototyping period is limited, such as if users are only provided mock-up screens without opportunities to work with them. In these cases prototyping can be accommodated within a single phase of a waterfall life cycle development process.

This approach is demonstrated by Monckemeyer and Spitta (1984, p. 126), who prescribe the following prototyping life cycle:

(1) Rough concept—detailed analysis of the organizational concept and first structuring of the functional and database aspects of the application system.

(2) Fine concept—requirement specification for each EDP package; in this phase

prototyping activities are performed depending on the complexity software to be developed.

(3) EDP techniques—modularization under EDP-aspects, database design.

(4) Realization—module specification and construction, programming, testing, integration.

(5) Introduction—in end user's environment.

(6) Optimization—correction of faults detected in phase (5) and improvement of system performance.

Monckemeyer and Spitta emphasize that phase (2) results in a contract with the end user and they say one rule must be strictly obeyed: 'Never change requirements after the end of phase 2' (p. 126). Clearly this view of the place of prototyping in the system life cycle is anathema to most of those who consider prototyping to be the new paradigm for systems development.[24]

There is a third type of prototyping approach which can complement the waterfall model. This is a form of vertical prototyping when the core system functions are developed in a traditional manner, but add-on functions are handled by prototyping.[25] IS provides users with what IS considers to be a well-structured system, using a traditional life cycle approach,[26] which represents only, say, 60–70% of user requirements. Further functions are added using a versioning approach. We believe this approach has been very common in the 1980s.

11.3.3 Changing the IS Specialists: Wanted Renaissance People?

In our surveys between 1980 and 1985 we noticed a strong move away from certain traditional roles within IS departments or divisions. These changes may be summarized as a shift towards a widening of the knowledge and experience base from which most IS staff work. This has occurred in two ways. First, more IS staff are being required to have an understanding of what goes on outside the confines of the IS department. Expectations for knowledge of user environments may be at several levels: knowledge of the functions performed by user departments; knowledge of the particular business in which the organization as a whole operates; and general knowledge of business. Second, IS staff are being expected to perform a wider range of IS tasks. In particular, to combine analysis and programming skills.

In our US survey in 1983 many IS managers indicated their interest in hiring generalists. 'We need Renaissance people, who can think and act with an open mind', said one IS manager (Friedman and Greenbaum, 1984, p. 134). In Britain computer science degrees have never been popular with IS managers in user organizations. In fact less than 5% of British IS managers wanted a computer science degree for trainee analysts, analyst/programmers or programmers (NCC 1984 survey, although 6.6% wanted trainee operators to have a computer science degree and 7.4% wanted technical support staff, mainly systems programmers, to have one). In the USA, where these degrees are more common, IS managers were also looking for people with general qualifications, in business administration or even liberal arts and humanities (Friedman and Greenbaum, 1984, p. 138).

This theme was well borne out in the NCC 1987 survey, which concentrated on IT skills shortages. While most large organizations preferred a higher degree for development staff, there was little preference for a particular discipline:

> The possession of a degree is taken as evidence of a certain amount of intelligence and an ability to learn. (Buckroyd and Cornford, 1988, p. 53)

When some preference for a degree discipline was declared, it was business studies, rather than computer science, which was most frequently cited.

Many IS managers emphasized social skills as well as technical skills required of new recruits. This was well summarized by one particular respondent from a large site, who said:

> During our two-day evaluation and selection procedure we are looking for people who have the capacity to acquire the technical skills, but we are also looking for people who will be able to work well in teams, cooperate with colleagues and, most important of all, to communicate well with an enormous variety of users. (Buckroyd and Cornford, 1988, p. 54)

It is worth noting that Couger and Zawacki found particularly low 'social needs strength' among computer systems developers. They stated that this 'may be a prime factor in the perpetual difficulty in maintaining satisfactory relations with users of DP' (1980, p. 26).

This move towards more business skills required of computer specialists may be thought of as a convergence of skills required of computer systems developers and users. As one IS manager responding to the NCC 1987 survey put it:

> Users will have to adopt some more computer training. DP departments will need more business training. (Buckroyd and Cornford, 1988, p. 59)

This has led to a greater emphasis on interchange of staff across the departmental boundary between computer systems developers and users.

A high proportion of IS managers in our NCC 1984 survey stated that they recruited individuals from user areas to work as analysts (52%) and as programmers (50%). Hiring people from user areas was very common during phase one; however, with the development of a labour market this method of recruitment declined in phase two. By the CEL 1972 study, 17% of programmers and 24% of analysts were recruited from non-DP positions within the firm. Mumford noted that DP staff recruited from user departments very quickly accepted 'EDP group values'. That is, according to Mumford, they lost sympathy with users (1972, p. 199). The value of this source of recruitment was mainly to ease general labour shortages as well as to lower the cost of judging the work habits of recruits. However, by phase three there was evidence that some IS staff were being hired from user departments because of their knowledge of user areas. This was relatively common where job rotation has been traditional, in central government departments (17%) and in what we have called central government agencies (30%, such as government research agencies).[27] We also found relatively high proportions reporting job rotation schemes where we might expect to find highly skilled users (although not necessarily computer-skilled users), as in process industries (19%) and professional services (18%). Further evidence of this move towards positively looking for recruits with experience of user areas comes from a perusal of job advertisements in the computing press. There appeared to be more job advertisements that specify experience in some user areas, such as banking systems or CAD systems (computer-aided design) during the mid-1980s.

Along with recruiting generalists and people from user areas, there is evidence that the range of skills being exercised by individual systems developers has been changing during phase three. Strongest evidence for this change has been the degeneration of the traditional division of labour between analysts and programmers (Friedman and Cornford, 1984, p. 23). The composite job category, analyst/programmer, appears to be repairing this division of labour (see section 12.1.1).[28]

Why is it that this division of labour, well established since phase one, is being abandoned in phase three? Let us first review why this division of labour was established in the first place. The separation of analysis from programming was founded on three premises:

(1) The tasks of analysis and programming are different.
(2) People who are good at one of these sets of tasks are not particularly good at the other set. Programmers were considered to be rather bad at communicating with users. Their image was of technical people, unaware or disdainful of the problems of people who were not computer-skilled.
(3) It was assumed that user requirements could be clearly embodied in specifications. In fact, during phase two, it was assumed that program or module specifications could be made so clear and so detailed that the programmer would become a 'mere coder' (Kraft, 1977).

However, changes in the types of users and uses during phase two meant that applications being attempted in many departments by phase three could not be specified clearly in advance. Uncertain and complex user requirements meant that changes to specifications at late phases had to be accepted as part of the development process. This meant that communication with users would have to occur throughout the development process. If user communication during programming phases had to be carried out via analyst intermediaries, it was likely that messages would be corrupted as well as delayed. This situation favoured the emergence of the analyst/programmer.

A further factor favouring the analyst/programmer has been the fall in the size of tasks during phase three. In part this is because many new applications rely on a base of systems and data which have already been implemented. In part it is because the proportion of work on maintenance, minor enhancements and answers to ad hoc inquiries from users has been rising.

Finally, the continuing fall in hardware costs has meant that the population of systems development staff is being continually altered owing to new departments being set up in smaller and smaller organizations, as well as by changes in the size and distribution of jobs within existing IS departments. These new departments in small organizations are also small departments, where it is difficult to schedule workloads between projects to ensure a steady flow of both analysis and programming work. Any strong specialization is likely to result in slack periods for the specialists concerned. We found a clear negative correlation between the size of IS department and the proportion of analyst/programmers (see Tables 12.1 and 12.2).

One further factor that has sustained the analyst/programmer job category has been the strategies DP managers had developed to retain staff. During phase two responsible autonomy management strategies towards development staff came to mean developing career structures within DP. Analyst/programmer job categories came to represent intermediate steps between programmer and analyst positions in many DP departments. Hansen and Penney noted that 'some' of the organizations in their NCC 1975 survey had recently introduced the analyst/programmer grade as a means of transition from programming into analysis (1976, p. 31). Programmers could be introduced to new roles while still retaining their valuable technical skills. Again this strategy is precisely the opposite of the approach to work organizations within DP which emphasizes deskilling and the creation of mere coders, i.e. direct control types of strategies.

Statistically changes in the proportion of computer systems developers called analyst/programmers have occurred because of stagnation in the number called (applications) programmers. Although some of the 'craft' aspects of application programming have been removed, other skills—skills of analysis, design, communication and implementation—are being added to the job.

The major technical changes (high-level languages, the growth of on-line development, editors, database management systems, software utilities and software libraries and generators) have *also* removed much of the 'detail' aspects of programming. It is easier to computerize detail activities, which individually require little skill, but together increase the variety/complexity of programmer tasks. Removal of the detail tasks tends to make the creation of a 'mere coder' a less attractive and viable proposition for management because there is less 'mere coding' to be done for the same amount of analysis and design. In some senses the mere coder was stillborn, automated out of existence before 'she' had properly come to life. Thus programmers are being transformed into analyst/programmers.

The other reason for growth in analyst/programmers is the overall growth in the population of computer systems developers into smaller organizations and user-oriented application areas involving smaller jobs. Analysts, on the other hand, have also been growing rapidly, stimulated by changes in the boundary between the mediating process and users.

11.4 CONCLUSIONS

A major difficulty for computer systems developers in user organizations during phase three has been that usage of internally generated IS solutions has become more discretionary. The development of the external market for IS services has meant that alternatives have increasingly become available. More important, new applications are increasingly aimed at improving the quality of management decisions, rather than simply executing those decisions. Whether or not such systems get used depends on whether managers believe they actually improve the quality of their decisions. Also, non-usage of the system or resistance to it cannot be passed off as simply reflecting inadequate end users, i.e. inadequate low-level clerical staff. End users and clients are being fused. Many end users are now people in powerful positions within user organizations. Giving users what they really need and implementing these systems smoothly have come to be primary measures of IS department success.

Coincident with this rise in discretion and the power of end users, the task of specifying user requirements clearly and accurately has become much more difficult. This has occurred for several reasons.

First, there is the sheer problem of complexity. As the capacity of computers to deal with exception conditions has developed, so has the demand for systems which could deal with complex requirements. Also many new systems have been intended for more than one set of users or one set of purposes. This too has added to the difficulty of setting out requirements clearly.

Second is the problem of developing systems for which user requirements are increasingly uncertain and unstable. Systems intended to help decision making are much harder to specify in advance. Whether a system will in fact help decision making is likely to be discovered once the system is being used and once the effects of decisions based on such systems can be evaluated.

These issues have led to the pursuit of a wide range of strategies aimed at improving the ability of IS to meet user needs. Some strategies tackle the user relations problem by allowing sophisticated users to cross the IS/user barrier (end-user computing more or less supported by information centres). Other strategies have tackled the problem by making it easier for computer specialists to cross the IS/user barrier, as individuals (hiring 'renaissance people', analyst/programmer job categories, job rotation schemes) or as project groups (standing project teams mirroring user functions, user support groups which may be called information centres) or as subdepartments (decentralized computing). Other strategies concentrate on directly breaking down the IS/user barrier by creating arenas

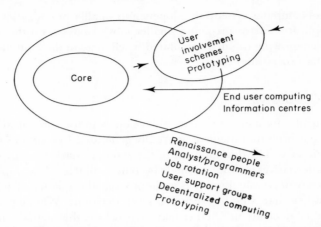

FIGURE 11.3 Phase three strategies for dealing with user relations problems

where internal interaction between computer specialists and users can occur (user involvement schemes). Prototyping may be thought of as a procedure to support mutual interaction types of strategies, but they may also support dealing with user relations problems by allowing computer specialists to cross the IS/user barrier. These three types of strategies are illustrated in Figure 11.3.

Strategies in relation to users appear to be having a number of important consequences on work organization within IS departments. Overall user relations strategies seem to encourage responsible autonomy strategies toward IS staff. The proportion of IS staff carrying out the more creative tasks is growing. Monitoring development work by users appears to be becoming more important than monitoring by IS management or senior management. Overall a concern with system quality rather than cost is encouraging IS management to adopt more flexible organization structures and to recruit staff who are able to carry out a wider range of tasks. Evidence for these claims is presented in the next chapter.

ENDNOTES

1. Different types of user involvement may be classified in other ways. They may be classified according to which stage in the system life cycle involvement occurs, according to which types of users become involved (section 7.3), according to what proportion of users become involved or according to the organizational form of involvement. One problem with the classifications relating to user influence is that each includes a wide range of possible types of involvement according to these other criteria, and these other criteria may also relate to user influence. Different organizations will all call their schemes user involvement, even though they differ widely in the degree of user influence they allow. This makes it difficult to compare installations. The problem is reminiscent of the problem with translating use of structured methods into a clear indicator of direct control strategies (see section 6.4.2).

2. For example, Rolf Høyer, Professor of Informatics at Bergen, Norway, distinguished three areas of end-user influence in the Scandinavian countries. These were (1979, p. 49):
   (1) social and humane considerations;
   (2) user involvement and participation in the design process;
   (3) co-determination, the right to be consulted and decide upon the properties of the new system.
   Other well-known European contributions are DeBrabander and Edstrom (1977) and DeBrabander and Thiers (1984).
   An important American exception has been Rob Kling and his associates in the URBIS group (see section 8.2.2). Kling analysed different theoretical perspectives adopted by social analysts of computing. He distinguished two major perspectives: systems rationalism and segmented institutionalism. Systems rationalists assume there is a major social goal relevant to computer use, while segmented institutionalists assume intergroup conflict is likely (1980, pp. 63–65). The latter group deal with power relations and conflict explicitly. Most references to writing from the segmented institutionalist approach in his survey are to work by Kling and his associates in the URBIS group. Another well-known American contribution to this area is Markus (1983).

3. In Sweden, consultancies specializing in providing worker-oriented support for end users have been flourishing during the 1980s. They have been supported by the 1977 Co-determination Act. However, Sweden is an exception, even in the Scandinavian countries.

4. However, in our surveys we discovered that formal post-implementation reviews rarely occur for any computer systems development projects. Others have found a similar dearth (McCosh and Scott Morton, 1978; Keen, 1980; Hogue, 1987).

5. Hirschheim (1983) notes this lack of portability and points out that it makes meaningful cross-section comparisons between organizations using participant design problematic. He found that organizations generally do not choose to use participative design a second time. One justification expressed by Hirschheim's respondents for this apparent 'inconsistency' was that they had not found a 'suitable' second case (p. 323).

6. A rapidly growing literature in the 1980s was reflected and encouraged by the appearance of new journals such as the *Journal of Management Information Systems* in 1983 and the *Journal of Information Systems Management* in 1984. Well-known specialist journals in this field which were established earlier are *MIS Quarterly* (1977), *Information and Management* (1976) and *Data Base* (1970).

7. Much of the research on end-user computing is concerned with how it should be organized, and particularly with the information centre. This is dealt with in section 11.3.1

8. The development of tools to automate the work of specialist systems developers has continued during phase three. During the late 1980s these tools have been receiving considerable attention in the literature under the label of CASE (computer-aided software engineering). These tools are discussed in section 13.5.1.

9. This has led some users to hold back on requests because of expected frustration with internal computer departments (Martin, 1985).

10. The provision of these tools was highly correlated with the size of installation. Growth between 1982/83 and 1985 was most marked for applications-building tools in medium-sized installations (10–29 systems developers). Among industry sectors, education institutions were outstanding, with 71% providing applications-building tools. Education, local government and utilities were high providers of tools for ad hoc inquiries (all 80–82%). The financial sector stood out as a particularly low provider of

facilities for ad hoc inquiries (40%) and was rather low on tools for applications building (20%).

11. Note the classification of users proposed by Rockart and Flannery (1983); see section 7.3.
12. There is considerable confusion as to when the information centre concept was first developed. Three dates suggested in different sources are 1972 (Horwitt, 1985, p. 38), 1974 (Necco *et al.*, 1987, p. 96) and 1976 (Wetherbe and Leitheiser, 1985, p. 3). All agree that it was first developed by IBM Canada.
13. Almost all of Wetherbe and Leitheiser's sample of information centres provided consultancy, training, trouble-shooting and new product resource services. Most also provided a newsletter (1985, p. 5).
14. Even the spread of PCs in organizations did not directly result in information centres. During our 1983 USA survey we found many installations had an individual or team providing software for user PCs and support for end-user computing without being formally designated as an information centre.
15. The median number of information centre staff has been reported as four by Wetherbe and Leitheiser (1985) and by Magal and Carr (1988).
16. This was highly correlated with the size of DP department (only 12% of departments with less than ten development staff, but 58% of those with more than 30). Financial institutions stood out, with around half (50–56%) reporting this form of organization structure.
17. For many terms in this field, connections with established meanings of words are sacrificed for salesmanship. Methodology sounds more impressive than method.
18. Reliable software will perform as expected under all normal conditions. This should minimize maintenance requirements. Modifiable systems are ones than can be changed with minimal impact on their structural characteristics (Colter, 1982, p. 75).
19. According to Boehm the waterfall model of the software life cycle was developed in the following sources: Air Force, 1966; Rosove, 1967; Royce, 1970.
20. The noun 'prototype' is used in other fields to mean the first of a type. It is a full-scale model of a product that is intended to be produced in quantity. It is intended to exhibit the essential features of the final product. It is used for testing, as a guide for further production, and sometimes as a demonstrator for potential customers. However, computer systems development generally leads to a single product. The prototype produced in this field is more strictly a version of the final product, or a pilot system (Rzevski, 1984). It is intended to allow the system to be demonstrated or tested, with the expectation that the test or demonstration will stimulate ideas for further refinement of the final product. The intention is to test or demonstrate the prototype with its eventual users. Therefore it is the catalyst for an early and informed dialogue with users which is the key value of the prototype. It is the process of learning user requirements or gaining user acceptance which is important, not the demonstration of a solution to a problem or a new type to be produced. For this reason the verb 'prototyping' has become more commonly used than the noun in the computer systems development field.
21. In terms of the longevity of a prototype we may distinguish three types of prototyping, according to Tavolato and Vincena (1984):

    (1) throw-it-away approach which emphasizes *rapid* prototyping;
    (2) evolutionary development approach by which the user is supplied with an early version of the system to experiment with and which will be modified;
    (3) plug-in or incremental delivery approach by which linear life cycle is pursued until the end of the functional specifications stage. Then parts of the system are delivered one at a time. User experiences with early parts may affect the implementation of later parts.

22. For example, in the introduction to the published papers from the 1983 Working Conference on Prototyping it was noted that in this field 'there are no "big names", few experts and few well-established methods, tools, experiences, etc.' (Züllighoven, 1984, p. v).

23. It may be that the most important criterion for deciding whether prototyping is likely to achieve its promised benefits (other than whether or not tools to support prototyping are available) is the size of the system being developed. The problem with using prototyping for very large new systems is that it takes such a long time to perform the required data analysis. The temptation is then to begin with what users want most and develop the system 'out' from that 'corner'. This can lead to a poorly structured system.

24. The last two phases of Mönckemeyer and Spitta's precribed life cycle is reminiscent of Bally *et al.*'s loopy linear life cycle (1977; see section 8.2.8).

25. In the traditional waterfall approach the problem of changing requirements or misunderstood requirements (which are discovered between the design and implementation phases) will be dealt with in three ways. First, they may be ignored. Second, if the change would lead to the invalidation of the original design and it must be incorporated, developers must return to the earlier phase and incorporate the change. Third, if the change can be dealt with as an add-on, a small 'river' may be run concurrently with the big waterfall. The add-on may be treated as a separate project. This third situation may be planned for by adopting this two-step approach to the development of large new systems.

26. Perhaps even an approach with an exaggerated absence of user involvement.

27. According to the NCC 1984 survey.

28. 'Analyst/programmer' is a label commonly used in Europe. In the USA they are more often called programmer/analysts.

Chapter 12

THE INFORMATION SYSTEMS FUNCTION IN PHASE THREE

In this chapter a picture of the information systems function is presented, primarily based on surveys in Great Britain. The surveys were carried out between 1982/83 and 1987 on the membership base of user organizations of the British National Computing Centre (see Data Appendix).

12.1 TASK ORGANIZATION

12.1.1 Division of Labour

During the 1980s the separation between analysts and programmers was already breaking down. About half (49·1%) of respondents to our NCC 1985 survey reported organization structures using analyst/programmers. Matched samples comparing NCC 1982/83 with NCC 1984 and NCC 1984 with NCC 1985 show some shifts towards organization structures using analyst/programmers. The main change has occurred because the size distribution of information systems departments has been changing. Departments have been getting smaller because of decentralization (see section 11.3.1) and because of the entry of more small departments into the population. Successively smaller organizations have come to be able to afford to computerize with their own staff and equipment owing primarily to the reduction in cost of purchased computer systems core. Table 12.1 shows the distribution of organization structures by size of computer installation.

The complete separation of analysts and programmers, either using separate teams or having a programming pool, has almost disappeared, accounting for only 8·5% of the sample. These traditional organization structures were common early in phase two. In Chapter 11 we suggested that the growing importance of user relations has been a major reason for the long-term recombination of this traditional division of labour between analysts and programmers.

Note that small installations were clearly more likely to use structures where all development staff were pooled together, as well as combining analysis and programming tasks into the analysts/programmer job category. However, while only a handful of larger installations used pools, over one-third used structures specifying analyst/programmers. The disposition towards analyst/programmers in smaller installations can also be seen from Table 12.2, which shows the percentage of staff in each job category by installation size.

Analyst/programmers accounted for 50% of computer systems developers in

TABLE 12.1 Which of the following best describes the organization of your development staff?

	Size of installation			
	0–9 (%)	10–29 (%)	30+ (%)	Total (%)
Teams of analysts and programmers	16.0	36.9	51.6	29.0
Separate teams of analysts	0.5	7.4	3.2	3.3
Teams of analysts and a programming pool	4.4	7.4	3.2	5.2
Teams of analyst/programmers	16.0	35.3	29.0	24.7
Pool of analysts and programmers	14.4	5.7	1.6	9.3
Pool of analyst/programmers	35.4	4.9	0	19.2
Matrix organization of analysts and programmers	4.4	2.5	6.5	4.1
Matrix of analyst/programmers	8.8	0	4.8	5.2
Structures using analyst/programmers	60.2	40.2	33.8	49.1
Structures using pools	49.8	10.6	1.6	28.5

Note: Size of installation is by number of computer systems developers (analysts, analyst/programmers and programmers).
Source: NCC 1985 survey.

small installations, but only 28% in large installations. Note that presence of technical support staff was correlated with installation size, and that IS management was negatively correlated with size.

During phase two, as the mediating process was being displaced by more sophisticated computer systems core, and as it spread deeper into the organization, the balance of job categories in installations began to change accordingly. By the

TABLE 12.2 Percentage of staff within different job category by installation size

	Size of installation		
	0–9 (%)	10–29 (%)	30+ (%)
DP management	21	14	8
Systems analysts	6	11	13
Analyst/programmers	17	16	11
Programmers	11	13	15
Technical support	2	7	13
Operations	28	21	25
Data preparation	15	18	15

Note: Size of installation is by number of computer systems developers (analysts, analyst/programmers and programmers). Technical support includes systems programmers, database administrators and network staff.
Source: NCC 1986 survey.

end of phase two it was clear that on-line systems were leading to a rapid decline in specialist data preparation staff located in information systems departments. Also more sophisticated operating systems and the spread of minicomputers meant fewer operators were required. Much of the basic locating, fetching and carrying of files have been automated. In contrast, analysts and programmers were growing to meet rising maintenance loads on existing systems and the growth of user demands for new applications. These trends have continued during phase three.

The changes in job categories described above have been transforming the overall character of IS departments. Generally it has been the *lowest*-level jobs in information systems departments that have been disappearing: data preparation and operators. Most recently the relative proportion of ordinary applications programmers within the development group have declined. Not only has the proportion of higher-level job categories been rising, but also the proportion of managers seems to be rising. This is because the distance between low-level management and ordinary IS staff is also being bridged. This may be considered to be another sign of responsible autonomy type of strategies, at least towards analysts or analyst/programmers. Overall the structure of job categories in information systems departments is coming to look like research or professional units within organizations, rather than the mass production departments predicted by Kraft. The base of the internal job pyramid is getting narrower, the upper middle levels wider (see Tables 12.3 and 12.4).[1]

The other strong division of labour that emerged during phase two, between applications and systems software specialists, has continued into the 1980s. Over 80% of installations reporting to the NCC 1985 survey had individuals or teams specifically responsible for systems software. Maintenance was a less clearly

TABLE 12.3 Changes in the DP department job pyramid during the 1980s

1980 version		1987 version
7.9	DP Management	8.9
10.8	Analysts	13.5
15.2	Analysts/programmers	20.6
15.1	Programmers	16.0
7.0	Technical support	9.6
18.8	Operators	17.9
25.2	Data preparation	13.5

Note: Technical support is a mixed category and difficult to represent. It should probably be placed just above or just below analyst/programmers, on average. However, we have placed them below programmers because we want to highlight changes among the groups we have been calling systems developers.
Source: NCC 1982/83 Survey.

TABLE 12.4 Changes in the DP department job
pyramid expected to 1990

1985 version		1990 version
7.6	DP Management	8.1
11.3	Analysts	13.8
17.4	Analyst/programmers	22.2
15.8	Programmers	17.2
8.1	Technical support	9.9
16.7	Operators	16.0
23.2	Data preparation	12.9

Note: Technical support is a mixed category and difficult to represent. It should probably be placed just above or just below analyst/programmers, on average. However we have placed them below programmers because we want to highlight changes among the groups we have been calling systems developers.
Source: NCC 1985 Survey.

specialized function. Over a third (36%) had no team or individual specifically responsible for maintenance.

In addition to these divisions, certain other specialisms that were emerging at the end of phase two were being assigned to individuals or to a team in the majority of installations, according to the NCC 1985 survey. Over 80% of installations had a specialist section working on communications and networks (although this was primarily the responsibility of a single individual). Over 60% had database design and administration specialists, and specialists to evaluate packages. As can be seen from Table 12.5, user relations was another important area to which most installations assigned individuals or whole teams.

The distinction between assigning an individual to one of these areas and the

TABLE 12.5 Do you have either a team or individuals within DP who are specifically responsible for the following areas?

	None (%)	Team (%)	Individual (%)
Applications maintenance	35.7	39.7	23.8
Systems software	16.2	47.7	36.1
Database design and administration	39.4	28.2	32.4
Communications/networks	19.6	32.8	47.6
Processing ad hoc requests from users	34.4	31.7	33.9
Evaluating packages	39.1	18.3	42.1
Training or assisting users to develop their own programs	45.1	21.3	33.6

Source: NCC 1985 Survey.

assignment of a team is mainly dependent on the size of the installation. A number of these functions are also strongly related to the size of installation. Systems software, database design and communications and network specialisms are all more likely to occur in the larger installations. For systems software, 94% of the installations with more than ten development staff had a specialist, compared with only 73% in the small installations. The pattern for database design and for communications was very similar with respect to size of installation. However, the incidence of specialists for user relations activities, maintenance and for evaluating packages was rather evenly distributed across size categories. These are not activities based on well-established technical skills. They may become established as peripheral activities within a computer installation in the sense of the more technical specialists being reserved to carry out other tasks.

12.1.2 New Technology

By the end of phase two we noted that database management systems, data dictionaries and report generators were diffusing rapidly. The proportions of installations reporting having database management systems (DBMS) and data dictionaries in the NCC 1985 survey were almost exactly the same as in the CEL 1981 survey (60% DBMS and 37% data dictionaries). The incidence of both are strongly correlated with installation size. Further diffusion among larger installations has been offset by the rise in smaller installations (as well as the better representation of smaller installations in all the NCC surveys compared with the CEL 1981 survey). Nevertheless our matched samples showed modest rises of 3% each.[2]

In spite of the high penetration of DBMS, the proportion of data items residing on the DBMS at installations with one was less than 20% for 78% of installations and above 80% for only 15%. Similarly, only 15% of installations had more than 80% of data items residing in their data dictionaries and 58% had less than 10%.[3]

Much higher than either database tools was the reported incidence of report or applications generators (72%, NCC 1985 survey). There was a slight positive correlation with size, but even among small installations over half had generators. According to our NCC 1984 survey, generators were most often used for ad hoc inquiries.

It is striking that structured methods, which were reported as being used by 70% of respondents to the CEL 1981 survey, were only reported by 40% of the NCC 1985 survey respondents. The use of methodologies was strongly correlated with installation size (only 18% of small installations using them, compared with 68% of large ones). They were used primarily in the public sector (excluding education) and among financial institutions. The size correlation is one reason why use of methodologies was reported by such a low proportion of the NCC 1985 survey, compared with the CEL 1981 survey. However, disappointment with these methodologies is another reason.

In the NCC 1985 survey we asked in which areas of systems development respondents expected to gain substantial benefits from the methodology they were using, and in which areas the benefits had been achieved. The answers are summarized in Table 12.6.

Of the reasons that were offered for using methodologies, ease of maintenance and system quality were most frequently indicated, by two-thirds of the methodology users. These were also areas in which the highest proportion of users (48% in the case of maintenance and 53% in the case of system quality) had achieved benefits. Productivity was cited by half of the users as an expected benefit, but was only achieved by one-third. For each of these areas of expected or

TABLE 12.6 Benefits expected and achieved from methodologies

	Expected benefit (%)	Achieved benefit (%)	Indicated expected but not achieved (%)	Disappointment index (col. 3 as % of col. 1) (%)
Project control	39.4	26.5	20.4	51.8
System specification	52.5	42.3	21.7	41.3
System testing	43.1	32.9	21.7	50.4
User involvement	38.4	25.5	20.4	53.1
Productivity	50.3	35.8	21.9	43.3
Ease of changes	61.3	42.3	28.5	46.5
Ease of maintenance	66.4	48.1	29.9	45.0
System quality	66.4	52.6	26.3	39.6

Source: NCC 1985 Survey.

achieved benefit there was a substantial number of respondents who indicated that they had expected benefits and not achieved them. These presumably must be put down as 'disappointed' users. There were also, for each area, a number who had achieved benefits that were not expected. These were presumably 'pleasantly surprised'. In every area the number of disappointed users exceeded the number pleasantly surprised. Note that user involvement and project control were relatively less likely to be cited as expected benefits and even more rarely cited as achieved benefits.

In a *Datamation* article about booming salaries in the DP field during the mid-1980s, it was noted that DP managers were trying to offset personnel shortages and high salaries by purchasing programmer productivity aids. However, several predicted that the productivity growth from improved technology would, at best, keep demand for skilled staff growing at a constant rate, rather than cause demand to fall, or even slow down its rate of increase (Marion, 1984, p. 88).

12.2 EMPLOYMENT RELATIONS

Labour shortages for development staff have continued during the 1980s. Although in the worst years of the recession (1981/82) there was some relief, shortages quickly re-emerged in Great Britain (see section 9.3.2). These shortages have continued to fuel labour turnover. According to the NCC 1987 survey, perceived shortages were highest for analysts and analyst/programmers, followed closely by programmers and systems programmers. Labour turnover was 16% for development staff. Analyst/programmers and programmers had the highest turnover rates, of 21% and 20% respectively (Table 12.7).

Note that perceived shortages were very small for IS managers, operators and data preparation staff. The difference between joiners and leavers was small for IS managers and operators but many more data preparation staff were leaving than were joining. Rather striking is the percentage of systems development staff joining IS departments, 21%. Clearly with such a high proportion of new staff every year, there are problems of integrating new people, as well as coping with the difficulty of dealing with the high proportion of leavers. Buckroyd and Cornford estimated that there was a shortage of 19 400 systems development staff among user organizations in the UK for 1987 (this figure excludes the IT 'supply' industry and the armed forces, 1988, p. 14).

As mentioned in Chapter 6, there are two sorts of responsible autonomy types of strategies that DP managers have been pursuing. One is to offer good salaries and fringe benefits as well as good working conditions (particularly evidenced by good opportunities to acquire experience and training with new techniques).[4] The second is to try to retain staff by offering a good career structure.[5]

TABLE 12.7 Labour turnover and shortage rates expressed as a
percentage of staff in post, 1987, analysed by job category

	Leavers (%)	Joiners (%)	Perceived shortage (%)
DP management	9.3	8.3	3.1
Systems analysts	14.3	18.9	15.7
Analyst/programmers	20.9	24.3	15.5
Programmers	20.0	30.2	13.3
Systems programmers	13.6	21.9	12.3
Network staff	8.7	24.1	8.4
Systems development staff	16.0	21.4	11.9
Operations	16.3	17.9	4.0
Data preparation	20.5	12.9	2.7
All jobs	16.7	19.4	8.9

Source: NCC 1987 Survey.

We have found no evidence to contradict the belief that organizations are attempting to pursue both sorts of strategies. The cover story in the 15 September 1984 issue of *Datamation* was displayed as 'DP Salaries: Bringing the Big Bucks Home' or 'The Big Wallet Era' (Marion, 1984). The recession of the early 1980s, like that of the early 1970s, resulted in a leveling off of DP salaries. However, both periods were short-lived.[6] *Datamation* reported salary rises during the 1980s significantly above both the general rate of inflation and above average salaries among professionals.

> Benefits such as reimbursement for education, company cars, and other perks continue to be popular, as noted last year ('1983 Dp Salaries—The Key Word is Perks' September, p. 82). But there is nothing like cash to attract people. (Marion, 1984, p. 86)

The worst shortages were reported for systems programmers, telecommunications staff and database staff in the *Datamation* surveys.[7] But shortages of project managers who had both technical and 'people skills' were also reported.

It is clear that the high salaries being paid were hardly part of a well thought out strategy in many organizations. A typical comment from the survey was, 'We have been paying higher prices than we would like to, higher than we feel they should be. We don't feel the skill level justifies the salary' (Marion, 1984, p. 86).

In the aftermath of the stock market crash of October 1987, salaries of IS staff have continued to grow.[8] According to *Datamation*, average annual salary increases to June 1988 were 6.6% for IS staff in the USA, compared with 4.8% for all American white-collar workers with a professional specialty or technical expertise (1 October 1988, p. 53). Again the biggest rises were reported for systems progammers. High demand was also reported for staff who could understand the technology and communicate with top executives (p. 54).

We note that the growth of the analyst/programmer job category is partly explained by its use as a transitional job category between programming and analysis. Respondents were asked if they ever recruited trainees (staff with no previous IS experience) into listed job categories. The results are shown in Table 12.8.

For many organizations trainees are recruited only for operator and programmer positions. The low proportion of trainees for other categories is either due to internal promotion or recruitment of experienced staff from other organizations. The low proportion of analyst/programmer recruitment reflects the higher incidence of this job category in small installations, which were generally less likely to hire trainees, as well as the position of the analyst/programmer as a position higher up the career structure than programmer. Notably, 33% of organizations had not recruited any trainees during the two years up to the survey data. However, only 12% reported difficulties in recruiting trainees.

We noted the problem of DP manager career prospects in Chapter 6.

TABLE 12·8 Installations that 'ever recruit IT trainees, analysed by job category

	Trainees recruited (%)
Systems analysts	10.7
Analyst/programmers	21.6
Programmers	56.8
Technical support	14.8
Operations	72.3

Source: NCC 1987 Survey.

12.3 STAFF CONTROL

In the section on task organization above we noted that only 35% of the NCC 1985 survey reported using methodologies for systems specification, design or programming. Of these only 39% expected benefits in terms of better project control. Only 27% reported that these benefits had been achieved (Table 12.6). One reason for low expected project control benefits from methodologies was clearly that many have been disappointed. Clearly the increased control which the methodologies of phase two promised were not being realized during the 1980s (at least by proprietary methodologies). As indicated in Chapter 6, one reason for this was that methodologies were rarely imposed strictly and in full.

In the NCC 1984 survey we asked the same question about standards and how they were enforced as was asked in the CEL 1981 survey. Results for the 1984 survey are given in Table 12.9.

The incidence of these standards was higher than the CEL 1981 survey, although in part this is because we offered the option of standards being enforced informally in the 1984 survey. Enforcement by inspection in walkthroughs was much lower in 1984. This may simply be due to some installations reporting informal enforcement as enforcement by inspection in walkthroughs if they did not have the informal option. Nevertheless, given the correlation between size of installation and incidence of these standards, along with the greater representation of small installations in the NCC surveys, we may conclude that the incidence of these standards was growing during the early 1980s.

It is notable that, in spite of the higher incidence of standards, the proportion of technical standards (avoid GOTO statements and control flow limited to sequence, selection and iteration) which were formally included in either written specifications or in the book of installation standards. occurred as frequently as in the CEL 1981 survey, but that standards concerning forms were much less frequently explicitly written down. It has been suggested to us that some falling off in incidence of explicit enforcement of what we would call direct control types of

TABLE 12.9 Do you encourage any of the following design and coding standards in your installation and if so how are they enforced?

	Informal (%)	Installation standards (%)	System or program specification (%)	Inspection by walkthroughs (%)	By any method (%)
Avoid GOTOs	32.7	29.2	2.0	4.1	63.3
Control flow limitation	23.8	21.7	2.7	4.1	49.0
Maximum module size	25.9	31.3	9.5	4.1	66.7
Requirements for commentary within code	25.2	56.5	2.7	8.2	86.4
Format conventions on program layout	21.2	55.1	1.4	8.2	80.9
Format conventions on output layout	21.1	44.9	15.7	4.1	80.3
Any of these standards	67.4	78.2	27.2	16.3	94.6

Source: NCC 1984 Survey.

strategies has occurred simply because the way systems developers have come to be trained leads them to follow these restrictions automatically. Table 12.9 lends some support to this hypothesis. In Chapter 6 we noted that almost all organizations followed some procedure for checking programmers' work other than by programmers themselves (according to the CEL 1981 survey). Table 12.10, based on the NCC 1984 survey, shows that this continued to be the case. [9]

Almost all (94%) of the respondents imposed some form of check on the work of programmers at some phase in the production of a program. Also 81% of the sample checked at the design phase and 80% at the test/debug phase. Some check

TABLE 12.10 Do you normally use the following methods to check the program design, coding and testing of a programmer who is writing a module or program?

	Design (%)	Coding (%)	Test/debug (%)	Used at any of these stages (%)
Clearance with senior required before further progress	66.4	28.2	56.4	82.5
Walkthroughs and reviews with peers	38.3	28.9	20.2	56.4
Clearance from user required before further progress	12.1	3.4	37.6	42.3
Any of these checks	80.5	51.7	79.9	94.0

Source: NCC 1984 Survey.

on coding was used in half of the installations. Clearance with a senior was the most common form of checking (81.5%), but walkthroughs were used at some phase (usually the design phase) in over half of the installations. Checking with users was confined mainly to testing and debugging.

The use of checking techniques was very strongly related to the size of the installations. This is probably due to two factors. One factor is the tendency to institute formal procedures in larger organizations. The other is a tendency for larger organizations to employ more trainees and inexperienced staff, who would require checks on their progress more often. The small installations were notable in their *closer* involvement between users and programmers, particularly at the test/debug phase of development.

The main method of checking continued to be by clearance with senior staff, but walkthroughs and reviews with peers had become as important as clearance with senior staff for checking coding for respondents to the NCC 1984 survey. This may indicate a slight move away from direct control strategies.

In Chapter 6 we also noted the high proportion of installations where this form of programmer checking by users was carried out. In the NCC 1984 survey we also asked directly if different job categories normally had contact with individuals in user areas after the phase of requirements analysis and agreement on the outline specification (Table 12.11).

The table indicates that the distinction between analysts and programmers, in terms of user contact, has continued. However, two features of the table are worth noting. First, in a large majority of organizations (83%) programmers have such contact at least sometimes. Few organizations seem to be following a policy of only allowing user contact through analysts. The smallest installations were more likely to have frequent contact with users by programming staff; 33.9% of installations with less than ten analysts and programmers reported programmer contact and 86.6% reported analyst/programmer contact with users, either always or usually.

Second, the pattern for analyst/programmers seems to resemble the analyst

TABLE 12.11 *After the initial requirements analysis and outline specification of a new application or enhancement is agreed with a user department, would the following DP staff normally have contact with individuals in user areas, prior to system testing?*

	Always (%)	Usually (%)	Sometimes (%)	Never (%)
Project leader	86.2	11.4	1.7	0.8
Analysts	61.7	35.0	1.9	1.3
Analyst/programmers	33.1	44.1	19.4	3.4
Programmers	5.4	17.5	60.2	16.9

Source: NCC 1984 Survey.

pattern more than the programmer pattern. While 97% of analysts had contact with users always or usually during the detailed development phases, compared with only 23% of programmers, the figure for analyst/programmers was 77%. As noted in Chapter 6, we would associate this high incidence of contact between lower-level development staff and individual users with responsible autonomy strategies towards development staff.

12.4 CONCLUSION

The data we have used in this chapter refer primarily to 1984 and 1985, only three or four years later than the main data used for our picture of DP departments late in phase two. Clearly we should not expect enormous changes in the organization of development staff during this short period. In addition the surveys used in this chapter are not directly comparable with the CEL 1981 survey. However, we would argue that the population has been changing in the same direction as the main difference in the NCC surveys compared with the CEL 1981 survey, i.e. towards greater inclusion of smaller installations.

In spite of these qualifications we would suggest that our early phase three picture differs from the late phase two pictures in a number of ways. First, and most important, is the further breakdown of the traditional division of labour between analysts and programmers. The further rise of the analyst/programmer category implies more user contact among ordinary development staff. We have associated this with responsible autonomy strategies. Second, while labour shortages continue to affect salaries and labour turnover, we note that the shortages are almost entirely for skilled and experienced staff, rather than raw recruits. This is due to increased supply of recruits from education institutions as well as rising demand for recruits with more generalist skills. Therefore the net of acceptable recruits has grown somewhat. However, at the other end, among incumbents, there is likely to be more pressure to face users and to develop a knowledge of user functions, as well as general social and communications skills.

ENDNOTES

1. Data for the two years represented in Table 12.3 are consistent in that they are based on the same sample of firms. However, the 1980 figure is an estimate of the situation two years before the survey and the 1987 figure is a forecast for five years after the survey. The different bases of the data may introduce a bias into the result. The five-year forecast in particular may be systematically inaccurate owing to the optimism or pessimism of respondents. However, almost all the general trends were confirmed by comparing estimates of the current year coming from 1982/83, 1984, 1985 and 1986 surveys. The relative rise in proportion of analysts, analyst/programmers and technical support, and the relative fall in proportions of operators and data preparation staff were generally confirmed. Although the major changes appear to have been in the right direction, the extent of the changes has generally been less than forecast, particularly for the decline in data preparation staff.

2. Nevertheless we expect the proportion of small installations having a DBMS to grow dramatically with the diffusion of IBM's new minicomputers series, AS/400, replacing its System/36 and System/38. The AS/400 has a DBMS built into its operating system, unlike the System/36. Also OS/2, IBM's operating system for the IBM PC 2, has this facility. The presence of a DBMS in the operating system supplied by hardware manufacturers may lead to under-reporting of the incidence of DBMS.

3. These figures are from the NCC 1984 survey. We expect these figures to rise much more slowly than the incidence of DBMS. Acquiring a DBMS is simply a matter of purchasing what is now recognized to be a useful, and fairly inexpensive, part of computer systems core. Using it requires a substantial change in practice and converting existing systems can be extremely expensive.

4. Couger and Zawacki think of these as two alternative strategies. 'The view that high salary and fringe benefits are the solution to the turnover problem is calamitous. Companies that concentrate solely on financial inducements will be disappointed in the results. The job itself is the major motivator' (1980, p. 4). Couger repeated the empirical work on which this quotation is based ten years later. Again he concluded that 'the number one motivating factor for IS personnel is the work itself' (1988, p. 62).

5. A third responsible autonomy strategy may be to hire staff who have already been socialized into the organization culture and who may be expected to retain a greater commitment to the organization than to their occupation for at least some time. This means hiring from user departments. Later on it means developing career structure, which includes prospects of returning to user departments via job rotation or by promotion back into user departments.

6. In the USA, federal government installations and installations in areas funded by the federal government (such as utilities and transport) were slower to join in the salaries escalation of the 1980s, although US public sector installations have traditionally paid lower salaries than those in the private sector, especially during the 1980s.

7. 'No matter how much money a dp manager has to offer, finding additional qualified systems programmers is an almost impossible chore these days' (Marion, 1984, p. 86)

8. Between these two surveys *Datamation* editors decided to change the label applied to their surveys from DP staff salary surveys to IS staff salary surveys.

9. Checking by requiring documentation before further progress was an option offered to respondents in the CEL 1981 survey but was, unfortunately, left off the NCC 1984 survey.

Part 4
PROSPECTS AND IMPLICATIONS

Chapter 13

THE FUTURE: WHITHER COMPUTER SYSTEMS DEVELOPERS?

The report of my death was an exaggeration.
(Mark Twain, cable from Europe to Associated Press, sometime before 1910)

The disappearance of computer specialists has been predicted regularly throughout the history of computer systems development. Often when discussing our research with academics during the 1980s we were advised to hurry and publish our results before our subject matter disappeared.[1] We have already cited predictions of the imminent disappearance of computer programmers made during phase one (Bosak, 1960; Hopper, 1962). After a short review of the three phases we have identified so far, we will discuss the prospects for computer systems development. This will be approached in two ways. First, we will consider effects that might be expected from sustained efforts to overcome user relations constraints, the major concern by which phase three has been identified. Second, we consider the emergence of a new set of constraints by which a future fourth phase might be identified. Finally we discuss our view of the prospects for computer systems developers in relation to recent reiteration of their predicted withering away.

13.1 THE PHASES OF COMPUTERIZATION: A REVIEW

Phase one, the hardware constraint period, covers the time from the emergence of the computer (late 1940s) until the mid-1960s. The high cost of computer equipment meant that only the largest organizations could afford one. Also cost and component technology limited the capacity of computers at that time. This meant that only applications that required relatively simple logic could be attempted. The comparative advantage of the computer was its ability to deal with high-volume problems, applications which handled a lot of data, but in straightforward or routinized ways—such as simple sorting operations. This meant that applications during phase one were those that took over existing clerical operations. There procedures were already relatively formalized and understood.

Not only did constraints in the computer systems core limit the penetration of computerization into further (smaller) organizations and into further (more complex) applications, but also the mediating activities were effected by hardware constraints. Programming work was constrained by the need to minimize the machine capacity required to run systems. This required writing programs that

ıd efficient. Programmers developed their own 'tricks' and 'techniques'
short cuts to improve program performance. Programmer creativity
٠.   ıuraged. The sorts of people hired to carry out such work were
mathematical or scientific 'types', who identified with the technology, rather than
the overall aims of their employers or the needs of the users. With the work
involving both creative and idiosyncratic procedures, as well as requiring
substantial mathematical and technical backgrounds, managers would often find
themselves only dimly understanding what their new specialists were doing.
Computer installations were often put under finance or accounting department
managers who knew little of computer systems development techniques. Even if
managers came from hardware manufacturers with strong technical backgrounds,
the pace of change in procedures developed within computer installations meant
that soon they too had to rely on the skill and judgement of systems development
staff. This encouraged responsible autonomy management strategies of a
particularly informal or lax type (management by neglect).

Responsible autonomy management strategies were also encouraged by the
shortage of experienced computer systems development staff which grew from the
outset of business computing in the mid-1950s. This strengthened staff's
bargaining position and allowed them to leave installations where working
conditions were not to their liking, without fear of being without a job for long.
However, the strongest encouragement for responsible autonomy strategies came
from the very low proportion of installation costs attributable to salaries during
phase one. At that time the job of computer department manager was primarily
thought of as one of evaluation, selection and servicing hardware, rather than
managing staff.

The influence of hardware constraints on the computerization process was not
static. During phase one these constraints were progressively relaxed owing to
remarkable technical improvements in hardware cost/performance ratios and
reliability. This allowed computers to spread to new firms, as well as to extend
applications. Not only did the computerization process expand by growth at its
outer edge, but also hardware improvements meant that certain activities which
had been carried out by computer specialists were incorporated into the computer
systems core. During the early part of phase one, programmers worked in machine
code. Gradually languages were developed by which programs were written using
mnemonic symbols. Such languages could only be used if a piece of software was
used to translate mnemonic symbols into machine code. By the second generation
computers were being sold including such software. Throughout all the phases of
computerization more and more basic functions have been taken over by the
computer systems core. Some programming tasks became so fundamental to the
computer that the commands were hard-wired into the system. The effect of this
automation of certain programming tasks was not to deskill the work of computer
systems developers. Tasks that required memory rather than creativity, such as the
need to remember commands in machine code, were automated.

Phase two, the software constraint period, began in the mid-1960s and continued until the early 1980s. A further effect of falling basic computer systems core costs was to increase visibility of the costs of mediating activities, primarily software development costs. In part this simply reflected slower productivity growth of software compared with hardware. In part it reflected rising software development content of new systems. Success with the basic applications during phase one, in terms of the delivery of computer systems which did in fact replace many aspects of certain manual systems,[2] encouraged attempts at more ambitious applications.[3] Many of the problems to which the computer was applied during phase two were less well understood and less formalized than before. Analysis and design aspects of the computerization process expanded accordingly. The software portion of DP department budgets overtook hardware costs during phase two.

This occurred at a time when DP department budgets as a whole were continuing to expand quickly due to stimulated user demands. During phase two, particularly during the 1970s, data came to be collected in user areas of organizations. Data were entered on-line, directly into the computer at source, rather than punching the data on to cards, tape, or disc within DP departments, and then entering it into the computer as a separate operation. This increased user awareness of the potential value of computerization and stimulated increases in user demands of the DP department.

Although DP department budgets were growing quickly, more and more incidents of serious budget overruns and of late systems delivery occurred. In part this was because of the rising complexity of newer applications. Less-structured problems were harder to deliver in a way which was difficult to estimate on the basis of experience with easier, more-structured problems. Delivery and cost problems were also encountered because of the rising proportion of DP department resources that had to be devoted to maintenance and minor enhancements of the accumulating collection of completed systems. This was exacerbated by changes in programming methods and personnel turnover that occurred between the time when systems were first completed and the time when they had to be maintained or enhanced.[4]

These problems, combined with rapidly rising DP department budgets, attributable to rising staff costs, led to a redefinition of the jobs of DP managers. They became primarily managers of people rather than equipment. New techniques were developed to deal with the software productivity constraint. Two rather different sorts of techniques were developed.

First, following the train of technical progress during phase one, certain mediating process functions which were closest to the computer systems core were automated. Either they were directly automated, by hard-wiring important programs into the computer, or software was developed, and provided with the computer, which allowed programming at a higher level. These included very high-level languages and software tools and utilities, such as program libraries, generators and database management systems. Automation techniques were generated primarily by traditional suppliers and innovators: the computer hardware manufacturers and their research collaborators in academic and military circles. The effect of these techniques was to shift the skill requirements of computer staff away from understanding of the inner workings of the computer when writing programs. Resources required for the mediating activities did not fall, because at the same time mediating activities were penetrating further into the needs of the organization. Knowledge requirements of computer staff were expanding in the user direction. This can be attributed mainly to the change of new applications towards dealing with less-structured problems and needs to integrate information across different departments of the organization.

Shifting mediating activities away from the core technology and towards users, particularly towards user department managers, increased both the need and opportunity to manage DP departments using strategies more in line with strategies being pursued in those user departments. Shifting skill requirements made it easier to recruit staff into DP departments without high mathematical or engineering skills. At the same time, particularly in the USA, education establishments claiming to supply staff with the required programming skills grew very quickly. This relieved the labour shortage somewhat, although rapid expansion of the computerization process limited this relief.

The second sort of techniques developed during phase two were those designed to support direct control strategies. These included the development of structured methods and chief programmer teams.

Both direct control and responsible autonomy strategies towards computer systems developers were formalized and elaborated during phase two. More formal career structures were set up to try to retain staff and to encourage them to internalize organizational goals. Arguably automation techniques also supported responsible autonomy strategies because the new technology was regarded as a draw to systems developers who wanted to work at 'state-of-the-art' installations and because the tasks automated were generally regarded as the more tedious aspects of development work. However, it was the techniques to support direct control strategies which received the widest attention in the literature. Overall we believe that there was a shift in management strategies towards direct control, compared with the lax types of responsible autonomy strategies of phase one.

Formal procedures in order to track project development and to account for staff time (worksheets, records of performance against targets) were increasingly introduced. The 'book' of standards (standards for programming, analysis, documentation, reporting, etc.) grew substantially. However, the actual shift was far less than was implied in the literature of the 1970s.

One main factor militating against this trend was the rapid pace of new-technology diffusion. Certainly the new technology did deskill certain computer specialists' work by separating conception from execution tasks. Particularly the separation between analysis and coding was sharpened. Nevertheless, a further effect was to automate routine execution tasks and therefore to remove them from the labour process altogether. The numbers of key-punch operators (employees who were most emphasized by Braverman (1974) as clearest examples of deskilling) had been drastically reduced by the end of phase two, owing to the switch to on-line data collection directly from user departments. Continued labour shortages and the need for a flexible labour force when technology was changing rapidly, encouraged DP managers to soften the effects of new techniques which were originally designed to deskill and to control computer specialists' work. Often controls were formally introduced, but informally ignored. DP managers would turn a blind eye to deviations from standard procedures. Often methodologies for structured programming and design were only introduced in part and computer staff were encouraged, rather than required, to adhere to the techniques.

Nevertheless the set of issues concerning DP managers during phase two was generally one of whether or not to introduce or strengthen direct control types of strategies. Even if many chose not to do so, or chose to move in that direction only half-heartedly, managerial strategies in DP departments generally did shift towards direct control during phase two.

Phase three, the user relations constraint period, began in the early 1980s and continues to characterize the field. Concentration on productivity in systems development during phase two did not remove the problem. Software productivity did not rise dramatically, as hardware productivity did during phase one (and later). Nevertheless the effects of changes during phase two were to displace the main areas of mediating activities further away from the computer systems core and towards users. In part this occurred because of new techniques introduced; on-line data collection and output were augmented by on-line (interactive) programming. Higher-level languages were developed and more basic functions were incorporated into systems software (such as database management systems and more sophisticated language compilers). Nevertheless the strongest reasons for shifting mediating activities towards users were connected to the types of applications being attempted, to the pushing out of the computerization frontier into less structured and more management- and planning-oriented functions. In consequence user needs became increasingly difficult to specify.

In addition user relations problems became more important to solve because users were becoming more knowledgeable and powerful. The spread of PCs into user departments and a general increase in computer awareness during the 1980s[5] has meant that computer systems developers have come to face users who have the confidence and sophistication to express their dissatisfaction with delivered systems in terms that cannot easily be dismissed or ignored. Furthermore the identity of end users has been changing. The line between system clients or patrons and end users clearly followed the division between managers and clerical staff in business computing during phase one and most of phase two. However, applications increasingly attempted from the late 1970s involved providing decision support directly to managers. Managers were becoming end users. Use of new systems by these end users was more discretionary. Dissatisfaction could powerfully be expressed by non-use. Finally, towards the end of phase two the development of the computer software industry and the spread of PCs into user departments increased the capacity for users to 'go-it-alone', to break the monopoly that centralized DP departments enjoyed in the 'market' for computer systems within their 'host' organizations.

All these changes contributed to the growth in concern about user relations among computer systems developers, among their managers and among top managers of organizations.

Three types of strategies are being pursued in order to alleviate user dissatisfaction. The *first* type may be thought of as strategies to allow IS specialists to be more sensitive to users, better equipped to understand their needs and more flexible in response to those needs. Managerial strategies towards information systems staff have changed in the direction of responsible autonomy. Job divisions, particularly between programmer and analysis functions, are being broken down in order to give programmers a greater awareness of user problems. Staff with generalist skills are being recruited. Candidates with liberal arts and business degrees are being sought and analysts are being recruited from user departments. General organization awareness skills are being encouraged among existing staff by short courses and job rotation schemes. Structured methodologies and chief programmer team techniques are being dropped, or softened, in favour of systems prototyping procedures that allow more concrete communication with users in the design process at early phases.

These policies may also be thought of, rather more suspiciously, as methods for allowing IS specialists to *appear* to accede to user demands without really doing so. That is, providing IS specialists with the jargon to respond to users in an outwardly sympathetic manner. To users the situation may be one where things change only just enough to allow them to remain, fundamentally, the same.

Other ways of encouraging IS specialists to be more sensitive to users are to organize the information systems function in ways that reflect user requirements. These include establishing standing project teams dedicated to particular user groups, establishing specialist user support groups to deal with post-development problems, and breaking up the information systems function and situating the parts in different user departments.

The *second* type of strategy may be thought of as ways of allowing users to take over traditional mediating process functions. End-user computing is being encouraged and supported. This strategy aims to provide a system or an environment that users can directly tailor to their own needs, independently of the IS department. The dream of end-user computing is very old (Bosak, 1960, Hooper, 1962). There has been a certain amount of end-user computing within business environments by highly sophisticated users (such as actuaries and production engineers) throughout the history of computing. End-user computing has always been common in the scientific and research communities. Recent growth has been very rapid because of widespread availability of high-level tools and the spread of cheap personal computers.

The *third* type of strategies are various schemes and procedures to involve users in systems development. This can involve joint project teams and user management of project teams, as well as user membership in steering committees. As noted in Chapter 11, these schemes may result in genuine user influence over the systems development process, but they may also result in a purely formalistic, insubstantial interaction.

13.2 THE PROSPECTS: EXTENSION OF CURRENT STRATEGIES FOR DEALING WITH USER RELATIONS PROBLEMS

All of the strategies for dealing with user relations problems outlined above are being pursued, more or less vigorously, in computer installations. Along with evidence of the extent to which these strategies are being pursued, we also noted important drawbacks associated with each strategy in Chapter 11. It is therefore unlikely that the future for computer systems development will be overwhelmingly shaped by the relentless pursuit of only one of these strategies or types of strategies. However, it will be instructive to sketch the future pattern of computer systems development which would be expected if one of the strategies did come to dominate efforts to solve user relations problems.

Consider what is arguably the most radical strategy for dealing with user relations problems, end-user computing. Figure 13.1 shows a likely scenario for an organization pursuing a highly developed end-user computing strategy.

Note first that sustained pursuit of end-user computing does not obviate the necessity for a mediating process. Computer specialists and information systems specialists are still required. Evaluation, purchase, maintenance and enhancement of computer systems core is still not only necessary, but likely to be done best by specialists. The enormous growth of technical support staff noted in section 12.1 reflects the continuing rise in sophistication and complexity of computer systems core existing in large organizations.[6] End users, even sophisticated end users, are not likely to want to become involved in this aspect of computing. Further specialists are required to support end users' efforts to develop particular applications, whether it be simple induction for novice users who want only to produce standard reports, or liaison with suppliers on behalf of sophisticated users who are stretching fourth (or fifth)-generation languages to their limits. Also specialist support for user purchases of computer systems core can result in substantial savings in search and evaluation costs. Even if the information centre were only to provide consultancy service to assist users to help themselves, there would be considerable demand for information centre staff.

A second thing to note about Figure 13.1 is its representation of strong links among users. In section 7.3 we noted Rockart and Flannery's (1983)

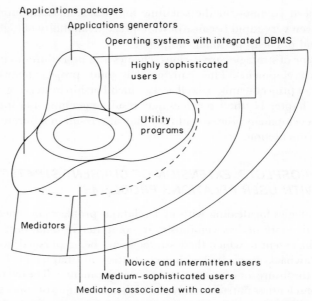

FIGURE 13.1 The future with end user computing dominant

categorization of end users into six levels. The category of functional support personnel is particularly interesting. These are sophisticated end users who act as IS specialists within their own functional area. They provide support to other end users on an informal basis. Casual empiricism suggests that this role is extremely important. It is an extension to end-user computing of the normal on-the-job training, which has always been so important for specialist computer systems developers in their first 18 months to two years in the field. This training has always been carried out in an informal master/apprentice pattern. It is likely that this role of trainer among staff within the user community would expand and become more formalized with a significant extension of end-user computing. We can foresee designated, sophisticated end users with a *formal* remit to spend some portion of their time supporting fellow users in their area of the organization, in addition to sophisticated end users who would provide such support on an informal basis.

The third feature of Figure 13.1 to notice is its similarity to the representation of scientific computing presented in Figure 9.3. If the path during phase three is to be primarily blazed by extension of end-user computing, then we would predict that the position of computer systems development in business organizations will come to resemble that in scientific or academic organizations. At universities, in spite of very sophisticated users carrying out their own development work since the beginning of computing, substantial computer centres have grown up providing the types of support outlined above. Not only do end users within university departments provide informal support to each other, but also some individual departments have hired specialist support staff on a full-time basis. Some have lecturers and researchers who are formally designated to spend part of their time providing support to other department staff.[7]

In this scenario the distinction between systems use and systems development would be broken down. The range in sophistication of end users will largely reflect experience (sophisticated end users will be either more frequent users or users who had undergone induction). Also the range of computer sophistication among individual end users and among individual IS specialists supporting them will overlap.

If user relations problems will be tacked primarily by user involvement strategies, we might expect a scenario as depicted in Figure 13.2 to develop in future.

In this scenario the distinction between systems development skills, and systems interaction or end-user skill requirements, will be maintained. Even though certain end users and systems developers join together, all end users will rarely be involved.[8] The proportion of end users in these schemes will vary. Procedures for end-user representation will have to be devised. For clerical and manual employee levels, existing trade union machinery may be used for this purpose, such as the data shop steward established in Norway and Sweden (see Chapter 8), although it is likely in the USA and UK that new systems of representation will be devised in

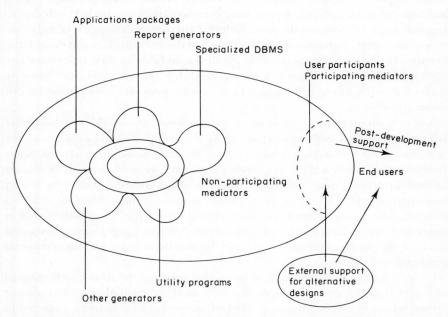

FIGURE 13.2 The future with user involvement schemes dominant

most organizations, based perhaps on expected frequency of use or seniority, rather than existing trade union machinery. Alternatively it may be that the managers of end users become the main participants in these schemes. The relationship between sophisticated users and novices in the strong end-user computing scenario is likely to be partly produced in the relationship between participants in user involvement schemes and other end users. User involvement participants will provide some degree of formal and/or informal post-development support.

If the user involvement strategy were to dominate in future, a number of supporting techniques and social arrangements are also likely to develop. In Chapter 8 we noted two different approaches to improving the end-user interface in the computing literature. One was a technical approach coming from the specialist end-user interface literature. These researchers concentrate on designing computer interfaces which are 'convivial'. That is, interfaces that are pleasurable to use and which give end users a feeling of control over the operations being performed, such as by trying to build the concept of direct manipulation or direct engagement into the interface (see section 8.2.8).

The other approach comes from the user as worker literature. These researchers emphasize organizational support which would allow end users to influence interfaces in a direction that would increase their control over their work (or at least reduce the likelihood of their work becoming deskilled; see section 8.2.4). This would require adequate support for user representatives participating in development work (not only to give these representatives computing skills, but to stimulate their awareness of the possibilities for alternative designs). It is likely that both of these approaches would be developed in this user involvement dominated scenario. In this scenario users would be supported both by their representatives participating in involvement schemes, and by outside agencies (possibly connected with trade unions), which would provide information about alternative designs.

A significant proportion of computer systems developers would have to change their style and their skills somewhat in this scenario, but the basic shape of the mediating process would not be altered from the early phase-three pattern. Some would have to adopt a more responsible autonomy view of users' work if users succeed in having real influence over the development process. Specialist developers would have to improve their communication skills in order to accommodate two-way or even user-centred communication, which was a source of concern during phase two. However, the basic programming work and much of the formal analysis would still be carried out by computer systems development specialists.

If user relations problems come to be tackled primarily by strategies that make computer systems developers more like users, and the mediating process a more faithful mirror of user departments, then we may expect a scenario as depicted in Figure 13.3 in future. In this scenario we would expect to see a proliferation of

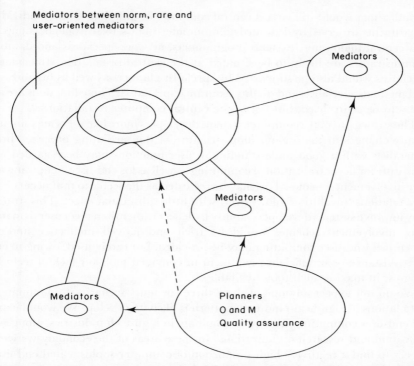

FIGURE 13.3 The future with internal adjustments to meet user demands
dominant

relatively small information systems sub-departments associated with different
user functions. We would expect the shape of those departments to resemble the IS
departments of smaller organizations depicted in Tables 12.1 and 12.2. These sub-
departments would have a majority of systems developers labelled as
analyst/programmers, and a substantial number of sub-departments would
organize them in a pool. Their education and experience background would be
much closer to that of end users in the department they are associated with.
Individual analyst/programmers would provide substantial post-development
support. The information systems specialist would become a jack of many trades.
As well as being able to carry out analysis and design functions and programming
in high-level languages, the information specialist would have to become familiar
with relevant organization databases. In addition to understanding the functions
carried out in the relevant user department, he or she would also need to be
sensitive to social and political situations in the relevant user department. In order
to perform this role of general organization change agent, specialist staff in these
sub-departments are likely to receive both technical and organization-oriented
support from more specialized groups and individuals. It is likely that large

organizations would still have a central computer installation. Even if individual departments are served by dedicated minicomputers of PCs, these would be connected to a central mainframe. Systems programmers, network specialists and database administrators are likely to be situated at the central installation. Information specialists would also be supported by specialist planners as well as organization and methods specialists and quality assurance specialists. These functions are also likely to be centralized, but not at the central computer installations.

The strategy to make computer systems developers more like users may not lead to any changes in the organization structure of the mediating process. Hiring generalists with a good understanding of user functions may be regarded as a substitute for decentralization of computing as well as for end-user computing and user involvement schemes. This may be regarded as the scenario that occurs if the user relations 'revolution' blows over, with little substantial effect. This strategy may improve systems developers' ability to deflect rather than meet user demands. User involvement schemes would be tried and judged ineffective and too expensive. End-user computing may be provided, but rarely used, owing to end-user resistance or insufficient investment in convivial tools (or lack of technical progress in making such tools available).

We do not expect any one of these three (or four) scenarios to dominate all installations. A significant industry pattern is likely to develop. We would expect the end-user computing strategy to dominate in high-tech industries, along with education and research organizations. In these areas of the economy we would expect to find a relatively high proportion of computer-sophisticated end users. The user involvement strategy would dominate where trade unions are strong, in public sector organizations (both government installations and within public utilities) and in traditionally militant industries such as the coal industry and the motor vehicle industry. It may also dominate where a high proportion of end users of computer systems interface directly with the clients or customers of the organization, such as in professional services organizations (like travel agents). In this cases the investment in reducing end-user confusion or resistance to computer systems can be justified by reduction of lost sales which may result from end-user dissatisfaction being translated into bad customer relations.

The scenario where the user relations revolution has little lasting effect on computer systems development may be expected in organizations where the investment in computer systems is traditionally low, and where it is highly concentrated on traditional operational systems. Where computer-based systems are exclusively for basic accounts, payroll and simple stock control, the fashion for user relations strategies may be half-heartedly followed for a time, or it may be ignored altogether. Where the organization's markets are stable, or where only a few large customers are served on the basis of long-term contracts, the need for improved management control and strategic decision support systems may not be keenly felt. In these circumstances end users are likely to remain low-level clerical staff and separate from system clients.

All of the scenarios outlined above are likely to embody a role for what is now called the information centre. The information centre would simply mean different things where different strategies dominate. The information centre could become primarily the location of support for end-user computing as its originators intended (see section 11.3.1), but it could also embody either the forum for user involvement schemes or the support group for participation representatives. It could also coincide with sub-department installations, or it could become synonymous with one of the groups supporting generalist computer systems developers, in the scenario where mirroring users dominates.

13.3 THE PROSPECTS: A FOURTH PHASE?

There is no strong reason to suppose that phase three will continue indefinitely. One possibility for the future is to revert back to the domination of earlier phase concerns. Further computerization may be constrained in future by hardware costs or by software productivity limitations. This will depend on ambitions for future computer systems.

High demand for supercomputers (such as produced by Cray) indicate areas of the computing field where hardware costs and capacity constraints are significant constraints.[9] The growth of organizations managing proprietary databases and agencies dealing with inter-organization transactions are likely to represent future sectors where hardware constraints are significant. One could easily imagine a future when prime computer systems core is no longer situated in each computer system user organization. Rather each user organization would contain a satellite core. Around this satellite core there may be facilities for end-user computing and groups of systems developers providing small development jobs and supporting end users. However, the main development projects would be undertaken in specialist organizations.[10] These specialist organizations would develop in a number of ways. Some would be set up by groups of user organizations. Some would be traditional service bureaus. Some would be bureau-like organizations selling access to particular databases, rather than access to computing power or sophisticated computer systems (leading to VANs or value-added networks).

Some would grow out of existing user organizations' central IS organizations in the way that many banks came to hive off sections of their DP departments dealing with certain systems carried out for bank customers during phase two (notably payroll systems). Configurations would look something like Figure 13.4.

There is considerable evidence that what is coming to be called EDI (electronic data interchange) is about to grow very quickly in the early 1990s. There is an Electronic Data Interchange Association (EDIA). User expenditures for EDI have been predicted to rise in the USA from $2·5 million in 1988 to $220 million in 1992 (Schatz, 1988, p. 56). In Europe, the coming of greater free trade and harmonization of business practices within the EEC in 1992 is expected to provide an added stimulus to EDI (Lamb, 1988).

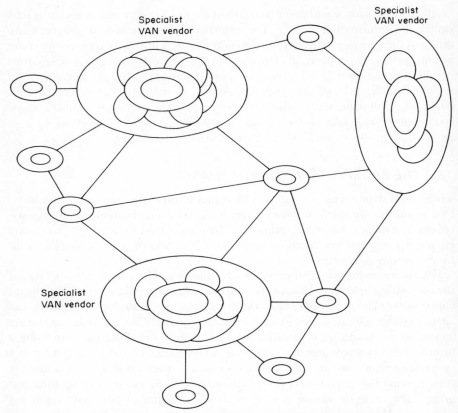

FIGURE 13.4 The future with hardware constraints dominant

If future computer systems will be primarily distinguished by their use of data of an inter-organization and super-organization kind, this sort of scenario is likely. The establishment of the EDI network will require considerable hardware resources and computer systems core expertise. However, we would expect the main hardware constraints to come from organizations providing services for which vector processing[11] is needed, such as systems that provide high-resolution graphical representations.[12]

With this future scenario we may expect the three turns of the helix, described so far for computer systems development *within user organizations*, to be repeated in the same order for the development of *inter-organizational systems*.

Inter-organizational systems represent only one direction in which future computer development efforts may be expected to proceed. This path requires a degree of cooperation among organizations that may not be forthcoming. Strategic systems designed to improve the organization's performance *against* other organizations may represent the more well-trod path in the future.[13] If demand for future computer systems is primarily in the direction of such strategic decision support systems, software production constraints may well return to dominance. Demand for these types of systems may be stimulated by the easing of user relations problems via the strategies outlined above. Usage of these types of systems is relatively discretionary. Non-use and under-use is a problem. However, rising computer sophistication among higher-level managers, improved user interfaces, better support for end users,[14] as well as improved salesmanship on the part of information systems specialists, may well result in a significant stimulation of demand for these systems.[15]

The scope for increased complexity of strategic decision support systems is enormous. Top managers must deal with rapidly changing and potentially hostile environments. They must be able to consider the consequences of a range of possible actions in response to environmental changes quickly. In order to do this, it would be of value to develop real-time systems that model the organization as it may be affected by environmental changes when the environment is critically affected by strategic moves by *specific* external agents. Strategic moves by external agents will be affected by the organization's own actions. Not only must the organization's internal structure be modelled, not only must conjectures about the threat or benefits from actions of these specific external agents be built into the system, but also the reactions of external agents to the organization's own strategic moves must be modelled. Moves, reactions, counter-moves, counter-reactions, etc. may be taken into account. Information about actual changes in supplier positions, changes in relations with the government, changes in competitors' initiatives, and information allowing such changes to be anticipated as it occurs must be processed, as well as conjectures about their counter-reactions to the organization's responses to those changes. The development of these types of systems come up against software production constraints.

Although the example is rather extreme, some of the difficulties encountered by the Strategic Defense Initiative (SDI) organization prefigure difficulties that will face developers of these decision support systems once they reach a certain size and sophistication. For example, Parnas notes the following problem characteristic of the SDI which makes the software very difficult:

> Fire-control software cannot be written without making assumptions about the characteristics of enemy weapons and targets. This information is used in determining the recognition algorithms, the sampling periods and the noise-filtering techniques. If the system is developed without the knowledge of these characteristics, or with the knowledge that the enemy can change some of them on the day of battle, there are likely to be subtle but fatal errors in the software. (1985, p. 1329)

A firm considering how to react to possible new product introductions by competitors, or to possible take-over threats, would face similar problems. Aspects of the environment that could be taken into account are vast. Many individual agents in the environment could be modelled; however, the difficulty of writing systems increases very quickly with increased size of the systems.

Although packages will undoubtedly be developed to provide such systems, the directly combative nature of these applications may well lead large organizations to insist on custom-made systems and on direct control over their production.

The two suggestions we have made about a fourth phase (one based on inter-organizational systems with attendant hardware constraints expected, and one based on strategic decision support systems with attendant software constraints expected) have two things in common. First, both are based on the assumption that the primary agent of change will be changes in computer applications. Second, both are based on computer applications that deal with the external environment of organizations.

It is likely that a fourth phase will be broadly associated with this second aspect of anticipated systems. Hardware and software constraints can only be binding if demands for inter-organizational and strategic decision systems generate many large-scale systems development projects. However, substantial numbers of large-scale projects of this nature have not materialized because of 'prior' constraints. These constraints have been due in part to technical and legal problems in establishing communications links between computer systems. One set of problems are those of system compatibility; notably the rather slow moves towards universal adoption of open systems interconnection (OSI) standards among hardware manufacturers.[16] The high cost of system compatibility must be borne by existing user organizations; high up-front costs of conversion to open systems and the UNIX operating system, and the uncertainty caused by more than one version of UNIX being backed by different UNIX vendors.

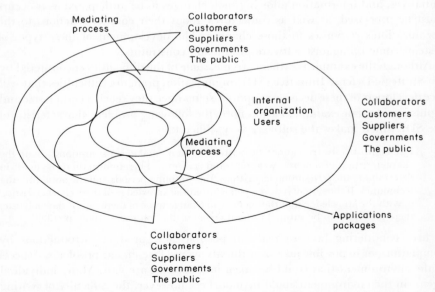

FIGURE 13.5 *The future with organization environment constraints*

Other problems have been related to the availability of communications linkages between organizations. However, significant progress has been made to alleviate this set of problems with the deregulation of communications between organizations during the 1980s.

'Demand-side' fourth-phase constraints are illustrated in Figure 13.5.

We would label this fourth phase the phase of organization environment constraints. Constraints arise from the interface between internal computing systems and specific agents in the environment of the organization. Agents include customers and clients, suppliers, competitors, cooperators, representatives and public bodies. Causes of constraints include the following problems:

(1) The problem of accurately identifying and accessing strategic information, particularly about hostile and potentially hostile agents.
(2) The problem of establishing sufficiently cooperative relations with complementary organizations.
(3) The problem of reducing supplier, and particularly consumer, resistance to operating through computer-mediated communication.
(4) The problem of agreeing and enforcing standards and protocols both for systems development and for use with cooperating organizations and customers.
(5) The problem of security, particularly as such systems become much more vulnerable to hackers and thereby to industrial espionage.

Inter-organizational systems and systems by which customers deal directly with organizations through computer-based systems have been developing rapidly in the financial sector during phase three. So far these systems have been primarily routine, high-volume applications. Customer resistance to straightforward transactions based on automatic cash points, for example, has been small (although most complaints to banks in the UK are due to 'errors' or 'crime' at cash points). However, the rapid growth of customer services sections of banks indicates resistance on the part of both customers and the banks to computer mediation of more complex transactions such as negotiation of loans (so far).

Whether the next phase of computerization leads to most attention being focused on 'demand-side' problems or 'supply-side' problems depends on the relative pace of demand or supply shifts. If the primary changes occur on the supply-side, i.e. if improvements in hardware cost/performance ratios and improvements in software production techniques stimulate attempts to introduce these organization–environment applications, before the fundamental problems with these applications outlined above are adequately resolved, we would expect this fourth phase of organization environment constraints to emerge. Organization environment issues would come to dominate the literature of the computing field, stimulating the establishment of a strong community of researchers and innovators dedicated to the removal of those constraints. If, on the other hand, the main pace of change occurs on the demand side, whereby strong demand for these sorts of systems emerges before the technical problems are sorted out, then new projects would be seen to fail for supply-side reasons leading to a reinforcing of existing research and innovation communities dedicated to the removal of hardware and software constraints. By and large we would predict the former case to be more likely, primarily because of the existence of strong communities dedicated to improving hardware cost/performance and software productivity.

13.4 MANAGEMENT STRATEGIES IN THE FUTURE

13.4.1 IS Management Strategies Towards IS Staff

We associated phase one with responsible autonomy strategies towards computer systems developers for three main reasons. First, high hardware costs tended to 'mask' labour costs. Productivity improvements arising from better allocation of labour, or better choice of staff, or better control over programming procedures, were small compared with the gains to be had from more careful evaluation of hardware purchases and better hardware maintenance procedures. Second, the novelty of the field meant that both labour supply and management techniques were undeveloped. Labour shortages, combined with lack of available management techniques, led computer managers to run installations in a loose manner. Third, hardware capacity constraints and rapid technological change meant that the nature of systems development tasks had to be open-ended. They had to be loosely defined and staff creativity had to be encouraged.

During phase two there was an elaboration of both types of strategies. On balance we believe there was a drift towards direct control strategies. This occurred because of the notable rise in proportion of computer installation costs attributable to staff, due to improved cost/performance of hardware and rising demands for more complex systems. Very ambitious new systems were attempted during phase two, encouraged by earlier successes with simpler replacements of existing manual systems. Especially systems labelled as management information systems were attempted without adequate appreciation of the systems development difficulties involved. Projects ran seriously over budget, they were delivered late, and even then they often did not deliver what was promised. Also the labour market changed somewhat. Particularly in the USA, a great extension of training in COBOL programming eased the shortage of *inexperienced* labour supply.[17] This encouraged managers to design 'mere coding' jobs for these recruits. However, rapid expansion of the field meant that the shortage of *experienced* systems developers remained. This made it difficult for organizations to retain mere coders in this sort of work once these people had accumulated the critical 18 months of experience. This, in turn, discouraged strict imposition of direct control techniques.

Expansion of the computer systems core during phases two and three has led to the automation of many of the mere coding tasks in installations. It has also led to the development of new specialties within IS departments. These specialties have *not* occurred as part of a deskilling exercise, from a hiving off of certain tasks from general all-round skilled jobs. Rather they have developed from the need for genuinely new skills, particularly in the networking area.

Management strategies in these new areas resemble phase-one strategies. These people work most closely with expensive computer systems core and they must often try to overcome hardware constraints. Their work is creative and not well understood by management. Rapid growth of these areas has led to extremely severe labour shortages. As a result during phase three, for a growing proportion of IS specialists, there has been a reversion to the kind of loose responsible autonomy strategies used for all systems developers during phase one.

Changes have also occurred in the character of systems demanded. More small jobs based on user requests are required. Rising user power and especially increasing discretion over system use has led to the need for development to proceed in a way that is more sensitive to subtle and changing user requirements. This has encouraged a recombination of analysis and programming tasks among the bulk of systems developers. It has thereby encouraged a reassertion of responsible autonomy strategies.

All of the scenarios outlined in section 13.2 and 13.3 above suggest that the trend towards responsible autonomy strategies will continue during phase three for the bulk of IS specialists. However, there are important differences. The end-user computing path would mean a rise in technical support staff and therefore a likely rise in the proportion of staff being treated with a loose (possibly management by neglect) type of responsible autonomy strategy. The growth of staff concentrating on user support is likely to lead to a more mixed pattern of management strategies. If they do in fact act purely as consultants (helping users to help themselves) and as overseers of corporate purchases of computer systems core and external services, then it is likely that the trend towards greater integration of these roles into general management will occur, with attendant responsible autonomy strategies. IS specialists would be interacting with sophisticated users and higher-level staff in this case. However, if user support tends to become more of a palliative involving pre- and post-development training of unsophisticated users (sophisticated users carrying out most of the development work with little support required), then the jobs may become downgraded, as are many of the 'caring' roles within organizations.

In the user involvement dominated scenario, we suspect that IS specialists will take on roles similar to the user support roles discussed above. The type and level of user representatives participating in these schemes may be expected to affect the management strategies developed to deal with IS specialists. The higher the level of users, the more likely responsible autonomy strategies will be strengthened. Career links will be made more easily between these tasks and general management. There would be some important differences between end-user support groups and participants in user involvement schemes from the IS specialist side. There would be more emphasis on working with groups of user representatives and perhaps a significant element of management consultancy and negotiation roles. The information systems department may come to liaise more closely with personnel and industrial relations functions. In this scenario, as with the end-user computing scenario, there is likely to be a growing technical support group where loose responsible autonomy strategies dominate.

With the mirroring users path, the prospects for technical support groups would be the same as in the other two scenarios. Similarly groups of analyst/programmers mirroring user functions are likely to have considered latitude to develop systems with little direct control over them. However, the small groups of analyst/programmers who come to work most closely with users may become so integrated with user department staff that the same management strategies come to be applied to both groups, particularly if these groups are decentralized. This is likely to lead to a shift towards direct control for computer systems developers.

If the fourth phase that we have outlined above comes, then we would roughly expect loose responsible autonomy strategies to dominate if hardware costs become the dominant constraint. If software costs come to dominate we would expect the tendencies towards direct control to return to prominence. Finally, if the demand-side issues come to dominate in the fourth phase, if organization environment constraints come to dominate the field, our prediction is that IS specialists would become more closely associated either with central, strategic planning functions or with purchasing and sales or marketing staff. If it is to be integration with central planning functions, we would expect formal responsible autonomy strategies to dominate in future. If it is to be integration with sales staff, the situation may be quite different. Sales staff generally enjoy considerable autonomy, but their employment position is often tied closely to results attributable to individuals. This can be precarious.

13.4.2 Top Management and IS Management

As computer systems development has come to support higher-level management functions, so the position in the organization hierarchy of the manager in charge of computer systems development has risen. From a section leader or sub-department head within the accounting or finance department in phase one, to the DP manager of a separate department reporting at board level in phase two, the head of computer systems development has risen, in many large organizations, to the level of MIS or IS executive in charge of a division during phase three. A few IS executives we interviewed in the early 1980s were board-level directors.

The fourth phase that we have painted would lead to a continuation of this trend, with more IS executives sitting on the board of directors and with more chief executive officers coming from IS backgrounds. Already there is considerable evidence that IS executives are becoming involved in the long-term planning process in large organizations, i.e. IS is taking on greater 'strategic' importance in these organizations (see McFarlan and McKenney, 1982; Piercy, 1986; Galliers and Somogyi, 1987; Griffiths, 1987; Earl, 1988).

Hirschheim *et al.* (1988) propose an evolutionary model to describe how IS is developing. In this model the focus of the IS executive shifts from internal IS concerns (trying to solve phase-three user relations constraints problems by delivering systems that will satisfy user demands); to relations with the rest of the organization, reorienting them towards an awareness of strategic opportunities afforded by IS; and then back to focus on the internal IS function to make it fit better with its new strategic role, with the new phase four concerns.

13.5 OTHER PREDICTIONS ABOUT THE FUTURE FOR COMPUTER SYSTEMS DEVELOPMENT

Two sorts of predictions are well known in the literature. The first and most common prediction is that identifiable specialist computer systems developers will disappear. For the most part their jobs will be automated out of existence by expanding computer systems core. What is left will be carried out by users. The only systems development work that takes place will be in specialist software firms, which will mainly produce packages. The second sort of prediction is that direct control strategies will lead to the work becoming deskilled. In the end IS specialists will suffer the same fate as many other craftsmen. They will become no different from other mass-production-type workers.

We have, I think, effectively dealt with the latter prediction in Chapters 11 and 12. It is rarely reiterated, other than by Kraft. However, the automation prediction is commonly restated.

13.5.1 The Automation Strategy and CASE Tools

A recent article in the *Wall Street Journal* headlined 'Software Writing Becoming Automated' began with the following statement:

> Computer programmers of the world, beware! You too could be replaced by a computer someday. (Wessel, 1986)

According to that article computer-aided software engineering, or CASE, is the instrument that will lead to the automation of software writing. Although most of the 'flock' of small software companies were automating only a part of the development process, one 'plans to introduce, within six months, a soup-to-nuts product that will automate everything from the early design work to the generation of computer code' (Wessel, 1986, p. 6).[18]

CASE is perhaps *the* major buzz-word in the computing literature of the late 1980s. Like all buzz-words, it is interpreted in many different ways. At its broadest

CASE is being interpreted as the automation of anything done by people with software (Stamps, 1987, p. 57). Three more specific meanings may be usefully distinguished. These should not be thought of as mutually exclusive categories of CASE, rather they are three different aspects of CASE which are emphasized by different writers.

Automation of analysis, design and coding

One way of looking at CASE is to interpret it as the automatic linking of analysis, design and coding.[19] With this interpretation, CASE is a clear extension of the automation strategy, which runs from 'low-level' language compilers developed in phase one, through third-generation language compilers, which spread early in phase two, and the generators and fourth-generation languages being developed toward the end of phase two and during phase three.[20] Historically it has been known by the label of automatic programming.[21] The addition to automatic programming that CASE provides may be thought of as steps in two directions. The first step is to attach code generation to *graphical* requirements definition and design languages. Rather than drawing boxes or bubbles on paper, they are drawn on the computer screen. The CASE tool then automatically generates code as well as checking for logical consistency. It will also automatically produce documentation. The second step is to extend this procedure to more than one stand-alone system development project by attaching these CASE tools to a database, or rather a data dictionary, a central repository that stores the various functional elements of a design in a way which allows them to be called upon for new projects. New designs can be checked for consistency with elements already held on the database. As with a corporate database management system, its value increases as the proportion of corporate data items residing in the database rises. However, the costs of putting data from previously developed systems into the database management system is very high (note section 12.1.2).

This approach to automation has a long history in the computing field. Early important proponents were the CODASYL systems committee (see section 4.2.4), which began its work in the 1950s and which stated as its objectives:

> To strive to build up an expertise in, and to develop, advanced languages and techniques for data processing, with the aim of automating as much as possible of the process currently thought of as systems analysis, design and implementation. (cited in Teichroew and Sayani, 1971, p. 28)

This line of thinking has been associated with the ISDOS project since the late 1960s. ISDOS (Information Systems Design and Optimization System) is a software package being developed at the University of Michigan under Daniel Teichroew. It begins with user requirements recorded in machine-readable form, the PSL (Problem Statement Language). PSL was derived at first from requirements definition languages developed during the early 1960s (see section 10.2).[22]

Statements written in PSL by someone ISDOS calls a problem definer are then analysed by a computer program called a problem statement analyser (PSA). The PSA checks the statements for consistency and produces a series of reports, including a data dictionary and a function dictionary (meaning structured listings of data and functions). These can be examined by a data administrator, which ensures standardization on names and characteristics as well as definition by functions (i.e. by types of computation). A system definer identifies system-wide requirements to eliminate duplication of effort by different problem definers. In this way PSA performs both static network analysis (ensuring completeness of derived relationships) and dynamic analysis (identifying time-dependent relationships and analysing volume specifications). The PSA then produces a 'complete' and 'error-free' statement of the requirements in PSL. It also produces a coded statement of the problem for use in the physical systems design and construction phases of development. The aim of the ISDOS project was then to use the computer to evaluate various design strategies and then to produce specifications for program modules, hardware requirements, data storage structures and scheduling procedures using a tool they called SODA (Systems Optimization and Design Algorithm). Output from SODA is then to be directed to two further modules. First, the data re-organizer receives the specifications for desired storage structure and hardware requirements from SODA, as well as the data defined by PSA, and combines it with the currently existing data and storage structure. It, in turn, produces further information for the data administrator required for file construction. Second, the program module specifications are received by a code generator. The generated code, the timing specifications from SODA and the file specifications from the data re-organizer are all finally received by the final module of ISDOS, the systems director, which produces the target information processing system.

The ISDOS team began marketing the PSL/PSA modules of their grand design as a separate package. In a report on PSL/PSA written in 1979, they cited ten major corporations (including IBM, AT & T and British Rail) using the package (Teichroew *et al.*, 1979, pp. 344–345).

Reusability

A second way of looking at CASE is to interpret it as development with reusable software. With this interpretation CASE is an extension of the software or subroutine libraries which have been in existence since the beginning of phase one (McClure, 1987; Joyce, 1988).[23] More experienced and more productive programmers can be distinguished by their extensive use of reusable software components and standard program forms (McClure, 1987, p. 2). This view links CASE to CAD (computer-aided design) systems.[24] With these systems the designer builds new products based on building parts called up from the CAD system database and combined or altered using CAD.

In order for CASE to follow this path, it is necessary to establish an appropriate way of representing software components that will allow them to be used again without undesirable side effects. In order for this to be achieved they must be written in a standard format. They should be well structured and documented. In addition individual components need to be constructed such that they can be easily and safely modified. Tools must not only allow them to be modified, but they must automatically analyse the impact of change. This means it is necessary to store information about where components have been previously used and how they were used. Then a scheme for classifying and selecting components must be established. Currently such schemes tend mainly to be application-specific. Also a large number are function-specific. They relate to particular systems development functions such as error processing or database access. The additional step for transferring CASE tools, thought of in this way, into the automation of computer systems development, is to develop systems of software component representation and classification out from application-specific groups of categories. Finally, tools to support the assembly and modification of reusable software components are needed (such as syntax-directed program editors, verification systems, timers and portability checkers).

Application of artificial intelligence

There is a third way of looking at CASE tools. That is as the application of artificial intelligence to the systems development process. Artificial intelligence is an even more diffuse term than CASE. Parnas (1985, p. 1332) neatly separates two meanings for the term 'artificial intelligence' (AI).

The first is the use of computers to solve problems that previously could be solved only by human intelligence. This defines AI as a set of problems. It has a sliding meaning. The meaning changes as new computer systems are developed.[25]

The second meaning of the term is the use of a specific set of techniques known as heuristic or rule-based programming. Human experts are studied to determine what heuristics or rules of thumb they use in solving problems. These rules are incorporated into a program so that the program will solve problems the way people seem to solve them. This defines AI as a set of techniques. This sort of AI is often called expert systems or knowledge-based tools. It is this meaning of AI that is being incorporated into systems development according to the third way of looking at CASE.

This approach to CASE is deliberately less ambitious than the total automation approach to CASE described above. Early projects taking this approach have been influenced by Terry Winograd (1973), who suggested that programmers trying to develop AI systems should apply AI systems to their own programming efforts. Two interrelated groups have been working on this approach since the 1970s, one at the Kestrel Institute in Palo Alto, California (the Chi Project), and the other at MIT (Programmer Apprentice Project). Both were influenced by the earlier Psi Project at Stanford (see Frenkel, 1985). These systems are often called programming environments or tools or shells.

Some of these systems have a particular notable characteristic. Rather than imposing a complete logic structure on human systems developers, they provide facilities that allow developers to act creatively and even to increase their own understanding of the system. This positive view of the effect of computers on work is reminiscent of the 'human–computer symbiosis' in which the computer is able to liberate people's creative energy, as described by Licklider (1960, 1965) in the early 1960s and by Martin (1973) in the early 1970s. In this view computers need not fulfil the fears described in Chapter 8 (especially sections 8.2.3 and 8.2.4), at least when the users are IS specialists.[26]

The key to this positive effect is what may be called a tool perspective to computerization. Tools may be distinguished by their connection with particular human practices. Tools may be distinguished from machines in that tools are strictly instruments of *manual* operation; they are usually thought of as held in and operated directly by the hand. Certainly computer systems are not tools in this strict sense. They are powered by a non-human source and they perform many actions without human intervention.[27] Many think of the computer as the ultimate machine, the machine that will eliminate human intervention from most traditional practices. However, we may think of the way computer systems are used in relative terms. Some computer systems can be more tool-like.

The tool metaphor has recently been employed by vendors of computer-aided programmer productivity aids (e.g. programmer tool box, or the general expression CASE 'tools'). Expert systems can contribute to human creativity in a number of ways. First, as with the 'outward' or hardware-towards-user approach that describes the actual progress of automation of the mediating process (as opposed to the top-down or user-requirements-to-hardware approach taken by the ISDOS project team), it is what are regarded as the more tedious, memory-taxing tasks to which CASE tools have been applied first.[28] Debugging is a particularly appropriate development task for the application of CASE tools because people find it boring (see Gupta and Seviora, 1984, p. 339).

Second, when these systems use their knowledge base to make inferences, the user, in this case the systems developer, can display the logical chain used by the expert system to come to a particular 'conclusion'. In this way systems developers *can* use the expert system as a tool to enhance their productivity and their skill. The key to the effect of these systems on developer skills is whether humans use them at their own discretion, for advice and support, or if the human developers simply monitor the system.

Two characteristics of expert systems, or of any computer systems, seem to be critical for their capacity to be worked with in a tool-like manner. First, they must automate only part of the systems development process. The smaller the proportion of the process they automate, the greater their capacity to be used like tools. Second, and most important, their use must be discretionary. Although many decry as serious limitations of CASE that they are mostly aimed at only a portion of the computer system life cycle, there are certain advantages to this, not only for computer systems developers as employees. One aspect of work which is lost in mechanization or automation is the time to reflect on a labour process as it proceeds. This may appear to be unproductive time, measured in terms of standard units of output (such as lines of code), but we have already noted several times the importance of system or program quality in the era of hardware constraints and in that of user relations constraints. Generally high-quality programs tend to be short programs. The quality of a program in the hardware constraints phase would have been measured by how little machine time and capacity were required to run the program. The quality of a program in the user relations constraints phase depends on how much it contributes to a system that provides users with what they really need and how user-friendly the interfaces are. These qualities may be achieved by intermediate activities which are, themselves, difficult to measure in terms of physical artifacts like lines of code. Thinking time, observation time, time to discuss on an informal basis, can lead to leaps in quality.[29]

The master/apprentice metaphor has also guided the developers of certain expert systems. The apprentice follows the master's practice, makes his or her own attempts, and receives correction and advice along the way. The apprentice (the expert system) may in this way be thought of as a junior partner for the human systems developer. It serves the master. However, most of those developing these expert systems seem to view the tool approach as merely a step along the path to total automation. As one of the researchers on the MIT Programmer's Apprentice Project stated: 'Eventually the apprentice should become a master' (C. Rich, cited in Frenkel, 1985, p. 579).

We note that the three ways of looking at CASE described above are not mutually exclusive. Many CASE tools combine the three approaches, but with varying degrees of emphasis.

Limitations of CASE

CASE tools are described in the literature in terms of providing a solution to the software productivity problem. Some have reported enormous productivity improvements using CASE.[30] As with structured methods, it may turn out that the really strong advantages with CASE will come in falling maintenance costs due to reduced coding errors.[31] Nevertheless there are certain problems that stand in the way of the automation dream being realized through CASE.

First, although maintenance costs due to programmer errors are substantial, as noted by DeMarco, most maintenance costs arise from errors or changes in requirements specifications (see Figure 11.2). The user relations problem still prevails. However, CASE tools can contribute to easing these problems by speeding up systems development and by supporting prototyping procedures.[32] In so doing CASE will contribute to the shift in systems development activities towards analysis and away from more straightforward, even boring, coding tasks.

Second, as noted above, in order for substantial productivity gains to be realized from CASE, it is necessary to use it extensively. This requires substantial changes to the way systems development is carried out. It requires a degree of standardization which, as we have noted in earlier chapters, simply does not exist in most installations:

> Despite its growing fascination with computer aided software engineering, corporate America, for the most part, is culturally unprepared to receive CASE technology. (declared Capers Jones, reported in Carlyle, 1987, p 23)

Connected with the lack of standardization, there is also no generally accepted way of measuring programmer (or analysts's) productivity for reasons well documented by Jones (1986).[33] This would not be so great a problem if CASE could be introduced with little outlay. If CASE simply involved reorganizing existing staff or sending a few people on a course, it would be diffusing much more rapidly. However, CASE involves large up-front investments for the tools themselves and, more importantly, for the changed procedures required.

Third, a particular problem with expert systems is that one can add more and more rules to the system, especially when trying to cover special cases. This leads to systems that are expensive in terms of required computer capacity. It also leads to greater complexity of the system and therefore greater unpredictability (note Parnas' comments about SDI, 1985).

Overall we believe that CASE tools will continue to spread. They represent another layer of core which does take over certain functions of the mediating process. However, they will not remove the need for systems developers, or even for programmers. They automate certain programming tasks, but they will also require other sorts of programmers to be hired. As operating systems require systems programmers and database management systems require database administrators, so CASE tools will require systems programmers. Perhaps they will also require 'knowledge engineers' to work 'on site' in order to incorporate further local human rule-like behaviour at user organizations into purchased CASE tools.[34] This pattern is all the more likely if CASE tools continue to be marketed by a wide range of companies. The different approaches to CASE described above lead us to expect that most tools marketed under the label of CASE will be incompatible with each other. CASE will lead to further standardization problems, rather than the solution to earlier lack of standardization.

13.5.2 The Automation Strategy and Independent Software Specialists: A 'Market' Solution

A rather more subtle recent example of the automation out of existence prediction is Dearden (1987). Dearden predicts:

> IS departments as they are currently constituted will be dismantled. Independent software specialists will dominate the development of systems, programming, and

other software. Users will completely control individual information systems ... If users can get both hardware and software support from another source, then there is no reason why they should not exercise complete control over their information systems. I believe within the next five years companies specializing in software will largely replace in house resources in U.S. companies because the cost will be far lower and the quality far higher than that which can be developed internally. (p. 87)

Independent specialists will win out because of the advantages of spreading their costs over many purchasers when they sell packages; because they can specialize by type of application and industry 'whereas an IS department must be a jack-of-all-trades'; and because they employ better people because their 'selection, evaluation and training will be better' (p. 88). Dearden allows that companies with existing IS installations will not dismantle them. Rather he predicts they will disgorge these departments. They will establish independent IS profit centres or independent subsidiaries which will compete both inside and outside the company. He then states, 'As far as users are concerned, though, dealing with subsidiaries should be no different than dealing with independent suppliers' (p. 87). He also envisions making IS departments into profit centres as 'the first step in an inevitable journey into oblivion' (p. 91).

We disagree with this prediction. What Dearden misunderstands is the importance of establishing close and regular relations with users in order to overcome the user relations constraint. He recognizes that systems development requires an intimate knowledge of management needs and of available information, but he assumes that typical IS departments will not have the expertise required for this task. Why? According to Dearden each system is different. Software houses can specialize in *different* types of systems and thereby bring much more concentrated knowledge and experience of similar systems to the design of packages (and custom systems) for any particular application. IS department staff cannot compete because their client base is too small and too diversified.

While there is some truth in this claim, and we would expect the independent software services sector to continue to grow, there are a number of problems with Dearden's version of the future. They are as follows:

(1) Dearden overestimates the extent to which users wish to become involved, either in end-user computing or in the management of IS specialists.
(2) Dearden underestimates the difficulties of external agents acquiring the intimate knowledge of management needs, which may not only be specific to a certain type of application or industry, but which are also *unique* to the particular client and end-user group for which the system is being developed.
(3) Dearden underestimates the capacity of existing IS departments to adapt to the user relations challenge. In particular the ability to hire staff which not only have the background to understand user needs, but which can also use external sources of supply as backup. Most centralized IS departments have

always hired specialists on a contract basis for special jobs (such as hardware conversion). The issue of centralized IS departments versus decentralized IS functions has generated a misplaced debate, in our opinion. The configurations we have predicted (Figures 13.1–13.5) generally envision a role for both a centralized IS installation and for decentralized IS functions. It is the balance between them which is in doubt, not their joint existence.

(4) Dearden misinterprets the trend towards making IS departments into profit centres. As noted in section 10.3, chargeout systems and the establishment of DP departments as separate profit centres, and even as separate service bureaus, has a long history in the computing field. According to the CEL 1972 survey 10% of user organizations ran their DP departments as profit centres and a further 5% were set up as separate service companies. In addition 45% provided DP services to external organizations. Some of the problems of setting up formal financial contracts between in-house IS departments and users were discussed in section 10.3).

13.6 SUMMARY NOTE

Predictions about the future for systems developers have tended to concentrate on supply-side changes rather than demand-side changes. They have focused on changes in computer systems core, rather than changes in applications, on growth of the 'inner boundary' of the mediating process (with computer systems core), rather than changes in the 'outer boundary' (with the users and the types of applications). This reflects the legacy of expertise generated by work on earlier constraints.

ENDNOTES

1. There is, to my knowledge, only one independent trade union exclusively representing computer specialists in the world. This is called PROSA (Programmers, Operators and Systems Analysts). It is a Danish trade union with about 6800 members (1988 estimate representing about 24% of computer specialists in Denmark). In 1987 the president of the union, Steffan Stripp, was sent an anonymous gift, a dinosaur. This was not thought to symbolize the sender's belief in the imminent demise of trade unionism in this field. Rather it was thought to represent the imminent demise of the union's constituency.
2. Such as payroll and the production of basic financial accounts.
3. Such as production control and general management information systems.
4. However, in part these problems simply became more obvious because there were more projects being undertaken. Budget overruns and late delivery also occurred during phase one.
5. Associated with government policy and with the spread of PCs into the home market and into education institutions.
6. In small organizations, or rather in organizations that do not choose to computerize more recent types of applications, core is likely to become simpler to deal with. A single integrated package may suffice. This could be maintained easily and cheaply on

contract with the supplier or with a specialist maintenance agency. The proportion of technical support staff is highly correlated with installation size (see Table 12.2). Although there is a tendency for older core functions to be integrated and simplified, there is a counteracting tendency to add core functions, increasing the variety and complexity of computer systems core.

7. All of these arrangements exist in the Economics Department at Bristol University. The formal combination of teacher/researcher with computer support responsibilities is a recent development.

8. Even if all prospective end users at the time of the user involvement scheme participated, end users joining the organization after the system is developed cannot participate.

9. Such as in the growing computer service bureaus sector, composed of firms that provide a range of very complex systems, and in scientific and military installations.

10. We believe that this is a possible scenario, but unlikely in the extreme form presented here; see section 13.5.2.

11. Computers which are able to deal with vectors of data entities all at once, rather than having to manipulate collections of data taking one element at a time. This is the facility which primarily distinguishes the new supercomputers such as the Cray.

12. The demand for supercomputers, once limited to scientific and military installations, is now growing rapidly among business users (see Gullo and Schatz, 1988).

13. Note that we are using the term 'strategic' in a more specific way than it is sometimes used in the computing field. Sometimes the term 'strategic information systems' refers to all computer-based administrative systems that are not purely aimed at reducing the costs of existing manual systems. Sometimes 'strategic' refers to having anything to do with a company's competitive environment. Sometimes 'strategic' refers to systems that are aimed at supporting higher-level management, and particularly with top management's concern with long-range planning (which is how we have usually used the term). In this section we refer to strategic systems in the way that economists sometimes use the term. It refers to systems intended to deal with other agents when it is assumed that those agents will actively respond to one's own initiatives. In relation to markets, it refers to systems that attempt to simulate specific reactions of competitors to one's own reactions.

14. Through schemes for their involvement in development and through the type of support available from information centres.

15. Many believe that this has in fact occurred and that the software backlog has continued to be the major problem in the computer field during the 1980s. Rapid growth of the information centre is taken as evidence of these demands. However, the demands referred to in this context are generally for ad hoc inquiries and minor enhancement requests from users. A backlog composed of these sorts of demands can be removed, at least in part, by expanding end-user computing facilities. The software constraints we envision in the future may be attributed to changes in the nature of systems demanded rather than a simple rise in the volume of demand. We envision new sorts of systems which will require very sophisticated software. They will not be developed by end-user computing.

16. Open systems are computer core that will allow the same program to run on any hardware. Unfortunately the term sometimes is used by hardware manufacturers in a limited way, to mean systems only open to certain types of hardware; for example, IBM's open systems architecture, called Systems Application Architecture (SAA), excludes UNIX, which is 'open' to most other hardware. An important advantage of open systems to user organizations is that it allows them to swap their hardware for cheaper or faster equipment without having to rewrite all their software. This is a

disadvantage for the largest hardware manufacturers (and most disadvantageous for IBM), who have used incompatibility with other manufacturers to protect their customer base, to force user organizations to stay with their equipment even if cheaper or better alternatives are available.

17. Much through private sector institutions dedicated to this purpose (although some were of dubious quality).

18. The company named was KnowledgeWare Inc.

19. '... the future success of CASE hinges upon this seamless interface between design and code generation' (Stamps, 1987, p. 58). Graphical tools to aid in design may not significantly speed up applications development unless they are linked with fourth-generation systems.

20. See sections 5.4.2 and 9.1.

21. Parnas notes that automatic programming in the 1940s was what became coding in assembler. In later years automatic programming referred to what came to be third-generation languages. 'In short, automatic programming always has been a euphemism for programming with higher-level languages than was then available to the programmer. Research in automatic programming is simply research in the implementation of higher-level programming languages' (1985, p. 1333).

22. Couger considered these earlier techniques (Information Algebra, TAG, SYSTEMATICS, ADS) and the first version of PSL to be third-generation systems analysis techniques. However, he calls ISDOS (the only) fourth-generation technique in the 1974 edition of the influential text *System Analysis Techniques*. In the 1982 version of the text ISDOS has been promoted to be (the only) fifth-generation technique.

23. McClure links CASE to subroutine libraries. '... subroutines were the first labor-saving technique invented by programmers. A subroutine for the *sin x* was written in 1944 for the Mark I calculator' (McClure, 1987, p. 2).

24. 'CASE which stands for Computer Aided Software Engineering is really the application of CAD/CAM technology to software development' (Wylie, 1988, p. 2).

25. As Parnas slightly overstates it, 'In the Middle Ages, it was thought that arithmetic required intelligence. Now it is recognized as a mechanical act. Something can fit the definition of AI-1 today, but, once we see how the program works and understand the problem, we do not think of it as AI any more' (1985, p. 1332; AI-1 refers to the first meaning of AI stated above).

26. A group of people who enjoy a particularly favoured labour market position.

27. A key characteristic that distinguishes a machine from a tool is that the machine imparts a fixed motion path to the implement and/or the work that is carried out with the machine (Braverman, 1974), p. 188).

28. This movement has been depicted in various figures showing the changing position of computer systems development in organizations (for example, Figure 4.2 or Figure 5.4).

29. See section 11.3.2 on the second category of problems with prototyping.

30. 'We found we can achieve a 600% productivity increase' reported DuPont's manager of information engineering, using a CASE tool called Application Factory (reported in Stamps, 1987, p. 56). Hartford Insurance reported improved overall productivity by almost 30% using an internally developed product (reported in Carlyle, 1987, p. 23). Ratheon reported achieving a 50% increase in productivity through the use of reusable code (Joyce, 1988, p. 102).

31. Even if the number of errors per line of code remain the same (although CASE tools allow better checking facilities, such as checking for data consistency), the number of functions per line of code rises using automated tools. Therefore the number of errors per function falls.

32. As Teichroew and Sayani stated back in 1971:

> Since new requirements or modifications to existing requirements could be implemented at computer speeds, [using an automated package like ISDOS] management would be able to get the information it asked for in a much shorter period of time. It would therefore be much less important to get the requirements right the first time since a change could be incorporated more easily than at present. The user would be closer to the requirements specification since the language is closer to one he is familiar with.

However, the last sentence in this passage is where CASE tools, especially those that promise total automation, often disappoint, as do other requirements definition languages. By concentrating on representation of user requirements in a machine-readable form, rather than elicitation of user needs, their assumption that the requirements definition language is sufficiently close to a language that users are familiar with has usually proven false (see sections 8.2.6 and 10.2).

33. The chief problem is the distinction between efficiency and effectiveness. Easily observable measures of programmer productivity or efficiency, such as lines of 'correct' code produced per unit of time, do not measure how 'good' the code is. 'Good' programs are usually shorter programs, ones which use less code and thereby appear to be the product of lower efficiency (Bergland 1981, p. 15; Jones, 1986).

34. The demand for knowledge engineers has been predicted to grow exponentially from the late 1980s (Johnson, 1984).

Chapter 14

CONCLUSIONS AND GENERALIZATIONS

In the first two sections of this chapter we return to a number of themes introduced in Part One. First we discuss explicit connections between some of the models introduced in Chapter 3. We then return to an evaluation of the other approaches to the history of computer systems development which were introduced in Chapter 2 and those referred to again in Chapter 13. In particular, we criticize the tendency of those adopting these approaches to assume that there is one best way for computer systems development to be managed.

In this book we have focused on computer systems development as a set of occupations. Computer systems development also involves the creation of new technology. What can be learned about the generation and direction of technical change in general from our consideration of the history of computer systems development? Is it advisable to generalize from the phases of computer systems development to a general model of technical progress? We will attempt to answer these questions in the next three sections of this chapter. In section 14.3 we discuss a particular characteristic of new technology generation in computer systems development, what we call the 'autogeneration' of new technology. In sections 14.4 and 14.5 we discuss, first, the relation between the literature in the computing field and the direction of technical change and, second, the advisability of generalizing from the factors contributing to the direction of technical change in computer systems development to the direction of technical change in other fields. Finally, we return briefly to comments made in Chapter 1 about the relation between technological change and social change.

14.1 MODELS OF COMPUTER SYSTEMS DEVELOPMENT

In Chapter 3 we presented models that have guided the historical and predictive material presented in Chapters 4–13. How do these models interrelate? Table 14.1 presents a summary of our model of the phases in terms of the emphasis of management strategies during each phase.

We may represent the main issues of each phase on a simple diagram of the position of computer systems development (Figure 14.1). In this simplified form of representation the 'outward' displacement of constraints appears very clearly. While we believe this to represent the general drift of change, we wish to emphasize that during *all* phases, *each* of these issues has concerned certain portions of the computer community. It is the relative degree of emphasis which has changed.

The phases of computerization growth and management strategies

.ses	Managerial strategies
Phase 1 Hardware Constraints	Loose responsible autonomy
Phase 2 Software Constraints	Elaboration of both responsible autonomy and direct control
	More emphasis on techniques for direct control
	Emergence of systems programmers as a separate group in user organization installations
Phase 3 User Relations Constraints	Reimposition of responsible autonomy, but on a more formal basis for generalist systems developers
	Greater integration with users and management strategies applied to them
	Separation of technical support (loose responsible autonomy)
Phase 4? Organization Environment Constraints	Integration with sales and marketing, and strategic planning staff and management strategies applied to them (responsible autonomy if planning, direct control if sales and marketing)
	Further separation of technical support from systems developers and dispersion of developers

During the earlier phases, 'outer issues' (issues relating to users both within organizations and outside them) were largely ignored, or occupied very few people. Changes in the key set of issues associated with each phase has been driven by the 'outward' expansion of both the inner boundary of the mediating process, the boundary with the computer systems core, and the outer boundary of the mediating process, the boundary with the users and with the organization's environment. However, as the computing field has passed through each phase, a significant and identifiable sub-community has been established, dedicated to solving the characteristic constraint of that phase. In later phases this sub-community does not disappear. Techniques aimed at solving 'earlier' chief problems continue to be generated. The problems of one phase are not 'solved' with the progression to the next phase. They are alleviated and other problems have become exacerbated. 'Earlier' chief problems no longer occupy the centre stage of attention in the field. Therefore there is still a demand for these innovations. In this way the direction of technological progress in the field reflects the chief issues of the past as well as current fashionable issues. We will return to a more detailed consideration of the direction of technological change in sections 14.4 and 14.5.

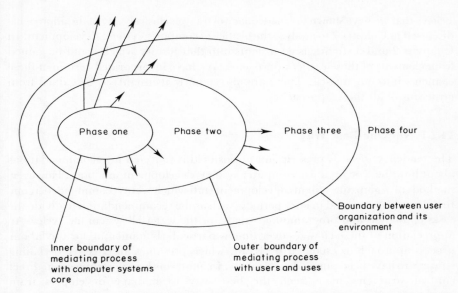

Phase one   Phase two   Phase three   Phase four

Boundary between user
organization and its
environment

Inner boundary of
mediating process
with computer systems
core

Outer boundary of
mediating process
with users and uses

FIGURE 14.1 The phases and displacement of the locus of computer systems
development

14.2 THE PHASES OF COMPUTERIZATION AND OTHER APPROACHES TO THE HISTORY OF COMPUTER SYSTEMS DEVELOPMENT

As formulated in Chapter 3, the phases of computerization are driven by several forces, several agents of change. We have shown that at different times certain agents of change have been more 'important' than the others. Importance may be thought of in two ways.

First, agents may push the field with different degrees of strength at different times. For example, competition against existing internal computer departments to supply systems to users within their host organizations was not strong during phase one. However, this competition has become stronger during phase three with the growth of software package suppliers.

Second, the effect of an agent on the field may become more or less potent because of general changes in the field over time. For example, rapid improvements in computer hardware cost/performance ratios have continued since phase one. However, the influence of hardware constraints, and of the relaxation of those constraints, on management strategies towards computer systems developers has lessened considerably since phase one. Other constraints have become more important.

By tracing the varying influences of several different agents of change, we believe that we have shown the inadequacy of using exclusively any of the approaches discussed in Chapter 2 to analyse the history of computer systems development. In Chapters 2 and 3 we discussed insights into that history which could be gained from elements of those earlier approaches. We have incorporated certain of these elements into our models. There are also important insights to be gained from criticisms of all those approaches.

14.2.1 No 'One Best Way'

The tendency towards prescription in this field is reflected in recommendations about how 'best' to organize computer systems development functions. However, methods of organizing systems development staff which were recommended at one time have been rejected in later periods (such as the recommendation to divide the tasks of analysis and programming strictly, or the waterfall system life cycle). An appreciation of these changes over time is particularly damaging for the labour process approach as espoused by Kraft, which presumes an effective deskilling strategy to have been pursued continually. In our terms Kraft presumes that direct control strategies have been the best way to manage developers from management's point of view throughout the history of computer systems development.

Nolan's version of organization-tied stages also reflects the one-best-way syndrome. While Nolan recommends that the balance between control and slack should alter systematically as organizations go through the stages, he does not allow the balance to alter in response to general changes occurring in the field. He also assumes that all organizations go through the same set of stages and within each stage he recommends one particular control/slack mix as appropriate (see section 2.3.4). Our material suggests that the set of techniques which seems to be appropriate for one installation may be completely different for another installation, even if those installations are of similar age. There are many reasons why we observe different strategies being pursued at different installations.

First, the agents of change we have described affect different installations with varying degrees of intensity, depending on particular circumstances of those installations. For example, larger installations will have more communications problems simply because of there being more people to be dealt with, more chances of misunderstanding among developers and between managers and development staff.[1] They will also be better able to reap the benefits of specialization, because they will have enough work to keep more specialists busy full time. These factors will encourage more formal methods and greater division of labour in larger installations. Similarly the type of industry the host organization is in and its location will affect the markets IS departments face, the types of systems being developed and the types of users (especially in terms of their degree of computer sophistication). These factors will also affect the types of management strategies likely to be pursued in relation to computer systems developers (see section 13.2).

Second, and perhaps most important, there has been considerable debate in the literature as to the value of various different strategies.[2] In part this is because the contingencies associated with any technique are often not spelled out (although contingency approaches are becoming more popular). In part it is because different techniques may be associated with different general strategies or philosophies or ideals about management strategies. The two broad strategies to managing staff that we have identified, responsible autonomy and direct control, are based on very different philosophies (even ethics) about how people should be treated and about the value of order. Those who espouse responsible autonomy emphasize that management should appeal to employees' humanity and to encourage their common feelings with management and their loyalty (such as Mumford; see section 8.2.3). Those who espouse direct control emphasize the need to apply engineering techniques to labour as well as other factors of production. They recommend a much more strict line be drawn between order givers and order receivers, between management responsibility and staff obedience (such as Brandon; see section 5.5.1). The two groups often recommend completely different techniques. There is little common ground for deciding which set of recommendations is 'best'.

This leads to a third reason for different strategies being pursued in different installations. Different management strategies not only reflect the different philosophies of those who generate techniques, nor do they only reflect the pressures managers face (both external and internal to the DP or IS department); they also reflect the styles of IS department managers who implement particular policies. Some managers may change their style in response to pressures in practice; some managers with particular styles may be removed by top managers if they do not meet particular targets; however, the degree of competition IS department managers face and the accuracy with which their performance is monitored by top managers are far from perfect. Many will be able to maintain their preferred strategies in spite of pressure to change.

A very clear demonstration of the no-one-best-way proposition was neatly illustrated by Robert Glass in a piece he wrote for *Computerworld* (Glass, 1978). Glass describes two (mythical?) computer installations run by managers with very different personal styles and management strategies. One, Stan Sorcerer, manager at Alchemy Chemical, is shown dressed in a suit, well shorn and with a determined look on his face. The other, Herb Bond, manager at Softli Paper, is bearded, beaded, ear-ringed and displays a smile of saintly understanding. Their management strategies neatly follow the distinction between direct control and responsible autonomy we have been using. Stan Sorcerer clearly pursues direct control:

> Stan Sorcerer runs a tight ship. His employees have a dress code, fixed working hours, specified coffee breaks and a strict behavior program. The standards defined for his programmers are profuse and rigid. Both documentation and listings are subject to periodic and surprise review. Fortran and COBOL are required languages for all

applications, and precompilers are used to both encourage and enforce structured programming standards. Management of tasks is by schedule, and if a programmer gets behind in his work he is expected to put in voluntary overtime to make it up. The atmosphere is tense, businesslike and productive ... From all appearances, Stan Sorcerer has built himself a software factory, and he runs his shop like an assembly line. (1978, p. 35)

Herb Bond clearly pursues responsible autonomy:

Herb Bond sees things differently. Herb's programmers' dress could best be described as neo-hippy. They come and go through the swinging doors of Softli at all hours of the day or night. Their standards manual would fit within the index of that used at Alchemy, and it uses words like 'can' and occasionally 'should' instead of 'shall' and 'will'. Herb uses peer code reviews but never conducts management code inspections. Fortran and COBOL are the predominant languages, but one of his ace programmers is coding a report generator program in PASCAL now, and loving it. Management of tasks is by progress reporting, with emphasis on product quality rather than schedule. The atmosphere at Softli is laid back, unbusinesslike, and resembles a graduate school seminar ... From all outside appearances, Herb Bond is herding a group of untamed craftsmen in the general direction of product completion. (1978, p. 35)

In the story Glass tells about these two computer installations there is a competition between the two places, a 'code-off'. Each company fields a team and the teams are set identical programs to be designed and coded; one straightforward and the other complex and tricky. The result was a draw, a 'standoff'. The Alchemy team did better with the more straightforward task and scored higher in terms of time to complete and cost to complete the tasks. The Softli team did better with the more complex and tricky task and scored higher on a matrix of quality attributes.

The no-one-best-way proposition runs even deeper than a stricture against assuming that all installations of a similar age should be run in the same way. Even installations in similar circumstances, installations of the same size and in the same industry, for example, may still be successfully run in different ways. There was no suggestion in Glass's story that Stan Sorcerer and Herb Bond faced different contingencies.

We have found that the no-one-best-way proposition often applies within computer installations. The programmer using PASCAL on his own at Herb Bond's installation is not atypical. In our interviews we often found IS managers unwilling to answer our questions in terms of general policies. The common expression we were given in the UK was 'It's horses for courses.' Policies pursued depended on the particular task at hand, and on the particular skills, experience levels and even *personalities* of the staff involved.

It is important to distinguish between the general no-one-best-way proposition and the presumption that we cannot establish any general relations between agents of change and managerial strategies, that we cannot predict changes in managerial strategies. We have suggested certain relationships such as the connection between uncertain environments or labour shortages and responsible autonomy strategies, or between severe competition based on cost reduction and direct control strategies. We believe these propositions to be true for the field as a whole, rather than for each and every installation. The pressures towards either responsible autonomy or direct control are real. However, whether they elicit the predicted response will depend on the complex set of agents of change we have distinguished, as well as factors relating to the internal history of individual installations and the philosophies, personalities and determination of both managers and staff.

It is important to appreciate the *limitations* of generalizing from the case of computer systems development to other labour processes. In this book we have shown that managerial strategies have changed in response to broad changes in the conditions faced by computer department managers; such responses to long-term changes have been demonstrated in other contexts (see Friedman, 1977). Here we believe we are on strong ground and we believe that generalization is appropriate. However, computer systems development is also a special field. Conditions that encourage responsible autonomy have been particularly important, much more than for most other fields. Computer systems development, especially as occurs in user organizations, is an activity that has been relatively protected from 'product' market competition. Also computer systems developers have been highly protected from labour market pressures by severe and continual labour shortages. This is an unusual situation. It has allowed a wider range of policies to coexist in this field than would be expected in conditions where market competition is more severe. Some sets of policies may be just as productive as widely different ones, as Glass's story implies. However, we do not believe that all policies pursued represent good practice simply because they exist (or even persist). Management problems, failures and errors are not only possible, they are central to our models of change in computer systems development. We will elaborate on this point in the next sections.

14.3 AUTOGENERATION OF NEW TECHNOLOGY

Our model of the phases of computerization does not follow a Schumpeterian pattern as discussed in Chapter 1. Each new phase is not the result of the innovation and diffusion of a new invention, discovered by some agent outside the field. The phases emerge from constraints and problems on the 'demand' side of technology generation. New technology is invented, not only in response to demands from the computer-using community (considered in its broadest sense) but also *by members of that community*. Certainly new technology has emerged from the academic community and from traditional specialist suppliers (especially in the hardware area), but it has also emerged from those engaged in the mediating process within computer user organizations. This we refer to as the autogeneration of new technology.

Computer systems development is a creative process. Even if developers in different organizations are producing systems that have exactly the same purpose, these systems will not be developed in exactly the same way. The procedures and techniques used will differ. The programs produced will also differ.

In part differences will reflect differential abilities of developers. In part they will also reflect development environments in different organizations. These development environments will themselves be generated and altered by past efforts on the part of those engaged in the mediating process; on their successes and the adjustments made in response to their failures. Each environment will therefore be unique. It will not merely reflect bought-in computer systems core.[3] Therefore a continual stream of new techniques are developed in the user organization sector of the computing field, among 'ordinary' developers.

In addition, when new techniques diffuse, whether they originate from outside the computer-user community or within it, they will be modified in the user setting. They may be degraded, as were certain structured methods according to their originators (see section 6.4.2). They may be enhanced, as is systems software in most large installations.

There are many instances of major new techniques being developed within the user community. Most of the literature about user involvement schemes and prototyping procedures come from case study reports from user organizations. One spectacular example of new technology generated within the user community is the operating system (see section 4.2.3). Most service bureaus have emerged from computer installations within user organizations. Many independent software houses have been founded by staff from within user organizations to market either products they have developed in those organizations, or industry-specific skills they have acquired in this way. Some of this new technology is generated by individual systems developers in the course of their ordinary work, without being explicitly directed to develop new technology.

In this we believe computer systems development to be unusual. Adam Smith believed that a major source of productivity growth, and ultimately of the growth in the wealth of nations, occurred due to machines which facilitate and abridge labour which were 'originally the inventions of common workmen' (Smith, 1776, p. 114). Smith was writing before the Industrial Revolution, before technical progress in the Schumpeterian model sense became so important. Clearly today technical progress, in terms of big breakthroughs (often developed outside the normal business community), is very important. However, the other type of technical progress, that which arises from the cumulation of individually minor improvements, is also important today. What distinguishes computer systems development is the extent to which technical change of this second type occurs. This is, in turn, dependent upon the inherent creativity which still characterizes systems development.

This means that the connection between demand factors stimulating new technology, and the supply of that technology, is very strong. Pressures for techniques to solve problems arising from computer usage and computer systems development are readily transformed into new technology in this field.

We are not suggesting that computer systems development is unique in the autogeneration of new technology. Rather it is an extreme case. The autogeneration of new technology is likely to be important in the wake of many major technological breakthroughs. That is, it is likely to be a feature of the early stages of many technological regimes (see Chapter 1, endnote 8). What distinguishes computer systems development is that it is at the centre of such an enormous technological regime. This is because the purposes to which computers may be applied are so general and because those applications have been anticipated by so many for so long (see section 14.5 below).

14.4 PERCEPTION OF PROBLEMS, FASHION, MANAGERIAL STRATEGIES AND TECHNOLOGICAL CHANGE

Our concentration on *problems* expressed in the computing literature may seem oddly negative.[4] The computing field has clearly experienced continual and spectacular growth. However, the history of computer systems development has not been linear. There have been several twists of the helix and undoubtedly there will be more.

It is our contention that those twists of the helix have been stimulated in broad terms by certain agents of change; changes in technology, changes in computer applications, and in types of computer systems users and changes in market conditions. These agents of change have, in combination with each other and with existing practice in the field, stimulated changes in managerial strategies towards computer systems developers. However, the changes in managerial strategies have not occurred automatically. The changes have not been smooth or straight-forward. The agents of change have not decreed that computer systems developers be managed in new ways, nor have they revealed, of themselves, what those new directions for work organization should be. Rather the agents of change have stimulated problems that appear as management errors or failures. It is these problems that act as the transmission mechanism which relates the phases to changes in management strategies. New constraints enter into the consciousness of IS department managers and stimulate their actions via the perceptions of problems. In individual installations these problems appear as disappointments, miscalculations and unexpected failures as systems arrive late, as budgets are overrun, as end users find systems difficult to work with, as clients find their needs are not being met, and as profitability, due to new systems, expected by top managers, is not achieved.[5]

The computing literature is important because it allows actions taken by some to be shared among others in the field. While it certainly does not provide a precise and accurate picture of what is going on in the field, as we have noted elsewhere (the problem of tenses), it does reflect many of the problems in the field.

More important, it influences practice. It creates, or at least stimulates, fashion. It provides decrees and revelations for new directions, while the real agents of change merely stimulate search for those new directions.[6] Therefore the literature provides clues as to the broad direction of change of managerial strategies in the field, as well as to concrete policies being pursued which reflect that direction of change.[7]

This is more important when considering the direction of technological change in the field. Problems encountered in individual installations may be alleviated by the development of new techniques as well as changes in management strategies. The ability of computer systems developers within user organizations to develop new technology (its 'autogeneration') is supplemented by information from the computing literature about new techniques generated elsewhere. The literature has a strong effect on techniques adopted in the field for a number of reasons. First, the literature is widely read, particularly the magazines and papers that thrive on job advertisements. Second, the literature is supplemented by word-of-mouth communication at the many seminars, conferences and short courses which are well attended. It is also supplemented by word-of-mouth through labour turnover. Third, a lot of money is available to try new techniques because of the rapid growth of the field and its perceived importance to user organizations.

Perceptions of problems and of 'fashionable' solutions to those problems enter into our view of the progress from one phase to another in the following critical manner. A particular set of constraints on computerization are perceived within the computing community as problems or failures. This generates changes in management strategies and in new technology, both from within the user community and from outside of it (magnified and made fashionable by the computing literature). It is these actions of the computing community, along with external agents of change, which leads to the alleviation of the original set of constraints and both the revelation and the imposition of a new set of constraints. This new set of constraints is then perceived as a different set of problems and generates different sorts of failures (in part because the criteria of success may change as part of the change in constraints; see section 7.1).

In Chapter 1 (endnote 6) we noted that in mainstream economics the direction of technological change had, at one time, been thought to be induced by relative factor costs; that high labour costs, compared with capital, would induce labour-saving technological change and vice versa (Hicks, 1932). This idea was effectively criticized by later writers, who noted that under perfect competition no factor can be thought of as more expensive than another from the firm's perspective, because each factor is paid the value of its marginal product. This clearly depends on the assumption of perfect information, a particularly inappropriate assumption when analysing the generation and introduction of new technology. The effect of the introduction of new technology can rarely be predicted with confidence. Therefore managers must rely on unscientific cues, on hearsay and fashion. The value of effort expended on generating new technology is even more difficult to predict. The value of the expected payoff will still affect which techniques are introduced and which ones are developed, but the value of the payoff will be mediated by managers' perceptions of which areas will most readily yield productivity benefits. This will depend on the nature of the 'problems' they are currently experiencing. This does not mean that new techniques introduced are *exclusively* concerned with alleviating the currently perceived chief set of constraints, or that new technology generated is *exclusively* in this direction. Rather the stream of techniques introduced into user organizations and, to a lesser extent, the stream of new techniques generated, will be in part diverted in this new direction.

Each phase stimulates the computing community to introduce and to generate new technology (and management strategies) to alleviate the chief constraints of the phase. As noted in section 14.1, with the emergence of a new phase and a new set of constraints, work on alleviating constraints previously considered to be most important is not entirely abandoned. Sub-communities continue to work on these problems. Work on improving hardware cost/performance ratios, on automating computer systems development, and on developing structures method, continue and coexist with efforts to alleviate user relations problems.[8]

14.5 TECHNOLOGY REGIMES AND THE COMPUTER SYSTEMS TECHNOLOGY REGIME

We may consider this view of the direction of technological change in general terms as being common to the development of other technology regimes. The pattern of technological change demonstrated by the history of computer systems development can provide certain insights into a general model of the type of technological progress described in Chapter 1; that is, change arising from the cumulation of minor improvements in techniques. This type of technological change often seems to accompany big breakthroughs in technology. Big breakthroughs lead to technology regimes. They stimulate a swarm of technical advances in products and processes affected by big breakthroughs in technology. The pattern of technological change we observe in computer systems development may be identified as the pattern followed in an important technology regime, the computer systems technology regime.[9]

The flow of new technology in the computer systems technology regime can be thought of as reflecting a combination of sets of constraints and problems, mirroring what may be thought of as the archaeology of problems in the field. This may be labelled a vintage model of the direction of new technology.

Older vintages of chief constraints still occupy important sub-communities. Their work may be found in academic journals. This work may be described as scientific research programmes, after Lakatos (1970). We prefer to use the term technological research programmes. According to Lakatos scientific activities occur in clusters or programmes. Individual theories do not stand alone. These programmes involve two types of propositions: the hard core and the protective belt. The hard core consists of the basic assumptions without which work in that programme would be impossible. These assumptions are not questioned by adherents. The protective belt consists of theories that are subjected to tests, and which may be rejected if they fail tests repeatedly. In a technological research programme the conviction that solving certain problems or alleviating certain constraints may be thought of as the hard core; that is, the unquestioned conviction among adherents that significant advances in the field can be achieved by dealing with certain problems rather than others. For example, within the structured methods community, progress in the field is identified with generating systems development methods that allow computer systems to be produced in a manner which is easily understandable, repeatable, modifiable and manageable. The core problem is to simplify systems development in order to achieve these aims. How that should be done is part of the protective belt (such as whether decomposition should be based on functions or data structures).

Technological research programmes should be distinguished from technology regimes. A technology regime is the whole constellation of activities around a significant new technology, such as computer systems. A technological research programme is the problems and ideas or theories that guide one subset of those activities, the activities of a sub-community working to develop new techniques within a technology regime. As constraints change, technological research programmes dedicated to alleviating past constraints seem to slip from what is thought of as applied research to basic research. Students complain that much of what they are taught in computer science degree courses, for example, is not relevant to practice in the jobs they get. However, these communities are capable of producing important breakthroughs in the field in later phases. The problems they work on persist in the field. Also advances against certain constraints may be used to alleviate other constraints via substitution (see endnote 8).

We do not believe that it is advisable to generalize from the phases of computerization to conclude that all major new technology regimes must pass through precisely the same phases. The phases are the outcome of a complex mix of what may be thought of as supply and demand factors. The direction of technological change has been 'pulled' by the perceived benefits from further computerization. This has been affected by the sorts of uses to which systems have been put, by the types of clients and end users demanding computer-based systems, and by the perceived major constraints to meeting those demands for computerization. Technical change has also been 'pushed' by the efforts of particular sub-communities dedicated to particular technological research programmes within the field, and by the logical paths of knowledge flow.

Two factors distinguish the computer systems technology regime from other technology regimes. First, as mentioned above, computers are extremely general in terms of the uses to which they may be put. Second, and more important, something like computers were imagined long before electronic computers appeared. The dream of creating a human-like artifact, or even better, one with super-human powers—one to 'think', one to 'do' as we command—has been a recurrent theme in the science fiction literature for the past hundred years or so. The dream is certainly older than this.[10] Furthermore the dream continues. Modern science fiction builds explicitly on existing achievements of computerization. These accounts, along with the semi-fictional claims of computer systems core suppliers, have (over)stimulated demand-pull pressures on the computer systems technology regime. The demand side has therefore normally provided impetus, rather than constraints. In this we believe computer systems development has been unusual.

Computerization has progressed very quickly. Yet it has also been distinguished by regular reports of problems and failures. These apparently contradictory statements can be reconciled by an appreciation of how high expectations have been in this field. Fired by dreams of the imaginable, computer systems developers and their clients have often attempted the improbable. Constraints have been important in this field, not because people have been bound by what is considered possible, but because inadequate attention has been paid to limitations. Constraints have therefore been experienced, rather than simply perceived. Experiences of failure have provided the detailed knowledge required to make later attempts with greater confidence and greater success. Failures have rarely held computer systems development back, because the gains perceived by those who have ultimately footed the bill have been so great.[11]

Although strong demand-side stimulation may mean that the detailed pattern of phases we have found may be specific to computer systems development, we believe certain characteristics of the historical pattern are common to most technology regimes. These may be summarized as two general principles of technology regime development.

The first we call the *principle of elaboration*; that new activities and structures often begin in a simple form, but come to be elaborated over time. This principle seems to have applied to the development of techniques for managerial strategies to control the work and employment conditions of computer systems developers. During phase one, particularly in the earliest years, the division of labour was simple (sometimes no more than a separation between operators and systems developers). Little attempt was made to monitor programming work. Little attempt was made to give systems developers a career structure. Both direct control and responsible autonomy strategies were undeveloped. Although we may characterize the general bias as strongly towards responsible autonomy, the way that responsible autonomy was encouraged was simply by lack of management intervention. We may characterize this situation as management by neglect.[12]

During phase two, although there appears to have been movement towards direct control strategies, the techniques of both direct control and responsible autonomy were either developed or imported from other areas of management ınto the mediating process. Arguably a further elaboration is occurring during phase three.

Similarly with regard to the sources of new technology there has been an elaboration. Although fashion is important, the number of sub-communities attempting to develop new technology along previously fashionable lines grows as the field acquires a more complex 'archaeology' (see section 14.4 above).

The principle of elaboration operates for two reasons. First, there is no one best way to organize the labour process. Over time many paths will be tried. Technologies supporting different ways of organizing the labour process will be developed. This does not mean that we can never say that one way of organizing the labour process is *better* than another. Rather a great number of contingencies must be held constant, a great number of the *ceteris paribus* conditions are necessary, in order to establish one set of management practices as better than another. Therefore when considering any substantial number of installations, the set of 'best' practices[13] becomes rather large. If all installations were organized in the same way, then a strong stimulus for the elaboration of different sorts of new techniques for computer systems development would be removed. If all labour processes ostensibly producing similar products were organized in the same way, then a strong stimulus for the elaboration of different sorts of new techniques would be removed.

The second reason for the principle of elaboration is that competition is never perfect. Another way of putting this is to say that the degree of elaboration is inversely related to the degree of competition. This works in two ways. First, pressure to adopt better techniques and to change management strategies in directions encouraged by the agents of change we have discussed is not perfect. We have already noted that computer systems development has been particularly marked by the weakness of these pressures. Second, information that would allow managers to judge which techniques and methods are better is not available. Such information as exists is notoriously unreliable.[14] A significant rise in the degree of competition in this field would lead to a significant fall in the variety of practices. We would *not* predict further elaboration of different management strategies and techniques to continue throughout the lifetime of a technology regime. To the extent that competition increases as technology regimes mature,[15] we would predict that the pattern of elaboration would be to contract as the technology regime approaches maturity, after expanding during the early phases.

The second principle is what may be called the *compensation principle*. There are two parts to this. First, in any technology regime certain parts get developed faster than others. Whether we are considering components of products or stages of processes, technical advances normally affect certain parts of products or processes more than others. This stimulates future technological change in varying combinations of three routes. The first two routes involve substitution of the improved part for less affected ones. One is a direct substitution—older parts are simply eliminated. The second is indirect, whereby the improved part is applied to functions normally carried out by less affected parts in order to reduce reliance on these latter parts. The third route is to stimulate search for improvements in less affected parts. All three routes may be thought of as ways of eliminating or alleviating a bottleneck in parts of a system which has been created or revealed by rapid technological progress in other parts of that system.

The principle of compensation has been discussed in various sections of this book in relation to several different divisions, or partitions, of the computer systems technology regime. Partitions considered include the effect of advances in electronic switches on circuitry, components on other parts of computer hardware, hardware on software, and computer systems core on the mediating process.

The replacement of vacuum tubes by transistors represented a major breakthrough in computer systems technology. However, the transistor only affected part of computer hardware—the switches (at first). They allowed more switches to be packed into a smaller space. This stimulated search for advances in the circuitry, particularly in the connections between wires and switches. In a sense the full potential of solid-state switches could not be realized because packing switches more closely together was limited by problems arising with the circuitry (such as heat production, space required for wires and mechanical connection failure). This stimulated search for ways of substituting solid-state techniques for the circuit wiring, which led to the development of integrated circuits. The use of integrated circuits, or chips, with greater and greater numbers of circuits packed on to them, i.e. the substitution of separate electrical wiring by solid-state circuitry, continued at a spectacular pace from the mid-1960s (see section 2.2.1).

Rapid technological change in components stimulated changes in other aspects of hardware, again by stimulating dissatisfaction with areas where the pace of development was slower. The developments in solid-state technology and other major advances primarily affected CPU and memory components of computer hardware in the early years. The input and output devices were still based on electromechanical components. Eventually chip technology was substituted for more and more of the electromechanical aspects of input and output devices (the development of modern video display units, VDUs). However, 'compensating' changes did not occur by the direct substitution route alone. With the use of buffers and spooling, input/output functions were translated into CPU and memory functions. These techniques created what may be thought of as holding bays, either in the CPU or on magnetic tape, which allowed input/output-like functions to be carried out within the hardware, in place of certain input/output operations which would have occurred between the hardware and its environment (see section 4.2.3).

All three routes by which the compensation principle operates are illustrated in the relation between hardware and software. Rapid improvements in hardware cost/performance ratios have stimulated direct substitution of hardware for software (hard-wiring of programs on to chips). It has also stimulated the use of hardware to carry out functions that had previously been carried out using software. For example, the use of high-level languages requires fewer lines of code to be written by the programmer in order to carry out most functions. However, the object code produced will generally be less efficient than that resulting from programs coded in lower-level languages (see sections 4.2.4 and 5.4.1). In addition hardware improvements have stimulated improvements in software itself, such as the separation of systems from applications software.

We can also see the three routes illustrated in the relation between computer systems core and the mediating process. First, the mediating process, at least for rather straightforward applications, may be effectively substituted by computer systems core with the use of applications packages. Second, software tools such as higher-level languages, database management systems and automated debugging tools substitute computer systems core for certain mediating process functions. The third route is represented by the development of strategies for managing computer systems developers (in both direct control and responsible autonomy directions).

The likelihood of all three routes of 'compensation' being pursued depends on how complex are the activities or parts of systems which are being pressed to compensate for rapid improvements elsewhere.[16] Simpler parts of systems, such as wires, are likely only to be directly eliminated by substitution. More complex components, such as software or the mediating process, are likely to be affected by developments along all three routes of compensation.

14.6 THE DIRECTION OF CAUSALITY: TECHNOLOGICAL AND SOCIAL INFLUENCES

While we have argued against technological determinism (see section 1.1), we certainly do not believe that technology has no influence on the social organization of work. The principle of compensation described above illustrates technological influences. Note that improved technology in one part of a system stimulates activity elsewhere in the system. It does not determine what that activity will be. There are choices. The route taken will depend on social factors. For example, the degree to which technological changes in computer systems core stimulated changes in the mediating process in the direction of productivity improvements through managerial strategies for organizing that work 'better' (as opposed to substitution routes) has been limited by labour shortages, by the market power of computer systems developers. This has also limited the extent to which productivity improvements could be achieved by direct control strategies. Technological changes represent one among several agents of change.

One way of looking at the relationship between technology and social factors is to view reactions to technological change as mediated by social factors.[17] We wish to go further than this. We also show how the direction of technological change has been shaped by social factors. The constraints of each phase may be attributed to the various agents of change. Mediated by the perceptions of these constraints as problems and failures, the technological research community is stimulated to develop new technology along lines that will alleviate constraints. However, some sub-communities continue to work along lines designed to alleviate older chief constraints. They persist against the tide of current fashion. They desire to persist because of personal dispositions towards certain lines of research and because of intellectual 'capital' invested in understanding the older technology research programme. They are allowed to persist because these sub-communities can become more or less protected from the need to produce profitable results, because old constraints do not completely disappear, because solutions to certain problems can be adapted to other problems (see section 14.4) and because of strategic institutionalization of those sub-communities. Thus, along with the more technically oriented principle of compensation, there is the more socially oriented principle of elaboration.

We can be more detailed than this. While we have concentrated on the effects of the agents of change on managerial strategies towards computer systems developers, we have also alluded to the effects of managerial strategies on those agents of change. New techniques are introduced and developed during certain periods in order to complement current managerial strategies. The development of structured methods and their diffusion, for example, occurred mainly during the late 1960s and the 1970s. They both stimulated and were stimulated by moves towards direct control strategies for computer systems developers.

We have analysed the history of computer systems development in relative isolation from the direct effects of wider social and technical events on that history. We believe that, at least until recently, computer systems have been developed in some isolation from concurrent broader social and technological movements. There are two reasons for this. First, we believe that any substantial technology regime will demonstrate a degree of independent dynamism. This in part reflects the principles of compensation and elaboration described above.[18] Second, the computer systems technology regime has developed particularly quickly. As noted above, demand-pull pressures have been strong. Certainly these pressures have wider social antecedents, as we have indicated. However, the effect of these strong demand-pull pressures has been to protect computer systems developers from external influence. A corollary of this is that the relation between the computing field and its wider social environment is notable for the strong *outward flow* of ideas and influence. We certainly have not neglected wider social issues, as may be seen in Chapter 8. However, the lines of literature discussed in that chapter were almost entirely about the social and economic effects of computer systems on their environment, on users. The recent outpouring of books and conferences and academic courses about computers and society or information technology and society are almost entirely concerned with the flow of influence that runs from computer systems to society, rather than the other way round (see sections 8.2.1–8.2.4 and Chapter 1, endnote 5). Nevertheless, we expect that wider social issues will become more important in future, reflecting the 'outward' movement of constraints on further computerization (to users recently, and increasingly beyond organizational boundaries in future; see section 13.3).

Klein and Hirschheim (1987) have suggested that recent challenges to what they call the information systems development orthodoxy have been stimulated directly by wider social change. They note that challenges to the narrow, purely 'technical' view of information systems, based on positivist scientific traditions, as represented by 'hard' computer scientists and software engineers, have recently come from several sources. Some authors view information systems as technical systems with social consequences, such as Mader (1979) and Davis and Olson (1985). Others, like Mumford, view them as part of socio-technical systems. Still others, like Ciborra (1981) and Goldkuhl and Lyytinen (1982), view information systems as social systems. These groups incorporate currently popular social theories into their research on information systems. For example, Mumford incorporates general socio-technical or humanistic management theory; Ciborra views information systems as social transaction architectures and uses neo-institutional economic theory; Goldkuhl and Lyytinen view information systems as formal language systems and incorporate linguistic theory.

According to Klein and Hirschheim, these challenges to the orthodox view of information systems development reflect more general social changes, which themselves are induced by changes in the image of social reality. These changes in the image of social reality may be discerned in recent books which are widely read and which show a remarkable consistency in their vision of society (books such as those by Toffler, 1980; Naisbitt, 1982; and Peters and Waterman, 1982). The new image is essentially one of a 'bottom-up' society, an egalitarian and democratic society, where individual effort and the realization of individual human potential is legitimated, prized and supported, rather than the dictates of tradition, custom or organizational efficiency.[19] We would interpret their thesis as a contention that a general change towards the values and philosophy underpinning responsible autonomy management strategies and away from those underpinning direct control has occurred in recent years and that this has influenced the computer systems development community. It is notable that Klein and Hirschheim do not attempt to explain why this fundamental change in the image of social reality has occurred.

We would agree with Klein and Hirschheim that certain individuals who have come to criticize the orthodox view of computer systems development have been influenced by currents of thought in other disciplines. However, what must be explained is the timing of the growth and partial internalization of these criticisms into the computer systems development community. It is only from the late 1970s, and during the 1980s, that this has occurred. While Klein and Hirschheim cite the three popular works of the early 1980s which express this responsible autonomy type of philosophy, we could also cite works expressing similar views which were popular earlier, particularly in the 1960s, such as McGregor (1960), Etzioni (1961) and Maslow (1964), but also others in the 1930s, with the origins of the human relations school of management (see Mayo, 1933; Roethlisberger and Dickson, 1939).[20]

There have always been substantial numbers with a vision of social reality that conforms with Klein and Hirschheim's description of an egalitarian and democratic society which supports individual pursuit of self-actualization. It has arguably been the dominant ideology of American society, the liberal or populist vision as expressed clearly by such as Jefferson, Jackson and Lincoln during the first century of the existence of the USA. Elsewhere I have traced the conflict between philosophies underpinning responsible autonomy and direct control to the early years of the Industrial Revolution (Friedman, 1977). Why should these ideas have been of so *little* influence in the field of computer systems development, say during the early 1960s, during late phase one, the part of the history of computer systems development when books expressing this ideal were arguably most popular?

We have also noted the general challenge to the technical and narrow view of computer systems development and moves towards responsible autonomy, both in strategies towards computer systems developers and towards users. However, we have connected it to the development of an appreciation of user relations constraints, especially in the area of implementation problems.[21] We have connected the change with developments which are part of a semi-independent internal dynamic of computer systems development, namely the rise in prominence of user relations constraints occasioned by changes in types of users and uses, further improvements in computer systems core technology, and rising market pressures.

We would like to make one final point about the relation between technological and social influences. We have concentrated on the interaction of social factors with the development of the computer systems technology regime. We have not mentioned social influence on the origin of that technology regime. However, social factors can be brought to bear.

The development of both electronic computers and of transistors were highly dependent on investment by the military in the years leading up to, and immediately following, these initial 'breakthroughs'. These investments were largely underwritten by the military demands of the Second World War and the subsequent Cold War. These military demands were directed towards working out shell trajectories, code breaking and the development of atomic weapons. It is difficult to imagine how these demands could have been otherwise. However, there was an important field of scientific and technological endeavour which was hardly stimulated at all by these wars, even though it was the field which had been traditionally stimulated by war since the discovery of gunpowder. After the terrible experiences of chemical warfare during the First World War, work in this field in response to military demands has been considered to be socially and politically unacceptable. This has not meant the total disappearance of military stimulation for research into chemical weapons, but since the 1925 Geneva Protocol against the use of chemical weapons this source of stimulation has waned significantly. We would argue that the fields of research that led up to the development of the computer benefited from this socially stimulated reduction in demands for the products of the main competing field of research.

ENDNOTES

1. Larger installations are likely to attempt larger systems development projects as well as a larger number of projects. This will exacerbate communications problems within project teams as well as between them.
2. We have indicated the differences of opinion with regard to strategies for dealing with user relations problems in Chapters 8 and 11, and differences of opinion regarding strategies for improving systems developer productivity in Chapter 5.
3. Although considerable variation in user organization environments is generated by the variety of computer systems core available.
4. At least this seems to be the picture outsiders have. Within the field reports of failures are commonplace, as we have shown throughout this book. There are many jokes about this in the field. Glass's collections of articles, *The Universal Elixir and Other Computing Projects Which Failed* (1977) and *Tales of Computing Folk: Hot Dogs and Mixed Nuts* (1978), provide many examples. A nice example is given by Taggart and Silbey (1986, pp. 278–279), who suggest that the 'real' development life cycle is made up of the following phases:
   (1) Wild Enthusiasm
   (2) Disillusionment
   (3) Total Confusion
   (4) Search for the Guilty
   (5) Punishment of the Innocent
   (6) Promotion of Non-participants
5. Changes will not occur through the perception of computer department managers alone. Pressure from top managers through their own perceptions (or those of users) of computer systems department failures often lead either to directives imposed on computer managers or to their removal.
6. The problem is, as noted in section 14.2.1, that the literature offers many and contradictory new directions, while also overexposing certain directions as though they are appropriate for all situations. In this latter way the literature creates fashion.
7. Examination of the literature must, of course, be supplemented with observations, with surveys and case studies, when attempting to ascertain the current position.
8. Some are 'sold' as methods for reducing user relations problems, such as automated tools for prototyping or structured design methods which allow users, as well as managers, to sign-off documents at different milestones marking the 'end' of system life cycle phases. An excellent example of a sub-community which has been working along an 'older' direction, but one which has recently made important advances, is the ISDOS group (see section 13.5.1).
9. Some may prefer to define the technology regime somewhat differently as the information technology regime or the microelectronics technology regime.
10. According to Greek mythology Pygmalion made an ivory image of Aphrodite when she would not lie with him and prayed that the image should come to life.
11. The process of overcoming constraints has been far from smooth. In the early 1970s in particular, confidence in computer systems development seemed to falter due in part to spectacular reports of failures. However this lack of confidence was short-lived.
12. Tracy Kidder, in his popular book about developing a new minicomputer at Data General, called the type of management used to deal with hardware engineers and software specialists 'mushroom' management. 'Put 'em in the dark, feed 'em shit, and watch 'em grow' (1981, p. 109). The case he was discussing was a phase-one situation for the software specialists. They were clearly working with serious hardware constraints.

13. Those for which there is no clear better set.
14. See Jones (1986) for an excellent account of the difficulties of measuring programmer productivity, and see section 13.5.1 for a discussion of the limiting effect this has had on the diffusion of CASE tools.
15. Due to factors such as widening knowledge of opportunities in the field attracting companies from elsewhere and saturation of the market for major products affected by the technology regime.
16. This depends in part on our own perception of bottlenecks. It depends on how broadly the bottleneck parts of the system may be defined.
17. This is the view taken by Wilkinson (1983) for example.
18. An analogy with changes in the character of people, which are affected largely by their own biological maturation process in early years, seems appropriate here. Certainly wider environmental factors are always present and always of some influence, but these influences are much less powerful compared with the normal process of maturation in early years of life.
19. The social changes Klein and Hirschheim point to are indeed wide-ranging and general. They include changes in societal attitudes such as the view that work is a right, rather than a burden to be endured (1987, p. 280); or that organizations are seen as valued sources of personal satisfaction, rather than social means to implement efficiency (p. 281); or that learning 'is now seen to occur by insight and feedback from practical experience. Preplanned curricula are notoriously out of date' (p. 282). They also include changes in organizational incentives away from 'bureaucratic incentives to achieve compliance with predefined policies' (p. 283) towards autonomy, self-motivation and intra-organizational entrepreneurship (p. 284).
20. Klein and Hirschheim also cite influential works published before the 1980s expressing similar views (such as Bell, 1973, and Schumacher, 1974).
21. See section 8.2.7 and Chapter 11, especially section 11.1.

Data Appendix

A large number of surveys have been used in this book. Many of these are not easily accessible. In this appendix we provide basic information about these surveys.

Early in phase two, three substantial surveys were carried out on computer specialists in the UK. Two originated in academic departments. One was headed by Enid Mumford at Manchester Business School (Mumford, 1972). The other was carried out by researchers at Salford University (Hebden, 1975). The third survey was carried out by a private company, Computer Economics Ltd, in cooperation with management consultants Peat, Marwick, Mitchell (Peat, Marwick, Mitchell and Computer Economics, 1972). We refer to this as the CEL 1972 survey. Computer Economics had been set up in 1968 to survey salaries of computer staff and to sell the results of the surveys to managers.

The three surveys were not carried out at precisely the same time. Mumford's fieldwork was carried out in 1969, Hebden's between 1969 and 1971 and the CEL 1972 survey was conducted early in 1972. As we are concerned with long-run patterns, the three and a half year span between surveys is not a serious drawback. Nevertheless, the period between 1969 and 1972 was a turbulent one in the labour market for computer staff. The only significant falling off in the demand for computer specialists throughout phases one and two occurred in 1971. At that time a general recession in the UK coincided with the growing awareness of computer department costs and certain well-publicized failures of computer departments to meet deadlines within budgets. As the Mumford study was carried out before 1971, we particularly concentrate on it when discussing employment relations.

Mumford's was the first study by a social scientist in the UK to consider computer specialists as an occupation group. Her data came from a survey of eight organizations: two computer manufacturers, three computer consultants and three computer user firms. The three computer user firms were a mail order company, a firm making industrial products and a large Civil Service department of the British government. Interviews were carried out on 266 systems analysts and computer programmers during 1969. Mumford's study, along with all others up to that time, suffered from the bias towards established, large and therefore relatively sophisticated computing organizations. The three user firms had, on average, over 100 people employed in their computing departments. Each had over 30 people who were analysts, programmers or managers. The mail order firm had used computers since 1956. Only the Civil Service department was relatively inexperienced, having recently set up their facility.

374

Hebden's results were based on responses from 334 DP staff to a mailed questionnaire. Respondents included a wide range of organizations (private industry, commerce, Civil Service, local government and university administration). Representivity was not discussed.

The CEL 1972 study was based on a mailed questionnaire completed primarily by DP managers in user organizations. The questionnaire was mailed to the client base for the Computer Economics DP salary surveys. These surveys are carried out twice a year. The authors attempted to establish how representative their sample was of the UK population of computer departments. They concluded that their sample was biased towards larger computer departments and also towards financial institutions and users in construction and distribution, at the expense of government, utilities and service industry firms. Overall they estimated their sample to represent 3% of computers in use and 10% of staff employed in user firms where the computer is used almost exclusively for internal processing work (1972, pp. 1–3).

In 1975 the National Computing Centre (NCC) carried out an interview survey of DP departments in 106 organizations. The results of this survey were reported in Hansen and Penney (1976). We refer to this as the NCC 1975 survey. The sample was not chosen from the NCC membership base. Rather they chose organizations that had been recommended to the authors as 'forward-thinking and progressive in their approach to DP' (1975, p. 7). This survey was therefore highly biased towards larger DP departments (40% of the departments had over 100 staff members). The authors gave no information about refusal rates.

Our picture of the situation *late* in phase two relies heavily on our own surveys of DP managers carried out during 1981. This involved face-to-face semi-structured interviews with DP managers (in-depth survey) and a mailed survey of Computer Economic's clients. We refer to the mailed survey as the CEL 1981 survey. The in-depth survey was carried out as a pilot study. Therefore the sampling technique was not carefully thought out. We generally tried to spread the interviews across different parts of England and different industries. The results are not used in a rigorous fashion.

The CEL 1981 survey was sent to Computer Economics' entire client base, 406 organizations, and 142 usable responses were received. The distribution of installations according to age is presented in Table A.1. The age distribution was gratifyingly well spread, with 24% beginning during phase one. As with the CEL 1972 survey, the CEL 1981 survey was somewhat biased towards larger computer departments and financial institutions, reflecting the Computer Economics client base.

A further mailed survey was carried out in 1981. This was a set of questions concerning current and planned usage of productivity aids conducted by *Computing* magazine and Urwick Dynamics. This will be referred to as the 1981 Urwick/Computing survey. Results from this survey were reported in Friedman and Cornford (1981).

TABLE A.1 CEL 1981 Survey distribution of respondents by age of computer department

Q: In which year did your firm install its first computer?

Date	Year first computer installed (%)
Before 1955	0
1955–1959	6
1960–1964	18
1965–1969	43
1970–1974	16
1975–1979	13
After 1979	2
No response or not applicable	3

The Urwick/Computing survey was part of a regular quarterly survey carried out by Urwick Dynamics for *Computing* magazine in the UK. The base questionnaire had been sent to a stable panel of 820 DP managers from September 1979. This questionnaire asked whether respondents thought their own budgets and staff levels and expenditures on particular items would increase, decrease or stay the same during the next 12 months. Our supplementary questionnaire concerning usage of productivity aids was sent with the March 1981 survey. That survey generated 476 usable supplementary questionnaires.

Our analysis of phase three is based primarily on the results of a series of mailed surveys in the UK carried out in cooperation with the National Computing Centre. The first survey was carried out between November 1982 and January 1983. The survey base was the 1583 class B (user organizations) members of the National Computing Centre. We refer to this as the NCC 1982/83 survey. This sample was not strongly biased by industry. Compared with the CEL-based survey there were significantly more government and public utility organizations and fewer financial institutions. The chief source of bias in the NCC base is the over-representation of installations using ICL as opposed to IBM hardware. This leads to a bias towards public sector installations. Although the size distribution is biased towards larger departments, as with all of the mailed surveys we know of, the bias is less than the CEL and earlier surveys. A substantial 21% of the NCC 1982/83 sample were computer departments with ten or less computer systems developers (12% had more than 100).

Two further mailed surveys using the NCC class B membership base were carried out in 1984 and 1985 (the NCC 1984 and NCC 1985 surveys). During 1985 Dominic Cornford went to work for the NCC. He ran the NCC 1985 survey and carried out further surveys with colleagues at the NCC in 1986 and 1987 (the NCC

1986 and NCC 1987 surveys). Response rates for all the mailed surveys for which we have information about the sample base are presented in Table A.2.

All of the sample size figures are those which were analysed. They all exclude not only poorly filled-in questionnaires, but also a number that were received after the date when analysis commenced. Sample sizes for the 1984 and 1985 surveys were, in fact, identical. The lower response rates for the 1986 and 1988 surveys reflect a more complex sampling procedure used. For the 1986 survey 2190 of the base organizations were NCC members; the rest were chosen randomly from an index of computers in the UK, maintained by NCC (the National Computer Index, NCI). The response rate from NCC members was 26·2%; from the NCI sample it was only 12.7% (see Cornford, 1987, p. 5).[1] For the NCC 1987 survey the sample was based on the NCI entirely. Questionnaires were sent to all installations whose site record had been updated in the last two years before the survey. This survey was more representative of smaller installations, with 58% of the sample employing less than ten DP staff and only 6% employing 50 or more.

The distribution of respondents to the different NCC surveys by size, industry and area were similar to each other. In Table A.3 the distribution for the NCC 1984 survey is presented.

The area distribution corresponds to major salary differentials as identified by Computer Economics. The bias towards public services and government was noted above in relation to earlier NCC surveys.

Table A.4 presents the number of computer specialists covered by the CEL 1972, NCC 1984 and NCC 1987 surveys, along with an estimate of the UK population of computer specialists employed in user organizations in 1972 and 1987. The 1972 sample figures are derived from 92 respondents for which staff figures were provided. The 1972 population estimate was derived from estimates of the numbers of computers in use, and the average number of computer staff per installation provided in a Select Committee report on the UK computer industry (Select Committee, 1970).

The population figure for 1987 is based on information from only 640 installations. The 1987 estimates of the population of computer specialists in the UK were derived from the NCI, supplemented by information contained in a census of installed computer equipment based on suppliers' shipments.[2] These sources provided estimates of the number and value of basic computer core in the installations included in the NCI. Then the number of sites in a set of value bands

TABLE A.2 Sample sizes and sample bases of CEL and NCC Surveys

	1972	1981	1982/83	1984	1985	1986	1987
Size	110	142	321	394	394	843	777
Base	380	406	1 583	1 500	1 600	4 310	6 000
Response rate (%)	28.9	35.0	20.3	26.3	24.6	19.6	13.0

TABLE A.3 Distribution of the NCC 1984 sample of installations

	% of total sample
Size of installation	
(number of DP personnel)	
0–9	19·0
10–29	26.8
30–49	18.8
50–99	17.4
≥ 100	18.0
Industry sector	
Private manufacturing	32.9
Private services	32.1
Public services	16.8
Government	18.2
Area	
London	13.9
Home counties	17.3
Major conurbations	42.8
Rural areas	26.0

TABLE A.4 Numbers of DP professionals and DP department staff in CEL and NCC Surveys with some estimates for the UK population of DP specialists (numbers in 1,000s)

	1972	1984	1987
Sample systems			
developers	2.7	7.8	7.0
(% of UK population)	n.a.	n.a.	(4.4)
Sample department			
staff	6.3	12.3	11.0
(% of UK population)	(10.0)	n.a.	(4.1)
UK systems			
developers	n.a.	n.a.	157.5
UK department			
staff	63	n.a.	266.4

(defined by the value of the largest installed computer) were calculated for the population as a whole and for the 1987 sample. The average number of staff for each value band was calculated from the sample responses and this average was then multiplied by the estimated number of installations in the UK population in each value band.[3] Only sites where the value of installed computer core exceeded £30 000 were included. Limitations of this method of estimating the UK population of computer specialists are discussed in Buckroyd and Cornford (1988, pp. 43–44).

Some results of the ICON survey of the USA are reported in this book. Detailed results of that survey may be found in Friedman (1986). This survey, which we label the USA 1983 survey, was carried out in the Boston and New York areas in the first half of 1983. Face-to-face, semi-structured interviews with DP managers and other IS executives were carried out. The sample was drawn mainly from the *Directory of Top Computer Executives*. The sample was stratified as strictly as possible by size of computer installation (measured by number of computer systems developers) and by industry sector (an equal distribution of financial institutions, computer services firms, public sector and other private companies). This sampling procedure was followed for all the ICON face-to-face surveys. The sample size for the USA 1983 survey was 95.

ENDNOTES

1. The NCI contains information about 36 000 computers installed at 9500 sites in the UK (1988 figures). It is estimated to cover 80–90% of the larger sites in the UK. With the diffusion of small computers, the NCI has become increasingly unrepresentative of the smaller end of the computer population. This is less of a problem for representivity of the population of the computer specialists.
2. This census is published annually by Pedder Associates Ltd.
3. Separate population figures for central government and defence were obtained from the Central Computing and Telecommunications Agency (CCTA).

Bibliography

Ackoff, R. L. (1960) 'Unsuccessful case studies and why', *Operations Research*, **8**, 259–263.

Ackoff, R. L. (1967) 'Management misinformation systems', *Management Science,* **14**, B147–156.

Adams, C. R. (1973) 'Attitudes of top management users toward information systems and computers', working paper 73-07, Management Information Systems Research Center, University of Minnesota.

Adams, C. R. (1975) 'How management users view information systems', *Decision Sciences*, **6**, 337–345.

Adler, M., and Du Feu, D. (1977) 'The implications of a computer based welfare benefits information system', in Parkin, A. (ed.), *Computing and People*, Edward Arnold, London, pp. 109–121.

Air Force Space and Missile Systems Organization (1966) 'Computer program subsystem development milestones', SSD Exhibit 61-47b, April.

Aitken, H. G. J. (1960) *Taylorism and the Watertown Arsenal*, Harvard University Press, Cambridge, MA.

Alavi, M., and Weiss, I. R. (1985–86) 'Managing the risks associated with end-user computing', *Journal of Management Information Systems*, **11**, 5–20.

Alavi, M., Nelson, R. R., and Weiss, I. R. (1987–88) 'Strategies for end-user computing: an integrative framework', *Journal of Management Information Systems*, **4**, 28–49.

Alter, S. (1981) 'Certification program for MIS systems analysts', in Cotterman, W. W., Couger, J. D., Enger, N. L., and Harold, F. (eds), *Systems Analysis and Design: A Foundation for the 1980's*, Elsevier, New York, pp. 521–535.

Anderson, A., and Hersleb, S. (1980) *Computer Manpower Outlook for the 1980's*, National Economic Development Office, London.

Anderson, R. G. (1974) *Data Processing and Management Information Systems*, Macdonald and Evans, Plymouth.

Anderson, R. G. (1978) *Data Processing and Management Information Systems*, (2nd ed.), Macdonald and Evans, Plymouth.

Anthony, R. N. (1965) *Planning and Control Systems: A Framework for Analysis*, Harvard University Press, Boston.

APEX (1985) *New Technology and Job Design*, Association of Professional, Executive, Clerical and Computer Staff, London.

Arbuckle, R. A. (1966) 'Computer analysis and thruput evaluation', *Computers and Automation*, January.

Argyris, C. (1957) *Personality and Organisation*, Harper & Row, New York.

Argyris, C. (1971) 'Management information systems: the challenge to rationality and emotionality', *Management Science*, **17**, B275–292.

Armer, P. (1965) *Computer Aspects of Technological Change, Automation and Economic Progress*, report prepared for the National Commission on Technology, Automation and Economic Progress, Washington, DC.

Arthur, M. (1977) *Computer People: An Occupational Perspective*, Computer Economics and Cranfield School of Management, London.

Auerbach (various years) *Auerbach Standard EDP Reports*, Auerbach Information, Philadelphia.

Babbage, C. (1832) *On the Economy of Machinery and Manufactures*, London.

Bàhl, H. C., and Hunt, R. G. (1985) 'Problem solving strategies for DSS design', *Information and Management*, **8**, 81–88.

Bairdain, E. F. (1964) 'Research studies of programmers and programming', unpublished studies, New York (cited in Mayer and Stalnaker, 1968).

Baker, F. T. (1972) 'Chief programmer team management of production programming', *IBM Systems*, **1**, 56–73.

Ball, L. D. (1985) 'Computer crime', in Forester, T. (ed.), *The Information Technology Revolution*, Basil Blackwell, Oxford, pp. 533–545.

Bally, L., Brittan, J., and Wagner, K. W. (1977) 'A prototype approach to information system design and development', *Information and Management*, **1**, 21–26.

Bannon, L. J. (1986) 'Issues in design: some notes', in Norman, D. A., and Draper, S. W. (eds), *User Centered System Design: New Perspectives on Human–Computer Interaction*, Lawrence Erlbaum, Hillsdale, NJ, pp. 25–29.

Bansler, J. (1987) *Systemudvikling—teorier og historie i skandinavisk perspektiv* (in Danish: *Systems development: theory and history from a Scandinavian perspective*), Studentlitteratur, Lund, Sweden.

Baran, P. (1968) 'Does the interconnected computer network pose a hidden threat of invasion of privacy?', in Orr, W. D. (ed.), *Conversational Computers*, Wiley, New York, pp. 195–205.

Baroudi, J., and Olson, M. H. (1986) 'An empirical study of the impact of user involvement on system usage and information satisfaction', *Communications of the ACM*, **29**, 231–238.

Beirne, M., and Ramsay, H. (1986) *Computer Redesign and 'Labour Process' Theory: Towards a Critical Appraisal*, paper presented to the Fourth Annual Labour Process Conference, Aston University, Birmingham, UK.

Bell, D. (1973) *The Coming of Post-Industrial Society*, Collier-Macmillan, New York.

Bell, T. E., and Thayer, T. A. (1976) 'Software requirements: are they a problem?', *Proceedings of the 2nd International Conference on Software Engineering*.

Benbasat, I. (1985) 'An analysis of research methodologies', in McFarlan, F. W. (ed.), *The Information Systems Research Challenge*, Harvard Business School Press, Boston, pp. 47–85.

Benbasat, I., Dexter, A. S., and Mantha, R. W. (1980) 'Impact of organizational maturity on information system skill needs', *MIS Quarterly*, **4**, 21–34.

Benbasat, I., Dexter, A. S., Drury, D. H., and Goldstein, R. C. (1984) 'A critique of the stage hypothesis: theory and empirical evidence', *Communications of the ACM*, **27**, 476–485.

Benington, J. (1976) *Local Government Becomes Big Business*, CDP Information and Intelligence, London.

Bennett, J. (1976) 'Integrating users and decision support systems', in White, J. D. (ed.), *Proceedings of the Sixth and Seventh Annual Conferences of the Society for Management Information Systems*, University of Michigan, Ann Arbor, pp. 77–86.

Berger, R. M., and Wilson, R. C. (1967) 'Computer personnel selection and criterion development: the computer position profile', Electronics Personnel Research Group, University of Southern California, Los Angeles, Technical Report No. 53.

Bergland, G. D. (1981) 'A guided tour of program design methodologies', *Computer*, October, 13–37.

Bernotat, R. K. (1977) 'Man and computer in future on-board guidance and control systems in aircraft', in Shackel, B. (ed.), *Proceedings of the NATO ASI on 'Man–Computer Interaction'*, Mati, Greece.

Bernstein, J. (1981) *The Analytical Engine: Computers—Past, Present and Future*, Morrow, New York.

Bikson, T. K., and Mankin, D. (1983) 'Factors in successful implementation of computer-based office information systems: a review of the literature', mimeo., Rand Corporation.

Bjerknes, G., Ehn, P., and Kyng, M. (eds) (1987) *Computers and Democracy*, Avebury, Aldershot, UK.

Bjørn-Andersen, N. (ed.) (1980) *The Human Side of Information Processing*, North-Holland, Amsterdam.

Bjørn-Andersen, N., Hedberg, B., Mercer, D., Mumford, E., and Sole, A. (eds) (1979) *The Impact of Systems Change in Organisations*, Sijthoff & Noordhoff, Alphen aan den Rijn, The Netherlands.

Blackburn, P., Coombs, R., and Green, K. (1985) *Technology, Economic Growth and the Labour Process*, Macmillan, London.

Boehm, B. W. (1973) 'Software and its impact: a quantitative assessment', *Datamation*, **19**, 48–59.

Boehm, B. W. (1981) *Software Engineering Economics*, Prentice-Hall, Englewood Cliffs, NJ.

Boguslaw, R. (1965) *The New Utopians*, Prentice-Hall, Englewood Cliffs, NJ.

Bohm, C., and Jacopini, G. (1966) 'Flow diagrams, Turing machines and languages with only two formation rules', *Communications of the ACM*, **9**, 366–371.

Bolan, R. (1967) 'Emerging views of planning', *Journal of the American Institute of Planners*, **33**, 233–245.

Boland, R. J. (1978) 'The process and product of system design', *Management Science*, **24**, 887–898.

Borum, F. (1980) 'A power-strategy alternative to organization development', *Organization Studies*, **1**, 123–146.

Bosak, R. (1960) 'Implications of computer programming research for management controls', in *Management Control Systems*, Wiley, New York.

Bouvard, J. (1970) 'The translation of user requirements into fourth generation software', in Gruenberger, F. (ed.), *Fourth Generation Computers: User Requirements and Transition*, Prentice-Hall, Englewood Cliffs, NJ, pp. 117–129.

Brandon, D. H. (1963) *Management Standards for Data Processing*, Van Nostrand, New York.

Brandon, D. H. (1967) 'The dark side of data processing', *Data Systems*, July.

Brandon, D. H. (1968) 'Personnel management: missing link in data processing', *Journal of Data Management*, **6**, June.

Brandon, D. H. (1970) 'The economics of computer programming', in Weinwurm, G. F. (ed.), *On the Management of Computer Programming*, Auerbach, Philadelphia, pp. 3–18.

Braun, E., and Macdonald, S. (1982) *Revolution in Miniature: The History and Impact of Semiconductor Electronics*, Cambridge University Press, Cambridge.

Braverman, H. (1974) *Labor and Monopoly Capital*, Monthly Review Press, New York.

Bridges, A. H. (1977) 'Architecture and computers: two twentieth century monsters?', in Parkin, A. (ed.), *Computing and People*, Edward Arnold, London, pp. 99–108.

Briefs, U. (1983) 'Participatory systems design as approach for a workers' production policy', in Briefs, U., Ciborra, C., and Schneider, L. (eds), *Systems Design for, with, and by the Users*, North-Holland, Amsterdam, pp. 311–315.

Briefs, U., Ciborra, C., and Schneider, L. (eds) (1983) *Systems Design for, with, and by the Users*, North-Holland, Amsterdam.

Brooks, F. P. (1975) *The Mythical Man-Month*, Addison-Wesley, Reading, MA.

Brown, G. (1977) *Sabotage: A Study in Industrial Conflict*, Spokesman Books, Nottingham.

Buckroyd, B., and Cornford, D. (1988) *The IT Skills Crisis: The Way Ahead*, NCC Publications, Manchester.

Budde, R., and Sylla, K. (1984) 'From application domain modelling to target system', in Budde, R., Kuhlenkamp, K., Mathiassen, L., and Züllighoven, H. (eds), *Approaches to Prototyping*, Springer-Verlag, Berlin, pp. 31–48.

Budde, R., and Züllighoven, H. (1983) 'Socio-technical problems of systems design methods', in Briefs, U., Ciborra, C., and Schneider, L. (eds), *Systems Design for, with, and by the Users*, North-Holland, Amsterdam, pp. 147–155.

Budde, R., Kuhlenkamp, K., Mathiassen, L., and Züllighoven, H. (1984) *Approaches to Prototyping*, Springer-Verlag, Berlin.

Bullock, A. (1977) *Report on the Committee of Inquiry on Industrial Democracy*, HMSO, London.

Burch, J. G., and Grudnitski, G. (1986) *Information Systems: Theory and Practice*, Wiley, New York.

Burns, T., and Stalker, G. M. (1961) *The Management of Innovation*, Tavistock, London.

Burnstine, D. C. (1979) 'The theory behind BIAIT', unpublished paper, BIAIT International Inc., Petersburg, New York.

Buxton, J. N. (1978) 'Software engineering', in Gries, D. (ed.), *Programming Methodology*, Springer-Verlag, New York, pp. 23–28.

Byrne, J. A. (1986) 'Business fads: what's in—and out', *Business Week*, 20 January, 40–47.

CAITS (1984) *New Technology and Trade Unions–Agreements–Human Centered Systems: Dossier for Trade Unionists*, Centre for Alternative Industrial and Technological Systems, London.

Calingaert, P. (1967) 'System performance evaluation: survey and appraisal', *Communications of the ACM*, January, 12–18.

Campbell, S. G. (1970) 'The generation gap', in Gruenberger, F. (ed.), *Fourth Generation Computers: User Requirements and Transition*, Prentice-Hall, Englewood Cliffs, NJ, pp. 169–177.

Canan, J. (1982) *War in Space*, Harper & Row, New York.

Canning, R. G. (1956) *Electronic Data Processing for Business and Industry*, Wiley, New York.

Carlson, E. D., Grace, B. F., and Sutton, J. A. (1977) 'Case studies of end-user requirements for interactive problem-solving systems', *MIS Quarterly*, March, 51–63.

Carlson, W. M. (1979) 'Business information analysis and integration technique (BIAIT): the new horizon', *Data Base*, **10**, 3–9.

Carlson, W. M. (1981) 'Making your work effective', in Cotterman, W. W., Couger, J. D., Enger, N. L., and Harold, F. (eds), *Systems Analysis and Design: A Foundation for the 1980's*, Elsevier, New York, pp. 25–40.

Carlyle, R. E. (1987) 'High cost, lack of standards is slowing pace of CASE', *Datamation*, 15 August, 23–24.

Central Computing and Telecommunications Agency (1980) *Principles for the Management and Organisation of Computing in Departments*, CCTA Report, HMSO, London.

Chandor, A. (1976) *Choosing and Keeping Computer Staff*, George Allen & Unwin, London.

Chapin, N. (1971) *Flowcharts*, Van Nostrand Reinhold, New York.

Chapin, N. (1974) 'Structured programming simplified', *Computer Decisions*, June, 28–31.

Chapin, N. (1979) 'Full report of the flowchart committee on ANS standard X3.5-1970, *SIGPLAN Notices*, **14**, 16–27.

Chapin, N. (1981a) 'Graphic tools in the design of information systems', in Cotterman, W. W., Couger, J. D., Enger, N. L., and Harold, F. (eds), *Systems Analysis and Design: A Foundation for the 1980's*, Elsevier, New York, pp. 121–162.

Chapin, N. (1981b) 'Structured analysis and structured design: an overview', in Cotterman, W. W., Couger, J. D., Enger, N. L., and Harold, F. (eds), *Systems Analysis and Design: A Foundation for the 1980's*, Elsevier, New York, pp. 199–212.

Christoff, K. A. (1985) 'Building a fourth generation environment', *Datamation*, 15 September, 118–124.

Christy, D. P., and White, C. E. (1987) 'Structure and function of information centers: case studies of six organizations', *Information and Management*, **13**, 71–76.

Churchill, N. C., Kempster, J. H., and Uretsky, M. (1969) *Computer-based Information Systems for Management: A Survey*, National Association of Accountants, New York.

Churchman, C. W. (1975) 'Theories of implementation', in Schultz, R. L., and Slevin, D. P. (eds), *Implementing Operations Research/Management Science*, Elsevier, New York, pp. 23–30.

Churchman, C. W., and Schainblatt, A. H. (1965) 'The researcher and the manager: a dialectic of implementation', *Management Science*, **11**, 869–887.

Ciborra, C. (1981) 'Information systems and transactions architecture', *Policy Analysis and Information Systems*, **5**, 304–324.

Ciborra, C. (1983) 'The social costs of information technology and participation in system design', in Briefs, U., Ciborra, C., and Schneider, L. (eds), *Systems Design for, with, and by the Users*, North-Holland, Amsterdam, pp. 41–50.

Ciborra, C. (1987) 'Research agenda for a transaction costs approach to information systems', in Boland, R. J., and Hirschheim, R. A. (eds), *Critical Issues in Information Systems Research*, Wiley, Chichester, UK, pp. 253–274.

Clark, N., and Juma, C. (1987) *Long-Run Economics: An Evolutionary Approach to Economic Growth*, Pinter, London.

CODASYL Development Committee (1962) 'An information algebra phase I report', *Communications of the ACM*, **5**, 190–204.

Cole, R. E. (1979) *Work, Mobility and Participation: A Comparative Study of American and Japanese Industry*, University of California Press, Berkeley.

Colter, M. A. (1982) 'Evolution of the structured methodologies', in Couger, J. D., Colter, M. A., and Knapp, R. W. (eds), *Advanced System Development/Feasibility Techniques*, Wiley, New York, pp. 73–96.

Connor, M. (1981) 'Structured analysis and design techniques', in Cotterman, W. W., Couger, J. D., Enger, N. L., and Harold, F. (eds), *Systems Analysis and Design: A Foundation for the 1980's*, Elsevier, New York, pp. 213–234.

Cooley, M. J. E. (1976) 'CAD: a trade union viewpoint', in *Proceedings of the Second International Conference on Computers in Engineering and Building Design*, IPC Science and Technology Press, London.

Cooper, R. B., and Swanson, E. B. (1979) 'Management information requirements assessment: the state of the art', *Data Base*, Fall, 5–16.

Cornford, D. S. (1987) *Information Technology Trends*, NCC, Manchester.

Cotterman, W. W., Couger, J. D., Enger, N. L. and Harold, F. (eds) (1981) *Systems Analysis and Design: A Foundation for the 1980's*, Elsevier, New York.

Couger, J. D. (1973) 'Evolution of business system analysis techniques', *Computing Surveys*, September, 167–198; reprinted in Couger and Knapp (1974), pp. 43–81.

Couger, J. D. (1982) 'Evolution of system development techniques', in Couger, J. D., Colter, M. A., and Knapp, R. W. (eds), *Advanced System Development/Feasibility Techniques*, Wiley, New York, pp. 6–13.

Couger, J. D. (1988) 'Motivating IS personnel', *Datamation*, 15 September, 59–64.

Couger, J. D., and Knapp, R. W. (eds) (1974) *Systems Analysis Techniques*, Wiley, New York.

Couger, J. D., and Zawacki, R. A. (1980) *Motivating and Managing Computer Personnel*, Wiley, New York.

Couger, J. D., Colter, M. A., and Knapp, R. W. (eds) (1982) *Advanced System Development/ Feasibility Techniques*, Wiley, New York.

Cragon, H. G. (1982) 'The myths of the hardware/software cost ratio', *Computer*, December.

Cross, E. M. (1971) 'Behavioral styles of computer programmers revisited', *Proceedings of the Ninth Annual Computer Personnel Research Conference*, Special Interest Group on Computer Personnel Research of the Association for Computing Machinery, New York.

Cyert, R. M., and March, J. G. (1956) 'Organizational factors in the theory of oligopoly', *Quarterly Journal of Economics*, February, 44–64.

Cyert, R. M., and March, J. G. (1963) *A Behavioral Theory of the Firm*, Prentice-Hall, Englewood Cliffs, NJ.

Dagwell, R., and Weber, R. (1983) 'System designers' user models: a comparative study and methodological critique', *Communications of the ACM*, **26**, 987–997.

Dahl, O. J., Dijkstra, E. W., and Hoare, C. A. R. (1972) *Structured Programming*, Academic Press, London.

Daly, E. B. (1977) 'Management of software development', *IEEE Transaction Software Engineering*, May.

Dambrine, M. (1981) 'The Warnier approach of EDP problems', in Cotterman, W. W., Couger, J. D., Enger, N. L., and Harold, F. (eds), *Systems Analysis and Design: A Foundation for the 1980's*, Elsevier, New York, pp. 342–371.

Danziger, J. N. (1979) 'The "skill bureaucracy" and intraorganizational control: the case of the data processing unit', *Sociology of Work and Occupations*, **6**, 204–226.

Danziger, J. N., and Kraemer, K. L. (1986) *People and Computers*, Columbia University Press, New York.

Danziger, J., Dutton, W., Kling, R., and Kraemer, K. (1982) *Computers and Politics*, Columbia University Press, New York.

Datamation Staff (1988) 'What are you worth in '88?', *Datamation*, 1 October, 53–66.

David, P. (1975) *Technical Choice, Innovation and Economic Growth*, Cambridge University Press, London.

Davis, G. B. (1973) *Computer Data Processing*, McGraw-Hill, New York.

Davis, G. B. (1974) *Management Information Systems: Conceptual Foundations, Structure, and Development*, McGraw-Hill, New York.

Davis, G. B. (1982) 'Strategies for information requirements determination', *IBM Systems Journal*, **21**, 4–29.

Davis, G. B., and Olson, M. H. (1985) *Management Information Systems: Conceptual Foundations, Structure, and Development* (2nd edn), McGraw-Hill, New York.

Davis, S. (1969) 'Internal recruitment and training of data processing personnel', *Computers and Automation*, September, 38–39.

Dearden, J. (1972) 'MIS is a mirage', *Harvard Business Review*, January–February, 90–99.

Dearden, J. (1987) 'The withering away of the IS organization', *Sloan Management Review*, Summer, 87–91.

DeBrabander, B., and Edstrom, A. (1977) 'Successful information system development projects', *Management Science*, **24**, 191–199.

DeBrabander, B., and Thiers, G. (1984) 'Successful information system development in relation to situational factors which affect effective communication between MIS users and EDP specialists', *Management Science*, **30**, 137–155.

DeCindio, F., De Michelis, G., Panello, L., and Simone, C. (1983) 'Conditions and tools for an effective negotiation during the organization/information systems design process', in Briefs, U., Ciborra, C., and Schneider, L. (eds), *Systems Design for, with, and by the Users*, North-Holland, Amsterdam, pp. 173–192.

DeJong, P. (1976) 'BDL', *IBM Systems Journal*.

DeMarco, T. (1978) *Structured Analysis and System Specification*, Yourdon Press, New York.

Department of Employment (1964) *Computers in Offices 1964*, HMSO, London.

Department of Employment (1972) *Computers in Offices 1972*, HMSO, London.

Diamond, S. (1979) 'Contents of a meaningful plan', *Proceedings of the Tenth Annual Conference of the Society for Management Information Systems*, Chicago.

Dickmann, R. A. (1966) '1966 survey of test use in computer personnel selection', *Proceedings of the 4th Annual Computer Personnel Research Conference*, Association for Computer Machinery, New York, pp. 15–27.

Dickson, D. (1974) *The Politics of Alternative Technology*, Universe Books, New York.

Dickson, G. W., Leitheiser, R. L., and Wetherbe, J. C. (1984) 'Key information systems issues of the 1980's', *MIS Quarterly*, **8**, 135–159.

Dijkstra, E. (1965) 'Programming considered as a human activity', *Proceedings of the 1965 IFIP Congress*, North-Holland, Amsterdam, pp. 213–217.

Dijkstra, E. (1968) 'GOTO statement considered harmful', *Communications of the ACM*, **11**, 147–148.

Dijkstra, E. (1972) '1972 Turing award lecture', ACM Annual Conference, Boston, 14 August 1972, in *Communications of the ACM*, **5** (citations from reprint in Yourden, 1979, pp. 113–125).

Donaldson, J. R. (1973) 'Structured programming', *Datamation*, **19**, December.

Dosi, G. (1982) 'Technological paradigms and technological trajectories', *Research Policy*, 147–162.

Dreyfus, H. L. (1967) 'Why computers must have bodies in order to be intelligent', *Review of Metaphysics*, **21**, 13–32.

Dreyfus, H. L. (1972) *What Computers Can't Do: The Limits of Artificial Intelligence*, Harper & Row, New York.

Dreyfus, H. L., and Dreyfus, S. (1986) *Mind Over Machine*, Macmillan/Free Press, New York.

Drury, D. H. (1983) 'An empirical assessment of the stages of DP growth', *MIS Quarterly*, June, 59–70.

Drury, D. H., and Bates, I. E. (1979) *Data Processing Chargeback Systems: Theory and Practice*, Society of Management Accountants of Canada, Hamilton, Ontario.

Duffy, N. M., and Assad, M. G. (1980) *Information Management: An Executive Approach*, Oxford University Press, Cape Town, South Africa.

Dutton, W. H., and Kraemer, K. L. (1977) 'Technology and urban management: the power payoffs of computing', *Administration and Society*, **9**, 304–340.

Dutton, W. H., and Kraemer, K. L. (1978) 'Management utilization of computing in American local governments', *Communications of the ACM*, **21**, 206–218.

Earl, M. J. (1978) 'Prototype systems for accounting information and control', *Accounting, Organizations and Society*, **3**, 161–170.

Earl, M. (ed.) (1988) *Information Management: The Strategic Dimension*, Oxford University Press, Oxford.

Eason, K. D. (1977) 'The potential and reality of task performance by man–computer systems', in Parkin, A. (ed.), *Computing and People*, Edward Arnold, London, pp. 55–62.

Eason, K. (1981) *The Process of Introducing New Technology*, HUSAT Memo No. 239, Loughborough University, Loughborough, UK.

Eason, K. D., and Corney, G. M. (1970) 'The evaluation of a small, interactive, management information system', *Proceedings of IEE Conference on Man–Computer Interaction*, National Physical Laboratory, September.

Eason, K. D., Damodaran, L., and Stewart, T. F. M. (1975) 'Interface problems in man–computer interaction', in Mumford, E., and Sackman, H. (eds), *Human Choice and Computers*, North-Holland, Amsterdam, pp. 91–105.

Eaton, J., and Smithers, J. (1982) *This is IT: A Manager's Guide to Information Technology*, Philip Allan, Oxford.

Edstrom, A. (1977) 'User influence and the success of MIS projects: a contingency approach', *Human Relations*, **30**, 589–607.

Ehn, P. (1988) *Work-oriented Design of Computer Artifacts*, Arbetslivscentrum, Stockholm.

Ehn, P., and Kyng, M. (1984) 'A tool perspectives on design of interactive computer support for skilled workers', unpublished manuscript, Swedish Centre for Working Life Skills, Stockholm.

Ehn, P., and Kyng, M. (1987) 'The collective resource approach to systems design', in Bjerknes, G., Ehn, P., and Kyng, M. (eds), *Computers and Democracy*, Avebury, Aldershot, pp. 17–57.

Ehn, P., and Sandberg, A. (1979) 'Systems development: critique of ideology and the division of labor in the computer field', in Sandberg, A. (ed.), *Computers Dividing Man and Work*, Arbetslivscentrum, Stockholm, pp. 34–46.

Ein-Dor, P., and Segev, E. (1982) 'Information systems: emergence of a new organizational function', *Information Management*, **5**, 279–286.

Elger, A. J. (1975) 'Industrial organizations: a processual perspective', in McKinlay, J. B. (ed.), *Processing People: Cases in Organizational Behavior*, Holt, Rinehart & Winston, New York, pp. 91–149.

Ellul, J. (1964) *The Technological Society*, Knopf, New York.

Elster, J. (1983) *Explaining Technical Change*, Cambridge University Press, London.

Emery, F. E. (1978) *The Emergence of a New Paradigm of Work*, Centre for Continuing Education, Australian National University.

Emery, F., and Thorsrud, E. (1976) *Democracy at Work: The Report of the Norwegian Industrial Democracy Program*, Martinus Nijhoff, Leiden, The Netherlands.

Emery, F. E., and Trist, E. (1969) *Form and Content in Industrial Democracy*, Tavistock, London.

Enger, N. L. (1981) 'Classical and structured system life cycle phases and documentation', in Cotterman, W. W., Couger, J. D., Enger, N. L., and Harold, F. (eds), *Systems Analysis and Design: A Foundation for the 1980's*, Elsevier, New York, pp. 1–24.

Etzioni, A. (1961) *A Comparative Analysis of Complex Organizations*, Free Press, New York.

Fagence, M. (1977) *Citizen Participation in Planning*, Pergamon, New York.

Feigenbaum, E. A., and McCorduck, P. (1983) *The Fifth Generation: Artificial Intelligence and Japan's Computer Challenge to the World*, Addison-Wesley, Reading, MA.

Fellner, W. (1962) 'Does the market direct the relative factor-saving effects of technological progress?', in Universities National Bureau Committee for Economic Research, *The Rate and Direction of Inventive Activity*, Princeton University Press, Princeton, NJ.

Fiedler, F. (1964) 'A contingency model of leadership effectiveness', in Bercowitz, L. (ed.), *Advances in Experimental Social Psychology*, Academic Press, New York.

Fishlock, D. (1983) 'Star Wars weapons research', *Financial Times*, 2 November.

Fitts, P. M. (1951) *Human Engineering for an Effective Air-navigation and Traffic-control System*, National Research Council, Washington.

Floyd, C. (1984) 'A systematic look at prototyping', in Budde, R., Kuhlenkamp, K., Mathiassen, L., and Züllighoven, H. (eds), *Approaches to Prototyping*, Springer-Verlag, Berlin, pp. 1–18.

Floyd, C. (1987) 'Outline of a paradigm change in software engineering', in Bjerknes, G., Ehn, P., and Kyng, M. (eds), *Computers and Democracy*, Avebury, Aldershot, pp. 191–210.

Floyd, C., and Keil, R. (1983) 'Adapting software development for systems design with users', in Briefs, U., Ciborra, C., and Schneider, L. (eds), *Systems Design for, with, and by the Users*, North-Holland, Amsterdam, pp. 163–172.

Forester, T. (ed.) (1980) *The Microelectronics Revolution*, Blackwell, Oxford.

Forester, T. (ed.) (1985) *The Information Technology Revolution*, Blackwell, Oxford.

Forester, T. (1987) *High-Tech Society*, Blackwell, Oxford.

Fox, A. (1974) *Beyond Contract: Work, Power and Trust Relations*, Faber & Faber, London.

Francis, A. (1986) *New Technology at Work*, Oxford University Press, Oxford.

Frank, W. L. (1968) 'Software for terminal oriented systems', *Datamation*, June, 30–34.

Frank, W. L. (1983) 'The history of myth no. 1', *Datamation*, May, 252–254.

Freeman, C. (1983) *Long Waves in the World Economy*, Butterworths, Borough Green, UK.

Freeman, C. (1988) 'Diffusion: the spread of new technology to firms, sectors and nations', in Heertje, A. (ed.), *Innovation, Technology and Finance*, Blackwell, Oxford.

Freeman, P. (1981) 'Why Johnny can't analyze', in Cotterman, W. W., Couger, J. D., Enger, N. L., and Harold, F. (eds), *Systems Analysis and Design: A Foundation for the 1980's*, Elsevier, New York, pp. 321–329.

Freiberger, P., and Swaine, M. (1984) *Fire in the Valley: The Making of the Personal Computer*, Osborne/McGraw-Hill, Berkeley, California.

Frenkel, K. A. (1985) 'Toward automating the software-development cycle', *Communications of the ACM*, **28**, 578–588.

Friederich, J., and Wicke, W. (1983) 'Design of an information system for workers', in Briefs, U., Ciborra, C., and Schneider, L. (eds), *Systems Design for, with, and by the Users*, North-Holland, Amsterdam, pp. 301–310.

Friedman, A. L. (1977) *Industry and Labour*, Macmillan, London.

Friedman, A. L. (1984) 'Management strategies, market conditions and the labour process', in Stephen, F. H. (ed.), *Firms, Organization and Labour*, Macmillan, London, pp. 176–200.

Friedman, A. L. (1986) *Software Industry and Data Processing in the USA: Work Organization and Employment Structure*, EEC, Brussels.

Friedman, A. L. (1987a) 'Specialist labour in Japan and the subcontracting system: the case of computer specialists', *British Journal of Industrial Relations*, **25**, 353–369.

Friedman, A. L. (1987b) 'Understanding the employment position of computer programmers: a managerial strategies approach', *CHIPS Working Papers*, No. 8, Copenhagen School of Economics.

Friedman, A. L. (1989) 'Management strategies, activities, techniques and technology: towards a complex theory of the labour process', in Knights, D., and Willmott, H. (eds), *Labour Process Theory*, Macmillan, London.

Friedman, A. L., and Cornford, D. S. (1981) *The Pursuit of Productivity in U.K. Data Processing Installations*, Work Organization Consultants, Bristol.

Friedman, A. L., and Cornford, D. S. (1982a) 'The use of generators and similar techniques in the UK', in Wallis, P. (ed.), *Programming Technology*, Pergamon Infotech, Maidenhead, UK, pp. 154–170.

Friedman, A. L., and Cornford, D. S. (1982b) *DP Survey Report, 1981*, mimeo. University of Bristol.

Friedman, A. L., and Cornford, D. S. (1984) 'Research in the U.K. reveals '80's revamp for jobs', *Computing*, 2 February, 23.

Friedman, A. L., and Cornford, D. S. (1985) 'Choosing the right programming job', *Information Management Journal*, 26–28.

Friedman, A. L., and Cornford, D. S. (1987) 'Strategies for meeting user demands: an international perspective', *International Journal of Information Management*, **7**, 3–20.

Friedman, A. L., and Greenbaum, J. (1984) 'Wanted: Renaissance people', *Datamation*, 1 September, 134–144.

Friedman, A. L., and Greenbaum, J. (1985) 'Japanese DP', *Datamation*, 1 February, 112–118.

Friedman, A. L., Greenbaum, J., and Jacobs, M. (1984) 'The challenge of users and unions', *Datamation*, 15 September, 93–100.

Friedman, A. L., Hørlück, J., Rieswijck, B., and Regtering, H. (1988) *Work Organization and Industrial Relations in Data Processing Departments: A Comparative Study of the United Kingdom, Denmark and The Netherlands*, EEC, Brussels.

Galbraith, J. K. (1967) *The New Industrial Estate*, Signet, New York.

Galliers, R., and Somogyi, E. (eds) (1987) *Towards Strategic Information Systems*, Abacus Press, Tunbridge Wells, UK.

Gane, C., and Sarson, T. (1971) *Structured Systems Analysis: Tools and Techniques*, Improved Systems Technologies Inc., New York.

Gatto, O. T. (1964) 'Autosate', *Communications of the ACM*, July, 425–432.

Gibson, C. F. (1976) 'A contingency theory of implementation: implications for research and practice', paper presented at the Implementation II Conference, University of Pittsburgh, 18–20 February.

Gibson, C. F., and Hammond, J. S. (1974) 'Contrasting approaches for facilitating the implementation of management science', paper presented at the Operations Research Society of America/Institute of Management Sciences Joint National Meeting, Boston, 22–24 April.

Gibson, C. F., and Nolan, R. L. (1974) 'Managing the four stages of EDP growth', *Harvard Business Review*, **52**, 76–88.

Gilfillian, S. C. (1935) *The Sociology of Invention*, 1970 edition, MIT Press, Cambridge, MA.

Gillis, W. K. (1968) 'Personnel requirements in data processing', *Computers and Automation*, September, 24–26.

Gingras, L., and McLean, E. R. (1982) 'Designers and users of information systems: a study of differing profiles', *Proceedings of the Third International Conference on Information Systems*, pp. 169–181.

Ginzberg, M. J. (1975) 'A process approach to management science implementation', PhD dissertation, MIT.

Glans, B. G., Holstein, D., Meyer, W. E., and Schmidt, R. N. (1968) *Management Systems*, Holt, Rinehart & Winston, New York.

Glass, R. L. (1977) *The Universal Elixir and Other Computing Projects Which Failed*, Computing Trends, Seattle.

Glass, R. L. (1978) *Tales of Computing Folk: Hot Dogs and Mixed Nuts*, Computing Trends, Seattle.

Goldkuhl, G., and Lyytinen, K. (1982) 'A language action view on information systems', *Proceedings of the Third International Conference on Information Systems*, Ann Arbor, December.

Goldstein, R. C., and McCririk, I. (1981) 'The stage hypothesis and data administration: some contradictory evidence', in Ross, C. (ed.), *Proceedings of the Second International Conference on Information Systems*, Cambridge, MA, pp. 309–324.

Göranzon, B. *et al.* (1982) *Job Design and Automatation in Sweden*, Centre for Working Life, Stockholm, Sweden.

Gould, J. D., and Lewis, C. (1985) 'Designing for usability: key principles and what designers think', in Shackel, B. (ed.), *INTERACT '84: First Conference on Human–Computer Interaction*, North-Holland, Amsterdam.

Grad, B., and Canning, R. (1969) 'Information process analysis', *Journal of Industrial Engineering*, November–December, 470–474.

Grayson, C. J. (1973) 'Management science and business practice', *Harvard Business Review*, **51**, 41–48.

Greenbaum, J. (1976) 'Division of labor in the computer field', *Monthly Review*, **28**, 40–55.

Greenbaum, J. (1979) *In the Name of Efficiency*, Temple University, Philadelphia.

Greenberger, M. (ed.) (1962) *Computers and the World of the Future*, MIT Press, Cambridge, MA.

Greiner, L. E. (1972) 'Evolution of revolution as organizations grow', *Harvard Business Review*, July–August, 37–46.

Griffiths, P. (ed.) (1987) *The Role of Information Management in Competitive Success*, Pergamon–Infotech, Maidenhead, UK.

Grindley, C. B. B. (1966) 'Systematics: a nonprogramming language for designing and specifying commercial systems for computers', *Computer Journal*, August, 124–128.

Grosch, H. R. J. (1970) 'Are we ready for progress?', in Gruenberger, F. (ed.), *Fourth Generation Computers: User Requirements and Transition*, Prentice-Hall, Englewood Cliffs, NJ, pp. 1–9.

Grosch, H. R. J. (1977) 'The way it was in 1957', *Datamation*, September, 75–78.

Gruenberger, F. (ed.) (1970) *Fourth Generation Computers: User Requirements and Transition*, Prentice-Hall, Englewood Cliffs, NJ.

Gruenberger, F. (ed.) (1971) *Expanding Use of Computers in the 70's: Markets, Needs, Technology*, Prentice-Hall, Englewood Cliffs, NJ.

Gullo, K., and Schatz, W. (1988) 'The supercomputer breaks through', *Datamation*, 1 May, 50–63.

Gupta, N. K., and Seviora, R. E. (1984) 'An expert system approach to real time system debugging', in *Proceedings of the 1st Conference on Artificial Intelligence Applications*, IEEE Computer Society, Silver Springs, MD.

Hansen, P., and Penney, G. (1976) *Job Trends in Data Processing*, National Computing Centre, Manchester.

Hart, S. G., Battiste, V., and Lester, P. T. (1984) 'POPCORN: a supervisory control simulation for workload and performance research', in *Proceedings of the 20th Annual Conference on Management Control*, National Aeronautics and Space Administration, pp. 431–454.

Hartmann, D. (1981) *Die Alternative—Leben als Sabotage*, Initiative Verlagsanstalt, Tübingen, FRG.

Hayes, J. P. (1978) *Computer Architecture and Organization*, McGraw-Hill, New York.

Head, R. V. (1985) 'Information resource center: a new force in end-user computing', *Journal of Systems Management*, February, 24–29.

Hebden, S. E. (1975) 'Patterns of work identification', *Sociology of Work and Occupations*, **2**, 107–132.

Hedberg, B. (1975) 'Computer systems to support industrial democracy', in Mumford, E., and Sackman, H. (eds), *Human Choice and Computers*, North-Holland, Amsterdam, pp. 211–230.

Hedberg, B., and Mumford, E. (1975) 'The design of computer systems: man's vision of man as an integral part of the system design process', in Mumford, E., and Sackman, H. (eds), *Human Choice and Computers*, North-Holland, Amsterdam, pp. 31–59.

Hershman, A. (1968) *Dun's Review*, January.

Herzberg, F. (1968) *Work and the Nature of Man*, Staples Press, London.

Hicks, J. R. (1932) *The Theory of Wages*, Macmillan, London.

Hilleglass, J. R. (1965) 'Hardware evaluation', *DPMA Proceedings*, **8**, 391–406.

Hingel, A. J. (1983) 'The challenge of new technology for European unions: a comparative approach', in Briefs, U., Ciborra, C., and Schneider, L. (eds), *Systems Design for, with, and by the Users*, North-Holland, Amsterdam, pp. 195–206.

Hirschheim, R. A. (1983) 'Assessing participative systems design: some conclusions from an exploratory study', *Information and Management*, **6**, 317–327.

Hirschheim, R. A. (1985) *Office Automation: Concepts, Technologies and Issues*, Addison-Wesley, Wokingham, UK.

Hirschheim, R., Earl, M., Feeny, D., and Lockett, M. (1988) 'An exploration into the management of the information systems function: key issues and an evolutionary model', in Jeffrey, R. (ed.), *Proceedings of the Joint Symposium on Information Systems*, March, Sydney.

Hogue, J. T. (1987) 'A framework for the examination of management involvement in decision support systems', *Journal of Management Information Systems*, **4**, 96–110.

Hollander, S. (1965) *The Sources of Increased Efficiency*, MIT Press, Cambridge, MA.

Holloway, N. J. (ed.) (1986) *Proceedings of the CSNI Workshop on Probabilistic Safety Assessment*, UK Atomic Energy Authority, Warrington.

Hooper, K. (1986) 'Architectural design: an analogy', in Norman, D. A. and Draper, S. W. (eds), *User Centered System Design: New Perspectives on Human–Computer Interaction*, Lawrence Erlbaum, Hillsdale, NJ, pp. 9–23.

Hopper, G. M. (1962) 'Discussion of Brown's contribution', in Greenberger, M. (ed.), *Computers and the World of the Future*, MIT Press, Cambridge, MA, pp. 271–287.

Hørlück, J. (1985) 'Formal availability and actual usage of methods and techniques in Danish computer installations', *ICON Working Papers*, **3**, 2–18.

Hørlück, J. (1986) '4th generation tools: the solution?', *ICON Working Papers*, **4**, 67–85.

Hørlück, J. (1988) 'Vi kan selvi' (We can do it ourselves—in Danish), *Nordisk DataNytt*, No. 3.

Horwitt, E. (1985) 'Redefining the information center', *Business Computer Systems*, September, 38–46.

Høyer, R. (1979) 'User participation: why is development so slow?', *Data*, **12**, 49–54.

Hruschka, P. (1987) 'Is there life after structured analysis?', in *Proceedings of the Fifth Annual Control Engineering Conference*, pp. 421–432.

Huff, S. L., Munro, M. C., and Martin, B. H. (1988) 'Growth stages of end-user computing', *Communications of the ACM*, **31**, 542–550.

Hutchins, E. L., Holland, J. D., and Norman, D. A. (1986) 'Direct manipulation interfaces', in Norman, D. A., and Draper, S. W. (eds), *User Centered System Design: New Perspectives on Human–Computer Interaction*, Lawrence Erlbaum, Hillsdale, NJ, pp. 87–124.

IBM (1971) *The Time Automated Grid System (TAG): Sales and Systems Guide*, GY 20-0358-1, IBM, White Plains, New York.

IBM (1973) *HIPO: Design Aid and Documentation Tool*, SR 20-9413-0, IBM, White Plains, New York.

IBM (1978) *Business System Planning: Information Systems Planning Guide*, GE 20-0527, IBM, White Plains, New York.

Iivari, J. (1984) 'Prototyping in the context of information systems design', in Budde, R., Kuhlenhamp, K., Mathiassen, L., and Züllighoven, H. (eds), *Approaches to Prototyping*, Springer-Verlag, Berlin, pp. 261–277.

Illich, I. (1974) *Tools for Conviviality*, Harper & Row, New York.

Ives, B., and Olson, M. H. (1984) 'User involvement and MIS success: a review of research', *Management Science*, **30**, 586–603.

Jackson, M. A. (1975) *Principles of Program Design*, Academic Press, London.

Jackson, M. A. (1981) 'Some principles underlying a system development method', in Cotterman, W. W., Couger, J. D., Enger, N. L., and Harold, F. (eds), *Systems Analysis and Design: A Foundation for the 1980's*, Elsevier, New York, pp. 185–198.

Jenkins, C., and Sherman, B. (1979) *The Collapse of Work*, Eyre Methuen, London.

Jenkins, J. P., and Glynn, J. C. (1987) 'Development and evaluation of a risk based interactive decision aid', in Salvendy, G., Sauter, S. L., and Hurrell, J. J. Jr (eds), *Social, Ergonomic and Stress Aspects of Work with Computers*, Elsevier, Amsterdam, pp. 173–180.

Johnson, T. (1984) *The Commercial Application of Expert Systems Technology*, Ovum, London.

Jones, C. (1986) *Programming Productivity*, McGraw-Hill, New York.

Jörgensen, A. H. (1984) 'On the psychology of prototyping', in Budde, R., Kuhlenkamp, K., Mathiassen, L., and Züllighoven, H. (eds), *Approaches to Prototyping*, Springer-Verlag, Berlin, pp. 278–289.

Joyce, E. (1988) 'Reusable software: passage to productivity?', *Datamation*, 15 September, 97–102.

Kasper, G. (1985) 'The effect of user-developed DSS applications on forecasting decision-making performance in an experimental setting', *Journal of Management Information Systems*, **2**, 26–39.

Katzan, H. Jr (1976) *Systems Design and Documentation: An Introduction to the HIPO Method*, Van Nostrand Reinhold, New York.

Kaye, D. (1971) 'Career paths in systems and data processing', *Journal of Systems Management*, **22**, 12–15.

Keen, P. G. W. (1980) 'Decision support systems: translating analytic techniques into useful tools', *Sloan Management Review*, **22**, 33–44.

Keen, P. G. W. (1981) 'Information systems and organisational change', *Communications of ACM*, **24**, 24–33.

Keen, P. G. W., and Scott Morton, M. S. (1978) *Decision Support Systems: An Organizational Perspective*, Addison-Wesley, Reading, MA.

Kelly, J. F. (1970) *Computerized Management Information Systems*, Macmillan, London, pp. 367–402.

Kensing, F. (1983) 'The trade unions' influence on technological change', in Briefs, U., Ciborra, C., and Schneider, L. (eds), *Systems Design for, with, and by the Users*, North-Holland, Amsterdam, pp. 219–239.

Kerner, D. V. (1979) 'Business information characterization study', *Data Base*, **10**, 10–17.

Keul, V. (1983) 'Trade union planning and control of new technology', in Briefs, U., Ciborra, C., and Schneider, L. (eds), *Systems Design for, with, and by the Users*, North-Holland, Amsterdam, pp. 207–218.

Keus, H. E. (1982) 'Prototyping: a more reasonable approach to system development', *ACM Software Engineering Notes*, **7**, 94–95.

Kidder, T. (1981) *The Soul of a New Machine*, Avon Books, New York.

King, D. (1984) *Current Practices in Software Development*, Yourden Press, New York.

King, J. L. (1988) 'The changing political economy of chargeout systems', *Journal of Information Systems Management*, **5**, 65–67.

King, J. L., and Kraemer, K. L. (1984) 'Evolution and organizational information systems: an assessment of Nolan's stage model', *Communications of the ACM*, **27**, 466–475.

King, J. L., and Kraemer, K. L. (1985) *The Dynamics of Computing*, Columbia University Press, New York.

King, W. R. (1978) 'Strategic planning for management information systems', *MIS Quarterly*, March, 27–37.

Klein, H. K., and Hirschheim, R. (1987) 'Social change and the future of information systems development', in Boland, R. J., and Hirschheim, R. (eds), *Critical Issues in Information Systems Research*, Wiley, Chichester, pp. 275–305.

Kling, R. (1978) 'Value conflicts and social choice in electronic fund transfer system development', *Communications of the ACM*, **21**, 642–656.

Kling, R. (1980) 'Social analyses of computing: theoretical orientations in recent empirical research', *Computing Surveys*, **12**, 61–110.

Kling, R. (1982) 'Citizen orientation of automated information systems', *Information Age*, **4**, 215–223.

Kling, R. (1987) 'Computerization as an ongoing social and political process', in Bjerknes, G., Ehn, P., and Kyng, M. (eds), *Computers and Democracy*, Avebury, Aldershot, pp. 117–136.

Kling, R., and Iacono, S. (1984) 'The control of information system developments after implementation', *Communications of the ACM*, **27**, 1218–1226.

Klockare, B., and Norrby, K. (1983) 'A Swedish model for systems development in public administration', in Briefs, U., Ciborra, C., and Schneider, L. (eds), *Systems Design for, with, and by the Users*, North-Holland, Amsterdam, pp. 119–129.

Knight, K. E. (1963) *A Study of Technological Innovation: The Evolution of Digital Computers*, PhD dissertation, Carnegie Institute of Technology.

Knight, K. E. (1968) 'Evolving computer performance, 1963–1967', *Datamation*, January, 31–35.

Knudsen, T. (1984) '*Det Store Systemet*', '*De Sma Syatemene*' og *Systemereren* (in Norwegian, '*The Big System*', '*The Small Systems*' and *The System Developers*), dissertation, University of Bergen, Norway.

Knudsen, T. (1986) 'Professions and development of strategic computer based systems', *ICON Newsletter*, **4**, 27–29.

Knuth, D. E. (1968) *The Art of Computer Programming*, Addison-Wesley, Reading, MA.

Knuth, D. E. (1974) 'Structured programming with go to statements', *ACM Computing Surveys*, **6**, 261–302.

Koestler, A. (1970) *The Ghost in the Machine*, Pan Books, London.

Konsynski, B. (1976) 'A model of computer aided definition and analysis of information system requirements', PhD dissertation, Purdue University.

Kraemer, K. L., and Dutton, W. H. (1979) 'The interests served by technological reform', *Administration and Society*, **11**, 80–106.

Kraemer, K. L., Dutton, W. H., and Northrop, A. (1981) *The Management of Information Systems*, Columbia University Press, New York.

Kraft, P. (1977) *Programmers and Managers: The Routinization of Computer Programming in the United States*, Springer-Verlag, New York.

Kraft, P. (1979) 'Challenging the Mumford democrats at Derby works', *Computing*, 2 August.

Kraft, P., and Dubnoff, S. (1986) 'Job content, fragmentation, and control in computer software work', *Industrial Relations*, **25**, 184–196.

Kubicek, H. (1983) 'User participation in systems design: some questions about structure and content arising from recent research from a trade union perspective', in Briefs, U., Ciborra, C., and Schneider, L. (eds), *Systems Design for, with, and by the Users*, North-Holland, Amsterdam, pp. 3–18.

Kyng, M., and Mathiassen, L. (1982) 'Systems development and trade union activities', in Bjørn-Anderson, N. *et al.* (eds), *Information Society: For Richer, For Poorer*, Elsevier, Amsterdam.

Lakatos, I. (1970) 'Falsification and the methodology of scientific research programmes', in Lakatos, I., and Musgrove, A. (eds), *Criticism and Growth of Knowledge*, Cambridge University Press, Cambridge.

Lamb, J. (1988) 'IBM eyes EDI in Europe', *Datamation* (International edition), 1 July, 48-11 to 48-16.

Land, F. (1982) 'Notes on participation', *Computer Journal*, **25**, 283–285.

Landes, D. S. (1969) *The Unbound Prometheus*, Cambridge University Press, Cambridge.

Langefors, B. (1963) 'Some approaches to the theory of information systems', *BIT*, **3**, 229–254.

Lanzara, G. F. (1983) 'The design process: frames, metaphors and games', in Briefs, U., Ciborra, C., and Schneider, L. (eds), *Systems Design for, with, and by the Users*, North-Holland, Amsterdam, pp. 29–40.

Laurel, B. K. (1986) 'Interface as mimesis', in Norman, D. A., and Draper, S. W. (eds), *User Perspectives on Human–Computer Interaction*, Lawrence Erlbaum, Hillsdale, NJ, pp. 67–85.

Lecht, C. P. (1977) *The Waves of Change*, McGraw-Hill, New York.

Levie, H., and Williams, R. (1983) 'User involvement and industrial democracy: problems and strategies in Britain', in Briefs, U., Ciborra, C., and Schneider, L. (eds), *Systems Design for, with, and by the Users*, North-Holland, Amsterdam, pp. 265–286.

Lewin, K. (1952) In Cartwright, D. (ed.), *Field Theory in Social Science: Selected Theoretical Papers*, Tavistock, London.

Licklider, J. C. R. (1960) 'Man–computer symbiosis', *IRE Transactions on Human Factors in Electronics*, **HFE-1**, March.

Licklider, J. C. R. (1965) 'Man–computer partnerships', *International Science and Technology*, May.

Likert, R. (1967) *The Human Organisation*, McGraw-Hill, New York.

Littler, C. R. (1982) *The Development of the Labour Process in Capitalist Societies*, Heinemann, London.

Livesey, P. B. (1984) 'Experience with prototyping in a multinational organization', in Budde, R., Kuhlenkamp, K., Mathiassen, L., and Züllighoven, H. (eds), *Approaches to Prototyping*, Springer-Verlag, Berlin, pp. 92–104.

Longley, D., and Shain, M. (1985) *Macmillan Dictionary of Information Technology* (2nd edn), Macmillan, London.

Loseke, D. R., and Sonquist, J. A. (1979) 'The computer worker in the labor force', *Sociology of Work and Occupations*, **6**, 156–183.

Lucas, H. C. (1973) *Computer Based Information Systems in Organizations*, Science Research Associates, Palo Alto.

Lucas, H. C. (1974) *Towards Creative Systems Design*, Columbia University Press, New York.

Lucas, H. C. (1975a) 'Behavioral factors in system implementation', in Schultz, R. L., and Slevin, D. P. (eds), *Implementing Operations Research/Management Science*, Elsevier, New York, pp. 203–215.

Lucas, H. C. (1975b) *Why Information Systems Fail*, Columbia University Press, New York.

Lucas, H. C. (1978) *Information Systems Concepts for Management*, McGraw-Hill, New York (2nd edn, 1982; 3rd edn, 1985).

Lucas, H. C. (1981) *Implementation: The Key to Successful Information Systems*, Columbia University Press, New York.

Lucas, H. C., and Sutton, J. A. (1977) 'The stage hypothesis S-curve: some contradictory evidence', *Communications of the ACM*, **20**, 254–259.

Lutz, B. (1982) 'Social endogeny of technical progress and the question of human labour', in Diettrich, O., and Morley, J. (eds), *Relations Between Technology, Capital and Labour*, EEC, Brussels.

Macro, A., and Buxton, J. (1987) *The Craft of Software Engineering*, Addison-Wesley, Wokingham, UK.

Mader, C. (1979) *Information Systems: Technology, Economics, Applications, Management* (2nd edn), Science Research Associates, Chicago.

Magal, S. R., and Carr, H. H. (1988) 'An investigation of the effects of age, size, and hardware option on the critical success factors applicable to information centers', *Journal of Management Information Systems*, **4**, 60–76.

Mambrey, P., and Schmidt-Belz, B. (1983) 'Systems designers and users in a participative design process: some fictions and facts', in Briefs, U., Ciborra, C., and Schneider, L. (eds), *Systems Design for, with, and by the Users*, North-Holland, Amsterdam, pp. 61–69.

Manley, J. H. (1975) 'Implementation attitudes: a model and a measurement methodology', in Schultz, R. L., and Slevin, D. P. (eds), *Implementing Operations Research/Management Science*, Elsevier, New York, pp. 183–202.

Mann, F. C., and Williams, L. K. (1960) 'Observations on the dynamics of a change to electronic data processing equipment', *Administrative Science Quarterly*, **5**, 217–256.

Marglin, S. A. (1974) 'What do bosses do? The origins and functions of hierarchy in capitalist production', *Review of Radical Political Economics*, **6**, 60–112.

Marion, L. (1984) 'The big wallet era', *Datamation*, 15 September, 76–88.

Markus, M. L. (1979) *Understanding Information System Use in Organizations: A Theoretical Perspective*, PhD dissertation, Case Western Reserve University, Cleveland.

Markus, M. L. (1983) 'Power, politics and MIS implementation', *Communications of the ACM*, **27**, 430–444.

Martin, J. (1973) *Design of Man–Computer Dialogues*, Prentice-Hall, Englewood Cliffs, NJ.

Martin, J. (1982) *Application Development Without Programmers*, Prentice-Hall, Englewood Cliffs, NJ.

Martin, J. (1985) *Fourth-Generation Languages*, Prentice-Hall, Englewood Cliffs, NJ.

Martin, J., and Norman, A. R. D. (1970) *The Computerized Society*, Prentice-Hall, Englewood Cliffs, NJ.

Maslow, A. (1964) *Motivation and Personality*, Harper, New York.

Mathiassen, L. (1984) 'Summary of the working group systems development and prototyping', in Budde, R., Kuhlenkamp, K., Mathiassen, L., and Züllighoven, H. (eds), *Approaches to Prototyping*, Springer-Verlag, Berlin, pp. 255–260.

Mathiassen, L., Rolskov, B., and Vedel, E. (1983) 'Regulating the use of edb by law and agreements', in Briefs, U., Ciborra, C., and Schneider, L. (eds), *Systems Design for, with, and by the Users*, North-Holland, Amsterdam, pp. 251–264.

Mayer, D. B., and Stalnaker, A. W. (1968) 'Selection and evaluation of computer personnel', *Proceedings of the 23rd National Conference, Association for Computing Machinery*, in Weinwurm, G. F. (ed.), *On the Management of Computer Programming*, Auerbach, Philadelphia (1970), pp. 133–157.

Maynaud, J. (1968) *Technocracy*, Faber & Faber, London.

Mayo, E. (1933) *The Human Problems of an Industrial Civilization*, Harvard Business School, Boston, MA.

McClure, C. (1987) 'Software reusability and CASE technology', *CASE Report*, October, 1–2.

McCosh, A., and Scott Morton, M. (1978) *Management Decision Support Systems*, Wiley, New York.

McCracken, D. D. (1981) 'A maverick approach to systems analysis and design', in Cotterman, W. W., Couger, J. D., Enger, N. L., and Harold, F. (eds), *Systems Analysis and Design: A Foundation for the 1980's*, Elsevier, New York, pp. 446–451.

McCracken, D. D., and Jackson, M. A. (1981) 'A minority dissenting position', in Cotterman, W. W., Couger, J. D., Enger, N. L., and Harold, F. (eds), *Systems Analysis and Design: A Foundation for the 1980's*, Elsevier, New York, pp. 551–553.

McFarlan, F. W., and McKenney, J. (1982) 'The information archipelago: maps and bridges', *Harvard Business Review*, September–October, 109–119.

McGregor, D. (1960) *The Human Side of Enterprise*, McGraw-Hill, New York.

McKinsey Corporation (1968) *Unlocking the Computer's Profit Potential*, McKinsey Corporation, New York.

McLuhan, M. (1964) *Understanding Media*, McGraw-Hill, New York.

Meador, C. L., and Keen, P. G. W. (1984) 'Setting priorities for DSS development', *MIS Quarterly*, **8**, 117–129.

Meyers, G. J. (1975) *Reliable Software Through Composite Design*, Mason Charter, New York.

Miller, A. R. (1971) *The Assault on Privacy*, University of Michigan Press, Ann Arbor.

Miller, R. B. (1968) 'Response time in man–computer conversational transactions', *Proceedings of the Fall Joint Computer Conference*, Thompson, Washington, DC, pp. 267–277.

Mintzberg, H. (1973) *The Nature of Managerial Work*, Harper & Row, New York.

Mintzberg, H. (1979) *The Structuring of Organizations*, Prentice-Hall, Englewood Cliffs, NJ.

Mitroff, I. I. (1975) 'On mutual understanding and the implementation problem: a philosophical case study of the psychology of the Apollo moon scientists', in Schultz, R. L., and Slevin, D. P. (eds), *Implementing Operations Research/Management Science*, Elsevier, New York, pp. 237–251.

Mohrman, A. M. Jr, and Lawler, E. E. (1985) 'A review of theory and research', in McFarlan, F. W. (ed.), *The Information Systems Research Challenge*, Harvard Business School Press, Boston, pp. 135–164.

Mönckemeyer, M., and Spitta, T. (1984) 'Concept and experiences of prototyping in a software-engineering environment with NATURAL', in Budde, R., Kuhlenkamp, K., Mathiassen, L., and Züllighoven, H. (eds), *Approaches to Prototyping*, Springer-Verlag, Berlin, pp. 122–135.

Moritz, M. (1984) *The Little Kingdom: The Private Story of Apple Computer*, William Morrow, New York.

Mumford, E. (1972) *Job Satisfaction: A Study of Computer Specialists*, Longman, London.

Mumford, E. (1979) 'Systems design and human needs', in Bjørn-Andersen, N., Hedberg, B., Mercer, D., Mumford, E., and Sole, A. (eds), *The Impact of Systems Change in Organisations*, Sijthoff & Noordhoff, Alphen aan den Rijn, The Netherlands, pp. 1–6.

Mumford, E. (1980) 'The participative design of clerical information systems: two case studies', in Bjørn-Andersen, N. (ed.), *The Human Side of Information Processing*, North-Holland, pp. 91–104.

Mumford, E. (1983) *Designing Human Systems*, Manchester Business School, Manchester.

Mumford, E. (1987) 'Sociotechnical systems design: evolving theory and practice', in Bjerknes, G., Ehn, P., and Kyng, M. (eds), *Computers and Democracy*, Avebury, Aldershot, pp. 59–76.

Mumford, E., and Banks, O. (1967) *The Computer and the Clerk*, Humanities Press, New York.

Mumford, E., and Hensall, D. (1979) *A Participative Approach to Computer Systems Design*, Associated Business Press, London.

Mumford, E., and Sackman, H. (eds) (1975) *Human Choice and Computers*, North-Holland, Amsterdam.

Mumford, E., and Ward, T. B. (1968) *Computers: Planning for People*, Batsford, London.

Munk-Madsen, A. (1983) 'System analysis with users', in Briefs, U., Ciborra, C., and Schneider, L. (eds), *Systems Design for, with, and by the Users*, North-Holland, Amsterdam, pp. 157–161.

Munro, M. C., Huff, S. L., and Moore, G. (1987–88) 'Expansion and control of end-user computing', *Journal of Management Information Systems*, **4**, 5–27.

Myers, G. J. (1975) *The Art of Software Testing*, Wiley, New York.

Naisbitt, J. (1982) *Megatrends: Ten New Directions Transforming Our Lives*, Futura, London.

Nashelsky, L. (1972) *Introduction to Digital Computer Technology*, Wiley, New York.

Nassi, I., and Schneiderman, B. (1973) 'Flowchart techniques for structured programming', *SIGPLAN Notices*, **8**, 12–26.

Naumann, J. D., and Jenkins, A. M. (1982) 'Prototyping: the new paradigm for systems development', *MIS Quarterly*, **6**.

Naumann, J. D., Davis, G. B., and McKeen, J. D. (1980) 'Determining information requirements: a contingency method for selection of requirements assurance strategy', *Journal of Systems Software*, **1**.

Naur, P. (1963) 'GOTO statements and good algol style', *BIT*, **3**, 204–208.

Naur, P. (1984) 'Comment' (on Jorgensen, 1984), in Budde, R., Kuhlenkamp, K., Mathiassen, L., and Züllighoven, H. (eds), *Approaches to Prototyping*, Springer-Verlag, Berlin, pp. 290–291.

Naur, P., and Randell, B. (1969) *Software Engineering*, Scientific Affairs Division, NATO, Brussels.

NCR (1961) *MAP-System Charting Technique*, National Cash Register Co., Dayton, OH.

NCR (1968) *A Study Guide for Accurately Defined Systems*, National Cash Register Co., Dayton, OH.

Necco, C. R., Gordon, C. L., and Tsai, N. W. (1987) 'The information center approach for developing computer-based information systems', *Information and Management*, **13**, 95–101.

Nelson, D. (1974) 'Scientific management, systematic management, and labor, 1880–1915', *Business History Review*, **28**, 479–500.

Nelson, R. R., and Winter, S. G. (1977) 'In search of a useful theory of innovation', *Research Policy*, 36–76.

Nelson, R., and Winter, S. (1982) *An Evolutionary Theory of Economic Change*, Belknap Press, Cambridge, MA.

Newell, A., and Simon, H. A. (1972) *Human Problem Solving*, Prentice-Hall, Englewood Cliffs, NJ.

Nickerson, R. S. (1969) 'Man–computer interaction: a challenge for human factors research', *Ergonomics*, **12**, 501–517.

Noble, D. (1977) *America By Design: Science, Technology and the Rise of Corporate Capitalism*, Knopf, New York.

Nolan, R. L. (1973a) 'Managing the computer resource: a stage hypothesis', *Communications of the ACM*, **16**, 399–406.

Nolan, R. L. (1973b) 'The plight of the EDP manager', *Harvard Business Review*, **51**, 143–152.

Nolan, R. L. (1977a) 'Controlling the cost of data services', *Harvard Business Review*, July–August, 114–124.

Nolan, R. L. (1977b) 'Restructuring the data processing organization for data resource management', in Gilchrist, B. (ed.), *Information Processing 1977*, North-Holland, Amsterdam, pp. 261–265.

Nolan, R. L. (1979) 'Managing the crisis in data processing', *Harvard Business Review*, March–April, 115–126.

Norman, D. A. (1986) 'Cognitive engineering', in Norman, D. A., and Draper, S. W. (eds), *User Centered System Design: New Perspectives on Human–Computer Interaction*, Lawrence Erlbaum, Hillsdale, NJ, pp. 31–61.

Norman, D. A., and Draper, S. W. (eds) (1986) *User Centered System Design: New Perspectives on Human–Computer Interaction*, Lawrence Erlbaum, Hillsdale, NJ.

Nunamaker, J. F. (1971) 'A methodology for the design and optimization of information processing systems', *Proceedings of the 1971 AFIPS Spring Joint Computer Conference*, AFIPS Press, Montvale, NJ, pp. 283–294.

Nunamaker, J. F., and Konsynski, B. (1981) 'Formal and automated techniques of systems analysis and design', in Cotterman, W. W., Couger, J. D., Enger, N. L., and Harold, F. (eds), *Systems Analysis and Design: A Foundation for the 1980's*, Elsevier, New York, pp. 291–320.

Nygaard, K. (1979) 'The "iron and metal project": trade union participation', in Sandberg, A. (ed.). *Computers Dividing Man and Work*, Arbetslivscentrum, Stockholm, pp. 94–107.

Nygaard, K. (1983) 'Participation in system development: the tasks ahead', in Briefs, U., Ciborra, C., and Schneider, L. (eds), *Systems Design for, with, and by the Users*, North-Holland, Amsterdam, pp. 19–25.

O'Donnell, D. J., and March, S. T. (1987) 'End-user computing environments: finding a balance between productivity and control', *Information and Management*, **13**, 77–84.

OECD (1985) *Software: An Emerging Industry*, OECD, Paris.

Opperman, R., and Tepper, A. (1983) 'Initiation and acceptance of the participation of persons affected in system development', in Briefs, U., Ciborra, C., and Schneider, L. (eds), *Systems Design for, with, and by the Users*, North-Holland, Amsterdam, pp. 71–84.

Orlicky, J. (1969) *The Successful Computer System*, McGraw-Hill, New York.

Ortner, E., and Wendler, K. (1984) 'Prototyping in an environment using several data management systems', in Budde, R., Kuhlenkamp, K., Mathiassen, L., and Züllighoven, H. (eds), *Approaches to Prototyping*, Springer-Verlag, Berlin, pp. 244–254.

Orwell, G. (1949) *Nineteen Eighty-four*, Secker and Warburg, London.

Paddock, C. E., and Swanson, N. E. (1986–87) 'Open versus closed minds: the effect of dogmatism on an analyst's problem-solving behavior', *Journal of Management Information Systems*, **3**, 111–122.

Parnas, D. L. (1972) 'On the criteria to be used in decomposing systems into modules', *Communications of the ACM*, **15**, 1053–1058.

Parnas, D. L. (1985) 'Software aspects of strategic defense systems', *Communications of the ACM*, **28**, 1326–1335.

Peat, Marwick, Mitchell and Computer Economics (1972) *Computer Management and Economics*, Computer Economics, London.

Peters, T., and Waterman, R. (1982) *In Search of Excellence: Lessons from America's Best-run Companies*, Harper & Row, New York.

Piercy, N. (ed.) (1986) *Management Information Systems: The Technology Challenge*, Croom Helm, London.

Pirsig, R. M. (1974) *Zen and the Art of Motorcycle Maintenance*, Bodley Head, Oxford.

Pugh, D. S., Hickson, D. J., Hinings, C. R., Macdonald, K. M., Turner, C., and Lupton, T. (1963–64) 'A conceptual scheme for organisational analysis', *Administrative Science Quarterly*, **8**, 289–315.

Pugh, D. S., Hickson, D. J., Hinings, C. R., and Turner, C. (1969) 'The context of organisation structures', *Administrative Science Quarterly*, **14**, 91–114.

Quintanar, L. R., Crowell, C. R., and Moskal, P. J. (1987) 'The interactive computer as a social stimulus in human–computer interactions', in Salvendy, G., Sauter, S. L., and Hurrell, J. J. Jr (eds), *Social, Ergonomic and Stress Aspects of Work with Computers*, Elsevier, Amsterdam, pp. 303–310.

Qvale, T. (1976) 'A Norwegian strategy for democratization of industry', in *Human Relations*, No. 5.

Regtering, H., and Riesewijk, B. (1987) *ICON Onderzock Nederland*, ICON Nederland, Nijmegen, The Netherlands.

Rhodes, J. J. (1973) 'Beyond programming', in Cougar, J. D., and Knapp, R. W. (eds), *Systems Analysis Techniques*, Wiley, New York.

Rice, A. K. (1963) *The Enterprise and its Environment*, Tavistock, London.

Riddle, W. E. (1984) 'Advancing the state of the art in software system prototyping', in Budde, R., Kuhlenkamp, K., Mathiassen, L., and Züllighoven, H. (eds), *Approaches to Prototyping*, Springer-Verlag, Berlin, pp. 19–26.

Rigal, J.-L. (1983) 'Consultation with users: a new paradigm and a new culture', in Briefs, U., Ciborra, C., and Schneider, L. (eds), *Systems Design for, with, and by the Users*, North-Holland, Amsterdam, pp. 51–58.

Rockart, J. F. (1979) 'Critical success factors', *Harvard Business Review*, **57**, 81–91.

Rockart, J. F., and Flannery, L. S. (1983) 'The management of end-user computing', *Communications of the ACM*, **26**, 76–84.

Roethlisberger, F. J., and Dickson, W. J. (1939) *Management and the Worker*, Harvard University Press, Cambridge, MA.

Rosen, S. (1969) 'Electronic computers: a historical survey', *ACM Computing Surveys*, March, 7–36.

Rosenberg, N. (1969) 'The direction of technological change: inducement mechanism and focusing devices', *Economic Development and Cultural Change*, October.

Rosenberg, N. (1975) 'Problems in the economist's conceptualization of technological innovation', *History of Political Economy*, **7**, 456–481.

Rosenberg, N. (1982) *Inside the Black Box: Technology and Economics*, Cambridge University Press, Cambridge.

Rosenbrock, H. (1979) 'The redirection of technology', paper given at International Federation of Automatic Control Symposium, Bari, Italy.

Rosin, R. F. (1969) 'Supervisory and monitoring systems', *ACM Computing Surveys*, December, 197–212.

Rosove, P. E. (1967) *Developing Computer-Based Information Systems*, Wiley, New York.

Ross, D. T. (1977) 'Structured analysis (SA): a language for communicating ideas', *IEEE Transactions on Software Engineering*, **SE-3**, 16–34.

Ross, D. T., and Schoman, K. E. (1977) 'Structured analysis for requirements definition', *IEEE Transactions on Software Engineering*, **SE-3**, 6–15.

Rostow, W. W. (1960) *The Stages of Economic Growth*, Cambridge University Press, Cambridge.

Royce, W. W. (1970) 'Managing the development of large software systems: concepts and techniques', *Proceedings, WESCON*, August.

Rudofsky, B. (1969) *Streets for People: A Primer for Americans*, Doubleday, New York.

Rule, J. (1974) *Public Surveillance and Private Lives*, Schocken, New York.

Rzevski, G. (1984) 'Prototypes versus pilot systems: strategies for evolutionary information system development', in Budde, R., Kuhlenkamp, K., Mathiassen, L., and Züllighoven, H. (eds), *Approaches to Prototyping*, Springer-Verlag, Berlin, pp. 356–367.

Sääksjärvi, M. (1985) 'End-user participation and the evolution of organizational information systems: an empirical assessment of Nolan's stage model', in Wetherbe, J. C. (ed.), *Proceedings of the Twenty-First Annual Computer Personnel Research Conference*, May, ACM Vol. 5, pp. 181–189.

Sackman, H. (1967) *Computers, System Science and Evaluing Society*, Wiley, New York.

Sackman, H. (1971) *Mass Information Utilities and Social Excellence*, Auerbach, New York.

Sackman, H. (1975) 'Computers and social options', in Mumford, E., and Sackman, H. (eds), *Human Choice and Computers*, North-Holland, Amsterdam, pp. 73–87.

Sackman, H., and Borko, H. (eds) (1972) *Computers and the Problems of Society*, AFIPS Press, Montvale.

Sackman, H., Erikson, W. J., and Grant, E. E. (1968) 'Exploratory experimental studies comparing online and offline programming performance', *Communications of the ACM*, **11**, No. 1.

Salter, W. E. G. (1960) *Productivity and Technical Change*, Cambridge University Press, Cambridge.

Samuelson, P. (1965) 'A theory of induced innovation along Kennedy–Weisäker lines', *Review of Economics and Statistics*, **47**, 343–356.

Sanders, D. H. (1973) *Computers in Society: An Introduction to Information Processing*, McGraw-Hill, New York.

Sanders, D. H. (1970) *Computers and Management*, McGraw-Hill, New York.

Sayre, D. (1962) 'Discussion of Brown's contribution', in Greenberger, M. (ed.), *Computers and the World of the Future*, MIT Press, Cambridge, MA, pp. 271–287.

Scharer, L. L. (1982) 'Systems analyst performance: criteria and priorities', *Journal of Systems Management*, **33**, 10–15.

Schatz, W. (1988) 'EDI: putting muscle in commerce and industry', *Datamation*, 15 March, 56–64.

Schein, E. H. (1961) 'Management development as a process of influence', *Industrial Management Review*, **2**, 59–77.

Schneider, L., and Ciborra, C. (1983) 'Technology bargaining in Norway', in Briefs, U., Ciborra, C., and Schneider, L. (eds), *Systems Design for, with, and by the Users*, North-Holland, Amsterdam, pp. 243–250.

Schneidewind, N. F. (1966) *Analytic Model for the Design and Selection of Electronic Digital Computers*, PhD dissertation, University of Southern California.

Schneidewind, N. F. (1967) 'The practice of computer selection', *Datamation*, February, 22–25.

Schulz, R. L., and Slevin, D. P. (1975a) 'Implementation and management innovation', in Schultz, R. L., and Slevin, D. P. (eds), *Implementing Operations Research/Management Science*, Elsevier, New York, pp. 3–20.

Schultz, R. L., and Slevin, D. P. (1975b) 'Implementation and organizational validity: an empirical investigation', in Schultz, R. L., and Slevin, D. P. (eds), *Implementing Operations Research/Management Science*, Elsevier, New York, pp. 153–182.

Schultz, R. L., and Slevin, D. P. (eds) (1975c) *Implementing Operations Research/Management Science*, Elsevier, New York.

Schumacher, E. F. (1974) *Small is Beautiful*, Sphere, London.

Schumpeter, J. A. (1934) *The Theory of Economic Development*, Harvard University Press, Cambridge, MA.

Seidel, K. P. (1970) 'Profiting from the past in software development', in Gruenberger, F. (ed.), *Fourth Generation Computers: User Requirements and Transition*, Prentice-Hall, Englewood Cliffs, NJ, pp. 131–140.

Select Committee (1970) *UK Computer Industry*, ref. no. 272, 13 May, HMSO, London.

Semprevivo, P. (1981) 'The art of interviewing', in Cotterman, W. W., Couger, J. D., Enger, N. L., and Harold, F. (eds), *Systems Analysis and Design: A Foundation for the 1980's*, Elsevier, New York, pp. 109–120.

Shackel, B. (ed.) (1985) *INTERACT '84: First Conference on Human–Computer Interaction*, North-Holland, Amsterdam.

Sharpe, W. F. (1969) *The Economics of Computers*, Columbia University Press, New York.

Shneiderman, B. (1982) 'The future of interactive systems and the emergence of direct manipulation', *Behaviour and Information Technology*, **1**, 237–256.

Shneiderman, B. (1983) 'Direct manipulation: a step beyond programming languages', *IEEE Computer*, **16**, 57–69.

Shurkin, J. (1984) *Engines of the Mind: A History of the Computer*, Norton, New York.

Simon, H. A. (1957) *Models of Man*, Wiley, New York.

Simon, H. A. (1960) *The New Science of Management Decision*, Harper & Row, New York.

Skalkum, S. (1967) 'Changes in performance of components for computer systems', unpublished, cited in Sharpe (1969), pp. 297–332.

Smith, A. (1776) *An Inquiry into the Nature and Causes of the Wealth of Nations*, reprinted as Pelican Classic (1974), Penguin, Harmondsworth, UK.

Smolawa, C., and Toepfer, A. (1983) 'A strategy for user participation in the development of future non-commercial services', in Briefs, U., Ciborra, C., and Schneider, L. (eds), *Systems Design for, with, and by the Users*, North-Holland, Amsterdam, pp. 85–92.

Sorensen, R. E., and Zand, D. E. (1975) 'Improving the implementation of OR/MS models by applying the Lewin–Schein theory of change', in Schultz, R. L., and Slevin, D. P. (eds), *Implementing Operations Research/Management Science*, Elsevier, New York, pp. 217–235.

Sprague, R., and Carlson, E. (1982) *Building Effective Decision Support Systems*, Prentice-Hall, Englewood Cliffs, NJ.

Sprague, R. H., and McNurlin, B. C. (1986) *Information Systems Management in Practice*, Prentice-Hall, Englewood Cliffs, NJ.

Stamper, R. (1975) 'Information science for systems analysis', in Mumford, E., and Sackman, H. (eds), *Human Choice and Computers*, North-Holland, Amsterdam, pp. 107–120.

Stamps, D. (1987) 'CASE: cranking our productivity', *Datamation*, 1 July, 55–58.

Sterling, T. O. (1979) 'Consumer difficulties with computerized billing systems', *Communications of the ACM*, **22**, 283–289.

Stewart, T. F. M. (1977) 'Side effects of computer aided problem solving', in Parkin, A. (ed.), *Computing and People*, Edward Arnold, London, pp. 65–71.

Stoneman, P. (1976) *Technological Diffusion and the Computer Revolution*, Cambridge University Press, Cambridge.

Stoneman, P. (1983) *The Economic Analysis of Technological Change*, Oxford University Press, Oxford.

Straussman, J. (1978) *The Limits of Technocratic Politics*, Transaction, New Brunswick, NJ.

Sullivan, T. A., and Cornfield, D. B. (1979) 'Downgrading computer workers: evidence from occupational and industrial redistribution', *Sociology of Work and Occupations*, **6**, 184–203.

Taggart, W. M., and Silbey, V. (1986) *Information Systems: People and Computers in Organizations* (2nd edn), Allyn & Bacon, Boston.

Taggart, W. M., and Tharp, M. O. (1977) 'A survey of information requirements analysis techniques', *ACM Computing Surveys*, **9**, 273–290.

Tavolato, P., and Vincena, K. (1984) 'A prototyping methodology and its tool', in Budde, R., Kuhlenkamp, K., Mathiassen, L., and Züllighoven, H. (eds), *Approaches to Prototyping*, Springer-Verlag, Berlin, pp. 434–446.

Taylor, F. W. (1911) *Principles of Scientific Management*, reprinted in *Scientific Management*, Harper, New York, 1947.

Taylor, R. N., and Benbasat, I. (1980) 'A critique of cognitive styles: theory and research', *Proceedings of the First International Conference on Information Systems*, pp. 82–90.

Teichroew, D., and Sayani, H. (1971) 'Automation of system building', *Datamation*, 15 August, 25–30.

Teichroew, D., Hershey, E. A., and Yamamoto, Y. (1979) 'The PSL/PSA approach to computer-aided analysis and documentation', reprinted in Couger, J. D., Colter, M. A., and Knapp, R. W. (eds) (1982) *Advanced System Development/Feasibility Techniques*, Wiley, New York, pp. 330–346.

The Economist (1971) 27 February, pp. i-xxxviii between pp. 50 and 51.

Thompson, P. (1984) *The Nature of Work*, Macmillan, London.

Toffler, A. (1980) *The Third Wave*, Morrow, New York.

Tomeski, E. A. (1974) 'Job enrichment and the computer: a neglected subject', *Computers and People*, **23**, 7–11.

Tomlin, R. (1988) 'A European IS culture for the 1990s', *Datamation* (International edition), 1 September, 48-14 to 48-20.

Trist, E. (1971) 'Critique of scientific management in terms of socio-technical theory', *Prakseologia*, **39**.

Trist, E. (1981) *The Evolution of Socio-technical Systems*, Ontario Quality of Working Life Center, Toronto.

Trist, E., Higgins, G., Murray, H., and Pollock, A. (1963) *Organizational Choice*, Tavistock, London.

Turner, J. A. (1981) 'Organizational models in information systems', in Cotterman, W. W., Couger, J. D., Enger, N. L., and Harold, F. (eds), *Systems Analysis and Design: A Foundation for the 1980's*, Elsevier, New York, pp. 492–497.

Turton, R. (1977) 'On the relevance of professionalism', in Parkin, A. (ed.), *Computing and People*, Edward Arnold, London, pp. 87–98.

Urwick, L. F. (1949) *The Meaning of Rationalization*, Nisbet, London.

Usher, A. P. (1954) *A History of Mechanical Inventions*, Harvard University Press, Cambridge, MA.

US House of Representatives (1966) *The Computer and Invasions of Privacy. Hearings before a Sub-Committee on Government Operations, July 26–28, 1966*, 89th Congress, 2nd Session, US Printing Office, Washington, DC.

Vertinsky, I., Barth, R. T., and Mitchell, V. F. (1975) 'A study of OR/MS as a social change process', in Schultz, R. L., and Slevin, D. P. (eds), *Implementing Operations Research/Management Science*, Elsevier, New York, pp. 253–270.

Vonnegut, K. Jr (1952) *Player Piano*.

Vyssotsky, V. A. (1979) 'Software engineering', keynote speech delivered at COMPSAC 79, 6–8 November, Chicago, cited in Bergland (1981).

Waddell, G. R. (1975) 'Information systems development in a local authority', in Mumford, E., and Sackman, H. (eds), *Human Choice and Computers*, North-Holland, Amsterdam, pp. 121–133.

Wagner, G. (1980) 'Optimizing decision support systems', *Datamation*, **26**, 209–214.

Wagner, H. M. (1971) 'The ABC's of OR', *Operations Research*, **19**, 1259–1281.

Wainwright, J., and Francis, A. (1984) 'Office automation: its design, implementation and impact', *Personnel Review*, **13**, 2–10.

Walker, P. F. (1983) 'Smart weapons in naval warfare', *Scientific American*, May.

Walter, C. J., and Walter, A. B. (1970) 'The significance of the next generation: technical keynote presentation', in Gruenberger, F. (ed.), *Fourth Generation Computers: User Requirements and Transition*, Prentice-Hall, Englewood Cliffs, NJ, pp. 11–29.

Ward, T. B. (1973) *Computer Organisation, Personnel and Control*, Longman, London.

Warnier, J. D. (1974) *Logical Construction of Programs*, Van Nostrand Reinhold, New York.

Watson, J. J., and Carr, H. H. (1987) 'Organizing for decision support system support: the end-user services alternative', *Journal of Management Information Systems*, **4**, 83–95.

Webb, S., and Webb, B. (1898) *Industrial Democracy*, published by the authors, London.

Weinberg, G. (1971) *The Psychology of Computer Programming*, Van Nostrand Reinhold, New York.

Weinwurm, G. F. (ed.) (1970) *On the Management of Computer Programming*, Auerbach, Philadelphia.

Weizer, N. (1981) 'A history of operating systems', *Datamation*, January, 119–126.

Wessel, D. (1986) 'Software writing is becoming automated', *Wall Street Journal*, 24 September, 6.

Westin, A. F. (1967) *Privacy and Freedom*, Atheneum, New York.

Wetherbe, J. C. (1979) *Systems Analysis and Design: Traditional, Structured, and Advanced Concepts and Techniques*, West Publishing, St Paul, MN (2nd edn, 1984).

Wetherbe, J. C., and Leitheiser, R. L. (1985) 'Information centers: a survey of services, decisions, problems and successes', *Journal of Information Systems Management*, **2**, 3–10.

White, K. B. (1984) 'MIS project teams: an investigation of cognitive style implications', *MIS Quarterly*, **8**, 95–101.

White Paper (1975a) *Computers and Privacy*, Cmnd. 6353, HMSO, London.

White Paper (1975b) *Computers: Safeguards for Privacy*, Cmnd. 6354, HMSO, London.

Wilkinson, B. (1983) *The Shopfloor Politics of New Technology*, Heinemann, London.

Williams, R. (1987) 'Democratising systems development: technological and organisational constraints and opportunities', in Bjerknes, G., Ehn, P., and Kyng, M. (eds), *Computers and Democracy*, Avebury, Aldershot, pp. 77–96.

Williams, R., and Steward, F. (1985) 'Technology agreements in Great Britain: a survey 1977–1983', *Industrial Relations Journal*, **16**, 58–73.

Williamson, O. E. (1975) *Markets and Hierarchies: Analysis and Antitrust Implications*, Free Press, New York.

Winograd, T. (1973) 'Breaking through the complexity barrier (again)', in *Proceedings of the SIGIR–SIGPLAN Conference*, November, ACM, New York.

Wirth, N. (1974) 'On the composition of well-structured programs', *ACM Computing Surveys*, **6**, 247–260.

Wylie, C. (1988) 'CASE rings in the new year', *Nyhedsbrev*, No. 6, 2–3.

Yearsley, R. (1969) 'Some thoughts on computer personnel and its solution', *Data Systems*, January, 30–31.

Yoritz, B., and Stanback, T. (1967) *Electronic Data Processing in New York City*, Columbia University Press, New York.

Young, J. W., and Kent, H. K. (1958) 'Abstract formulation of data processing problems', *Journal of Industrial Engineering*, November/December, 479.

Younger, K. (1972) *Report of the Committee on Privacy*, Cmnd. 5012, HMSO, London.

Yourden, E. (ed.) (1979) *Writings of the Revolution: Selected Readings on Software Engineering*, Yourden Press, New York.

Yourden, E., and Constantine, L. L. (1975) *Structured Design*, Yourden Press, New York.

Zand, D. E., and Sorensen, R. E. (1975) 'Theory of change and the effective use of management science', *Administrative Science Quarterly*, **20**, 532–545.

Zierau, E. (1988) *An Empirical Study of User Involvement in Systems Development Work Organization: Analysis and Evaluation of an ICON Case Study*, unpublished Master's degree thesis, University of Aarhus, Denmark.

Zmud, R. W. (1979) 'Individual differences and MIS success: a review of the empirical literature', *Management Science*, **25**, 966–979.

Züllighoven, H. (1984) 'Approaches to prototyping: an introduction', in Budde, R., Kuhlenkamp, K., Mathiassen, L., and Züllighoven, H. (eds), *Approaches to Prototyping*, Springer-Verlag, Berlin, pp. v–vi.

Zwass, V. (1987–88) 'Editorial introduction', *Journal of Management Information Systems*, **4**, 3–4.

Index